Pandia Press
R.E.A.L. Science Odyssey

Read ☀ Explore ☀ Absorb ☀ Learn

RSO Physics
(level one)
for grades 3-6

Written by Dahlia Schwartz BS, MA, JD

Written by Dahlia Schwartz
Illustrated by Terri Williams

© 2015, 2017 Pandia Press
ISBN: 978-0-9798496-9-5

www.pandiapress.com

WHAT'S INSIDE THIS BOOK?

*Denotes lab or activity

Pandia Press

About the Author and Dedications

Dahlia Schwartz has been interested in physics since her family acquired a cheap telescope when she was a child. She graduated from Michigan State University with a Bachelor's Degree in Electrical Engineering and Computer Science and worked for the Space & Communications group at Hughes Aircraft Company for five years. A few degrees, decades, and careers later, Dahlia started homeschooling her two children. She now helps to run a homeschool co-op where she has had a wonderful time developing science classes that encourage kids to think outside the usual box, such as a world-building class in which students create their own planet, from the big bang to the development of language, culture, and technology, learning about subjects such as physics, chemistry, biology, linguistics, and anthropology. Dahlia lives in Michigan and enjoys teaching, reading, complex origami, playing guitar and, when the Michigan weather permits, taking out her newer, bigger telescope to marvel at the universe.

This book is dedicated to every child who has been curious about the world around us, and especially to my children, Aliana and Itamar, who taught me that even young children are capable of comprehending precise and complex scientific ideas. Thanks to them, I have discovered that true wonder and excitement about science spring from being exposed to the deep questions that science asks and to the ideas that are often, mistakenly I believe, reserved for advanced science classes. This book is also dedicated to my spouse, who patiently endured not only my many hours spent writing, but also lived with various science experiments inhabiting our shared office space during the last few years.
—Dahlia Schwartz, BS, MA, JD

Introduction to RSO Physics

Almost everyone who has ever spent any time with a baby has played "the gravity game." The rules go something like this: The baby seems bored. You hand her an interesting object. She promptly drops it. So, you pick it up and hand it to her again. She promptly drops it. Repeat indefinitely. It seems babies could play this game for hours, certainly for longer than most adults continue to enjoy it.

We know that the baby is actually actively learning and studying—learning about cause and effect, studying how the people around her behave and internalizing some of the deepest concepts in physics without even being aware of it. Without language or math, we learn when we are quite young how the physical world behaves—that some force pulls things toward the ground, that balls arc when we throw them, that it is harder to push heavy objects than lighter objects, that, overall, objects behave in fairly predictable ways.

Yet, by the time we get to high school, only about 30% of us study physics—the very science that fascinates us as babies. Our lack of engagement with physics as we get older is not because most of us think it is just too easy, but rather, because for some reason we have been led to believe that it is really quite difficult, too difficult in fact. This is unfortunate because physics is not only incredibly fascinating, but an understanding of physics also allows us to look at everything in the world around us in new and deeper ways.

I have given a lot of thought to how and when and why to teach physics, and more generally science to elementary and middle-school-aged students. Many science programs I have seen and tried either turn the learning of science into something like learning a foreign language—memorize these words, these rules, these formulae—or focus on unconnected, flashy, and interesting experiments at the expense of depth, consistency, and true understanding. In both cases, children never gain the exposure they need and deserve from the essence of real science—wonder, exploration, problem-solving, understanding, and application to the world they live in.

It is this sense of wonder and exploration that I have striven to incorporate into every lesson of RSO physics. Students will not only learn Newton's three laws of motion but they also will experiment with them and develop simple models of real-world applications such as automobile safety and rocket engines. In studying simple machines, the emphasis is placed on building each type of machine with common household objects, experimenting with how the machines make work easier for people, and discovering that, after careful observation and experimentation, it is possible to predict how these machines will behave in new situations.

Science is a precise academic discipline, but it is also a story—a story of discovery, of mistakes that seem ridiculous to us now but that halted scientific development for centuries, of great intuitive leaps that opened doors to entirely new realms inside the atom or out in the depths of space. Therefore, I have also striven to incorporate a sense of the history of physics into this course—through stories of scientists such as Archimedes, Aristotle, Newton, Goddard, and Einstein.

I have heard it said that one cannot really learn or appreciate physics without knowing calculus. It is true that some of the beauty of science lies in the amazing fact of being able to describe the physical world with formulas and numbers, and I hope that many of the students who take this course will someday go on to learn calculus and college physics and experience that beauty. But even young students with basic arithmetic skills can appreciate that with a simple formula such as "weight = mass x gravity," they can figure out how much they, or their sister, or their family car, would weigh on any planet in the solar system. Therefore, formulas are introduced, but primarily as a way to show the power of describing physical laws through mathematics.

One of the most important ideas that young people should take away from studying science is that our understanding of the world and of the universe is still incomplete. How exactly are protons, which should repel each other, held together inside the nucleus of an atom? Can a magnet be made so small that it has only one pole? Can we reimagine some of the simple machines to invent new ways to generate energy or do work without polluting our planet? I hope, most of all, that studying physics inspires your students to think about the world around them in new ways and instills in them the belief that they can experiment, create, and improve the world.

<u>A Note About Grade Level:</u> The target grade level for this course is 4th (approximately 9- to 10-year-olds). However, with some minor adaptations, this course may be successfully utilized with children as young as 3rd grade, and as old as 6th grade. For younger children, you might need to eliminate some of the math (or do the calculations yourself). Don't worry about a few of the more abstract concepts like those found in the study of quantum physics. Focus on the main concepts, the "Big Ideas," with younger children.

Older students should grasp all the main concepts and details of each lesson, the "Big Idea" and "Small Stuff" list that starts on page 9. For older students, I also recommend requiring at least three formal lab reports while completing the course. There is a reproducible lab report form on page 485. Older students should also complete several of the "More Lab Fun" ideas found on the instructor pages. Many of these activities elicit higher-level thinking and delve deeper into science concepts. Finally, for older students, I suggest you assign research outside the course for at least one topic (or scientist) of the student's choosing, and require a written report.

THE UNIQUE PAGES IN THIS BOOK

<u>For My Notebook Pages</u>
1. All the student pages have a boxed outline around the material presented. That way it is easy to identify what is for the child and what is for the parent or teacher.
2. The For My Notebook (FMN) pages are the lesson pages that present the majority of new material to the student. They are intended to be read aloud. Some students, who are good readers, may want to read the FMN pages aloud themselves to the parent or class. However orchestrated, these pages are intended to be read aloud and not silently, to encourage discussion and questions.
3. New vocabulary words are underlined. You will notice that many of the vocabulary words are not presented with a classic dictionary definition. Instead, the explanation is given in context, so it is "felt" rather than memorized. Formal definitions for the vocabulary words are offered in the back of the book.
4. If you wish, FMN pages can be removed along the perforated binding, three-hole punched, and then placed in a three-ring binder along with completed Lab Sheets and Notebooking pages to create a Physics Notebook.

<u>Lab Sheets</u>
1. The lab sheets are those pages that the student writes on. They also have a boxed outline because they are intended for the student, not the parent/teacher, to complete.
2. The lab sheets not only reinforce the material presented in the FMN pages, but they are also the vehicle through which this course reinforces and formalizes scientific method. On the lab sheets, students will be making hypotheses based on questions formed during the lesson. Students record observations and lab results, and make conclusions based on those results. They will also practice sketching details of their lab experiences, an important process that reinforces observation skills.
3. If you are working with a student who isn't writing yet, have him dictate the information to be written on the lab sheets. If your student is unable to draw (meaning physically incapable; I'm not referring to artistic

abilities), then have him describe in detail his observations as you create them on the lab sheet.

4. If you wish, Lab Sheets can be removed along the perforated binding, three-hole punched, and then placed in a three-ring binder along with completed FMN pages and Notebooking Pages.

The Instructor Pages

1. The instructor pages contain the supply lists for the labs or activities and procedure instructions.

2. These pages are written for the parent/teacher, but the procedure is often written as if for the student. For example, "Complete the hypothesis portion of the lab sheet," is instruction for the student, not the parent.

3. Most instruction pages include a prompt to read aloud to students. A great deal of course instruction is found in these prompts. If you dislike prompts, then be sure to present the information in your own words.

Notebooking Pages and Creating a Physics Notebook

As an optional addition to the course, Notebooking Pages have been added. Notebooking is a method of organizing coursework (FMN pages and completed lab sheets) along with notes, drawings, photographs, questions, independent research, and projects on a particular subject, all in one binder. Notebooking tends to involve more creative and visual elements than traditional "taking notes" on a course, and a student's notebook on a subject can become a keepsake to revisit over the years. For a good introduction to notebooking, just look at the first results from an Internet search on that term.

Blackline masters of the Notebooking Pages are provided in the Appendix of this book. This means that you are free to make as many copies of these pages as you need for your child. These pages are essentially templates such as Venn Diagrams and Definition Pages, and suggestions are given in many of the units for using the templates or for open-ended notebooking assignments. When students build simple machines or perform other experiments, you might consider taking pictures of the work completed and pasting them on sheets of paper. You will also find a lab report form on page 485 for optional use with more advanced students.

When the course is complete, students can assemble the many pages they have completed in one large three-ring binder to create their own Physics Notebook. There is a cover sheet on page 475 that may be cut out, colored, glued to a sheet of construction paper, and then used as the front cover for a Physics Notebook. Encourage students to share their Notebook with family and friends. Showing others their work and teaching others are excellent ways for students to review the material and further reinforce the science concepts studied. Many families choose to have the pages bound into a book at a copy shop.

What's The Big Idea?

Whenever you study a subject, there are main ideas and details to learn. It's true, that in science, there is a lot of new material to discover. If you are using a classical education approach to teaching, you will cover every subject three times throughout your child's education. Because of this, don't sweat the small stuff. This outline gives you the big ideas that your child should get from each unit, and the small stuff is an added bonus. If you and your child are timid scientists, just have fun as you try to learn the big ideas. If you and your child have a strong science background, work on learning the small stuff as well as the big ideas. There are many challenging words in this course that are used because they are the right words, and after hearing them over and over, they will "sink in." They are not here for your child to memorize the first time around. Use difficult words and science concepts gently, not with force, and your child will enjoy his science experience.

BI = BIG IDEA　　　　　SS = SMALL STUFF

UNIT 1: WHAT IS PHYSICS?

<u>PHYSICISTS USE SCIENTIFIC METHOD</u>

BI =　Everything around us is made of matter.

Physicists are scientists who study how matter behaves using the scientific method.

The scientific method is a cycle—observe, record, analyze, hypothesize, experiment, and start over again.

SS =　Matter has characteristics that help us to describe it.

<u>PHYSICISTS, IT TAKES ALL SORTS</u>

BI =　There are many types of physicists.

A thought experiment is one in which you imagine what would happen if you did an experiment.

SS =　Experimental physicists tend to spend their time performing experiments.

Theoretical physicists tend to spend their time coming up with ideas.

Albert Einstein is famous for his thought experiments about the nature of time and space.

UNIT 2: WHAT MATTERS

<u>MASS: IT REALLY MATTERS</u>

BI =　Mass is a measure of how much matter is in an object.

Weight is a measure of the strength of gravity pulling on an object.

SS =　The mass of an object is the same everywhere—Earth, the moon, Jupiter.

The mass of an object will change only if you add something to or take something away from an object.

Weight = gravity x mass

<u>WHAT FLOATS YOUR PLANET?</u>

BI =　One characteristic of matter involves whether it floats in water or not.

Sometimes, larger, heavier objects float while smaller, lighter objects sink.

Density is one of the most important characteristics in determining whether an object will float.

Density is a description of how much matter is packed into the space, or volume, that the object takes up.

SS =   Saturn would float in water, but Earth would not.

The characteristics of matter that determine whether it will float include: volume, density, and volume of water displaced.

Density = Mass ÷ Volume

An object will float if the volume of water it displaces weighs more than the object weighs.

UNIT 3: NEWTON'S LAWS

A FORCEFUL INTRODUCTION

BI =   A force is any push or pull on an object.

Gravity is a force that pulls all objects toward the center of the earth.

When an object isn't moving, it is at rest. For an object to be at rest, all the forces acting on it must be in equilibrium.

SS =   A contact force is any force that requires touching an object.

An action-at-a-distance force is a force that pushes or pulls without touching an object, such as gravity or magnetism.

MOVING WITH NEWTON

BI =   Isaac Newton was a mathematician and scientist who lived in the 1600s in England.

Newton figured out that the gravity that caused objects to fall to the ground is the same force that causes the moon to orbit Earth.

A scientific law describes what always happens given certain conditions.

SS =   Newton invented a form of mathematics called calculus that he used to describe the effects of gravity on an object both on Earth and in space.

Newton used math to develop his laws of motion: these laws predict how matter behaves when at rest and in motion.

Newton's laws do not work under all conditions. They fail to predict what will happen at speeds close to the speed of light and at sizes smaller than an atom.

NEWTON'S LAWS: THE FIRST LAW OF MOTION—INERTIA

BI =   The first law of motion has two parts:

An object at rest tends to remain at rest unless an extra force is applied to it.

An object in motion tends to remain in motion unless an extra force is applied to it.

An object's mass determines how much force is needed to change whether it is at rest or in motion.

SS =   This law was hard to figure out because on Earth there are many extra forces that we don't see, such as gravity and friction.

The tendency of an object to stay at rest or in motion is called inertia, which even affects how your body behaves.

NEWTON'S SECOND LAW—FROM ARISTOTLE TO NEWTON

BI =   Velocity is the scientific term for the speed of an object in a particular direction.

Newton's second law describes how forces change the speed or direction of an object.

Aristotle incorrectly believed that for an object to keep moving at a constant velocity, one had to apply a constant force to the object.

SS =   Acceleration is the scientific term for a change in velocity.

NEWTON'S SECOND LAW: MOMENTOUS MOMENTUM

BI =   There are three parts to Newton's second law:

1) An object will move in the direction it is pushed.

2) The harder you push an object, the faster it will go.

3) The more mass an object has, the harder it is to push.

We say that a moving object has a lot of momentum if it is hard to change its speed or direction.

Momentum depends on an object's mass and speed and can be transferred from one object to another.

SS =   Momentum is the tendency of an object to keep moving in the same direction.

Momentum even affects objects in zero-gravity environments.

NEWTON'S THIRD LAW: LIFT-OFF!

BI =   Newton's third law states: every action has an opposite, but equal, reaction.

Rocket ships work because of Newton's third law.

SS =   When you stand on the earth, the action is your shoe pushing down on the earth from the force of gravity. The reaction is the force of the earth pushing back.

Vectors are arrows that physicists use to illustrate forces. Vectors have both quantities (size) and direction to show how much force is being applied and in what direction.

UNIT 4: FRICTION

FRICTION—IT CAN RUB YOU THE WRONG WAY

BI =   Friction is caused when irregularities in two surfaces rub against each other.

Friction is a contact force that resists motion and always involves two pieces of matter rubbing against each other.

Without friction, it would be impossible to walk or to get cars to move.

SS =   It is almost impossible on Earth to make a perfectly smooth surface.

Friction can be caused by liquids, gases, or solids. For example, air molecules cause friction when objects move through the air.

A tribologist is a scientist who studies friction.

The coefficient of friction is a number representing how much friction exists between two particular surfaces.

FRICTION IN REAL LIFE: AUTO SAFETY

BI =   The science of physics goes into the design of the treads on car tires in order to maximize friction in slippery conditions.

Friction generates heat.

Tire treads are designed to help prevent hydroplaning, which can occur if a thin layer of water forms between a wheel and a road.

Motor oil helps prevent too much friction in automobile engines.

UNIT 5: WORK: PLANE AND SIMPLE MACHINES

WORKING HARD AND HARDLY WORKING

BI = Work is done when an object is moved by a force from one place to another.

Energy is the capacity to do work.

Kinetic energy is the energy of a moving object.

Potential energy is the energy stored up by an object when you move it against a force like gravity.

SS = Work is accomplished even when a force-at-a-distance such as gravity moves an object.

SIMPLE MACHINES: PLANES & WEDGES

BI = Simple machines are devices used to make work "easier," either because a machine changes the direction of force needed or because it changes the amount of force needed.

In physics, there is always a trade-off. If less force is needed, that force probably needs to be applied over a longer distance.

One group of simple machines is made of planes—or flat surfaces. These include: ramps (inclined planes), wedges, and screws.

SS = Archimedes described how simple machines work mathematically and helped people to understand and use simple machines.

Great things can be accomplished with simple machines. The pyramids and the Parthenon were constructed using primarily simple machines.

A ramp or inclined plane is a plane that is at an angle. A wedge is a ramp that moves.

WHAT DO STAIRS AND SCREWS HAVE IN COMMON?

BI = Stairs are a sort of ramp. They make work easier than lifting ourselves straight up, but we have to travel farther.

A screw is like an inclined plane, or staircase, wrapped around a cylinder.

SS = Threads are the grooves on a screw. More threads mean less force is needed, but the screw needs to be turned more times.

LEVERS: HOW TO MOVE THE PLANET WITH A REALLY LONG STICK

BI = Levers make it easier to lift objects. A lever is a stick or board placed on a fulcrum.

The fulcrum is the rock or object it rests on.

The load is what you are trying to move.

The effort is the amount of force you push with to move the object.

SI = Archimedes claimed that he could move the planet with a large enough lever.

LUGGING LOADS WITH LOTS OF LEVERS

BI = The fulcrum's location relative to the load and effort determines whether a lever is a first-, second-, or third-class lever.

The load arm is the length from the load to the fulcrum.

The effort arm is the length from the effort to the fulcrum.

SS = In a first-class lever the fulcrum is between the load and the effort, such as in a teeter-totter.

In a second-class lever the load is between the fulcrum and the effort, such as in a wheelbarrow

In a third-class lever, the effort is between the fulcrum and the load, such as in a broom.

LAWFUL LEVERS

BI = Archimedes described a mathematical formula that predicts how levers behave.

The formula tells us that: for all classes of levers, if you increase the load on the lever, you will have to either increase the distance you move the lever or the amount of force you apply to move that load.

SS = Archimedes's formula is called "The Law of the Lever." The formula is: (size of effort arm) x (amount of force applied at effort) = (size of load arm) x (weight of load).

DIZZY LEVERS: WHEELS & AXLES

BI = An axle is a stick to which a wheel has been attached such that when the wheel turns, the stick turns, and vice-versa.

Axles make work easier either by decreasing the amount of force needed (e.g., a truck winch) or increasing the distance moved (e.g., automobile wheels).

SS = A wheel and axle is actually a type of a lever.

PULLEYS

BI = A pulley is a wheel with a groove in it for a rope or chain.

Fixed pulleys do not move and help do work by changing the direction of force.

Moveable pulleys help do work by changing the amount of force.

SS = A block and tackle or compound pulley system is a group of pulleys working together. These machines can multiply the advantages and disadvantages of using a single pulley.

UNIT 6: AERODYNAMICS

AN INTRODUCTION TO THE INVISIBLE

BI = Air is a gas made up of molecules which are constantly in motion.

Like any gas, air is made of matter, and therefore it has mass and takes up space.

SS = Two objects cannot occupy the same space at the same time. This means, for example, that to get water into a cup, the air has to be pushed out of the way.

IF HOT AIR WERE A SUPERHERO

BI = Heat is a form of energy which causes molecules in a gas like air to move more quickly.

Hot air rises because it has less mass than cool air.

SS = Hot air has less mass than cool air because its molecules are moving more quickly, leaving fewer molecules in any given space.

The interaction of air with different temperatures is one of the main causes of weather.

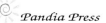

STANDING UP UNDER PRESSURE

BI =   The atmosphere is the air surrounding a planet.

The atmosphere is made of matter and therefore presses down on us with a lot of pressure.

SS =   Heat and cold increase and decrease air pressure in a closed space.

Differences in air pressure can create dramatic results, such as crushing a plastic bottle or creating a water fountain.

AIR FORCES WITHOUT UNIFORMS

BI =   Aerodynamics is the study of what happens when objects move through air.

The four basic forces that push or pull on objects in the air are: weight, drag, thrust, and lift.

SS =   Drag resists movement through air and is largely dependent on the shape of an object.

Bernoulli's principle is a partial description of how an airplane's wing shape, thrust, and lift interact to create a difference in air pressure and get planes off the ground.

UNIT 7: ENERGY AND WAVES

LET'S CATCH A WAVE, DUDE

BI =   A wave is energy carried from one location to another in the form of a distortion through a medium, such as the energy carried in a wave in the ocean.

SS =   The parts of a wave are the crest and the trough.

IT'S SOUND. IT'S A WAVE. IT'S A SOUND WAVE!

BI =   Sound waves consist of energy traveling through the medium of air molecules.

The amplitude, or height, of a sound wave determines how loud it is.

SS =   When sound travels through the air, it is energy that goes from one place to another, not air molecules.

THE SPEEDS OF SOUND

BI =   The distance between one wave and the next wave is called the wave's "wavelength."

When waves seem close together, we say that they have a higher frequency than waves that are farther apart.

SS =   Sound travels through different mediums at different speeds.

The speed with which a wave travels through a medium is different than the wave's frequency.

Higher-pitched sounds are created from waves with a higher frequency.

AMPLIFICATION: CAN YOU HEAR ME NOW?

BI =   Amplification means increasing the amplitude, or loudness, of a sound wave.

To increase amplification, one must increase the amount of energy in a wave.

Amplifiers such as stethoscopes or megaphones increase amplitude by focusing a lot of energy into a small space.

SS =   René Laennec invented the stethoscope when he realized that listening to a patient's heartbeat through a rolled-up piece of paper amplified the heartbeat's sounds.

UNIT 8: MAGNETISM

INTRODUCING MAGNETISM

BI =   In physics, a "field" is an area in which a force exists.

A magnet is a substance that produces a magnetic field. An object is magnetic if it can be attracted by a magnet.

Some magnets are stronger than others.

SS =   All magnetic objects have metal in them, but not all metals are magnetic.

Magnetism is an action-at-a-distance force.

Quantitative observations are those that involve measuring with numbers—such as temperature or distance. Qualitative observations involve describing something's qualities—such as whether or not it is magnetic.

MAGNETS AND POLES

BI =   All magnets have two "poles"—north and south. Like poles always repel one another, and unlike poles always attract one another.

SS =   Physicists believe that magnetism is ultimately caused by how electrons in different substances behave.

MAGNETS: SMALL, SMALLER, AND SMALLEST

BI =   When a magnet is cut in half, it creates two magnets, each with two poles.

Ferromagnetic materials are attracted by magnets and can be magnetized temporarily.

SS =   Magnetic domains are regions in a material in which the magnetic fields of the atoms making up the substance are aligned in one direction.

OH NO! I THOUGHT THIS WAS THE NORTH POLE!

BI =   The planet Earth behaves like there is a giant magnet running through the center of the planet.

Scientists believe the magnetic field around the earth is caused by molten iron spinning within the earth's outer core.

SS =   In reality, the magnetic poles of the earth move around quite a bit—on the order of hundreds of miles per century.

The North Pole is actually the south pole of the earth's magnetic field. We call it the North Pole because the north poles of our magnets point to it.

UNIT 9: ELECTRICITY

LET'S START INSIDE THE ATOM

BI = Atoms are composed of protons, neutrons, and electrons. Protons have an electrical charge of +1, electrons have an electrical charge of -1, and neutrons have no electrical charge.

Electrons exist in an orbit around the nucleus of the atom, which contains the protons and neutrons.

SS =   Normally positive charges repel each other. It is the strong nuclear force which holds the protons together in the nucleus of the atom and is immensely stronger than the force of gravity.

Scientists sometimes use models when they can't study something directly.

STATIC: IT'S ELECTRIFYING

BI =   A static electrical charge is created by a "pool" of electrons—a bunch of electrons that are not flowing through a substance.

          An electrical current is created by flowing electrons.

SS =   Sometimes, electrons are transferred between atoms and molecules. For example, when you rub a balloon on a wool sweater, electrons are transferred from the wool and "pool" on the balloon.

          An electroscope is a device used to detect static electricity.

ELECTRICITY RULES: PLAYING IT SAFE

BI =   Always follow the safety rules when experimenting with electricity.

ELECTRICAL CURRENT: GOING WITH THE FLOW

BI =   Electrical current is caused by electrons flowing through empty spaces in atoms' electron shells.

          Conductors are materials that allow electrons to flow freely. Insulators are materials in which electrons have a very hard time flowing.

          An electrical circuit is a loop through which electricity flows.

SI =   Batteries get current flowing through wires by creating a difference in a type of potential energy—electrical potential—between one end of the battery and the other.

          There are many types of electrical components—such as wires, batteries, switches, and light bulbs.

POWERING UP!

BI =   When electrical components are connected in series, they are connected one after the other.

          When electrical components are connected in parallel, there are two or more components connected to the same component.

SI =   Electricity is measured in power (wattage), amount of electrical charge (amperes), and electrical potential (voltage).

ELECTROMAGNETISM

BI =   Both electricity and magnetism are created by the motion of electrons and create fields of force around this motion. Because of this, electrical fields affect magnetism and magnetic fields affect electric current.

SS =   Electric motors transform electrical energy into motion. Magnets can be used in electrical generators to transform the motion of the magnet into electric current.

          Ferromagnetic materials can be made into magnets by running an electrical current around them.

UNIT 10: NEW WORLDS TO EXPLORE

EVERYTHING IS RELATIVE

BI =   Motion is relative. If you are in a car moving at 10 miles per hour and there is another car traveling next to you at the same speed and in the same direction, it will appear as if the other car is not moving relative to your car. The observation of speed and direction of an object will depend on—be relative to—the speed and the direction of the observer.

          Einstein imagined traveling with a beam of light and realized that the speed of light is not relative. It is constant regardless of whether an observer is moving. This realization led to Einstein's theory of special relativity.

Einstein also imagined various thought experiments involving acceleration and gravity. He realized that an observer experiences both acceleration and gravity the same way. This realization led to Einstein's theory of general relativity.

SS =   Objects (and people) traveling close to the speed of light experience time more slowly than observers not traveling close to the speed of light.

Objects traveling close to the speed of light contract, or get smaller, in the direction in which they are traveling.

These two effects are necessary for the speed of light to remain constant to all observers.

LIGHT: WHEN DOING THE WAVE JUST WON'T WORK

BI =   Isaac Newton theorized that light was composed of particles. Thomas Young theorized that light was composed of waves of energy. Both theories were supported by experimental evidence and everyday observations.

Albert Einstein wrote a paper about the photoelectric effect demonstrating that light behaves more like particles. This was an important step toward understanding that light exhibits both wave- and particle-like behavior.

SS =   Quantum physics is the study of the behavior of matter on the extremely small scale of subatomic particles.

Thomas Young demonstrated the wave nature of light by shining a focused light through small slits to create a wave-like pattern on the wall.

The photoelectric effect occurs when certain metals eject electrons from their surface when exposed to light of different wavelengths.

QUANTUM WEIRDNESS

BI =   Thomas Young used a light beam in his double-slit experiment. When scientists tried the experiment with electrons, rather than light, the results were startling. These experiments suggested that electrons, which are made of matter, behave like waves under certain circumstances, and like particles under other circumstances.

Ultimately, scientists concluded that light and electrons have a dual nature—they exhibit both wave- and particle-like behavior.

Scientists were amazed to discover that the act of measuring and detecting the results of their experiments changed the results of those experiments—forcing the electrons to behave like particles.

SS =   Physicists hypothesize that when an electron is fired toward double slits, the electron exists in a state of superposition: It exists as a set of possible outcomes such as going through the left slit, going through the right slit, or going through neither slit.

Schrodinger devised his famous cat experiment to demonstrate how absurd these quantum effects would seem if they occurred in the everyday world that we perceive. Rather than disproving quantum weirdness, Schrodinger's thought experiment became the basis for different interpretations of how measuring quantum behavior affects the outcome of experiments.

Lab Supply List (see page 2 regarding RSO supply kits from Home Science Tools)

Items are listed by unit in the order in which they are first needed. + means an item will be needed for later labs also. The amounts listed are totals for the entire course. Most items are common household items.
* means the item requires some explanation. Ordering hints and explanations are given on page 21.

UNIT	EQUIPMENT / MATERIAL	AMOUNT	UNIT	EQUIPMENT / MATERIAL	AMOUNT
1	Similar, not identical, toys	2	3+	Ruler/tape measure	1
1+	Colored pencils	pack	3	Clothespin (optional)	1
2+	Calculator	1	4	Book with dust jacket	1
2	Bathroom scale	1	4	Heavy book	1
2+	Kitchen scale	1	4+	Stiff foam board	1 @ 4' x 2'
2	Low- and high-density objects	6 each	4+	Meter stick	1
2+	Wide, short, clear glass	1	4	Aluminum foil	1 roll
2	Dry-erase marker	1	4+	Magnifying lens	1
2+	Polymer Clay	1 pack	5+	Rubber bands	5
2+	Glass of water	1	5	Flour	1 cup
2+	Teaspoon and tablespoon	1	5+	Spoon	1
3+	Drawing materials (e.g. markers)	pack	5	Paper plate	1
3+	Toy with wheels (small, flat top)	1	5	Box of tissues	1
3	Toy figure (small)	1	5+	Spring scale*	1
3	Cardboard (small, rectangular)	1	5	Door wedge	1
3+	Masking tape	1 roll	5	Large building blocks	2
3+	Flat, smooth surface		5+	Large sheet of paper	3
3+	Paper cup	2	5+	Corrugated cardboard, 12" square	3 sheets
3+	Permanent marker	1	5	Sharpened pencil with eraser	1
3	Toy with wheels (medium-size)	1	5+	Scissors	1
3+	String	2 rolls	5	Variety of screws	few
3+	Marbles (2 sizes)	at least 5	5	Bolts w/ different threading	2+
3	Cardboard from paper towel roll	1	5	Stiff ruler	1
3	Basketball	1	5	Pennies	50
3	Tennis ball	1	5	Internet access (optional)	
3	Outdoor paved space		5	Car owner's manual (optional)	1
3	Straws	3	5	Hole puncher	1
3+	Balloons (round and long ones)	16+	5	Shoebox	1

UNIT	EQUIPMENT / MATERIAL	AMOUNT
5	Whisk broom	1
5	Heavy object (e.g. jug of water)	1
5	Lighter object (e.g. empty jug)	1
5	Household objects that are levers (e.g. tweezers, pliers, rake)	10+
5	Stiff foam board or cardboard	1 @ 30" x 10"
5	Duct tape	1 roll
5	Drawing compass	1
5	Thin wooden dowels	4 @ 12-18" 2+ @ 3-4"
5	Straw that will fit over dowel	1
5	Household objects that are wheel & axle simple machines (e.g. screwdriver, doorknob, pencil sharpener, fan, etc.)	5
5	Wooden clothes hanger and place to hang it	1
5	Bendable metal wire	12"
5	Wire cutter	1
5+	Glue	1 bottle
5	1-liter bottle of soda or water	1
6+	Paper towels	1 roll
6+	Sink or plastic tub	1
6	Empty plastic 2-liter bottle	1
6	Heat source (e.g. light bulb or burner)	1
6	Sheet of newspaper	1
6+	Table surface	1
6	Empty plastic water bottle with cap	2
6	Freezer access	
6+	Large index card	2
6+	Sheets of copy paper	15+
6	High place from where to drop things (e.g. staircase, ladder, chair)	
6	Empty soda cans	2
6+	Paper clips (optional)	few

UNIT	EQUIPMENT / MATERIAL	AMOUNT
6	Stopwatch (or watch w/ second hand)	1
6	Wide-open space to fly paper airplanes	
7	Metal Slinky (or Mardi Gras beads)	1
7	Plastic, round food container	1
7	Rubber band that will fit over plastic, round food container	1
7	Plastic wrap	1 roll
7	Fine sugar or salt	pinch
7	Construction paper	8 sheets
8	Magnets (at least 2 bar-type, 1 disk-shaped, and 1 horseshoe-shaped)	5+
8	Household objects- magnetic and nonmagnetic	10-15
8+	Metal paper clips (that are magnetic)	5+
8	Colored tape	2 colors
8	Iron fillings*	
8	Iron or steel nail	1
8	Cork (e.g. wine bottle cork)	1
8	Needle (that is magnetic)	1
9	Self-hardening or polymer clay	2 colors, small packs
9	Glass jar	1
9	Piece of wool (or wool clothing)	1
9	Insulated wire	5-6 feet
9	Wire cutters	1
9	D-cell battery	2
9	D-cell battery holder*	2
9	Miniature light bulb*	1
9	Miniature light bulb receptacle or socket*	1
9	Card stock	5" x 1"
9	3" to 4" nail or screw that is attracted by a magnet	1
9	Needle-nosed pliers	1

UNIT	EQUIPMENT / MATERIAL	AMOUNT
10	Pencil lead for mechanical pencil	3 sticks
10	Laser light	1
10	Dark room with clear wall space	

*Ordering Hints and Explanations:

Spring Scale: You don't need to spend a lot of money on a spring scale (a $4-$10 one is all you need). These are readily available online at Amazon and from science supply companies. Look for one that has a 5-10 lb (about 2 kg-5 kg) capacity.

Iron Fillings: readily found in education supply stores, and even some toy stores in the "science" section. These can also be ordered online from many companies, including Amazon. Enter "iron fillings" in your search engine and you will find iron filings for sale in little shaker bottles like the type spices come in.

Electricity Supplies: D-cell battery holder, miniature light bulb**, and miniature light bulb receptacle: These items can be found at your local home improvement store or electronics store, such as Radio Shack. They are also readily available from online companies like Amazon. In lieu of purchasing all these items individually, you could purchase one or two basic electricity kits, such as those found in toy stores. Make sure you have at least 2 battery holders, a light bulb, and a bulb holder. These kits generally use AA batteries instead of D-cell, and they are more flimsy than one you could put together yourself, but they are still a possible alternative.

**Which miniature bulb should I buy? Students are going to be making circuits to illuminate a flashlight bulb. A decade ago, this was a simple proposition, as there was really only one type of flashlight bulb available, an incandescent bulb. Now, because of environmental concerns, incandescent bulbs are no longer being produced, and LED and other bulbs such as halogen, xenon, and krypton bulbs are replacing them. Halogen, xenon, and krypton bulbs look and function similarly to the old incandescent bulbs. The best bulb to use for this experiment is the bulb out of an old flashlight. The only bulb that absolutely won't work well is an LED bulb because the voltage requirements for LED bulbs are so low that one needs to use an extra component, a resistor, with regular batteries. You may have to experiment with one or two bulbs, but the worst that will happen is that you will burn out a flashlight bulb, or the exposed ends of the wires might become hot.

Suggested Weekly Schedule

The following schedule is suggested for those wishing to complete this course in a 36-week school year, teaching science twice a week. General supplies needed for each week are listed. Refer to the lesson or supply list for specifics on supplies including quantities.   * **indicates a lab or activity**

Week	Day	Lesson / Lab	Supplies Needed for the Week	Dates / Notes
1	Day 1	Physicists Use Scientific Method *Acting Like a Physicist	Similar toys (2), Colored pencils	Unit 1
	Day 2	Physicists, It Takes All Sorts *Thinking about Drinking Water		
2	Day 1	Mass: It Really Matters *Weighing in Around the Solar System	Calculator, Bathroom scale, Kitchen scale, Low- and high-density objects (6 each)	Unit 2
	Day 2	What Floats Your Planet? *Density: All Objects, Large and Small		
3	Day 1	*Water Displacement: It'll Float Your Boat!	Wide, short, clear glass; Dry erase marker; Polymer Clay; Glass of water; Teaspoon or tablespoon	Unit 2
	Day 2	A Story about Density: Archimedes and the Crown		
4	Day 1	A Forceful Introduction *An Object in Equilibrium	Glass of water, Drawing materials	Unit 3
	Day 2	Moving with Newton		
5	Day 1	Newton's Laws: The First Law of Motion—Inertia	Drawing materials, Toy with wheels, Small toy figure, Cardboard, Tape, Flat surface	Unit 3
	Day 2	*Inertia and You!		
6	Day 1	Physics in Action: Preventing Injuries in Car Accidents *Inertia Can Be Dizzying!	Paper cup, Permanent marker, Toy with wheels, String, Flat area	Unit 3
	Day 2	Newton's Second Law—From Aristotle to Newton *You've Got to Keep It Moving		
7	Day 1	Newton's Second Law: Momentous Momentum	Marbles, Cardboard from paper towel roll, Magic marker, Basketball, Tennis ball, Flat surface, Tape, Outdoor paved space	Unit 3
	Day 2	*Giving the Gift of Momentum		
8	Day 1	Newton's Third Law: Lift-Off! *Rocket Science Newton's Brain Teasers	String, Straws, Balloons, Ruler or tape measurer, Strong tape, Marker, Clothespin (optional)	Unit 3
	Day 2	Newton's Laws of Motion: A Summary		
9	Day 1	Friction - It Can Rub You the Wrong Way	Drawing materials	Unit 4
	Day 2	*Activity: Slip Sliding Away		
10	Day 1	*How Much Is Enough?	Book with dust jacket, Heavy book, Stiff foam board, Toy vehicle, Meterstick or yardstick, Aluminum foil, Magnifying lens, Tape, Calculator	Unit 4
	Day 2	Friction in Real Life: Auto Safety Friction: A Summary		
11	Day 1	Working Hard or Hardly Working? *Working It Out	Rubber bands, Marbles, Paper plate, Flour, Spoon, Ruler	Unit 5
	Day 2	*You've Got a Lot of Potential!		

Pandia Press

Week	Day	Lesson / Lab	Supplies Needed for the Week	Dates / Notes
12	Day 1	Simple Machines: Planes & Wedges *It's Plainly a Plane!	Box of tissues, Spring scale, Ruler, Foam board, Colored pencils, Door wedge, Large building blocks, Sheet of paper, Corrugated cardboard, Pencil w/ eraser, Magnifying lens (optional)	Unit 5 See p. 21 re. spring scale
12	Day 2	*All Wedged In *More Wedges		
13	Day 1	*Those Screwy Planes	Sharpened pencil, Sheets of paper, Scissors, Inches ruler, Screw(s), Bolts and fitting nuts, Permanent marker, String	Unit 5
13	Day 2	What Do Stairs & Screws Have in Common? *The Nuts & Bolts of Screws		
14	Day 1	Levers: How to Move the Planet . . . *Large, Little, and Long Levers	Stiff 12" ruler, Pencil, Pennies, Tape, Internet or car owner's manual (optional), Calculator	Unit 5
14	Day 2	Lugging Loads with Lots of Levers *First-Class Levers—Large, Larger & Largest		
15	Day 1	*Second-Class Levers: Wheeling It In	Stiff 12" ruler, Paper cup, Hole puncher, String, Pennies, Shoebox, Whisk broom, Heavy object (e.g. jug of water), Lighter object (e.g. empty jug), Masking tape, Tape measurer	Unit 5
15	Day 2	*Third-Class Levers: It's a Clean Sweep!		
16	Day 1	Lawful Levers *Lever Detector	Household objects that are levers (e.g. tweezers, pliers, rake), Foam board, Scissors, Wooden dowels, Duct tape, Drawing compass, Magic marker, Ruler	Unit 5
16	Day 2	Dizzy Levers: Wheels & Axles *Going in Circles		
17	Day 1	*A Dizzy First-Class Lever	String, Roll of packing or duct tape, Straw, Scissors, Helper, Tape, Ruler, Household objects that are wheel & axle simple machines (e.g. screwdriver, doorknob, pencil sharpener, fan, etc.)	Unit 5
17	Day 2	*Going in Circles in the Real World *Wheel & Axle Wrap-up		
18	Day 1	Pulleys *Fixed Pulleys- Which Way Did It Go? (begin)	Wooden clothes hanger and place to hang it, Bendable metal wire, Wire cutter, Corrugated cardboard, Drawing compass, Scissors, Wooden dowels, String, Glue, Pencil, 1-liter bottle of soda or water, Spring scale, Ruler	Unit 5
18	Day 2	*Fixed Pulleys- Which Way Did It Go? (complete)		
19	Day 1	*Moveable Pulley- How Does It Do That?	Spring scale, Ruler	Unit 5
19	Day 2	*It's a Block! It's a Tackle! It's a Block & Tackle! Simple Machines: They're Simply Fantastic!		
20	Day 1	An Introduction to the Invisible *It Can't Be Nothing if It Weighs Something	Balloons, String, Rubber bands, Meterstick or yardstick, Glass cup, Sink or plastic tub, Paper towels	Unit 6
20	Day 2	*Is the Glass Half Empty or Half Full?		
21	Day 1	If Hot Air Was a Superhero *Hot Air Is Cool!	Empty plastic 2-liter bottle, balloons, Access to hot and cold water, Tape, Colored pencils, String, Scissors, Heat source (e.g. light bulb or burner)	Unit 6
21	Day 2	*Taking Hot Air for a Spin		
22	Day 1	*Are You Stronger than a Piece of Paper? *Differences Matter *The Magic of Pressure *A Water Fountain That Defies Gravity!	Newspaper, Stiff ruler, Table surface, Empty plastic water bottle with cap, Access to a freezer, Glass of water, Large index card, Sink or basin, Straw, Water, Clay	Unit 6
22	Day 2	(Complete anything unfinished from the Quartet of Quick Experiments on Day 1)		
23	Day 1	Air Forces without Uniforms *Dropping Stuff Is a Drag	Sheets of copy paper, High place from where to drop things (e.g. staircase, ladder, chair), Scissors, Empty soda cans, Tape measure, Paper clips (optional), Stopwatch or watch w/ second hand, Wide open space	Unit 6
23	Day 2	How Do Planes Fly? *Hey, Bernoulli, Can You Give Me a Lift? *Take Off!		

Week	Day	Lesson / Lab	Supplies Needed for the Week	Dates / Notes
24	Day 1	Let's Catch a Wave, Dude! *Doing the Wave	Metal Slinky (or Mardi Gras beads); Large hard surface; Plastic, round food container; Plastic wrap: Large rubber band; Fine sugar or salt	Unit 7
	Day 2	It's Sound. It's a Wave. It's a Sound Wave! *Making Big Waves		
25	Day 1	The Speeds of Sound *Hitting the High Notes	Construction paper, Tape, Scissors, Crayons or markers (optional)	Unit 7
	Day 2	Amplification: Can You Hear Me Now? *Can You Hear Me Now?		
26	Day 1	Introducing Magnetism *Tracking Attraction	Magnets, Household objects- magnetic and nonmagnetic, Metal paper clips, Ruler, Flat surface, Tape	Unit 8
	Day 2	*The Measure of a Magnet		
27	Day 1	Magnets and Poles	Magnets, Colored tape (2), Iron Fillings, String	Unit 8 See p. 21 re. iron fillings
	Day 2	*Searching for Poles		
28	Day 1	Magnets: Small, Smaller, and Smallest *Is It a Magnet or Isn't It?	Magnets, Metal paper clips, Iron or steel nail, Cork, Bowl of water, Metal needle	Unit 8
	Day 2	Finding the North Pole *Oh No! I Thought This Was the North Pole!		
29	Day 1	Let's Start inside the Atom *Atomic Super Models (begin)	Self-hardening or polymer clay (2 colors), Colored pencils	Unit 9
	Day 2	*Atomic Super Models (complete)		
30	Day 1	Static: It's Electrifying	Aluminum foil, Scissors, Glass jar, Large Index card, Tape, Balloon, Piece of wool (or wool clothing), Hole puncher (optional)	Unit 9
	Day 2	*Static Detector		
31	Day 1	Electricity Rules: Playing It Safe Electrical Current: Going with the Flow	Insulated wire, Wire cutters, D-cell battery, D-cell battery holder, Miniature light bulb, Miniature light bulb receptacle or socket	Unit 9 See p. 21 re. electrical supplies
	Day 2	*Going with the Flow		
32	Day 1	*Switch It On	Insulated wire, Wire cutters, Metal paper clips, Tape, Card stock, D-cell batteries, D-cell battery holders, Miniature light bulb, Miniature light bulb receptacle or socket	Unit 9
	Day 2	Powering Up! *Power Up!		
33	Day 1	Electromagnetism *Creating a Force Field	Nail or screw that is attracted by a magnet, Insulated wire, Wire cutters, D-cell batteries, D-cell battery holders, Paper clips, Magnet, Tape, Needle-nosed pliers, Cardboard	Unit 9
	Day 2	*That's Right, I Made an Electric Motor! (begin)		
34	Day 1	*That's Right, I Made an Electric Motor! (complete)	Insulated wire, Wire cutters, D-cell batteries, D-cell battery holders, Paper clips, Magnet, Tape, Needle-nosed pliers, Cardboard	Units 9 and 10
	Day 2	Everything Is Relative *Dropping Rocks Around the Universe		
35	Day 1	Light: When Doing the Wave Just Won't Work * Quantum Experiments	Pencil lead for mechanical pencil, Laser light, Dark room with clear wall space	Unit 10
	Day 2	Quantum Weirdness * Schrodinger's Cat		
36	Day 1	Final Thoughts Begin Assembly of Your Physics Notebook	Completed Lab sheets, FMN pages, Photos from class, 3-hole punch, 3-ring notebook, Craft supplies: colored pencils, glue, scissors, etc.	See Introduction for info on creating a Physics Notebook
	Day 2	Complete Assembly of Your Physics Notebook and Show It off!		

Further Reading and Exploring

The following are suggestions for those who want to explore further. Most public libraries will have a children's section about physics which includes picture books about particular subjects, such as "gravity" or "pulleys." Almost all of these are good, solid books. The resources listed below are those that are exceptional or stand out in some way for each of the subjects covered. I have also included a few books for adults who would like an overview of physics.

Unit 1 - WHAT IS PHYSICS? (AND GENERAL PHYSICS)
> *What's Physics All About*, by Kate Davies
>
> *Junk Drawer Physics: 50 Awesome Experiments That Don't Cost a Thing*, by Bobby Mercer
>
> *A Brief History of Time*, by Stephen Hawkings (for adults)
>
> *Mr Tomkins in Paperback*, by George Gamow (for adults--an older, classic book explaining post-Einstein physics to lay people)

Unit 2 - WHAT MATTERS
> Audio recording: *Jim Weiss: Galileo and the Stargazers* (includes the story of "Archimedes & the Crown")
>
> *The Magic School Bus: Lost in the Solar System*, by Joanna Cole
>
> *Archimedes and the Door of Science*, by Jeanne Bendick

Unit 3 - NEWTON'S LAWS & UNIT 4: FRICTION
> *Car Science*, by Richard Hammond
>
> *Isaac Newton and Physics for Kids: His Life and Ideas with 21 Activities*, by Carrie Logan Hollihan
>
> *Forces Make Things Move*, by Kimberly Brubaker Bradley

Unit 5 - WORK: PLANE & SIMPLE MACHINES
> *The New Way Things Work*, by David Macaulay & Neil Ardley
>
> *The Best of Rube Goldberg*, by Ruben Lucius Goldberg
>
> Websites: On Wikipedia, look up "Hero of Alexandria," and look into the inventions on this page. Hero invented the first vending machine, steam engine, and hydraulic water fountain—2000 years ago!
>
> For kids who are into video games, this one provides a series of puzzles that require you to design various contraptions: http://www.fantasticcontraption.net/

Unit 6 - THE INVISIBLE WORLD OF AIR
> *The Flying Machine Book: Build and Launch 35 Rockets, Gliders, Helicopters, Boomerangs, and More*, by Bobby Mercer
>
> *The World Record Paper Airplane Book*, by Ken Blackburn
>
> *Flight! Make It Work!*, by Andrew Haslam

Unit 7 - SOUND AND WAVES
> *Rubber Band Banjos and a Java Jive Bass: Projects and Activities on the Science of Music & Sound*, by Alex Sabbeth

Unit 8 - MAGNETISM and Unit 9 - ELECTRICITY

Electricity! Make it Work!, by Andrew Haslam

Batteries, Bulbs, and Wires, by David Glover (covers similar material as this text, but in a bit more detail)

Awesome Experiments in Electricity and Magnetism, by Michael DiSpezio

Hands-on: Snap Circuits toys and kits are easy ways for kids to build electronic devices as complex as radio receivers

Website: http://deciwatt.global: This is the site of the GravityLight—a clever device which uses gravity and the principles of electromagnetism to power lamps in areas without electrical power.

Unit 10 - NEW WORLDS TO EXPLORE

Website: Dr. Quantum's video on quantum effects is fabulous:
https://www.youtube.com/watch?v=DfPeprQ7oGc

Albert Einstein and Relativity for Kids, by Jerome Pohlen

For older students & parents who are really intrigued by these ideas, I suggest reading any of Michio Kaku's books

Unit 1

What Is Physics?

Unit 1- What Is Physics?

For my notebook

Physicists Use Scientific Method

Look around you. You probably already know that everything around you, that almost everything in the universe, is made of <u>atoms</u> and <u>molecules</u>. This piece of paper, your body, whatever you're sitting on—all these things are made of atoms and molecules. Even things you can't see, like the air you breathe, or things you can't touch, like the clouds in the sky, are made of atoms and molecules. You might even know that there are a few things made of particles that are smaller than atoms and molecules.

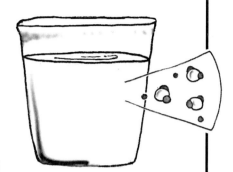

Scientists call any thing that exists, any thing that is made of any sized particle at all, <u>matter</u>. You are made of matter. The sun and other stars are made of matter. The food you eat and the liquids you drink are made of matter.

<u>Physicists</u> are scientists who try to understand why different forms of matter behave in certain ways. Physicists try to figure out why things fall when you drop them, why different objects move at different speeds when you push them, why magnets pull and push things, how electricity moves through a wire, and countless other questions. The science of <u>physics</u> is the study of matter and the forces and energy that affect matter.

There are many different types of physicists and many different ways that physicists study matter and its behavior. All physicists, though, use the <u>scientific method</u>. This means that they carefully observe the world around them. They examine things not only with their senses, but also with equipment that can measure different qualities of matter such as electrical current, brightness, speed, and weight. Then, they record their <u>observations</u> by writing them down in a lab book, just like you will when you do the experiments in this book.

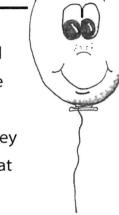

Once physicists have made observations and recorded their observations, they can analyze these observations—the <u>data</u>. They think about what they have seen and compare it with what they already know about how the world works. They think of questions that they might want to answer about what they've observed.

For example, a physicist might observe that a helium balloon slowly floats upward when she lets go of it. Then, she might compare this observation to the knowledge that almost everything else in the world falls toward the ground when you let go of it. She might wonder why the balloon rises. Is it because it is tied to a string? Is it because of the helium gas inside the balloon? Is it because of the substance the balloon is made from?

The physicist will come up with an idea about what is most likely the cause for the observation. Perhaps the physicist will develop an idea—a <u>hypothesis</u>—that the balloon rises because of the helium inside of it. The physicist will then develop experiments to test this hypothesis. The physicist might observe what happens if a balloon is filled with gases other than helium. Or, the physicist might experiment with filling objects other than balloons with helium. Eventually, the physicist will make additional observations and reach a <u>conclusion</u> about the hypothesis. Perhaps in our example the conclusion will be that helium causes the balloon to rise. Even if the conclusion is that the hypothesis was wrong, the scientist has still learned something valuable and can develop more experiments to understand more about the world.

In the next activity, you're going to practice the most valuable skill a scientist can have—the ability to observe the world around you carefully and precisely.

What Is Physics? Lab #1: Acting Like a Physicist
- instructions

Materials:
- Lab sheet, pencil
- Two similar, but not identical, toys. For example: two toy cars, two alphabet blocks, two dolls

Aloud: All matter has <u>characteristics</u>. A characteristic is some feature of an object that helps us to describe that object. For example, some characteristics of an apple are: it is round; it is red; it is composed of cells; and, it is healthy to eat. Can you think of other characteristics of an apple?

Physicists and other scientists use characteristics to help them compare different types of matter to each other. They might observe, for instance, that a magnet attracts iron but not wood. Scientists also use characteristics to describe what happens to a single type of matter in different situations. For example, water at room temperature has the characteristic of being a liquid. But when you boil it, it becomes a gas.

Two important skills scientists have are being able to notice details and being able to describe what they notice. Take a minute to look closely at one of your toys. What color is it? Is it big or small? Is it heavy or light? Would it travel a long way if you pushed it on a flat surface? Would it bounce or break if you dropped it? Now, fill in your lab sheet.

Procedure:
1. Lay the objects on a table or the floor where everyone can see them.
2. Fill in the lab sheet.
3. Conclusion / Discussion:
4. Talk about which of the characteristics are the most important in telling one toy from another. For example, with something like marbles, color and size are probably more important than shape.
5. Are these characteristics different from ones that help you know what to do with a toy? For example, if you compare two cars, you would notice that they both have wheels and can roll. These characteristics wouldn't help you to distinguish between the two cars, but they would help you to determine what to do with the toy cars.
6. Are these characteristics any different from the characteristics that tell you how a toy would behave? Which characteristics tell you things like whether a toy bounces; whether it rolls; whether it is sturdy or delicate?

More Lab Fun:
Here's a game you can play with characteristics: Have one player think of an object in the room. Don't tell the other player what it is. The second player should ask questions about what the object is, based only on its characteristics, such as: What is its color? Is it heavy or light? This is like 20 questions, but focuses on observations you can make about objects.

[continued]

Notebooking Ideas:

Reproducible notebooking pages are found in the Appendix.

1. Use a Venn Diagram page to diagram the characteristics of two people you know well. One circle should be labeled "Characteristics of _____" (the first person); the second should be labeled "Characteristics of _____" (the second person). The intersection is the characteristics these two people share.

2. Use a definition page to define any of the following words:

    Matter
    Physicist
    Scientific Method
    Data
    Hypothesis

Acting Like a Physicist

The two toys that I observed are:

_____ and

_____ .

Fill in the chart. Add whatever characteristics you'd like to the list. You should be able to come up with at least 10.

Characteristic	Toy 1	Toy 2
Color		
Bounces?		
Rolls?		

Circle the characteristics that would help you to distinguish one of your toys from the other.

Unit 1- What Is Physics?

For my notebook

Physicists, It Takes All Sorts

All physicists work with some or all of the parts of the scientific method. Some spend their time focusing on making observations. They might observe the universe by looking through telescopes, by tracking the motions of objects in the sky, or by listening to radio waves from objects in space. Or, they might observe what happens when they smash atoms together at very high speeds in order to find out what atoms are made of.

There are physicists who perform lots of experiments. Some of the astronauts who perform experiments in space are physicists. Some physicists might try to figure out how to speed up atoms when they smash them together. Other physicists might devise experiments that use electricity and magnets to help us understand more about how the world works.

There are also physicists who do none of these things. A <u>theoretical physicist</u> could work by sitting in an office all day long looking at mathematical equations that describe how matter behaves. He develops ideas based on previous observations and experiments and based on the ideas of other physicists. A theoretical physicist tries to develop a hypothesis that experimental physicists can test, using experiments.

One very famous theoretical physicist was **Albert Einstein**. He thought about what would happen if we could perform experiments that just weren't possible to perform at the time. In one of these thought experiments, he tried to figure out what would happen if one of two twin brothers were sent off into space and traveled at a speed that was close to the speed of light. He hypothesized that the brother who traveled into space would experience time more slowly than the brother who stayed on Earth—that when the traveler returned, he would be younger than his twin brother!

Albert Einstein

Scientists were shocked by Einstein's hypotheses. Many of his thought experiments were even more surprising than this one. So, experimental physicists figured out ways to test some of Einstein's ideas. Instead of sending a person into space, they put a very precise clock into an airplane that traveled at a very high speed. They kept an identical clock on the ground. When the plane landed, they compared the two clocks. Time actually had slowed down for the clock that was on the plane, just as Einstein's thought experiment predicted. All sorts of physicists were needed to demonstrate that many of Einstein's ideas were correct.

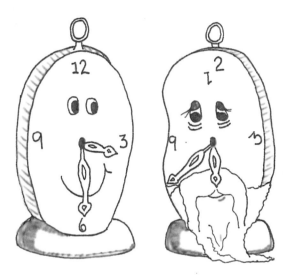

In the next activity, we're going to learn a little bit about how to conduct thought experiments of our own—just as Einstein did. Later in this course, we'll get to devise an experiment to test the ideas that we develop in this thought experiment.

What Is Physics? Lab #2: Thinking about Drinking Water - instructions

Materials:
- Lab sheets, pencil
- Colored pencils
- Imagination

Aloud: Albert Einstein used thought experiments as a way to help him think about what would happen if he could do things that were impossible—things like traveling at very high speeds in a rocket, or flying close to a very heavy object like the sun. Another reason that physicists use thought experiments is to help them think through a problem. By thinking about a scientific question before rushing to do a real experiment, physicists can make intelligent guesses about which experiments will be most helpful. This is the kind of thought experiment we're going to do today.

Here's the thought experiment: What happens when you drink through a straw? Sounds pretty simple, right? But, as a scientist, you would have to think about why each step happens the way it does. When you pour liquid into the glass, why does it stay there? Why does it take on the shape of the glass? When you put the straw into the glass, how much liquid fills the straw? What else is in the straw? Try to draw each step and label what you think is happening and what types of matter (air, water, glass) are involved. Try to do all this without actually having a glass of water and a straw in front of you. In another lesson, we'll do an experiment to see if the ideas from your thought experiment turn out to be correct.

Procedure:
Fill in the lab sheet

Note to Parents and Teachers:
 It is helpful to have a toy block on hand when starting the next unit, What Matters.

Thinking about Drinking Water

If I were to put a straw into a cup filled part way with water, this is what I think I would observe: (Show where you think water will be. Where will air be? Can you explain why matter might behave this way?)

_____

_____

_____

_____

_____

_____

_____

If I were to suck through the straw, this is what I imagine would happen. And, here's a description of why I think it would happen that way.

_____

_____

_____

_____

_____

_____

_____

Describe an experiment that might test your ideas:

_____

_____

_____

_____

_____

_____

_____

_____

_____

_____

_____

_____

_____

Unit 2

What Matters

Unit 2- What Matters

For my notebook

Mass: It Really Matters

It is helpful to have a toy block available for this lesson.

Pick up a toy block and hold it in your hand. It might feel heavy or light, but it definitely <u>weighs</u> something. It feels like something is pulling it down toward the earth. In fact, if you weren't holding onto the block, it would fall down. As you probably know, Earth's <u>gravity</u> pulls all objects. In which direction does gravity pull objects? I think that most people would answer, "down." Physicists have a slightly more precise way to answer this question. They say that gravity on Earth pulls all objects toward the center of the planet.

Let's look at your toy block. You can see that it contains a certain amount of matter—either wood, plastic, foam, or whatever it is made out of. You can *feel* the weight (the matter) in your hand. What would it feel like in outer space, though? Here's an experiment you might try: Catch a ride on the space shuttle and take the block into space with you. Wait. That could be a bit difficult. Let's try this as a thought experiment instead: *Imagine* catching a ride on the space shuttle with your toy block. You escape from Earth's gravity, and everything is floating. You take hold of the block: Does it feel like it weighs anything?

If you've ever seen videos of astronauts in space, you probably answered, "No. It feels weightless." If that's what you thought, you're correct. But now, let's say you look at the block. It still contains the same amount of matter as it did on Earth. No pieces of it have disappeared. You've just demonstrated the difference between <u>mass</u> and <u>weight</u>.

An object's mass is the amount of matter it is made of. The mass of an object doesn't change unless you actually add something to the object or take it away from the object. Your block's mass would be the same on Earth, out in space, or even under the very heavy gravity of Jupiter!

This is very different from an object's weight. The weight of an object is actually a way to measure how much gravity is pulling on the object. The weight of an object changes whenever the force of gravity changes. The weight of an apple would be less on the moon than it is here on Earth. But, where gravity is stronger, like on Jupiter, the weight of the apple would be greater than it is on Earth.

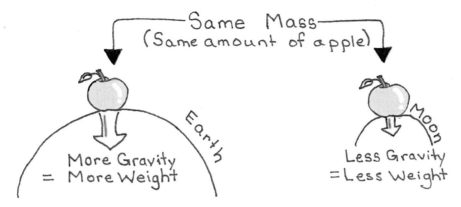

The difference between mass and weight is very important for physicists. Mass is an essential characteristic of matter. How objects behave when they are pushed and pulled depends on their mass. Weight, for physicists, is not really a characteristic of matter. Weight, instead, is just another force pulling on an object—the force of gravity. Physicists use a mathematical equation to describe how mass and weight relate to each other. Here is the equation:

$$weight = mass \times gravity \ (w = m \times g)$$

Cool Science Fact!

Gravity decreases the farther you get from the center of an object. Because Earth bulges, or is fatter, near the equator, you're slightly farther away from the center of mass of the earth at the equator than at the North Pole. So, your weight would be slightly less at the equator than at the North Pole!

Unit 2- What Matters

Pandia Press

What Matters Lab #1: Weighing in Around the Solar System - instructions

Materials:
- Lab sheets, pencil
- Calculator
- Bathroom scale

Aloud: Imagine that you could take a scale and travel to the other planets in our solar system and to the moon and the sun. If you could land at all of these places, even the gas giants like Jupiter, Saturn, Uranus, and Neptune, what would happen if you stepped onto the scale and weighed yourself? Would your weight stay the same? Would it change? How would it change?

What if there were a way to measure your mass—how much matter you're made of? Would that change when you went to different planets? Would there suddenly be more or less of you just because you are on another planet? Of course not. Your weight might change as the gravity around you changes, but your mass will not.

Because you're learning physics, you can figure out what the scale would read wherever you imagine going. All you need to know is how much you weigh on Earth and how strong gravity is on other bodies in our solar system. Remember, we just learned that weight = mass x gravity. Here on Earth, we define gravity as being equal to one. Because any number multiplied by 1 is just that number, our weight on Earth is pretty much equal to our mass. Because we're stuck on Earth when we do experiments, we'll usually think of mass and weight as the same number.

But, on other planets where gravity is greater or lesser than that of Earth, weight and mass are not the same. In our next activity, we'll figure out how much you would weigh at different spots around the solar system. We can use the equation above to do this. You may need to use a calculator because a lot of the numbers have decimal points.

Procedure:
1. Weigh yourself in pounds. *(see notation on next page)
2. Use this knowledge to fill in the lab page. Circle the places where you would weigh the least and where you would weigh the most.
3. Complete the thought experiment page.

Possible Answers:

Below is how the chart would look for a person who weighed 80 pounds:

	Force of gravity compared to Earth's	Mass x Force of Gravity (use your weight on Earth as your mass for this exercise)	My weight would be:
Mercury	.38	80 x .38 =	30
Venus	.91	80 x .91 =	72.8
Earth	1	80 x 1 =	80
Mars	.38	80 x .38 =	30
Jupiter	2.54	80 x 2.54 =	203.2
Saturn	1.08	80 x 1.08 =	86.4
Uranus	.91	80 x .91 =	72.8
Neptune	1.19	80 x 1.19 =	95.2
Pluto (dwarf planet)	.06	80 x .06 =	4.8
Moon	.17	80 x .17 =	13.6
Sun	27.9	80 x 27.9 =	2232

Conclusion / Discussion:

1. Talk more about the difference between mass and weight. Can you think of any ways you might be able to change your mass? (Some ideas: eat a meal, breathe out, etc.). These actually change the amount of matter that makes up your body.
2. What would be the dangers of living somewhere with much greater gravity than Earth's? What would be the dangers of living somewhere with much less gravity than Earth's?

More Lab Fun:

1. If you're interested in what it's like to live with very little gravity, look online for information about it, and new videos of the astronauts on the International Space Station. Try to find out what these astronauts have to do to stay healthy in zero gravity. Are the dangers of low gravity what you thought they would be?
2. Look up the weight on Earth of something very heavy (like a blue whale) and something very light (like a head of lettuce). Figure out what they would weigh on the sun and on the moon.

Notebooking ideas:

1. Use a definition page to define: *mass* and *weight*.
2. Use a piece of lined paper to write about what astronauts need to do to overcome the effects of low gravity on the human body.
3. Use an Equation page to copy and explain the formula that relates mass to weight.

Note to Parents and Teachers:

*We aren't going to worry about the fact that pounds technically measure weight, and kilograms measure mass. The point here is that as gravity changes, so does weight.

NAME _____ DATE _____

Weighing in Around the Solar System

On Earth, I weigh: _____ pounds

	Force of gravity compared to Earth's	Mass x Force of Gravity (use your weight on Earth as your mass for this exercise)	My weight would be:
Mercury	.38		
Venus	.91		
Earth	1		
Mars	.38		
Jupiter	2.54		
Saturn	1.08		
Uranus	.91		
Neptune	1.19		
Pluto (dwarf planet)	.06		
Moon	.17		
Sun	27.9		

On the moon, I would weigh _____ pounds. I would be much lighter than I am now, and gravity's pull on me would be much less. This is what I imagine I could do on the moon:

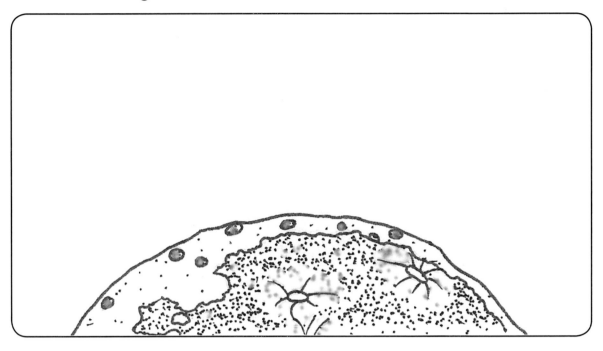

On the sun, I would weigh _____ pounds. I would be really heavy. The force of gravity would pull down a lot on me. If the sun weren't so hot, this is what I imagine things would be like:

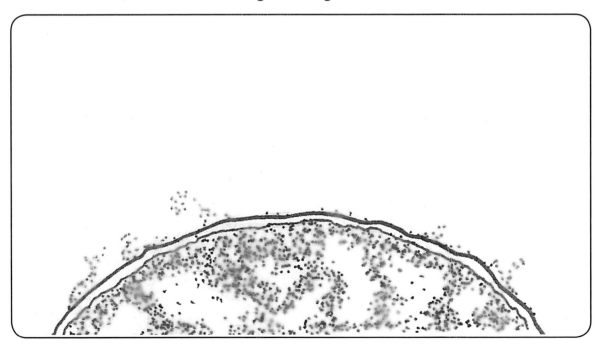

For my notebook

What Floats Your Planet?

Here's an amusing thought experiment for you. You get a really big bathtub—one as large as the sun. Then, you fill it with water, lots and lots and lots of water. Next, you drop planet Earth into the bathtub. Other than a really big splash, what do you think would happen? Take a moment to imagine your answer. After you take Earth out of the bathtub and dry it off, you decide to throw Saturn in next. Now what do you think would happen?

Part of the answer may surprise you. Earth, as you may have guessed, will sink to the bottom of the bathtub, just as a stone sinks to the bottom of a bucket of water. Saturn, which is more than nine times as large as Earth, however, will float!

How can this be? Doesn't Saturn contain more matter, and therefore more mass, than Earth? Doesn't Saturn weigh more? These are good questions, and the answer to both of them is "Yes." To understand why Saturn would float in water but Earth wouldn't, let's bring our thought experiment down to Earth. Instead of planet Earth and planet Saturn, imagine that you have a model of Earth (a small rock) and a model of Saturn (an inflated beach ball). These are appropriate substitutes because, in reality, Earth is a solid and Saturn is made mostly of gases. Also, Saturn really is much larger than Earth.

If you put the rock into your bathtub, it's pretty obvious that it would sink. But, if you were to put the inflated beach ball into your bathtub, it would float. This would be true even if the overall weight (and mass) of the beach ball were greater than that of the stone. The question is: Why does the larger object float and the smaller object sink?

The answer to this question is complicated, and involves a number of different characteristics of matter. In the following labs, we're going to learn about these characteristics—<u>volume</u>, <u>volume of water</u> <u>displaced</u>, <u>density</u>, and <u>buoyancy</u>. When we're done, you'll be able to explain why Saturn would float in water, but Earth would not.

A Science Riddle!

Q: What weighs more, a pound of feathers or a pound of bricks?

A: They both weigh one pound, so they weigh exactly the same!

Think about it: Which would take up more space, though, a pound of feathers or a pound of bricks?

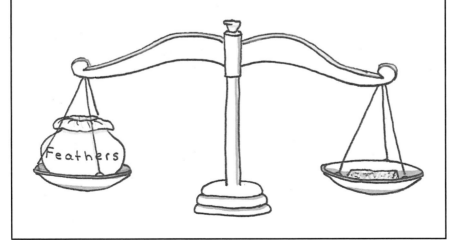

What Matters? Lab #2:
Density: All Objects, Large and Small - instructions

Materials:
- Lab sheet, pencil
- Balance or kitchen scale (or any type of sensitive precision scale that measures down to ounces and/or grams)
- At least 6 low-density and 6 high-density objects from around the house, as described below

Aloud: Scientists call an object's size (the amount of space that it takes up) its <u>volume</u>. Some objects seem to have a lot of mass for their volume—like heavy rocks. Other objects seem to be very light compared to the amount of space they take up—like inflated beach balls. This relationship between an object's mass and its volume is called an object's <u>density</u>. Scientists calculate an object's density by dividing its mass by its volume, like this:

$$DENSITY = MASS \div VOLUME$$
$$D = M / V$$

Because on Earth, mass is pretty much the same as weight, you could also think of it as:

$$DENSITY = WEIGHT \div VOLUME$$

Either way, a small rock is much more dense than an inflated beach ball. Its weight is large and its volume is small, so its density is pretty large. A beach ball takes up a lot of volume, but weighs very little. Therefore, its density will be pretty small.

Today, you're going to go on a scavenger hunt around your house. You'll be looking for small objects that you think are really dense—that are quite heavy for their size. And, you'll look for objects that you think have a low density—that are light for their size. The objects you find should all fit on your balance scale. I think that you'll discover that you already know quite a bit about the density of different objects.

Suggestions for objects if you're stumped:
High-density: small cup of water, coasters made of sandstone, filled up stapler, paperweight, roll of packing tape, ball bearings.

Low-density: Styrofoam cup, Styrofoam ball or packing materials, inflated balloon or beach ball, whiffle ball, loosely crumpled aluminum foil, an empty plastic container.

Procedure:
1. Try to guess which pairs of objects are such that a smaller object weighs more than a larger object. For example, a small cup of water might weigh more than a larger Styrofoam ball.
2. Fill in the lab sheet with your guesses. Then, use the scale or balance to test whether your ideas were correct.

Conclusion / Discussion:
1. Can you explain in your own words why some smaller objects are heavier than some larger objects? Does this give you a clue about why Saturn might float in water but Earth would not?
2. Make sure that students understand that density involves the relationship between the size and mass of an object. Large size, small mass = low density; and small size, large mass = high density.

[continued]

More Lab Fun:

Take a survey of 10 to 20 people that you know. Ask them the riddle: "Which is heavier? A pound of feathers or a pound of bricks?" Mark down how many people answer "a pound of bricks" and how many answer that they weigh the same. Why do you think some people are confused about this? Place your results in your notebook.

Notebooking Ideas:

1. Use a definition page to define *density* and *volume*.
2. Use an Equation page to copy and explain the equation used to calculate the density of an object.

NAME _____ DATE _____

Density: All Objects Large and Small

Larger object	Smaller object	The object I think will weigh more	The object that did weigh more

When a small object weighs more than a larger object, we know that the smaller object has a greater density than the larger object. You could summarize the results of your experiment by writing your conclusions in the following sentences:

1. I discovered that _____ has a greater density than

_____ .

2. I discovered that _____ has a greater density than

_____ .

3. I discovered that _____ has a greater density than

_____ .

What Matters Lab #3:
Water Displacement: It'll Float Your Boat! - instructions page 1

Materials:
- Lab sheets, pencil
- A wide glass that you can see through, filled ¾ way with water
- A dry-erase marker or small piece of soap (you'll be writing on the glass with it)
- A small piece of polymer clay that makes about a 1-inch diameter ball. (Don't use one of the really lightweight clays like Model Magic. You need something that will sink.)
- An additional small cup of water
- A teaspoon or tablespoon

Aloud: You now know about three of the characteristics of matter that are important in figuring out whether (and why) an object floats: mass, volume, and the relationship between mass and volume—density. The next important characteristic for you to consider is called the volume of water displaced. This sounds pretty complicated, but it really isn't. We've already learned what volume means—it's the space an object takes up. I probably don't need to explain what water is. Displaced is a word that you can take apart to figure out what it means: "dis" means "apart," so displaced means to place apart or to move away. Let's put all these pieces together now.

If you drop an object into water, regardless of whether it sinks or floats, it will push some water out of the way, displacing that water. You've probably noticed, for example, that when you sit down in a bathtub, the water level seems higher than it was. That's because your body moved some water out of the way—water that took up a certain amount of space, or volume, and that water had to go somewhere else. The volume of water that is pushed out of the way is called the volume of water displaced.

There are several ways to measure the volume of water displaced by an object. You could fill a container to the very top with water and place the object into the water. Then, you could collect the water that overflows the container and measure it. This method can be a bit messy and imprecise without special equipment, so we're going to use a different method—marking the water level on a container with and without the object inside of it.

As you can probably guess, the amount of water an object will displace—or move out of the way—depends a little bit on characteristics you've already studied—mass, volume, and density. But, there's one more factor to consider, and that's what we're going to explore in this lab.

Procedure:
1. Pick up the piece of clay and roll it into a ball. Draw an outline of the ball about the same size as the ball in the first box on your lab sheet. Now, play with the clay and make it into three different shapes—a snake, a teddy bear, whatever you'd like. The only rule is that you need to use all of the clay each time. For each shape you make, draw a sketch of it on your lab sheet. Try to make your sketch the same size as the actual object; you can even trace it if you want.

2. Answer questions 1 & 2 on your lab sheet and fill in the HYPOTHESIS section.

3. Mark the water level on the glass. Make sure that you bend down so that your eye is at the level of the water. This is the most accurate way to mark the water level.

[continued]

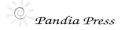

4. Roll the clay into a ball and fill in the first line of the chart on your lab sheet. You will notice that part of this has been done for you. When you are ready, gently place the ball of clay into the water, using a spoon so that you don't splash any water out of the glass. Mark the waterline now that the ball of clay is in the water. Record your observations on the chart.

5. Take the clay out of the water. If some water spilled and there's not enough water to reach your original waterline, add more water with a teaspoon until you have the same amount as you started with.

6. Make another shape with the clay—this time, the shape of a boat, like a canoe. Gently place the clay boat into the water. Fill in the next row on the chart. You don't need to mark the waterline; just observe whether it is higher or lower than it was when you placed the ball in the water. Repeat step 5.

7. Make another shape with the clay—this time, the shape of a flat boat, like a raft. Fill in the chart again. Repeat step 5. Make up a couple of shapes of your own to try. Record your observations on the chart.

8. Fill in the MY OBSERVATIONS section of the lab sheet.

Possible Answers:
  #1: the same
  #2: matter

My Observations:
  all of these, different amounts,
  shape, more

One more thing:
  sink

Analysis & Conclusions:
  #1: air, water
  #2: lighter
  #3: air

Aloud: Something strange is happening here. How could whether an object floats depend on its shape rather than on its weight? How can a piece of clay that has the exact same amount of matter displace different amounts of water depending on its shape? Now you see that sometimes the experiments that scientists perform can lead to new questions and new experiments. We're going to perform one more short experiment to see if we can figure out what's going on with our piece of clay.

9. Wipe off the waterlines you've made on the cup. Refill it to about ¾ and make a new waterline.

10. Make a shape that will float and could hold water—something like a little canoe or rowboat. Test that it floats and also mark a line for the amount of water displaced by the clay while you do this.

11. Now, use a spoon to take water from a second cup and place it little by little into the clay shape that is floating. Observe what happens and record your observations under ONE MORE THING and ANALYSIS & CONCLUSIONS.

[continued]

Conclusion / Discussion:

Aloud: You've discovered that you can make some shapes that float in water and some that don't—all with the same piece of clay. You now have all the pieces of a scientific puzzle: Why do some objects float while others sink? The answer has to do with all sorts of properties of matter: volume, mass, volume of water displaced, and density. There's a simple way to determine whether an object will float. Here it is: an object will float if the volume of water it displaces weighs more than the object weighs.

Let's think about this for a while. The clay weighed the same and had the same mass, no matter what we did to it. But when we floated it on water, it sometimes had lots of air taking up some of the space inside the clay sculpture (like when it was a boat) and sometimes no air at all (like when it was a ball). When there was air taking up space, as in the clay boat, the clay boat displaced more water and floated. When there was no air taking up space, such as when we shaped the clay like a ball, less water was displaced, and the boat sank. It's important to realize that the mass, volume, and density of the clay stayed the same no matter what we did. But, the overall mass, volume, and density of the boat and its contents changed.

Steel is very heavy and dense. Now that you understand why some objects float, can you explain why large steel cargo ships can float?

More Lab Fun:

1. Salt water is heavier than just plain water because it has the weight of the salt and the water together. You can experiment with what happens if you float your clay boats in water and then start adding salt. Does the waterline change? How?

2. Build a bigger clay boat and then try to load it with cargo, such as marbles. Does it still float? Can you make changes to the boat that allow it to float better and carry more cargo?

Notebooking Ideas:

1. Look up *buoyancy* in a dictionary and write its definition on a Definition page.

2. Design a ship that you think will float no matter how much load it carries. Draw a picture of your ship and explain why you think it will float.

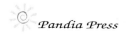

Water Displacement: It'll Float Your Boat!

From my piece of clay, I made:

Circle or underline the word(s) to make the sentences correct:

1. When I made these clay sculptures, I always used **the same** / **different** amounts of clay.

2. This means that even if the sizes of the clay sculptures are different, the clay always had the same amount of **matter** / **shape**.

Hypothesis: I think that changing the shape of the clay **will** / **will not** affect whether the clay floats in water.

Data:

Description of clay shape	Did I think this would float?	Did it float?	Did this displace more or less water than the clay shaped as a ball?
Ball			╳
Canoe			
Raft			

My Observations: Some of the shapes made from the clay floated, but some of them sank. All of the shapes had the same amount of clay. This means that they all had the same **volume / mass / weight / density / all of these**. Different shapes displace **different amounts / the same amount** of water. This means that the amount of water displaced depends on the **shape / mass of the object**. The shapes that floated displaced **less / more** water than the shapes that sank.

One More Thing: When I added water to the clay boat, it began to **sink / float**.

Analysis and Conclusions:

1. When I added water to the clay boat, the clay boat itself stayed the same shape. Whether it floated or sank depended on what it was filled with. When it floated, it was filled with **air / water**. When it sank, it was filled with **air / water**.

2. Air is **heavier / lighter** than water. (If you're not sure, think of how much a blown-up balloon weighs compared to a water balloon.)

3. If I were to experiment further, filling different clay shapes with air and different clay shapes with water, I think that the ones filled with **air / water** would be more likely to float.

For my notebook

A Story about Density: Archimedes and the Crown

Archimedes was one of the greatest physicists ever. He lived in Syracuse more than 2,000 years ago (c. 287 BCE-212 BCE) and was a cousin to King Hiero II. There's a wonderful story about Archimedes, King Hiero II and, of all things, density! We don't know if the story really happened this way, but it's a great story nevertheless.

One day, King Hiero commissioned, which means he hired for pay, a goldsmith to make him a crown—a golden crown shaped like a wreath of laurel leaves. The goldsmith told King Hiero that the crown was crafted from the purest gold. Indeed, the crown was amazing: Even the tiniest veins in the laurel leaves had been carved into the gold.

King Hiero, however, had heard that the goldsmith was a thief. The king began to worry about his crown. Perhaps it wasn't really made of pure gold. Perhaps the goldsmith had substituted some other metal for some of the gold and kept some gold for himself. But, the only way to find out for certain would be to melt the crown into a lump of gold to see if it weighed the same amount as another lump of gold with the same volume. King Hiero couldn't bring himself to destroy the crown just to prove that it was, or was not, pure gold.

The king mentioned his problem to his cousin Archimedes, a great scientist, inventor, and mathematician. Archimedes said that he would think about the problem and get back to the king. Some time later, Archimedes went to take a bath. As he stepped into the bathtub, he noticed something. He noticed that the water level rose every time he lowered himself into the tub. And, the water level dropped every time he stood. You can try this in your own bathtub.

Eureka!

Archimedes shouted, "Eureka!" *Eureka* in Greek means "I have found it!" He was so excited that he ran out of the bathhouse without a stitch of clothing on. He ran straight to King Hiero, whom we hope gave him a robe to wear. Then, Archimedes explained his discovery. He said something that went like this, "King Hiero, the problem with figuring out whether your crown is pure gold is that we need to know not only the weight of the crown, but also its volume. Does it weigh exactly the same as a lump of gold with the same volume? We thought that to figure out the volume of gold in the crown, we would have to melt the crown into a lump. I have discovered another way. All we need to do is fill a tub to the very brim with water. Then, we place the crown into the water slowly, until it sinks to the bottom. If we catch the amount of water that overflows the tub in a pan and measure the amount, that will tell us the exact volume of the crown."

The king, who didn't at all understand that density is the relationship between mass and volume, nodded politely. Archimedes performed his experiment and discovered that the crown was not, in fact, pure gold. The crown displaced a certain volume of water. Archimedes found a lump of pure gold that displaced exactly the same volume of water. This lump of gold, however, did not weigh the same as the crown. The volume of the crown and the volume of the lump of pure gold were the same, but their weights were different. In other words, the density of the crown was not equal to the density of pure gold.

We don't know what happened to the goldsmith or to the crown. But, we'll be hearing more about Archimedes, a man who discovered amazing things about physics just by observing the world around him. And, if you keep a history timeline, you might want to put Archimedes on it.

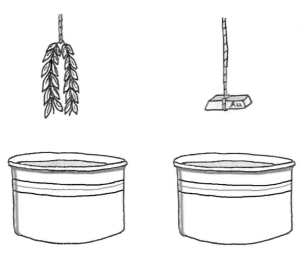

Unit 3

Newton's Laws

NAME _____ DATE _____

For my notebook

A Forceful Introduction

So far we've learned a lot about matter. We've seen that different types of matter have different characteristics. Some have a lot of mass in a small space, some have very little mass in a large space. Some bounce. Some are red. Some roll, and some don't. We had some fun learning that one needs to consider a number of characteristics of matter to figure out if an object will float.

But floating a hunk of matter is only fun for so long. And just looking at a hunk of matter sitting still on a table isn't very interesting. It's when we start doing things to matter—pushing it, pulling it, dropping it, throwing it, crushing it, crashing one piece into another—that physics gets really exciting!

Scientists call any push or pull on a piece of matter a <u>force</u>. When you push a toy car, you're exerting a force on it. When you throw a ball, pick up a glass of water, pull open a door—all these are examples of forces applied to matter.

We can divide forces into two general categories. The first type of force is called a <u>contact force</u>. Any force that we apply to an object by touching the object is a contact force. So, pushing a car, picking up a glass of water, and opening a door all involve contact forces. Can you think of a few more examples of using a contact force?

The other type of force is called <u>action-at-a-distance force</u>. This is a big name for a simple idea. Any force that pushes or pulls on something without touching it is an action-at-a-distance force. Take a minute to think of what kinds of forces you know about that might be action-at-a-distance forces.

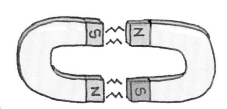

Did you think of any examples? Here are a couple you probably know a lot about already:

magnetism and gravity. If you've ever played with magnets, you know that they push and pull each other even when they aren't touching each other. Another action-at-a-distance force is gravity. Gravity is a force that pulls things toward the earth. Gravity doesn't need to reach out and touch an object to make it fall. It acts on matter from a distance.

When an object is at rest, when it's holding still, we say that all the forces acting on it are in equilibrium. That means that all the forces pushing on it and pulling on it balance out, and leave the object where it is. If you look around the room, you'll see a whole bunch of objects in a state of equilibrium—chairs, books, table, a cake, toys, the room itself. They're all just staying still, not appearing to do anything. It's really important to realize, though, that just because an object, like a cake on your table, is sitting still, there are still lots of forces acting on it. In fact, we're about to explore that idea a bit further in our next activity.

But first, see if you can identify four forces acting in equilibrium that keep the cake, pictured below, on the table. One of the forces, gravity, is the action-at-a-distance force, and it is labeled for you. The other three are contact forces; can you identify them?

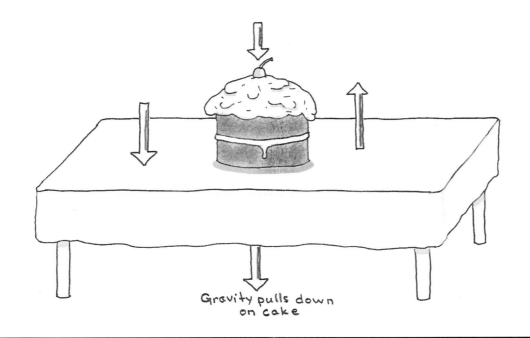

Gravity pulls down on cake

Unit 3- Newton's Laws

Newton's Laws Lab #1: An Object in Equilibrium

Materials:
- Lab sheets, pencil
- Glass partly filled with water, placed on a table
- Drawing materials

Aloud: When most people look at a glass of water, they don't think much about it. Physicists, though, think it's pretty exciting. Really. Think about all the forces involved in keeping that cup of water on the table. For some reason, the glass doesn't fall through the table onto the floor. What's pushing up on the glass to keep it there? Why doesn't the glass float away? Why doesn't the water climb out of the glass and spill? There must be a number of forces acting on that glass of water to keep it in a state of equilibrium, at rest. In this activity, you're going to draw a picture of the glass of water and show all the forces you can think of that are keeping it in equilibrium. Use arrows to indicate in what direction the forces are acting. The first one is drawn in for you.

Procedure:
1. Observe the glass and draw arrows (and words) on the glass of water on the lab sheet showing the forces as described above.
2. Fill in the set diagram listing which forces are contact forces and which are action-at-a-distance forces.
3. Complete the final drawing showing what would happen to the glass of water if one force was removed.

Possible Answers:
For my notebook: Forces acting in equilibrium in cake picture:

* Note: Technically, air pressure is pushing on the cake and the table from all directions. Students shouldn't be expected to know much about the properties of air at this point. Air pressure and how it affects objects on Earth will be discussed in Unit 6.

Lab sheet:
Some of the forces to consider:

The pull of gravity on the water in the glass, the glass, the table, the floor (all action-at-distance forces)

Air pressure (from many directions) on the water and on the table (contact force)

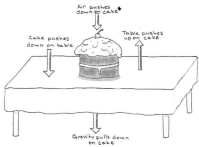

The water pushing outward against the walls of the glass (contact force)

The glass pushing back on the water (contact force)

The table pushing upward on the glass (contact force)

Note: Don't worry if not all the forces mentioned above are drawn in. The important thing is that students understand that lots of forces push and pull in different directions to keep an object in equilibrium.

Conclusion and Discussion:
1. Look around you. What other things are in equilibrium? Are there things you see that are not in equilibrium? Are there things you can think of that aren't in equilibrium? What "extra" force is being applied to them so that they move?
2. Think about yourself when you're sitting still. What forces are pushing and pulling on you?

An Object in Equilibrium

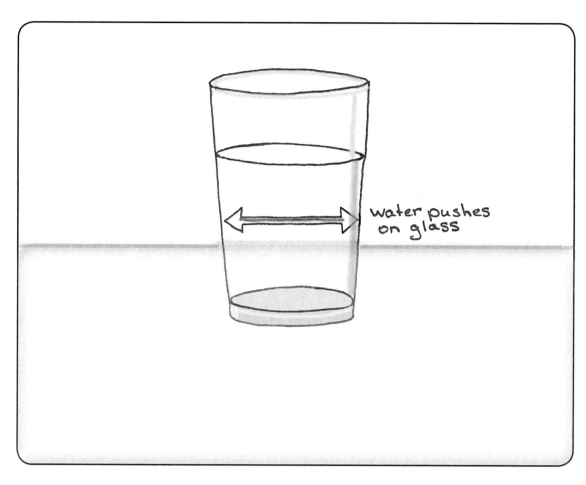

water pushes on glass

These are contact forces.   These are action-at-a-distance forces.

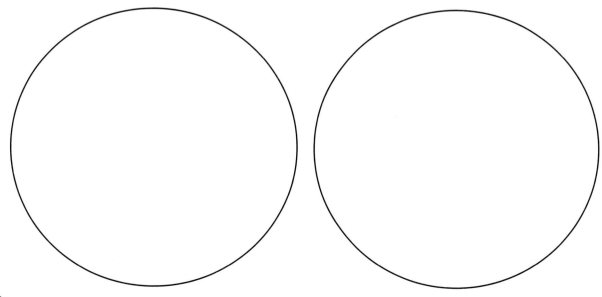

Draw a picture, or describe in words, what would happen if you took away one of the forces acting on the glass of water. Here are a couple of my favorite examples to imagine: What would happen if gravity no longer pulled on the water in the glass? Or, what would happen if the table stopped pushing up against the glass?

What force did you decide to remove? _____

What would happen if that force were removed?

Notice how removing just one force can take an object out of equilibrium and get things moving.

Unit 3- Newton's Laws

For my notebook

Moving with Newton

In 1643, **Isaac Newton** was born in England. He grew up, went to school, and then went to college in Cambridge, England. Just as he was finishing his studies at Cambridge University, which still exists today, all the schools in England were closed. The year was 1665, and a sickness called "the plague" was spreading throughout Europe. To prevent people from making each other sick, the government ordered that all big, public places where lots of people gather, be closed. So Newton left Cambridge and went to live in the country for a few years.

There's a famous story about Newton which may or may not be true. It is said that one day, while living in the country, Newton was out in an apple orchard when an apple fell on his head! Most of us would just say, "Ouch," eat the apple, and go on about our day. But, according to the story, Newton gave that apple a great deal of thought. He wondered what made it fall. What made it fall down instead of up or sideways? Why did other objects always fall toward the earth? Why didn't the moon fall to Earth like the apple?

In the two years Newton spent living in the country, he thought and thought about questions like these. During that time, Newton described what <u>gravity</u> is and how it works. He figured out why objects move the way they do. He also developed an entire area of mathematics called <u>calculus</u>, which is still used today.

We're going to spend a lot of time learning about the answers that Newton figured out to his questions about how objects move. His answers are now called <u>Newton's laws of motion</u>. Newton's laws are very different from laws that make it a crime, say, to steal something. A <u>scientific law</u> describes what always happens given certain <u>conditions</u>. Every time you stand in front of your house and drop a stone with nothing in the way, it will fall to the ground. This is something we know from the <u>law of gravity</u>, another scientific law attributed to Newton.

A scientific law also lets us <u>predict</u> what will happen. Using the laws of motion, I can predict that when I push a toy car across the floor, it will go for a certain distance and then stop. But in order to make this prediction, I need to know that certain conditions exist. I need to know that I'm pushing the car on Earth, where there's gravity. I need to know that I'm holding relatively still. As conditions change, the results that a scientific law predicts might change.

You should know that there are certain conditions under which even Newton's laws fail to predict what will happen. Newton's laws of motion are valid in almost every circumstance you or I will encounter in our lives. But, if we were to fly on a spaceship going almost as fast as the speed of light, which is much faster than any spaceship has ever gone, we would find that Newton's laws don't quite work. Or, if we were really, really tiny, smaller than even an atom, Newton's laws would also cease to predict what would happen. However, as none of us is currently traveling as fast as light or has shrunk to a subatomic size, we'll do just fine using Newton's laws to study forces and matter.

For my notebook

Newton's Laws: The First Law of Motion—Inertia

The first of Newton's laws is probably something you've understood all your life without really giving it much thought. Newton basically thought about what happens to objects when nothing happens to them! That is, he figured out what objects do when they're left alone. First, he broke this problem into two smaller problems:

(1) What happens to objects that are sitting still?

(2) What happens to objects that are moving at a constant (not slowing down or speeding up) speed?

Think about what happens to a book when you put it on the table. That doesn't take a lot of thought, does it? The book just lies there. And it remains there unless some outside force, some push or pull, occurs to move it. This is a demonstration of one part of Newton's <u>first law of motion</u>: **An object at rest tends to remain at rest unless an extra force is applied to it.** What does that mean? It means that if matter is holding still, it's going to keep holding still unless something pushes or pulls on it. The toy duck, below, will stay at rest unless a force is applied to it.

The next part of Newton's first law of motion is a bit trickier. What happens to an object that's moving if no other force acts on it? Think about throwing a ball. The ball is moving while it's in the air, and perhaps for a few seconds while it rolls on the ground. Does this mean that an object in motion tends to come to a rest? For centuries, people thought the answer was yes.

But Newton's answer was the correct, and very surprising answer: No! An object in motion does not tend to slow down and come to a rest! The second part of Newton's <u>first law</u> of <u>motion</u> states that: **An object in motion tends to remain in motion unless an extra force is applied to it.** The toy duck is rolling now, and it will continue to roll along unless an extra force is applied to stop it or slow it down.

So why when you throw a ball up into the air, does it land on the ground and just sit there? Shouldn't it continue to move? The main reason is that there is a force acting on it—gravity. Gravity pulls the ball to the ground whenever you throw it into the air. But what if there were no gravity? What if that ball were out in space, where there is no gravity to pull it and where there are no air molecules to push against it? Newton's law tells us that if the ball were moving in a gravity-free area of space without any air, it would keep on moving forever unless it encountered some force, like a planet's gravity, or another ball crashing into it. Basically, Newton's law states that an object tends to keep doing whatever it's doing unless something happens to change that. Newton called this tendency to stay at rest or in motion <u>inertia</u>, which is what our next experiment is going to explore.

Note to Parents and Teachers: You may have noticed the phrase "extra force" in this reading. An object at rest has many forces acting on it—as was discussed in a previous lesson. In physics, this is actually called a <u>net</u> <u>force</u>—meaning that the net force must change in order for an object at rest to move, or vice versa. The idea of an "extra" force that causes an object to change from rest to motion was used to help younger students understand the concepts.

Newton's Laws Lab #2: Inertia and You! - instructions

Materials:
- Lab sheets, pencil
- Drawing materials
- A toy vehicle with wheels and a relatively flat top, something a bit larger than a tiny matchbox car
- A small toy figure (a small plastic figure of a person or animal, 1-2 inches tall)
- Small rectangle of cardboard or card stock, about the size of the toy car
- Tape
- A flat, smooth surface like a wooden floor or tabletop.

Aloud: It's probably no big surprise to you that objects that are staying still tend to stay still, and that objects that are moving keep moving unless something pulls or pushes them. Newton, however, wasn't satisfied to describe <u>inertia</u> in this general way. He asked himself several questions (scientists are ALWAYS asking questions): How much does an object tend to stay at rest or in motion? How hard is it to change an object from standing still to moving? Do some objects in some situations have more inertia than other objects? Does this make it more difficult to move them if they are at rest?

Think about these questions for a moment. If a brick and a block of foam are sitting on the table, which one is easier to push? Which of the two resists a change in its resting state more? What makes the brick different from the foam? Can you think of a rule that would help us to predict which objects have more inertia and which have less?

If you figured out that an object's mass is what determines its inertia, you came to the same conclusion as Isaac Newton. The heavier an object, the harder it is to change its state—to move the object if it's at rest, or to stop it if it's already moving. Because the brick has more mass than the foam, the brick is harder to push from a state of rest. This would be true even in space! Because of this, we say that the brick has more inertia than the foam block. Inertia isn't some distant characteristic of matter that only physicists think about. Inertia affects almost everything we do here on Earth. For example, inertia is very important to engineers and scientists who design cars. In this experiment, we're going to find out why the safety of passengers in moving vehicles depends so much on the effects of inertia.

Procedure:
1. Tape or attach a rectangle of cardboard onto the top of the toy car or truck. The idea is to make a platform that you can stand the other little toy on top of.
2. Place the car on a flat surface and stand the toy figure on the middle of the platform you made.

3. Fill in #1 on your lab sheet.
4. Watch carefully as you put your finger on the back of the car and give it a gentle push. Be careful to push only the car and not the toy on top of it. Watch what happens to the toy on top of the car.
5. Fill in #2-#4 on your lab sheet.
6. Fold the back of the cardboard platform up so that it makes a little seat-back for your toy figure.
7. Before you give the car a push, fill in #5 on your lab sheet.
8. Now, give the car a gentle push and observe what happens. Fill in #6-#8 on your lab sheet.

[continued]

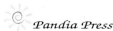

Aloud: The first time you pushed the car, the toy figure's inertia caused it to be left behind—falling backward as the car moved forward. This was because it was trying to stay at rest and not move with the car. The second time you pushed the car, there was a seat-back behind the figure. Because the cardboard seat was attached to the car, when you pushed the car, you were also pushing the seat. And the force of the seat moving forward was strong enough to push the toy figure as well—overcoming its inertia.

When designing cars, safety engineers have to think about what will happen to the people in the cars as the cars move forward and backward. They also need to think about what will happen to the people in the car if the car is moving forward but comes to a sudden stop. We're going to model what happens by pushing our car with a seat and a toy figure into a wall. But before we do, use what you know about inertia to come up with a hypothesis of what you think will happen. Remember—the car, the seat, and the figure will all be in motion when they hit the wall.

9. Fill in #9 on your lab sheets.
10. Place the car on the ground a few feet from a wall. Place the figure on the seat, toward the rear of the car. Give the car a gentle push toward the wall and watch what happens to the figure when the car hits the wall.
11. Complete the remainder of the lab sheets.

Possible Answers:
#2: the figure should fall backward
#3a: at rest; #3b: at rest; #3c: stay at rest; #3d: started moving; #3e: stay still
#4: backward
#6: moved along with the car
#7a: at rest; #7b: was not attached; #7c: the back of the seat
#8: strong enough
#10: was thrown forward
#11: came to rest
#12: stay in motion / keep moving forward until it hit the wall

Conclusion and Discussion:
1. Using words like "force" and "inertia," talk about what happened to the toy figure when the car was pushed and when the car hit the wall.
2. You may not know this, but about 30 years ago, most of the seat belts in cars were "lap belts." They only went around a person's waist. When people were in a car crash, they would often injure their head. Can you figure out why, now that you understand inertia?
3. Once engineers developed shoulder seat belts, there were fewer head injuries. But other kinds of injuries were common, such as neck injuries and injuries to parts of a person's torso. Can you figure out what was happening? Do you know what we use now to solve this problem?

More Lab Fun:
1. The next time you go on a car ride, pay attention to how inertia works. When the car starts moving, can you feel your seat back push against your back? When the car comes to a stop, do you feel yourself pushed forward a bit? What do you think your body wants to do when the car goes around a curve? See if you can pay attention and find out.
2. Try running as fast as you can in a straight line. Is it hard to come to a sudden stop? Once again, inertia is propelling you forward when you're trying to stop. Cool!

Notebooking Ideas:
1. Use a definition page to define *inertia* and *equilibrium*.
2. Make a list of some of the things you do during the day to overcome inertia.

NAME _____ DATE _____

Inertia and You!

EXPERIMENTING WITH A FIGURE AT REST ON A MOVING PLATFORM:

1. **Hypothesis:** When I push the car, I think that the toy figure will **move along with the car / fall backward / fall forward**.

2. **Observation:** When I pushed the car, the toy figure **moved along with the car / fell backward / fell forward**.

3. **Data Analysis:**
   A. Before I pushed the car, the car was **at rest / in motion**.
   B. Before I pushed the car, the toy figure was **at rest / in motion**.
   C. According to Newton's first law of motion, an object at rest will **tend to stay at rest / start moving until something pushes or pulls on it**.
   D. I pushed on the car, so it **stayed still / started moving**.
   E. I didn't push on the toy figure, so it tried to **stay still / move forward**.

4. **Conclusion:** Because of inertia, the toy figure fell **backward / forward** when the car was pushed.

EXPERIMENTING WITH A FIGURE AT REST ON A MOVING SEAT:

5. **Hypothesis:** When I push the car, I think that the toy figure will **move along with the car / fall backward / fall forward**.

6. **Observation:** When I pushed the car, the toy figure **moved along with the car / fell backward / fell forward**.

7. Analysis:

A. The car and the toy figure began **at rest / in motion**.

B. The seat I made out of cardboard was attached to the car. So when I pushed the car, I was also pushing the cardboard seat. But, the toy figure **was also attached / was not attached to the car**.

C. When I pushed the car with the seat, the toy figure moved along with the car because it was pushed by **gravity / the back of the seat**.

8. Conclusion: Although the toy figure started at rest and wanted to stay at rest, it started to move with the car and the seat. The force of the seat back pushing on the figure was **strong enough / too weak** to overcome the toy figure's inertia.

EXPERIMENTING WITH A FIGURE IN MOTION:

9. Hypothesis: When the car with the figure in the cardboard seat runs into the wall, I think the figure will **stop where the car stops / be thrown forward / be thrown backward**.

10. Observation: When I pushed the car into the wall, the toy figure **stopped where the car stopped / was thrown forward / was thrown backward**.

11. Data Analysis: When I pushed the car, the car, the seat, and the figure all moved from being at rest to being in motion. When the car hit the wall, aside from any bouncing, the car **came to rest / kept moving forward / made a huge hole in the wall**.

12. Conclusion: The figure in the seat wasn't attached to the car. Once it was in motion, Newton's first law says that it would tend to **stay in motion / come to rest**. Therefore, Newton's first law would predict that the figure would keep moving forward until it **hit the wall / stopped when the car stopped**. And that is what happened!

Unit 3- Newton's Laws

NAME _____   DATE _____

Physics in Action: Preventing Injuries in Car Accidents

Putting It All Together:

Now that you understand how inertia works, you know a lot about what engineers need to think about to prevent injuries during an automobile collision. Can you invent a new way to prevent injuries in head-on collisions if we didn't use seatbelts? What would it look like? What part, or parts, of the body would it protect? Draw a picture of your "inertia protection invention" below. Then turn over the page and describe your invention; explain how it protects against the effects of inertia.

Physics in Action: Preventing Injuries in Car Accidents - page 2

My Inertia Protection Invention

Newton's Laws Lab #3: Inertia Can Be Dizzying! - instructions

Materials:
- Lab sheets, pencil
- Paper cup (you need to write on it with marker or pen, so a plastic cup might not work)
- Permanent marker or pen

Aloud: Inertia affects not only the world around you, but also the world inside of you! You might not know this, but inertia plays a role in how your brain and body work together. Do you know why you get dizzy when you spin in circles? The answer might surprise you: It's because of how inertia affects some liquid inside your ear! There's an area inside your ear called, appropriately, your <u>inner ear</u>. Your inner ear is covered with a layer of tiny little hairs, called <u>cilia</u> (sil-ee-uh). This space is partially filled with liquid. As you move around, the liquid in your ear moves around. And as the liquid in your ear moves around, the tiny cilia swish around. Your brain detects this motion and uses it to keep track of where your head is, and whether it is moving, holding still, or tilting in some direction or another. Your brain uses this information to interpret what your other senses perceive, like what you see around you, and whether the world you see is moving, holding still, or tilting.

We're going to make a simple model of your inner ear to investigate what happens to the liquid when different forces are applied.

Procedure:
1. Get a paper cup. The paper cup is going to be your model of an inner ear.
2. Take your marker and make little lines or dots all over the inside of the cup. These little lines or dots represent the hairs (the cilia) in the inner ear. Make sure they are everywhere inside the cup— on the bottom of the cup and on all sides of the inside of the cup.
3. Fill the cup about one third of the way with water.
4. You've made a lovely model of an inner ear. Are you surprised that a model can be so simple? Sometimes, scientists use very simple models to focus closely on just one aspect of what they are studying. Draw a picture of your model in the space provided on the lab sheet.
5. Think about having something like the model inside your ear. What would happen to the liquid if you jumped up and down? Which of the "hairs" would sense liquid swishing past them? What if you tipped your head to the left? To the right? What if you spun around in circles? Imagine doing these things and fill in #1-#4 on your lab sheet. Don't forget about inertia when you fill in #4.
6. Pick up the cup and tilt it a little way to the left. Mark your observations on the lab sheet (#5). Notice how different "hairs" are touched by the water when the cup is tilted. Tilt your head a bit to the left and think about how the liquid in your inner ear behaves like the liquid in your model.
7. Repeat step 6, but tilt the model to the right. Fill in #6 on the lab sheet.
8. Pick up the cup and swish the water in circles. Stop, and immediately put the cup on the table. Observe the water. Record what happens (#7), paying attention to whether the water stops moving at the same instant you stop moving the cup. Think about what the hairs in the inner ear would be sensing if this were happening inside your ear.
9. Fill in #8-#11 on the lab sheet.

[continued]

Aloud: Now you can see how gravity and inertia interact with each other in your inner ear. The liquid in your inner ear stimulates different hairs depending on how you're holding your head—straight up, sideways, or tilted in one direction or another. When you move around, the liquid in your inner ear moves as well, just like the little figure we placed on the car shifted forward when the car moved in the previous experiment. Sometimes, because of inertia, the liquid in your inner ear needs some time to catch up with what your body is doing. For example, when you spin in circles, the liquid is pushed from a state of rest to a state of motion, swishing around inside your ear.

When you stop spinning, the liquid in your ear takes a few seconds to stop spinning around because an object (liquid) in motion tends to stay in motion unless another force (like gravity) acts on it. So, when you stop spinning, the liquid in your ear keeps spinning for a few seconds. You may be holding perfectly still, but your brain receives the message that your head is moving in circles! Let's find out what your brain makes of this situation.

10. Find an open, safe space. Spin around in circles a few times, until you get just a bit dizzy. Open your eyes and look at the room. What do you see? Are you actually moving? Is the room actually moving? When you feel steady again, fill in #12 and #13 on the lab sheet.

Possible Answers:

#7. keeps moving for a moment
#8. starts moving
#9. inertia, gravity
#10. keeps swishing around before coming to a stop
#11. still turning in circles
#12. the room still turning in circles
#13. the liquid in my inner ear is still spinning even though I have stopped, because of inertia

Conclusion / Discussion:
1. Liquids, like all matter, obey Newton's laws of motion. Talk about why this results in confusion when you spin around.
2. We learned how observing the world closely is an important part of science. But as we just saw, sometimes even our eyes can fool us. This is why scientists use not only all of their senses but also measuring devices to make their observations. Can you think of some examples of scientific measuring devices?
3. Can you think of other times when inertia "fools" your brain?

More Lab Fun:
1. Watch a video of a skater or dancer spinning in circles. How do such performers spin so quickly without getting dizzy? The answer involves what they do with their head and eyes while spinning. Watch closely to see if you can figure it out.
2. If you're interested in how our brains and eyes work together to interpret our world, you might want to get a book from the library about optical illusions. Try to find a book that explains why our brains misinterpret the illusions.

Inertia Can Be Dizzying!

Draw your model of the inner ear here. Be sure to show how high the water reaches.

Hypotheses:

1. When the model of the inner ear is still and sitting on a flat surface like a table, the waterline looks like this:

2. I think that if I were to tip the model to the left, the waterline would look like this:

3. I think that if I were to tip the model to the right, the waterline would look like this:

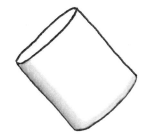

4. If I were to spin the model in circles and then stop spinning it, I think the water would (describe what you think would happen):

_____

_____

_____

_____

_____

Inertia Can Be Dizzying! - page 2

Observations:

5. When I tip the model to the left, the waterline looks like this:

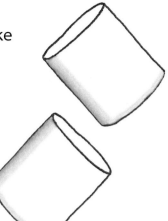

6. When I tip the model to the right, the waterline looks like this:

7. When I swish the water around in circles and then stop, the water

_____.

Data Analysis and Conclusions:

8. Newton's first law says that an object in motion tends to stay in motion. When I swish the water in the cup, the water **starts moving** / **holds still**.

9. When I stop swishing the water, the water's **inertia** / **gravity** keeps it moving in circles until the **inertia** / **gravity** of Earth causes it to settle back down.

10. The inner ear sends messages to my brain based on what the little hairs inside my inner ear sense. If I were to turn around in circles and then stop, the liquid in my inner ear would **stop immediately** / **keep swishing around before coming to a stop**.

11. So even if I were standing still, my brain would be getting messages that I was **running forward** / **still turning in circles** / **floating away**.

So What?

12. When I spin in circles and then stop and look around, I see: _____

_____.

13. This happens because _____

_____.

For my notebook

Newton's Second Law—From Aristotle to Newton

When people talk about how fast an object, like a car, can move, they usually talk in terms of how far it can go in a certain amount of time. For instance, you've probably seen road signs indicating that the speed limit for cars is 55 MPH, or 55 miles per hour. That means that if a car were traveling at that speed, it would travel 55 miles in one hour. Physicists call the speed of an object in a particular direction its <u>velocity</u>.

We can rephrase Newton's first law of motion using the idea of velocity: An object's velocity remains the same unless some net force acts on it. This is just the same as saying that an object that is holding still (with a velocity of zero) will continue to hold still until something pulls or pushes it in a particular direction. It is also the same as saying that an object that is moving will continue to move until something pulls or pushes it in a particular direction. Newton's first law has to do with how objects behave when they're left alone.

Newton's <u>second law of motion</u> describes what happens when objects are pulled or pushed by a force. **The second law talks about how a force can change the speed and direction of an object**. <u>Acceleration</u> is the word that physicists use to describe a change in speed or velocity. Any time something speeds up or slows down, it is experiencing acceleration. Some people say that slowing down is called deceleration, but we'll just call any change in velocity, acceleration. You may have heard people talk about a fast car that "goes from zero to sixty miles per hour in 10 seconds." What this is describing is how quickly the car accelerates, how quickly it changes its velocity from zero (holding still) to 60 MPH (going pretty fast).

This all might seem pretty straightforward, but the difference between velocity and acceleration confused the brightest minds for hundreds of years. Think about this statement for a moment: In order to keep an object moving at the same speed, a force needs to be applied to it continuously. For example, to keep a toy duck moving at the same speed, you need to keep pushing or pulling it. Do you think that statement describes how objects behave?

The famous Greek philosopher and scientist **Aristotle** thought that was an accurate statement (though he probably thought about toy chariots instead of ducks). And as far as observations of objects on Earth go, just about everyone thought that Aristotle was correct: If you push a toy duck (or a toy chariot), it will slow down and then stop. To keep it moving, it seems that you must keep pushing or pulling on it.

But there was a big piece of the picture that Aristotle was missing. He never thought about what happens to objects in an area with no outside forces—no gravity or air molecules pulling or pushing against objects. As you know, if you give a car a push out in space, it will keep going at the same speed forever unless it runs into something like a planet with gravity. Even for objects on Earth, Aristotle wasn't precisely correct, as we'll discover in our next experiment.

Newton's Laws Lab #4- You've Got to Keep It Moving - instructions

Materials:
- Lab sheets, pencil
- A toy with wheels. The toy should have a place you can tie or tape a string to pull it along behind you.
- A piece of string about 5 feet long
- A large flat area

Aloud: According to Aristotle, if I keep pulling on an object with the same amount of force, I'll keep that object moving at a steady speed. He would say that the velocity would remain constant and there would be no acceleration. Newton disagreed. According to Newton, an object in motion tends to stay in motion—without needing some force to keep pulling or pushing it. Newton would say that if I were to keep pulling on an object with the same amount of force, its velocity would change. In scientific terms, Newton would say that the object would accelerate and start to move more quickly if I continued to apply a force to it.

     Let's find out whether Aristotle or Newton is correct.

Procedure:
1. Tie the string around the toy (or tape it to the toy) so that you can pull it along and the wheels can still turn freely. Usually tying the string to the front of the toy toward the center works best.
2. Fill in #1, #2, and #3 on your lab sheet.
3. Go to one side of a large flat area. Walk in as straight a line as you can at a steady pace and pull the car behind you. Observe what happens: Does the toy keep going at the same speed (leaving the string straight), or does it start going a bit faster, so that the string becomes slack and is no longer pulling on it?
4. Fill in #4 and #5 on your lab sheet.
5. Complete #6 and #7 on the lab sheet.

Possible Answers:
#1: Aristotle believed that the object would keep moving at a constant speed.
#2: Newton believed that the object would accelerate, its velocity would change.
#4: The string should be drawn taut.
#5: The string should be drawn loose (and the toy is moving faster, so it is closer to the child)
#6: The toy accelerated. As I walked, the string became less taut and the toy started to catch up to me.
#7: Newton was correct.

Conclusion/Discussion:
1. Imagine that you are planning the first spaceflight to the moon. What difference would it make in your plans if you believed Aristotle was correct rather than Newton? How would this change your spaceship design? [Hint: If you are having trouble figuring this out, think about it this way: Once your spaceship is in space and traveling at a constant velocity, what would Aristotle have said about whether you need fuel or engines to keep it going? What would Newton have said?]

[continued]

2. Make sure that you understand that objects on Earth slow down because there are extra forces acting on them—forces like gravity and friction. Can you think of circumstances in which it would appear that Aristotle's ideas are correct? (Hint: other forces, like gravity and friction, would have to cancel out exactly a constant force on an object.)

Notebooking Ideas:
1. Use a definition page to define *velocity* and *acceleration*.
2. Draw a picture or write a story about what would happen if physicists had believed in Aristotle's idea of motion as described in #1 of the lab sheet.

NAME _____ DATE _____

You've Got to Keep It Moving!

1. What did Aristotle believe would happen if a person kept pushing on an object with the same amount of force?

_____

_____

_____

2. What did Newton believe would happen in the same circumstances?

_____

_____

_____

3. **Hypothesis:** Who do you think is correct, Aristotle or Newton? Can you explain why you think this person is correct?

_____

_____

_____

_____

Observations:

4. Draw what the string looked like just as you started pulling the toy.

5. Draw what the string looked like at the end of pulling it.

6. Describe what you observed. How did the toy and the string behave when you pulled at a constant speed?

_____

_____

_____

_____

_____

7. **Conclusion:** Who turned out to be correct, Aristotle or Newton?

_____

_____

For my notebook

Newton's Second Law: Momentous Momentum

Newton's first law is all about what objects will do if no new force disturbs them. If an object is at rest and no new force is applied to it, it will hold still. If an object is moving and no new force is applied to it, it will keep moving. But what happens when we don't leave objects alone? Newton's answers to this question make up his second of law of motion. I think these answers will seem pretty obvious to you.

First, **an object will move in the direction it's pushed**. Push a basketball away from you and it rolls away from you. It doesn't roll toward you, off to the left or right, or jump up into the sky. So the change in the basketball's direction depends on the direction of the force you applied to it.

Second, **the harder you push an object, the faster it will accelerate**. If you push the basketball harder, it will move more quickly than if you push it gently. In more scientific terms, the basketball's acceleration depends on the amount of force you use to push it.

Third, **the more mass an object has, the harder it is to push**. If a giant beach ball were rolling toward you, you could easily push it off in another direction. But what would happen if a giant ball of concrete the same size as the beach ball were rolling toward you? It might be traveling at the same velocity, but it will take a lot more force to push it out of the way because the concrete ball has a lot more mass than the giant beach ball.

Now you know what Newton's second law of motion tells us, and you're probably thinking, well that's obvious! You could say all of this is very obvious. Why did it take someone like Isaac Newton to discover something like "an object will move in the direction it is pushed" and "heavy things are harder to push than light things"? The answer is that Newton didn't really "discover" these laws. What he did was to find a mathematical way to describe and measure how an object behaves when a force is applied. He called the tendency of an object to keep moving in whatever direction it is moving <u>momentum</u>. The more momentum an object has, the harder it is to change its velocity or direction.

If you look closely at the three parts of Newton's second law of motion, you can probably figure out how to tell if an object has a lot of momentum or a little momentum. How much momentum an object has depends on two things—how fast it's moving and how much mass it has. An object that's moving quickly, even if it doesn't have a lot of mass, will have a lot of momentum. A fast baseball is much more difficult to stop than a baseball that was tossed gently into the air. And objects with a lot of mass have more momentum than objects with less mass. That's why the rolling ball of concrete is more difficult to push out of the way than the rolling beach ball, even if the rolling ball of concrete is moving slowly toward you.

The effects of momentum exist even in a zero-gravity environment like space. Rocket ships may weigh nothing because without gravity, there is no weight. But a fast-moving spacecraft will have a lot of mass and a lot of velocity. That means it will have a lot of momentum, so it will take a great deal of force to change speed or direction, even in space.

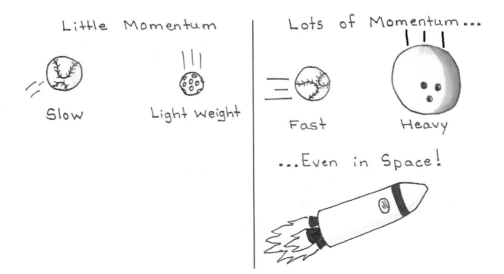

Unit 3- Newton's Laws

Newton's Laws Lab #5- Giving the Gift of Momentum
- instructions

Materials:
- Lab sheets, Do Your Own Experiment sheet (located in the Appendix), pencil
- Several marbles—at least three of the same size, and at least two of different sizes
- Cardboard roll from paper towel or wrapping paper—you'll need to cut this, so not a really thick cardboard roll
- Pen or marker
- Basketball
- Tennis ball
- Flat surface
- Tape
- An open space to bounce a basketball (such as a driveway) with nothing breakable too close by. This part of the experiment is best done outside, because the height reached is often higher than a ceiling.

Aloud: So far most of what we've learned about Newton's second law of motion and momentum has probably seemed pretty obvious to you. But there's another aspect of momentum that I find truly amazing: momentum can be transferred from one object to another. Have you ever played with the balls on a pool table or crashed one marble into another marble? When a moving ball hits a ball that's holding still, the moving ball tries to transfer its momentum to the ball that was holding still. If the balls are exactly the same size and shape and mass, the moving ball will stop, having transferred its momentum to the other ball. The ball that was at rest now has the momentum and starts rolling.

This makes sense if you remember that momentum depends on two things: mass and velocity. If a moving object crashes into an object that is holding still, the moving object transfers all the momentum it can to the object at rest. We can observe how much of the momentum is transferred by watching how the velocity of the two objects changes. If the two objects are about the same mass, then the moving object will transfer pretty much all of its momentum in the form of velocity—it will stop moving and the object it hits will start moving.

Really amazing things start to happen when objects of different mass and velocity try to transfer momentum to each other. Let's see what those amazing things are.

Procedure:
Preparation (can be done ahead of time)
1. Cut the cardboard roll down the middle lengthwise so that you have two "canals" in which you can roll marbles.

2. Place the two halves end to end and tape together. Try your best not to have a bump in the middle that will interfere with marbles rolling. You're trying to make a longer track in which to roll marbles. Place the assembly on a flat surface.

3. Make a mark about an inch or two in from one end of your marble run. This is the starting mark. On the same half of the marble run, make another mark at the middle of that cardboard tube-half.

Marbles of Equal Mass
4. Get two marbles of the same size. Place one marble at the "starting mark" you made at one end of the marble run. Give it a medium-strength push with your finger. Try to push it straight along the marble run. Record your results (#1).

5. Using the same marble and another of the same size, place one at the starting line and one on the other mark you made in the middle of the tube half. Fill in #2 and #3 before you do anything else.

[continued]

6. Give the marble at the starting line a medium-strength push with your finger. Try to make it as close to the same kind of push you did in step 4. Watch what happens. Try this a few times to see if you always get the same results. Sometimes, you might not push the marble exactly in a straight line, so your results might change. Figure out what usually happens. Record your observations (#4 and #5).

7. Play around with how hard you push the marble. If you push it harder, does the marble that began at rest move faster? What if you give the marble a very gentle push? Fill in #6.

Aloud: If everything in this experiment were perfect, the marble you pushed would stop exactly on the spot that the other marble sat. With practice, you can probably make this happen. But lots of factors can interfere with this experiment. Your cardboard tubes might not be perfectly smooth or level. Your push might not have been perfectly straight. The marbles might not have exactly the same mass. Most of the time, you should see the marble you push stop or roll a little ways after colliding with the marble that began at rest. This is because it will have transferred its momentum—mass x velocity—to the marble that started at rest. Because both of the marbles have about the same mass, most of this transfer takes the form of velocity—sending the second marble rolling--just about as fast and as far as the first marble would have, had there not been something in its way.

8. Fill in your analysis and conclusions (#7 & #8).

More Marble Experiments

9. Now that you understand how to set up a momentum experiment, you're going to set up a few of your own. There are some "Do Your Own Experiment" sheets included with the notebooking pages. You should design an experiment to test further what happens with marbles and momentum. You can use one experiment sheet to do the following: hit a smaller marble with a larger marble, place two marbles of the same size touching each other, and then roll a third marble into them, and one collision you design yourself. Fill in the "Do Your Own Experiment" sheet and write down your results. Pay attention to how far and how fast the different marbles roll.

Momentum Is So Cool

Aloud: You now have a pretty good sense of how the transfer of momentum works with marbles. Did you figure out that when a larger marble crashes into a smaller marble, two things happen? First, the larger marble doesn't stop—it keeps rolling, just more slowly. Second, the smaller marble not only starts to roll, but it actually ends up rolling more quickly than the larger marble does! If you didn't notice this, try it again and watch carefully.

Another thing you might have noticed is what happens when two marbles at rest are touching each other and a third marble crashes into them. In an instant, all the momentum from the moving marble is transferred to the marble in the middle. In that same instant, the momentum in the marble in the middle is transferred to the last marble, which rolls off down the marble run.

What do you think would happen if one of the marbles were not just a little more massive, but a whole lot larger than the marble it crashed into? We're going to find out by using a basketball and a tennis ball.

10. Go outside onto a surface on which you can bounce a basketball. Hold the basketball straight out in front of you and let it drop. Watch what happens. Try to remember about how high the basketball comes up the first time it bounces.

11. Repeat step 12 with the tennis ball. Don't throw it down on the ground. Let it drop.

[continued]

12. Fill in #9 and #10.

13. Take a moment and think about this experiment: You're going to place the tennis ball on top of the basketball and let them drop. The basketball will hit the ground and bounce up. What will happen to the tennis ball? Write down your hypothesis in #11.

14. Try the experiment. Hold the basketball in front of you with one hand. Balance the tennis ball on top of it with the other hand. Let go of both balls at the same time. What happens? Were you surprised? Fill in #12 and #13.

Possible Answers:

#1: Will depend on what happens, but you should push hard enough to get the marble to travel all the way along the marble run.

#4 & #5: The marble that is pushed should either stop at the point of collision or travel a little bit farther. The marble that started at rest should start rolling and travel about as far as the marble that was simply rolled, with no other marble in the way, travelled. If you're having trouble, try pushing a little more gently or with a little more force.

#6: faster, faster

#7: momentum

#8: about the same, velocity

#12: The tennis ball should shoot off toward the sky, much higher than you'd anticipate.

#13: inertia, a lot, velocity

Conclusion/ Discussion:

1. Momentum depends on two characteristics—mass and velocity. Talk about how momentum changes from an object with a tiny mass to an object with a very large mass. How does this affect how we try to change those objects' movements? You could compare how we handle ping-pong balls to how we handle bowling balls.

2. Talk about how velocity affects momentum. Would you be able to catch a speeding baseball with your bare hand? Why or why not? What if it were a gently tossed baseball?

3. Remember that momentum can be transferred from one object to another. Talk about how this happens in the experiments you just performed. Do you think the energy and speed of the tennis ball in the tennis ball experiment could be used, say, to launch a rocket? Why or why not?

More Lab Fun:

1. Ideas for momentum experiments are endless. Experiment with lining up five marbles and roll two marbles toward them. What do you think will happen? What does happen? Why? If you find this fun, you might invest in a Newton's Cradle. This is the device that Isaac Newton used to experiment with momentum. It has swinging balls instead of marbles and offers a fabulous demonstration of the transfer of momentum.

2. Build a giant marble run using cardboard tubes, rolled-up paper, whatever you can find. Use what you know about physics to get it to work. Can you make a marble run that rings a bell at the end? That knocks over a paper cup? Give it a try!

[continued]

Notebooking Ideas:

1. Use a definition page to define *momentum* and *transfer of momentum.*
2. Add momentum = mass x velocity (momentum = m x v) to an equation notebooking page.
3. Write story about what it would be like to be an ant on top of the tennis ball during the tennis ball/ basketball experiment. This is not as silly as it seems. Physicists imagine this kind of thing all the time to understand how things look from the "frame of reference" or perspective of a particular object.

 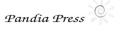

NAME _____ DATE _____

Giving the Gift of Momentum

<u>MARBLES OF THE SAME SIZE AND MASS</u>

Control:

1. When I push the marble along the marble run with nothing in the way, the marble **holds still / travels part way down the marble run / travels all the way down the marble run**.

Hypotheses:

2. When I push the marble at one end into the other marble, I think that the marble I pushed will **travel just as far and as fast as it did without a marble in the way / stop / travel a little less and a little more slowly than it did without a marble in the way**.

3. I think that the marble that was sitting still will **travel to the end of the marble run / stay still / travel part way down the marble run and stop**.

Observations:

4. When I pushed the marble at one end into the other marble, the marble I pushed **travelled just as far and fast as it did without a marble in the way / stopped / travelled a little less and a little more slowly than it did without a marble in the way**.

5. The marble that started out sitting still **travelled to the end of the marble run / stayed still / travelled part way down the marble run and stopped**.

6. The harder I push the marble, the **faster / slower** it goes. If I push the marble faster, the marble that gets hit travels **faster / slower**.

Data Analysis and Conclusions:

7. Without a marble in the way, the marble I pushed would have kept going toward the end of the marble run. Because there was a marble in the way, the marble I pushed transferred its **gravity / momentum / inertia** to the marble that started at rest.

8. The marbles have **about the same / very different** masses. Momentum depends on mass and velocity. Because the mass stayed the same, I saw a change in the **mass / velocity** of both marbles after they collided.

MOMENTUM IS SO COOL.... A BASKETBALL AND A TENNIS BALL

9. When I drop the basketball, it bounces up to about my

_____. (knee, waist, neck—fill in whatever body part applies)

10. When I drop the tennis ball, it bounces up to my _____.

11. **Hypothesis:** When I drop the basketball with the tennis ball on top of it,

I think the tennis ball will _____

_____.

12. **Results:** When I dropped the basketball with the tennis ball on top of it,

this is what happened: _____

_____.

13. **Conclusion:** When a large object collides with a smaller object, it transfers **momentum / inertia / gravity** to the smaller object. Here, the basketball has a lot more mass than the tennis ball. When they collide, the basketball is moving upward after bouncing and the tennis ball is traveling downward from being dropped. They collide with a whole lot of velocity, so that the momentum involved is **a lot / not very much at all**. Because there's so little mass in the tennis ball compared to the mass in the basketball, the momentum transfer takes the form of an increase in the **velocity / mass** of the tennis ball.

For my notebook

Newton's Third Law: Lift-Off!

Newton's <u>third law of motion</u> is the easiest to state, but probably the toughest to understand. Here's what it says: **Every action has an opposite, but equal, reaction.** Let's look at this one a little bit at a time.

Imagine that you are hopping up off the ground. To keep things simple, we'll look at the interaction between two objects—your shoe and the ground. In this example, what does <u>action</u> mean? It means a force applied by one object to another object. When you jump, your shoe pushes down against the ground. That pushing force is an action.

So, what is a <u>reaction</u>? You probably know that in everyday language, "reaction" means that one thing happens in response to another thing. When your hand touches something that's too hot, you react by pulling your hand away. When you are happy, you react by smiling. When the dinner gets burned, you react by ordering pizza.

In Newton's third law of motion, reaction means that another force is applied in response to an initial force. Newton's third law describes what happens when two objects act on each other. When your shoe pushes down on the ground, the ground pushes back on your shoe. If it didn't push back, your shoe would go straight through the ground!

Newton's third law tells us that every action has an <u>equal and opposite reaction</u>. So, when you hop, the ground pushes back on your shoe with exactly the same amount of force as your shoe uses when it pushes down on the ground. That is why the reaction is called equal. And the ground pushes back on your foot in exactly the opposite direction as your shoe pushes on the ground. That is why the reaction is called opposite.

We can show these actions and reactions using a picture. The arrows in the picture represent forces—pushes or pulls. You might notice that the two arrows are the same size. This shows that they are equal forces. And you probably noticed that the arrows are pointing in opposite directions. This shows that the two forces are opposite.

Shoe pushing down on ground

Ground pushing up on shoe

Physicists use arrows like these all the time to illustrate forces and their directions. The technical name for such arrows is <u>vectors</u>. There's a lot of advanced mathematics involved in using vectors, but for our purposes, it's enough to understand that the arrows show in which direction the force is acting and that the length of the arrow shows how big the force is. In the next experiment, you're going to use vectors to show some of the forces involved in propelling rocket ships.

Newton's Laws Lab #6- Rocket Science - instructions

Materials:
- Lab sheets (pp. 103-108: Rocket Science and Newton's Brain Teasers), pencil
- String, try to get 20-30 feet
- A few straws
- Several (6+) balloons of various shapes and sizes (some round balloons and some of the longer ones)
- Ruler or tape measure
- Strong tape
- Marker
- Clothespin (optional)

Aloud: One of the ways in which scientists use Newton's third law of motion is in propelling rocket ships. Inside the rocket ship's propulsion chamber, fuels are mixed and heated in order to produce lots and lots of gases—that's the smoke you see when a rocket blasts off. All of these gases are pretty much squirted out the bottom of the rocket at a very high speed. As you know, for every action (gases rushing out of the rocket) there is an opposite, but equal, reaction. So, the rocket is propelled upward by those gases shooting downward. Let's see if we can use these ideas to make our own little rocket ship.

Procedure:
1. Put the string through the straw. Tie the string to doorknobs, chairs, whatever you can find to make it taut and straight. If you have several people, you can take turns holding the string. For this experiment, try to get the string fairly level, so that it is parallel to the ground and not slanted up or down.
2. Use a marker to mark a "starting line" on the string. This starting line should be about 18 inches from one end of the string.
3. List the balloons you've gathered up on the first three columns on the chart on your lab sheet. You'll want to focus on their shapes and sizes. You're going to send these balloons racing along the string. What characteristic of the balloons do you think will affect which one goes the farthest? Which balloon do you think will go the farthest? Write down your HYPOTHESES (#1).
4. Now blow up one of the balloons, but don't tie off the end. While holding the end shut (a clothespin can help with this), tape the straw to the balloon as illustrated.
5. Line up the front of the straw with the starting line. Let go of the balloon and let the air out. Watch the little rocket go!
6. Measure how far the rocket went by measuring from your starting line to the point that the front of the straw reached on the string. Record your measurement on the last column of the chart. Complete the lab sheet.

Possible Answers:
5: To answer this question, children should understand that they could test two balloons of the same size and shape but of different colors.

Conclusion / Discussion:
1. Why does the balloon travel along the string when it is released? Talk about this in everyday language (the air pushes it) and in terms of Newton's third law—using words like action, equal, opposite, and reaction.
2. Does the fact that a reaction has to be "equal" help you to understand why some balloons travel farther?
3. Do you think this method would work in space? Why or why not? You'll be finding out the answer soon.

[continued]

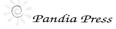

Newton's Laws Lab #6- Rocket Science - instructions page 2

More Lab Fun:
1. Why do you think we used the string for this experiment? What happens if you release the balloon and it's not forced to travel along the string? Try it.
2. Can you figure out a way to get the balloon to travel straight up? Write down your design in your notebook and give it a try.

NEWTON'S BRAIN TEASERS (pp. 107-108): First, allow students to think through the brain teasers themselves using what they have learned about Newton's laws. Then read the following:

1. <u>Jumping</u>. Aloud: You might remember from Newton's second law that more massive objects take more force to move than less massive objects. When you push your left hand against your right hand, the right hand pushes back with approximately equal force. Your left hand isn't significantly stronger or more massive than your right hand, so the two forces hold each other in equilibrium and your hands don't really move. On the other hand, Earth's mass is about 6,000,000,000,000,000, 000,000,000 (six septillion) kilograms. Your mass is probably around 30 to 40 kilograms. That's a HUGE difference in masses. When you push against Earth, you don't push with nearly enough force to cause a noticeable acceleration of Earth. But when Earth pushes back with the exact same force, it's enough to move your relatively little bit of mass up into the air a little ways. In fact, you do cause Earth to accelerate, but because of the huge difference in masses, the acceleration is so teeny-tiny, it pretty much can't be detected. Next time you jump, think about the fact that even a kid like you can move the whole planet, just a teeny-tiny bit.

2. <u>Rocket Ships</u>. Aloud: Here's a very interesting bit of history for you. More than 200 years after Newton described the laws of motion, people were still struggling to understand them. In the 1920s, a rocket scientist named Robert Goddard thought about Newton's third law when he was trying to figure out how people could travel to the moon. He realized that when the rocket pushes gas out of its engines, the rocket's acceleration is NOT caused by the air pushing against the ground. There are two objects interacting—gas and the rocket. The rocket pushes the gas out in one direction, and the gas itself pushes the rocket in the opposite direction. Robert Goddard realized that this meant that a rocket could propel itself through a vacuum without a problem. Even though this is a clear and easy example of Newton's third law, people made fun of Robert Goddard for his idea. But he was absolutely correct, and today NASA's Goddard Space Flight Center is named after him.

3. <u>Flies in a jar</u>. Aloud: Many people will answer that the jar weighs less when the flies are in the air than when they're all sitting on the bottom of the jar. But we know that the mass of the jar and the mass of the flies stay the same, right? Whether the flies are on the bottom of the jar or flying around, we haven't added or taken away any of the matter in the jar. The weight of the jar should stay the same.

   Why do many people think that the jar will weigh less when the flies are in the air? Probably because they think that the weight of the flies—the force of gravity pulling the flies down—is no longer pushing on the bottom of the jar. But this isn't entirely true.

   Something is keeping those flies flying around and not on the ground—the flapping of their wings. Every time they flap their wings, the wings push down on air. And, as we've learned from Newton's third law, the air pushes right back, keeping the flies aloft. Meanwhile, an air current has been created that pushes against the bottom of the jar with about the same force as gravity on the fly. So, the weight of the jar stays pretty much the same, whether all the flies are on the bottom or all the flies are in the air.

Note to Parents and Teachers: Have some aluminum foil handy for the first reading in Unit 4.

NAME _____ DATE _____

Rocket Science

1. **Hypotheses:** I think the balloon that is

   _____ -colored, _____

   -shaped, and _____ -sized will travel the

   farthest. I think the **size / shape / color** of the balloon will

   affect how far the balloon travels (you may choose more

   than one characteristic). I think the **size / shape / color** of the

   balloon will NOT affect how far the balloon travels.

Observations:

Balloon Color	Balloon Shape	Balloon Size	Distance Traveled

2. What were the characteristics of the balloon which traveled the farthest

   distance? _____

   _____

   _____

3. What were the characteristics of the balloon which traveled the least

   distance? _____

   _____

   _____

4. Why do you think some balloons traveled farther than others? _____

   _____

   _____

5. How might you find out if the color of a balloon makes a difference in how far it travels? _____

_____

_____

Draw a picture illustrating how your experiment was set up. Show the balloon, the string, and the straw. Use vectors to illustrate in what directions the forces on your balloon were applied. Don't worry about the size of the vectors for now.

Explain how this experiment illustrates Newton's third law of motion—that every action has an opposite, but equal, reaction.

_____

_____

_____

_____

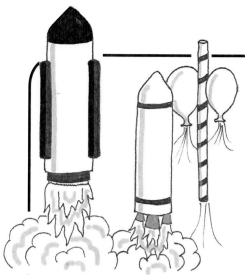

Here's a challenge for you:

Can you design a rocket that will travel farther than any of the ones on your chart? Maybe you could use two balloons? If so, what combination do you think will work best? Can you use the information you gathered earlier about the balloons to come up with some ideas?

Here's a sketch of what I tried:

Rocket Science - page 4

Here's a description of what happened. Try to describe not only how far your invention traveled but why you think it traveled farther or less far than the balloons in the first part of the experiment.

For my notebook

Newton's Brain Teasers

Newton's third law of motion is one of my favorite parts of physics. Why? I think it's because this law, more than almost any other, can make a person think really hard about how the world around us works. In fact, there's a whole series of puzzling questions that physics students have tried to figure out almost since Newton came up with his laws. So, get ready to think!

1. **Jumping**: Try pushing your hands against each other with about equal force. They don't move, right? But we've learned that when we jump into the air, our feet push down on the ground and the ground pushes up on our feet with equal force. Why is this different than when our hands push on each other? Why do we actually move upward when we jump? And, if we move up into the air a few inches, why doesn't Earth move downward a few inches?

2. **Rocket Ships**: We've learned that rocket ships are propelled upward by forcing gases at a high velocity out of their engines. A lot of people think that the gases push off of the ground (or off the air in the atmosphere) to keep the rocket moving. If this were true, rockets could not move around in the vacuum of space using their engines. What do you think? Can rockets move around in space by propelling gas out of one end? If so, why?

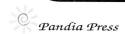

3. **Flies in a jar**: Imagine you could put 20 houseflies into a jar. Then, you put the jar into the refrigerator for a bit, to put the flies to sleep. With all the little critters asleep on the bottom of the jar, you weigh the jar on an extremely accurate scale. Then you wait for a while, until all the flies wake up and start buzzing around in the jar. You manage to find a time when they are all flying in the air in the jar and weigh the jar again. Does the jar weigh more than, less than, or the same as the jar did when all the flies were lying on the bottom? How come?

I hope you had some fun with these brain ticklers. The world around you is full of puzzlers like these. All you need to do is to look around and think about the forces at work on the objects you see. What happens when the car you're in comes to a sudden stop? What happens when you jump up in an elevator? What forces are at work when you pull on a wagon or ride a bike? Think about these or other questions, and write about your thoughts in your science notebook.

Newton's laws tell us so much about the world that it's really important to understand and remember them. The next page summarizes Newton's laws for you so you can have them all in one place in your science notebook. If you do copy work, you might want to copy these rules yourself. Try illustrating each law with a picture of an example.

Unit 3- Newton's Laws *Pandia Press*

For my notebook

Newton's Laws of Motion: A Summary

Newton's First Law of Motion

A body at rest tends to stay at rest

A body in motion tends to stay in motion

Scientific statement: An object at rest tends to stay at rest. An object in motion tends to stay in motion.

In everyday language: If something is sitting still, it will keep sitting still until something changes. If something is moving, it will keep moving, until something changes.

Also known as: Inertia

Examples: A cake sitting on a table stays there until you move it. A spacecraft will travel at the same speed through a gravity-free vacuum forever unless it runs into some force like the gravity from a planet. The liquid in your inner ear keeps spinning for a moment even when you've stopped spinning.

Newton's Second Law of Motion

Scientific statement: The acceleration of an object is in relation to the force acting on the object and moves the same direction as the force.

In everyday language: 1) The more massive an object is, the harder it is to move. 2) Objects move in the same direction as you push (or pull) them. 3) The harder you push (or pull) an object, the more it speeds up.

Also known as: Momentum

Examples: A brick is harder to push than a beach ball. If you kick a ball forward, it goes forward, not left or right or backward. The harder you push (kick) on a ball, the faster it goes.

Newton's Third Law of Motion

Balloon forces air to the left   Air forces balloon right

Scientific statement: Every action has an opposite, but equal, reaction.

In everyday language: When one object pushes on another, the second object pushes back in the opposite direction and with just as much force as the first.

Also known as: Conservation of Momentum*

Examples: A rocket ship blasting off, you standing on the ground without falling through, jumping off the ground, flies in a jar.

*This complicated name is because momentum in a system, like a rocket blasting off, is "conserved" in the following way: When momentum is given to the gases expelled from the rocket, equal and opposite momentum is given to the rocket to propel it forward. This way, no momentum is added to or subtracted from the "system" of the rocket and the gases being expelled. Therefore, physicists say that momentum has been "conserved."

Unit 4

Friction

NAME _____ DATE _____

For my notebook

Friction - It Can Rub You the Wrong Way

(Before beginning this reading, grab a roll of aluminum foil.)

An object in motion tends to stay in motion. Yet when you give a toy car a gentle push across the floor, it will come to a stop. Why? We've already learned one answer to this question. The car slows down and comes to a stop because the force of gravity is also pulling down on the car. This answer, though, is not complete.

Pick up two pieces of aluminum foil. Try to keep them as smooth as possible. Rub one piece against the other. They slide past each other pretty easily, right? Now, imagine you have a really powerful microscope that can zoom in so much that you see little bumps and dips on the surface of the aluminum foil. Why are there bumps and dips? The answer is that on Earth, it's almost impossible to make a perfectly smooth surface.

Surface of foil as
it looks with your eye

Surface of foil at very
high magnification

What does the foil look like really close up? There's an easy way to make a model of the surface of the foil at very high magnification. Take both of your pieces of foil and crumple them all up. Then, open them again, but don't try to smooth out the wrinkles. There! You have a model of a microscopic surface that's not perfectly smooth. It has bumps and dips and points and crinkles. This is what most of the surfaces in our lives are like extremely close up.

Try to rub the two pieces of foil together now. Is it harder or easier than it was to rub the two smooth pieces together? The bumps and dips on each piece of foil now get caught on each other, and it becomes harder to rub the two pieces together. This is what happens whenever two objects move against each other. All the irregularities on the objects' surfaces bump and grind against each other opposing your effort to move them.

For the most part, scientists don't worry about the details of how each little bump or dip pushes against another. If we zoom out from our microscopic view again, all we notice is that when we try to push one crinkled piece against the other, there is some force resisting our push, making it harder to push than smoother surfaces would be. Scientists call this force that resists motion <u>friction</u>. Whenever you try to push an object in some direction, friction acts to push it in the other direction. To move an object, the force you use has to be stronger than the force of friction.

Direction of push

Resistance from friction

Friction is a <u>contact force</u>, so it acts only when two objects are touching each other. Here on Earth, friction is literally everywhere. When you toss a ball into the air, the ball experiences friction as it whizzes past and rubs against air molecules and dust particles. We use motor oil in cars in order to reduce the friction between the various moving parts in a car engine. Without oil, the engine parts would rub against each other so much that they would start to break pieces off each other.

Friction is not all bad, though. Think for a moment about what the world would be like if there were no friction. Without friction, all the surfaces in the world would behave like the slipperiest ice. Car tires wouldn't push against the ground to make the car go forward: they would just spin and spin in the same spot. You couldn't pick anything up: everything would slip right out of your slippery hands. Friction makes some things more difficult, but we couldn't live without it.

Strange Science Words

Did you know that friction is so important that scientists who study friction have a special name? A <u>tribologist</u> is a scientist who studies friction.

Unit 4- Friction

Activity: Slip Sliding Away

Below, draw a picture showing what it would be like to try to eat dinner in a world without friction. Turn over the page and write a short story describing a day in your life without friction. (Your story is friction fiction, thank goodness!)

My Day without Friction

by _____

Unit 4- Friction Pandia Press

Friction Lab #1: How Much Is Enough? - instructions

Materials:
- Lab sheets, pencil
- Two books, one that has a dust jacket that you can remove and a cloth-type cover underneath—a child's picture book would be perfect. The other book should be a heavier book, like a dictionary.
- A stiff board—several feet long (3 to 4) and a couple of feet wide. This can be made of anything, but the thick foam core boards from the craft store work quite well and are light enough for children to use. You should hold onto this, as we'll be needing to use it again in future experiments.
- Small or medium-sized toy vehicle
- Meterstick, yardstick, or tape measure (Metric is preferred in science, but you could measure in inches if you don't have a metric ruler.)
- Roll of aluminum foil (you'll be covering part of the board with it)
- Magnifying lens (don't worry about quality—anything you have will do fine)
- Tape
- Calculator

Aloud: In science, it's not always enough to describe friction in everyday terms. You might be able to say, "This brick is very hard to push across the concrete but much easier to push across ice because of friction." Scientists, though, want to be able to measure exactly how much friction exists between two surfaces. To do this, they use a number called the <u>coefficient of friction</u>. The coefficient is just a fancy term that tells us how one object moves across a surface of another object. The higher the coefficient of friction, the more resistance there is and the harder it is to move across. Take bike riding for an example. Let's say one day you ride your bicycle on a gravel road. The next day you ride your bicycle on a smoothly paved sidewalk. Which would you expect to be a higher coefficient of friction—between your bike tires and the gravel road, or between your bike tires and the sidewalk? The gravel road, of course, and you had to work harder to pedal across it, too. Physicists use the lowercase letters "fr" to represent the coefficient of friction.

There's a pretty simple way to figure out the coefficient of friction between an object and a surface, for example, between a block and sandpaper. First, cover a board with the surface whose friction you're interested in testing. Lay the board flat on the ground. Place the object toward one end of the board. Start to lift that end of the board very slowly. Eventually, the object will start to move. When this happens, stop lifting and have someone measure the height of the top of the ramp, and also measure the base of the triangle formed by the ramp.

[continued]

The coefficient of friction is equal to the height divided by the base.

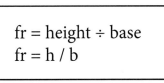

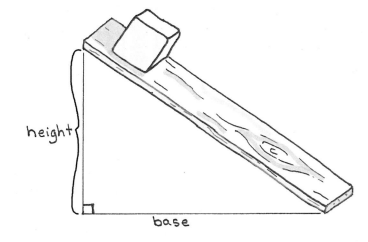

If you take a moment to think about it, the more friction there is between the board and the object, the higher you'll need to lift the ramp before the object starts moving. This means that the coefficient of friction will be a higher number if you have to lift the board higher. By taking measurements, you can figure out with precision just how much friction exists between two objects. We're going to use this knowledge in the next experiment to figure out which characteristics of objects affect the amount of friction.

Procedure:

1. Lay the board on a flat surface. Toward one end, make some kind of mark to indicate a "starting point" for your experiments.
2. Fill in #1 and #2 on the lab sheet.

Friction and Smoothness of Surface

Aloud: We're going to test how much friction exists between the board and a book with and without its dustjacket. The first question to answer is: Which is smoother, the book's surface with the dust jacket or without it? How could you find this out? Before you read further, take a moment to think of ways to use at least two of your senses to answer this question. The ideas I had were (1) to look closely at the two surfaces with a magnifying glass, and (2) to feel both surfaces with the tips of my fingers. Do both of these now and fill in #3 and #4 on your lab sheet.

3. Use the following procedure for finding the coefficient of friction for the following objects:
   a. The book with its dust jacket on
   b. The book with its dust jacket off
4. Procedure for finding the coefficient of friction:
   a. Lay the ramp flat on the ground.
   b. Place the object toward one end of the ramp at the starting point.
   c. Start to lift that end of the ramp very slowly. Eventually, the object will start to move.
   d. When this happens, stop lifting the ramp, and have someone measure the height of the top of the ramp and the base of the triangle formed by the ramp (see the illustration above). You can measure in inches or centimeters; just be consistent.
   e. Record this data on the table (first OBSERVATIONS AND DATA table).
   f. Calculate the coefficient of friction, which is equal to the height divided by the base. Record the coefficient of friction in the table.

[continued]

5. Get out the aluminum foil. You're going to try to cover a path down the board with crumbled foil. So, tear off a strip a bit longer than the board and crumple it up. Tape it to the board or secure it with clips of some sort. You may need two or three strips to make a surface wide and long enough to test the coefficient of friction between crumpled aluminum foil and the book.

6. Repeat steps 3 & 4 using the board covered with foil.

7. Fill in #5 & #6 on the lab sheet.

Friction and Weight

Aloud: You've seen how to conduct an experiment to find out how roughness and smoothness affect friction. Do you think you could design an experiment to find out how weight affects friction? Take a moment to think about your answer. Remember, you want to be able to compare weight and nothing else, so you'll want to do as much as possible to keep the surfaces you're testing the same and change only the weight on those surfaces. Write your thoughts in #7 & #8 on the lab sheet. I've designed one experiment that we're going to do next. If yours is much different, you should try it, too. I've left some extra room on the lab sheet for you!

8. Take the aluminum foil off the foam board.

9. Using the procedure in step 4, recalculate the coefficient of friction for the book you used earlier without its dustjacket on. We're repeating this part of the experiment so that the comparison between this step and the next are as good as possible.

10. Instead of placing just one book on the starting point, place the same book you just used, and then place a heavy book on top of it. Now the two surfaces we're testing are the same as last time—the board and the book without the dust jacket. However, the weight pressing down on the surfaces is greater because of the extra book. Calculate the coefficient of friction and fill in your observations (second OBSERVATIONS AND DATA table). Use the two empty rows in the table if your student has created his own method to test the change in weight on friction. Fill in #9 on the lab sheet.

Friction and Shape:

Aloud: So far, we've investigated how roughness and weight on a surface affect friction. Next, we're going to investigate whether the shape of the surfaces affect friction. To do this, we want to compare situations in which everything is the same except the shape of the area where the two surfaces touch each other. Can you think of a way to do that? Fill in #10 & #11 on the lab sheet. I've left some room again for you to try your experiment if yours is different than mine.

11. Using the procedure in step 4, calculate the coefficient of friction of the toy vehicle. Place it so that it will roll easily down the board when you lift the board. Stop as soon as it starts to roll. Record your results on the table.

12. Now, turn the toy vehicle upside down. Notice that we are using the same object, with the same mass and weight, but the shape of where the board and the toy vehicle touch each other is different. Calculate the coefficient of friction with the toy vehicle upside down (third OBSERVATIONS AND DATA table). Use the two empty rows on the table if your student has created his own method to test the change in shape on friction.

13. Fill in #12 on the lab sheet.

[continued]

Possible Answers:

#3: The cloth cover of a book should appear rougher than the dust jacket does. If the child is having difficulty with this, make sure to explain how there are bumps and grooves you can see on the cloth cover but not on the dust jacket.

#4: without

#5: rougher

#6: rougher

#7: Talk about the student's ideas. The key idea to try to get across in this part of the exercise is that you want to change only the characteristic you're curious about—in this case, the weight. Thus, if the child suggests trying to compare, say, a bowling ball and a feather, the experiment might yield confusing results. The two objects will have different smoothness/roughness of surface. They are different shapes, etc.

#9: increased

#10: see #7

#12: did

Conclusion and Discussion:

1. Recall that you used more than one sense to determine what was rougher and what was smoother. Many of us have a tendency to think that scientific observations can be made only with our eyes, but a number of important discoveries have evolved using other senses as well. Are there good aspects to using more than one sense in an experiment? What are they?

2. Why do you think we use wheels to move heavy objects? How does the smaller amount of surface contact cause less friction? Here's one important part of the answer: When the car is right side up, at any given time, only a very small part of the wheel is in contact with the ramp. When the car is upside down, the whole top of the car is in contact with the ramp. Where there is more of each of the surfaces rubbing together, more friction is created.

3. Make sure that you understand that the coefficient of friction depends on two surfaces in contact with one another. A particular object doesn't have its own coefficient of friction. This number only makes sense with respect to two surfaces rubbing against each other.

More Lab Fun:

1. Look at the first part of your lab sheet where you tried to form a hypothesis about which characteristics of matter might change the amount of friction. Now that you know all about calculating the coefficient of friction, pick out a few of these and design your own experiments to test out your ideas.

2. Try changing the surface of the board in different ways. What happens if you cover it with a soft towel?

3. Try placing the toy vehicle right side up, but sideways. Are the results the same as when it was facing forward? Can you explain the results you got?

Notebooking Ideas:

1. Use an equation page to copy down the formula for finding the coefficient of friction.
2. Use a definition page to define *coefficient of friction*.
3. Use some lined paper to tell a story about the day friction stopped working.
4. Use some "Design Your Own Experiment" pages to test different characteristics of objects.

Note to Parents and Teachers: Access to a parked car, a pitcher of water, and a little cooking oil would be useful (but not necessary) props for the next reading.

How Much Is Enough?

CHARACTERISTICS OF FRICTION

Hypothesis:

1. I know that matter has a lot of different characteristics. I think the following characteristics will affect how much friction there is between two objects. (Circle the characteristics you think will affect friction.)

Weight	Color	Smoothness		Size
Shape	Bounciness	Prettiness	Cost	Age

FRICTION AND SMOOTHNESS OF SURFACES

Hypothesis:

2. I think that smoother surfaces will have **more** / **less** friction than rougher surfaces.

Observations:

3. Using the magnifying glass, I observe that the book **with** / **without** the dust jacket has the roughest surface.

4. Using my finger tips, I feel that the book **with** / **without** the dust jacket has the roughest surface.

Observations and Data:

Surfaces	Height of triangle when object moves	Base of triangle when object moves	Coefficient of Friction between the two surfaces: fr = height ÷ base
Book with dust jacket & board	÷	=	
Book without dust jacket & board	÷	=	
Book with dust jacket & crumpled aluminum foil	÷	=	
Book without dust jacket & crumpled aluminum foil	÷	=	

Analysis and Conclusion:

5. The two surfaces that had the highest coefficient of friction were the: _____ and the

   _____.

   These two surfaces were **rougher** / **smoother** than the surfaces with lower coefficients of friction.

6. Therefore, I conclude that the **rougher** / **smoother** the surface, the more friction there is.

FRICTION AND WEIGHT

7. I want to figure out how weight affects friction. I could perform the following experiment to find this out:

   _____

   _____

   _____

Hypothesis:

8. I think that the heavier an object is, the **higher** / **lower** its coefficient of friction with another object.

Observations and Data:

Surfaces	Height of triangle when object moves	Base of triangle when object moves	Coefficient of Friction between the two surfaces: fr = height ÷ base
Book without dust jacket & board	÷	=	
Book without dust jacket + heavy book on top & board	÷	=	
	÷	=	
	÷	=	

Unit 4- Friction

Analysis and Conclusions:

9. The surfaces in contact this time were the book without a dust jacket and the board. The only thing I changed was the weight with which the book was pressing on the foam board. This **increased** / **decreased** the friction between the two surfaces.

FRICTION AND SHAPE OF SURFACES IN CONTACT

10. I want to figure out how shape affects frictions. I could perform the following experiment to find this out:

_____

_____

_____

_____

Hypothesis:

11. I think that the shape of the surfaces touching each other **will** /**will not** affect the friction between the two objects.

Observations and Data:

Surfaces	Height of triangle when object moves	Base of triangle when object moves	Coefficient of Friction between the two surfaces: fr = height ÷ base
Vehicle right side up & board	÷	=	
Vehicle upside down & board	÷	=	
	÷	=	
	÷	=	

Analysis and Conclusions:

12. This time, the object and its weight on the board were the same. I didn't really change the roughness of the surfaces involved, either. The biggest change was the shape of the area where the car was touching the board. Changing the shape of the area of contact **did** / **did not** change the friction between the two surfaces.

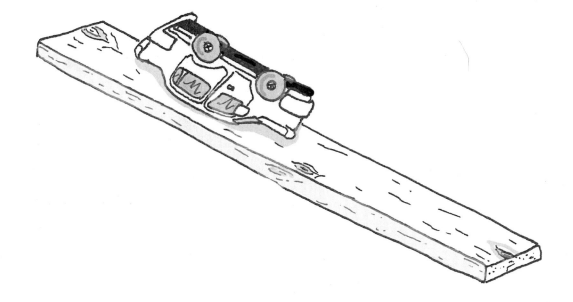

For my notebook

Friction in Real Life: Auto Safety

Props could be used to make this lesson a demonstration, or students can use their imaginations. Access to a parked car, a pitcher of water, and a little cooking oil would be useful (but not necessary) props.

Most of us use automobiles pretty frequently. We might drive to the store, to a friend's house, or to a museum. Automobile engineers spend a lot of time finding ways to make the cars we drive safer. One of the big issues automobile engineers have to think about is friction. We're going to consider two areas in which friction plays a big role in how cars are designed.

Think about what a car's tires look like. If it's convenient, you could even step outside and look at a car. Are the tires smooth? Are they rough? If you have access to a car, run your hand along the tire, applying some pressure. Is there a lot of friction? Very little friction?

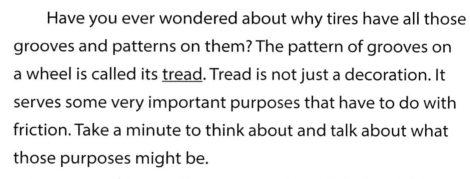

Have you ever wondered about why tires have all those grooves and patterns on them? The pattern of grooves on a wheel is called its <u>tread</u>. Tread is not just a decoration. It serves some very important purposes that have to do with friction. Take a minute to think about and talk about what those purposes might be.

To answer this question, you need to think about driving in all kinds of weather because you don't usually change the tires on your car from "sunny day tires" to "rainy day tires." And, most people no longer change their tires in the winter to "snow tires." This means that the tire treads you see on your car have to work well on dry pavement, on wet pavement, and on snow. Each of those surfaces probably has a very different coefficient of friction with the tire. So, tires have a complicated job. On snow, a tire should generate a lot of friction as it comes into contact with the snow, so that the car doesn't slip and slide. On pavement, the car should generate just the little bit of friction needed to keep it moving across the pavement, but not too much friction or the tires will wear down and more energy will be needed to move the car. In the rain, it's important to keep the rain from forming a layer of slippery wetness between the tires and the pavement. When that happens, it's called <u>hydroplaning,</u> and it's a very dangerous way to discover what happens when there's almost no friction between a car's tires and the pavement.

You may have noticed that when you move your hand against the tires, they're rubbery. The rubber surface seems to grab on to surfaces like concrete and your hand. This characteristic of the tire generates a good deal of friction. You can see how this would help in snowy weather to keep the car from sliding around. So, the material from which the tires are made is one factor that engineers consider in making safer tires.

Now, imagine what happens when water is poured over the tires. If you have access to a car, try pouring water over a tire. Can you picture the water running through all the little grooves and channels? This is the part of the tire tread's design that helps it to maintain friction on rainy days. To keep the water from forming an unbroken slippery surface between the pavement and the tires, the grooves draw the water into the channels and let it run out in a more controlled and predictable way.

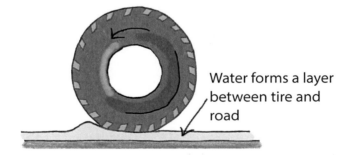

Water forms a layer between tire and road

How does the design of car tires help us out on sunny days? There are lots of answers to this question that I'm sure you can think of, but I'll offer just one. Tires are round. Because they're round, only a small bit of the tire is in contact with the road at any time, so we don't need to create too much energy to move the car. But the small part of the tire that is in contact with the road has a lot of friction—enough to keep the car moving and not sliding.

If you've discovered a new appreciation for tire tread design, you might want to experiment further. You could test various shoe treads against various surfaces now that you know how to measure friction. Bowling shoes have much different treads than hiking boots. Why?

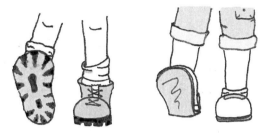

There's one more aspect of automobile safety we should think about while we're on the topic of friction. Imagine being inside the engine of a car.

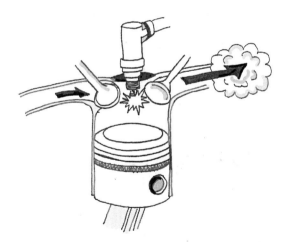

Here is what it would be like: There are metal rods that get pulled up to take in air and gasoline, just like a syringe draws up medicine. Then, the metal rods push the air and gasoline closer together, mixing them up. Next, something called the spark plug lights a little fire, a spark, that sets the gasoline and air mixture on fire, creating a tiny explosion. The tiny explosion forces the metal rod down, and the cycle starts again. The up-and-down motion of the cylinder, and others like it, is what eventually turns the car's tires.

I don't know about you, but I imagine that people who are concerned with automobile safety think a lot about this engine—a tiny place where there's gas and air and flames and explosions happening all the time. On top of all that, there's friction—the friction of all the moving metal parts rubbing against each other.

Why does this matter? Well, try rubbing your hands together, really quickly. Getting warm? Friction generates <u>heat</u>. The faster and harder two surfaces rub against one another, the more friction there is and the more heat is generated. On a cold day, friction's ability to generate heat might be nice to know about. Rubbing your hands together is a great way to keep them warm, though I think that gloves are even better. But what about inside our engine? Do you think it's a good idea to let friction generate lots of heat where there's gasoline around just waiting to explode? Well, it's certainly not a safe idea.

This is one reason why we use motor oil in our cars. It greatly reduces the amount of friction between moving parts in the engine. You could try a simple experiment to demonstrate that this works: Get some cooking oil and rub it on your hands. Now rub your hands together. I imagine they're not getting as hot as when you rubbed them together the first time. This is because the oil reduced the friction, just as it does in a car. Now, don't forget to wash the oil off your hands!

For my notebook

Friction: A Summary

We've learned a lot about friction. You might want to transcribe the following in your science notebook so you can remember the most important things about friction.

1. Friction is the force that opposes motion when one surface is being moved across another surface.

2. We couldn't live without friction. It keeps us from sliding around. It allows us to pick up objects. It affects our everyday lives in countless ways.

3. Friction is measured using the coefficient of friction or "fr."

$$fr = height \div base \ (fr = h \ / \ b)$$

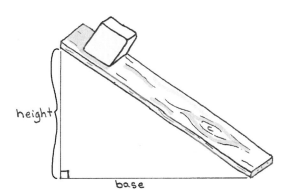

4. There is more friction when an object weighs more.

5. There is less friction when an object has less of its surface in contact with another surface.

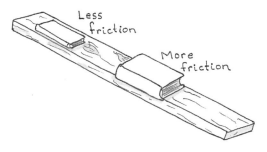

6. Friction generates heat energy.

Unit 4- Friction

Unit 5

Work: Plane and Simple Machines

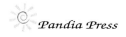

For my notebook

Working Hard or Hardly Working?

What do you think of when you hear the word "work"? A lot of kids might think about doing chores around the house as work—like setting the table, cleaning up a bedroom, or taking out the garbage. Grown-ups might think of work as going some place or doing something to earn money—like working as a nurse, going to meetings at an office, or repairing broken machines.

Physicists have their own definition of *work*. For physicists, <u>work</u> is what is done when a force moves an object from one place to another place. As you can see, there are two parts to this definition. First, for work to be done, something must move from one place to a different place. Second, the movement must occur because some force was applied, a push or a pull. The way that physicists define work can result in some surprising conclusions about work.

For example, I would say that I'm doing hard work when I stare for a long time at a difficult math problem and think intently about how to solve it. I would also say that I am working if I try with all my might to push a car that won't budge. A physicist, though, would say that I was doing no work at all when I studied really hard or tried to push the car, because I didn't move anything from one place to another.

Here's another strange outcome of the physicists' definition of work: did you ever bump the dinner table, causing a cup of water or milk to fall on the floor, making a big mess?

I imagine that your family thought it was a lot of work to clean up. But did you know that work was accomplished when the cup fell on the floor? An object was moved—specifically, the cup and the liquid inside of it. And a force caused that movement: gravity pulled the  cup to the ground. In fact, for physicists, work can be done without any people involved—as long as there is a force (including action-at-a-distance forces like gravity and magnetism) and movement. Can you think of some unusual examples that scientists would consider work? How about an apple falling from a tree, a cloud moving across the sky, or a helium balloon floating up in the air? These are all examples of work because a force moved something from one place to another.

Energy is another tricky word for physicists. Try to come up with your own definition of energy. I find it almost impossible to describe without using the word "energy" itself. Physicists say that energy is the capacity, or ability, of something to do work. If you pull a bowling ball on a rope up to the top of a tree house, you've definitely done work by moving matter from one place to another. You've also used some energy.

What if you drop the bowling ball? Well, you've done exactly as much work as when you pulled it up—you moved the same object the same distance. Did it take as much energy? Definitely not! It's much easier to drop something than to pull it up against gravity.

To explain this strange difference in energy, physicists talk about an object's potential energy and its kinetic energy. When you lift the bowling ball to the top of the tree, all the energy you put into pulling it up against gravity is said to be stored in the ball. The energy has the potential to be used when you decide to drop the ball. This is the ball's potential energy. When you do drop the ball, it starts moving not because of energy you're using as you drop it, but because of the energy you've already stored in it by pulling it up against gravity. Once it starts moving, its energy is *kinetic*, which is just a word meaning, "relating to motion."

So while scientists have different terms to describe the energy used to lift a bowling ball up a tree and then to let it fall to the ground, both activities (lifting and dropping) are considered work, and the amount of work is the same because the ball moved the same distance. Let's explore the physics of work and energy.

Unit 5- Work: Plane and Simple Machines   *Pandia Press*

Work Lab #1: Working It Out - instructions

Material:
- Lab sheets, pencil

Aloud: The scientific definition of *work* is different from how we think about work in our everyday lives. The most important thing to remember about the scientific definition is that it has two parts. First, for work to be performed, an object must move from one place to another. Second, the cause of the object's movement must be a force—a push or a pull on the object.

Procedure:
Lab Day
1. Fill in the lab sheet.

Possible Answers:
#1: there is a person using force (pushing or pulling) to move the can to the curb
#2: movement
#3: object, force, movement
#4: shows that work is being done because a force is moving an object: the static electricity of the balloon is a force that is pulling the hair on the boy's head up.

Conclusion / Discussion:
1. The word *work* can be used in an everyday sense and in a scientific sense. Sometimes, the two ways of using the word lead to similar conclusions. But sometimes they are very different.

2. Talk about everyday activities that you do. Which of these would physicists consider work? Which would most people consider work? Come up with reasons for your answers.

Notebooking Ideas:
1. Use a Venn Diagram Notebooking Page to show what things most people think of as work, what things physicists think of as work, and what things both physicists and nonscientists think of as work.
2. Use a Definition Notebooking Page to define *work*. Remember to include the two parts of the definition.

Note to Parents and Teachers: Technically, the amount of work done depends on the angle of the force. Because this concept is difficult and requires an understanding of trigonometry, all of the examples we use in discussing work will involve forces that are applied in the same direction as an object's movement. For example, when pushing a block forward you push in the direction that the block moves.

Unit 5- Work: Plane and Simple Machines

NAME _____ DATE _____

Working It Out

Let's find out why the activities below would (or would not) be thought of as work by a physicist.

1. A physicist would think that taking out the trash is work
   because _____
   _____
   _____.

   Most people would **agree / disagree** that taking out the trash is work.

2. A physicist would NOT think that holding a 100-pound block over
   your head is work because although there is an object, there is no
   _____ from one place to another.

   Most people would **agree / disagree** that holding a 100-pound
   block over your head is not work.

3. A physicist would NOT think that figuring out the answer to 458 times
   239 in your head is work because there is no _____ that is
   pushed or pulled by a _____, and therefore, there is
   no _____.

   Most people would **agree / disagree** that figuring out the
   answer to 458 times 239 in your head is not work.

4. **Challenge:** A physicist would say that this picture **shows / does not show** work being done:

Explain why this is, or is not, an example of work: _____

_____

_____

_____

_____

5. Write and illustrate your own activity that a physicist would consider work:

_____

_____

_____

_____

Work Lab #2: You've Got a Lot of Potential! - instructions

Materials:

- Lab sheets, pencil
- Rubber bands (a few in case of breakage; 1 is all that is needed)
- 2-3 marbles
- Paper plate
- 1 cup of flour
- Spoon
- Ruler

Aloud: It takes energy to do work. Sometimes, the nature of this energy is simple to understand. When you push a shopping cart, you've used some energy to move the cart from one place to another—to do work. But when you drop a bowling ball from a tree, something I strongly suggest you refrain from doing, it's harder to tell where the energy to move the ball has come from. You might answer that the energy comes from gravity, the force which is moving the ball. But gravity is a force and we're looking for some way to talk about the *energy* that underlies that force's ability to do work.

Scientists have come up with the idea of <u>potential energy</u> to describe this energy that seems to be stored in an object because somehow it got pushed or pulled into a position despite some other force acting upon it. The bowling ball in the tree has a lot of potential energy because someone lifted it despite and against gravity. Now, all it will take to get the ball to the ground is to let it fall. When it falls, it will give up its potential energy. Once it's on the ground, the bowling ball will have no potential energy left until someone lifts it up again. This is called <u>gravitational potential energy</u>.

Another type of potential energy is called <u>elastic potential energy</u>. Have you ever heard someone call a rubber band an "elastic"? An object is elastic if it can go back to some original shape after being pushed or pulled into some different shape. Springs and rubber bands are elastic. When you pull on a rubber band, you've stored some energy in the rubber band. To get it to snap back very quickly, you don't have to do anything but let go. And once you've let go and the rubber band resumes its original shape, it has used up its elastic potential energy until the next time someone pulls on it.

Procedure:

1. Prepare by putting about a quarter of an inch of flour onto the paper plate. You need only enough to drop some marbles into it to see what happens.

2. Fill in the hypothesis section of the lab sheet (#1-#5).

3. Place the rubber band by the ruler. Stretch it until it is almost taut. Observe where it ends on the ruler. Pull it ¼" (a little more than half a centimeter) more. Let go of the end you pulled on (it should snap softly back to your other finger). Record your observations (#6).

4. Pull the rubber band ½" (a little more than a centimeter) this time. Let go of the end you pulled on and record your observations.

5. Pull back the rubber band almost as far as it can go. Don't let go of the end you pulled unless you want it to snap back hard and hurt your finger! Just gently allow it to return to its original position. Record your observation.

6. You're finished with the rubber band.

[continued]

Work Lab #2: You've Got a Lot of Potential!
- instructions page 2

7. Now stand over the plate with the flour in it. Smooth the surface of the flour using a spoon. Lift a marble about an inch above the flour and drop it. Record your observations (#7) and smooth the surface of the flour again.

8. Repeat step 7, lifting the marble to the different heights specified on the lab sheet before dropping it. Record your observations.

9. Fill in the remainder of the lab sheet.

Possible Answers:

#1: potential, position

#2: Answers may vary.

#3: more, Answers may vary.

#4: lifting it up

#5: Answers may vary.

#6 and #7: Answers will vary, but basically the farther you pull the rubber band, the more forceful the snap. And the higher you drop the marble, the greater the effect on the flour.

#8: a little, distance moved

#9: more, more, potential

#10: more of an effect, size, and/or weight (mass)

Conclusion / Discussion:

1. We've learned about various types of characteristics of objects. Some characteristics don't change unless the object itself changes—such as color, shape, mass, and density. But an object, such as a bowling ball, has other characteristics important to physicists, such as its position relative to a person and the amount of potential energy it has stored. Can you think of characteristics of an object that might change even if the object stays the same mass, shape, density, etc.? (Some potential answers: weight, velocity, acceleration.)

2. Why might it be useful to scientists to understand potential energy? (Some hints: Think of how much potential energy an orbiting spacecraft might have. Would this affect what needs to happen when it lands? How much potential energy does an Olympic skier who has climbed to the top of a ski run have? Does this affect his skiing?)

3. Imagine a bowling ball sitting 40 meters up in the air. It has enough potential energy to come crashing down to the ground when released. Does the amount of potential energy in the bowling ball depend on how the bowling ball got up there? (i.e., if someone used a ramp to get the ball up there, or pulled it up, or used an elevator to get it there?) (Answer: no!)

Notebooking Ideas:

1. Use a Definition Notebooking Page to define *potential energy*, *gravitational potential energy*, and *elastic potential energy*.

2. Draw a comic strip about a boulder getting lifted from the ground, up to the top of a mountain, and then dropped back down again. Use thought bubbles to show the boulder thinking about how much potential energy it has at each stage of its journey.

NAME _____ DATE _____

You've Got a Lot of Potential!

Hypotheses:

1. I've just learned about **electrical / magical / potential** energy. This is energy that depends on an object's **color / position / shape**.

2. A rubber band has the ability to store potential energy. If I do work by stretching a rubber band and forcing it into a new position, it will store the energy I put into it. When I let go, I think the potential energy will **remain in the rubber band / be released** and the rubber band will **not move / fly away / snap back into its original position**.

3. If I pull the rubber band farther back, I think it will store **more / less** potential energy. Because of this, I think it will snap back **more quickly / less quickly**.

4. I can also put potential energy into a marble by: _____
   _____
   _____.

5. I think that if I lift a marble higher and higher, it will get **more and more / less and less** potential energy.

Observations:

6. Observations of Elastic Potential Energy

How far I pulled the rubber band	**What happened**
¼ inch (about ½ a centimeter)	It snapped back **not at all / gently / forcefully**
½ inch (about 1 centimeter)	It snapped back **not at all / gently / forcefully**
Almost all the way:	I didn't let go because I could tell there was a lot of energy stored up and I know it would have snapped back **not at all / gently / forcefully**

7. Observations of Gravitational Potential Energy

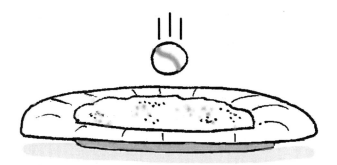

Height from which I dropped the marble	Effect on the flour
1 inch (about 2 ½ centimeters)	Marble made a **teeny / small / medium-sized / large** crater.
2 inches (about 5 centimeters)	Marble made a **teeny / small / medium-sized / large** crater. It was **bigger than / about the same size as / smaller than** the crater when dropped from 1 inch.
6 inches (about 15 centimeters)	Marble made a **teeny / small / medium-sized / large** crater. It was **bigger than / about the same size as / smaller than** the crater when dropped from 2 inches.
12 inches (about 30 ½ centimeters)	Marble made a **teeny / small / medium-sized / large** crater. It was **bigger than / about the same size as / smaller than** the crater when dropped from 6 inches.
24 inches (about half a meter)	Marble made a **teeny / small / medium-sized / large** crater. It was **bigger than / about the same size as / smaller than** the crater when dropped from 12 inches.

Analysis and Conclusions:

8. When I moved the rubber band just a little, it seemed to store **a lot of** / **a little** potential energy. So the **color** / **distance moved** must be related to the amount of potential energy.

9. When I dropped the marble from higher heights, **more** / **less** work was done because **more** / **less** flour was moved or made into a crater. So the distance I moved the marble against Earth's gravitational field must be related to the amount of **potential** / **electrical** energy stored in the marble.

10. Imagine what would happen if, instead of a marble, you dropped a bowling ball into the flour from 24 inches. Would it have more of an effect or less of an effect on the flour than the marble did? _____
So in addition to distance moved, what characteristic of an object do you think is related to its potential energy? _____

For my notebook

Simple Machines: Planes & Wedges

Do you remember **Archimedes**, the ancient Greek scientist who discovered that King Hiero's crown was not made of pure gold?   Archimedes also figured out that people can use certain types of <u>simple machines</u> to make work easier. To understand what physicists mean by "making work easier," let's do another thought experiment.

Imagine that you need to get one of your parents 5 meters (about 15 feet) up off the ground. You're going to accomplish this by applying some force to that parent—pushing or pulling him (or her) into the air. If you were tall enough, you could simply lift your parent 5 meters into the air. You can imagine how much force it would take to lift an adult so high up. Here's an idea: Maybe you could build a ramp and push your parent up the ramp.

Which of these two methods do you think would be easier: lifting your parent up, or using a ramp? I think it would be a lot easier for me to push someone up a ramp than to try to lift that person straight up. But here's the tricky part: It may be easier to use the ramp, but does it require less work? What do you think?

Well, your muscles don't need to work quite so hard at any given time as you push your parent up the ramp. In terms of physics, you'll need less force—less intense pushing—to get to the top of the ramp than you would need if you lifted your parent straight up. So, the job seems easier. However, there's a trade-off. One of the great rules of physics is that you can't get something for nothing. You can't use less force to accomplish the same job unless you have to use more of something else. What do you think that something else is?

Here's a hint: Think about how far you have to push your parent in both examples. If you lift your parent straight up, you're pushing over a distance of 5 meters. But if you roll your parent up the ramp, you're pushing over a distance of 10 meters! So, to push about half as hard, you have to push about twice as long. In other words, the work may seem easier to you—the pusher, but it is the same amount of work to get your parent 5 meters into the air no matter how you do it!

This is what Archimedes discovered. Using simple machines, people can make their work seem easier, either by changing the amount of force needed to do a job, or by changing the direction of the force. But no matter what simple machine you use, the amount of work needed to move a particular object a particular distance will be the same.

In the next sections, we're going to find out about and build a lot of simple machines to help accomplish work. In each case, you'll see that there's a trade-off of some kind. One part of the work will seem easier, but another part of the work will seem harder. Nevertheless, simple machines can accomplish amazing feats. The Egyptians built the pyramids, and the Greeks built the Parthenon with little more than simple machines, muscle power, and great ideas.

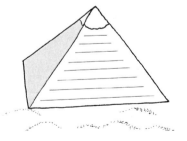

Work Lab #3: It's Plainly a Plane! - instructions

Materials:
- Lab sheets, pencil
- Opened box of tissues
- Spring scale
- Ruler, yardstick, meterstick, or tape measure
- Foam board (at least 6 inches wide and 3 feet long)

Aloud: Earlier, we discussed using a ramp to accomplish the work of moving one of your parents 5 meters above the ground. A ramp is a type of a simple machine called an <u>inclined plane</u>. The word *incline*, as you may know, means "to lean" or "to slope." The word *plane*, as we're using it here, doesn't refer to a vehicle that flies through the air. A plane is a flat surface. So, an inclined plane is a flat surface that's leaning or sloped—in other words, a ramp. Now let's prove that using an inclined plane makes work seem easier.

Procedure:
1. Fill in the Hypothesis.

2. Explore how the spring scale can measure force. Pull very gently on the spring. Note the measurement. Pull harder, and watch how the spring scale registers a higher number. The harder you pull, the more force you apply. Thus, the spring scale provides us with a way to quantify—or put into numbers—force.

3. Use the spring scale to figure out how much force would be needed to lift the tissue box. To accomplish this, hook the hook of the spring scale onto the opening of the box. Take your reading from the scale. Write what you found on the lab sheet (#1).

4. To demonstrate that this is how much force is needed to move the box straight upward at a constant speed, keep the box hooked onto the scale. Lift it slowly, but steadily, about a foot into the air. The measurement shouldn't change at all if you're moving perfectly steadily, but it may change a tiny bit because it's really difficult to move your arm at a perfectly steady speed. Record your answer (#2).

5. Now, set up your inclined plane by leaning your flat board against something about 1 foot off the ground. This means that there will be a very gentle slope.

6. Using a ruler or tape measure, record on the middle column of the chart how high up you could get an object using this inclined plane. (Measure from the top of the ramp to the ground.)

7. Using a ruler or tape measure, record in the last column of the chart how far the object would have to travel if it started at the bottom of the inclined plane and was pushed or pulled all the way to the top of the inclined plane. (Measure the length of the ramp.)

8. Place the tissue box on the bottom of the inclined plane with the spring scale still attached. Pull the tissue box slowly and steadily up the inclined plane and observe how much force the scale registers. Make certain you're pulling on the same angle as the inclined plane (i.e., the scale should be about parallel to the inclined plane and the tissue box should not lift up off the board). Record this data in the first column on the chart.

9. Change the inclined plane's slope by leaning it against something several feet high. Repeat steps 4-6. Record data in the second row on the chart.

[continued]

10. Complete the rest of the lab notes.

Possible Answers:

#1, #2: The measurements should be nearly identical.

Chart: Answers will vary, but the force needed to pull up a plane (steep or gentle) should be less than the force recorded in #1 or #2. And the force is greater for a steep incline than for a gentle incline.

Conclusion: Lifting is easier when using an inclined plane in the sense that it takes less force to pull the object to a particular height. It is harder in the sense that one must pull the object over a longer distance.

Conclusion / Discussion:

1. Think about ways in which inclined planes are used in our daily lives. How do they help people in wheelchairs? How do they help us to drive up steep mountains? How do they help truck drivers load or unload trucks? Can you think of other uses? In each case, talk about the trade-off between the force needed to move the object and the distance over which the object needs to be moved.

2. Talk about why it is helpful to have a simple machine that decreases the amount of force needed, even though it increases the amount of distance one needs to travel to lift an object.

More Lab Fun:

Using longer ramps and higher heights, you can take measurements of force, height, and distance in a number of positions. If you like finding math patterns, make some observations. Then see if you can predict how much difference ramps of various heights will make in the amount of force needed to pull an object.

Notebooking ideas:

1. Write down the definition of *inclined plane*.

2. Draw a picture showing some of the ways in which we use inclined planes. Explain how the inclined plane helps us in these situations.

Notes to Parents and Teachers:

1. In physics, a plane refers only to the flat surface of an object, not the thickness of it. A plane is a flat surface that goes on infinitely forever. So, the surface of a piece of paper is a plane, but it's only a portion of a plane that is infinitely wide and long.

2. Technically, force is not measured by a spring scale, but is expressed either in pounds or kg-meters / (seconds)^2. But the amount registered by the spring scale will be directly proportional to the measure of force, so for our purposes, it provides a way for the students to take relative measurements of force applied.

3. The unit used to measure work is the joule, abbreviated "J." Because the joule is a product of force multiplied by distance, it is technically thought of as a newton-meter, with a newton being the unit of force is kg-meters / (seconds) ^{2}. You can see why I decided not to introduce the issue of units into the discussion of work in this section. For the time being, just let your students work with the numbers and their magnitudes relative to each other (e.g., this takes twice as much pulling as that does).

It's Plainly a Plane!

Hypothesis: The amount of force needed to pull a tissue box a certain height straight up in the air will be **less than** / **more than** / **the same as** the amount of force needed to pull it up an inclined plane.

Observations:

1. How much force does it take to hold the tissue box in the air at the end of the spring scale? _____

2. How much force does it take to raise the tissue box straight up at a slow, steady speed? _____

	Force needed	Height off the ground of the top of the inclined plane	Distance the object has to travel to get from the bottom to the top of the inclined plane
Pulling up a gentle inclined plane			
Pulling up a steeper inclined plane			

Conclusion:

Pulling an object up an inclined plane seems easier because

_____

_____

_____

_____

_____.

But pulling an object up an inclined plane is harder in another way because

_____

_____

_____

_____

_____ .

Work Lab #4: All Wedged In - instructions

Materials:
- Lab sheets, pencil
- Colored pencils
- Door wedge (the kind used to keep a door open); if you don't have one, you could use a triangle-shaped building block (one with a right angle would be best).
- Two building blocks, the larger the better
- Piece of paper, large enough to place the two blocks on

Note: It is recommended that this lab and the next be completed on the same day—both are short and are related to each other. These labs might seem basic and simple, but the concepts taught are important to the understanding of work and force in physics.

Aloud: We've seen how an inclined plane can make work seem easier because it changes how much force is needed to get an object to a particular height. There's another simple machine which is closely related to the inclined plane. It's called the <u>wedge</u>. An inclined plane holds still, and we use force to push or pull things up or down along it. A wedge is two inclined planes put together that can be moved to exert force. By pushing, or wedging, inclined planes underneath something, we can make work easier in an entirely different way. Let's find out how.

Procedure:
1. On a flat surface like a table, place the two blocks side by side and touching each other on top of the piece of paper.
2. Using a pencil, mark the position of the two blocks (i.e., trace around them).
3. Fill in the HYPOTHESIS section on the lab sheet.
4. Place the thin part of the wedge just touching the crack between the two boxes. Now, push down on the wedge. Mark in a different color where the boxes are now.
5. Record your OBSERVATION on the lab sheet.
6. Fill in the CONCLUSION on the lab sheet.

Possible Answers:
Observation: The diagram should look something like this (below). Sometimes, one block will move, but not the other. As long as it is clear that pushing down on the wedge causes horizontal movement, that is fine.

Conclusion: direction

Conclusion / Discussion:
Now that you know how the wedge pushes things, why do you think that wedges help to keep doors open? Watch closely what happens to a door when you push a wedge under it next time (but watch your fingers!).

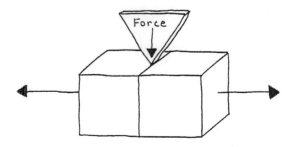

[continued]

Work Lab #4: All Wedged In - instructions page 2

More Lab Fun:

1. Play with the wedge by using it to wedge apart blocks or other objects that are of different weights. Does this change the result at all? You can also try using the wedge with the straight edge pointed the other way. Does this change how the blocks move?

2. If you have two wedges, put them back-to-back so they make a triangle. Try to push this new two-sided wedge between some boxes. Does it work differently now?

Notebooking Idea:

1. Draw a picture of a wedge and two blocks. Use arrows to show how, when you push down on the wedge, the wedge pushes outward on the blocks.

2. Write down the definition of *wedge*.

All Wedged In

Hypothesis: (Write and illustrate on the drawing.)

This is what I think will happen when I put the tip of the wedge between the two blocks and push down: _____

_____

_____

_____

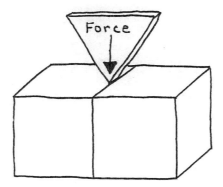

Observation: When I pushed down on the wedge, the blocks moved (use arrows to show the direction the wedge moved, and the direction the blocks moved):

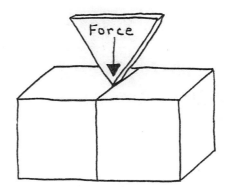

Conclusion: A wedge helps us do work by changing the **direction** / **amount** of the force applied.

Unit 5- Work: Plane and Simple Machines

Work Lab #5: More Wedges - instructions

Materials:
- Lab sheets, pencil
- Piece of scrap corrugated cardboard
- Pencil with an eraser that is dully sharpened… not so sharp that the point breaks easily if pushed on
- Optional: Magnifying glass

Aloud: A wedge is a simple machine that helps us to do work by changing the direction of the force applied. When you pushed down on the wedge in the previous experiment, it pushed the blocks outward. But how does this really help make work easier for us? Here's one example: Imagine that you want to poke a hole into something relatively thick, like a piece of cardboard. You can't get inside the cardboard to push open a hole from the inside. Instead, you need something you can push down on, something that will then push apart the cardboard to open up a hole. Wow! That sounds like what a wedge does.

We're going to use a pencil to see how a wedge can help us with tasks like this. First, though, think about how the point of the pencil is a type of wedge. It's like lots of very skinny wedge shapes arranged in a circle, all coming to a point.

Procedure:
(students might need assistance with this):

1. Fill in the HYPOTHESIS section of the lab sheet.

2. Carefully try to push a hole through the cardboard using the eraser end of the pencil. Don't jab the pencil at the cardboard. Just put the eraser against the cardboard and push. You might also try twisting the pencil back and forth. Write down what happens on the lab sheet, #1.

3. Carefully try to push a hole through the cardboard using the sharp end of the pencil. You might also try twisting the pencil back and forth. You should be able to poke a hole without too much trouble. Write down what happens on the lab sheet, #2.

4. Examine the hole you made closely. If you have a magnifying glass, use it to examine the hole. Look around on the floor for loose pieces of cardboard. Write down what you observe on the lab sheet, #3.

5. Fill in the CONCLUSION section of the lab sheet.

Possible Answers:
#1: It should be difficult, or impossible, to punch a hole through the cardboard this way.

#2: It should be fairly easy to push a hole through the cardboard this way.

#3: The pencil point pushed the cardboard to the sides to make way for the hole. It did not just punch a hole out of the cardboard like a hole puncher punches paper.

CONCLUSION: when I push down on the pencil, the wedge-shaped point pushes outward to force open a hole.

Conclusion / Discussion:
1. Wedges work by changing the direction of a force. When you push down on a wedge, the wedge shape pushes outward. Discuss further how this helped to make a hole in the cardboard.

[continued]

Work Lab #5: More Wedges - instructions page 2

2. Think of other ways in which wedges are used. For example, chisels help to break rocks apart, sharp chef's knives are wedges that cut food, and nails create holes in wood. There are even wedges in our mouths—our front teeth act as wedges to break up food.

More Lab Fun:

1. Repeat the above experiment, using a nail and hammer. How does the tip of the nail act as a wedge?

2. Eat an apple and pay close attention to how your teeth act as wedges to push the pieces of the apple apart.

Notebooking Idea:

Draw pictures of how wedges are used in our lives. Use arrows to show how the wedge changes the direction of the force.

NAME _____ DATE _____

More Wedges

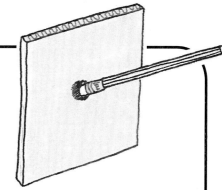

Hypothesis: I think it will be **easier / harder** to poke a hole in the cardboard with the pointy end of the pencil than it is to poke a hole with the eraser end of the pencil.

Observations:

1. Describe what happened when you tried to poke a hole in the cardboard with the eraser end of the pencil.

_____

_____

_____

2. Describe what happened when you tried to poke a hole in the cardboard with the sharp end of the pencil.

_____

_____

_____

3. Does it look like the pencil punched a circle-shaped piece of cardboard out of the sheet of cardboard, or does it look like the pencil pushed cardboard away from the pencil point to make the hole? What observations support this idea?

_____

_____

_____

Conclusion: The pencil point acts like a wedge which helps to make a hole in the cardboard because:

_____

_____

_____.

Unit 5- Work: Plane and Simple Machines

Work Lab #6: Those Screwy Planes - instructions

Materials:
- Lab sheets, pencil
- A new sharpened pencil at least 7 inches long (a standard #2 pencil is long enough)
- Few pieces of paper
- Scissors
- Ruler marked in inches
- Screw or several different screws to look at

Aloud: Inclined planes help us to do work because they change the amount of force needed to push something to a certain height. Wedges help us to do work because they change the direction of force. Now, here's a really tough thought experiment: Imagine an inclined plane that you could wrap around in a spiral. Add a sharp point at one end, like the wedge that is at a pencil point. What do you think you'd get? As you will discover in the next couple of labs, you get another incredibly useful simple machine!

Procedure:

1. Prepare triangles.

Aloud: To prepare for this lab, we're going to make a series of right triangles. A right triangle is a triangle that looks like the inclined plane we made, with one side of the triangle flat against the ground, the second side going straight upward, and a third side connecting the other two . . . like this:

To make these triangles, get four sheets of copy/printer paper.

A. On each sheet of paper, pick a corner to be the corner of your triangle. Make a mark so you remember where your corner is.

B. On the short edge of each sheet of paper, mark a spot 4 inches along the edge from your mark in the corner.

C. On the long edge of the first piece of paper, mark an edge 6 inches from the mark in the corner.

D. Repeat this, as follows: (You will end up with 4 triangles, with perpendicular sides of 4" x 6", 6" x 6", 8" x 6", and 10" x 6".)

      a. second piece of paper: 6" x 6"

      b. third piece of paper: 8" x 6"

      c. fourth piece of paper: 10" x 6"

E. Connect the marks you've made on the edges with a straight line to form a triangle.

F. Cut out the triangles. On each triangle, label the length of the sides you measured. Color a thick line along the diagonal (the longest) edge. Do this on both sides of your triangles.

G. You'll have 4 right triangles that look like this:

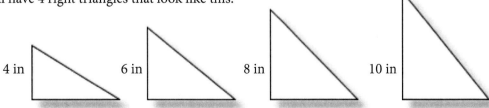

2. Look at your triangles. Talk about how they are essentially flat inclined planes.

3. Fill in the HYPOTHESIS section of the lab sheet.

[continued]

4. Pick up the smallest triangle. Hold the six-inch edge along the pencil, and wrap the triangle around the pencil over and over until there's no more triangle left.

5. Fill in #1 & #2 on the lab sheet.

6. Look at the screw you have. Talk about how the paper wrapped around the pencil is similar to the screw.

7. Look at one side of the pencil. Count the lines you see. The lines going around a screw in a spiral are called the thread of the screw. Counting the lines gives you the number of threads (plus or minus one or two, which we don't need to worry about).

8. Play with the piece of paper, scrunching it all close together so that the threads are close to each other. Count the threads. Stretch it out, so the threads are far apart. Count the threads. Fill in #3-#5 on the lab sheet.

9. Using the triangles and pencil, fill in the rest of the lab sheets.

Possible Answers:
#2: It should look like a spiral, screw, spiral staircase, candy cane, or something along those lines.
#3: Answers may vary, but probably between 5 and 8.
#4 & #5: Answer should be "a little difference." If it isn't, make sure that you've pulled the paper tightly around the pencil each time and try to count lines with the same side facing you.
Conclusion: greater

Note to Parents and Teachers: The exact number of threads will depend on the diameter of the pencil you use and how well the kids are able to wrap the triangles around the pencils. If you aren't sure just yet, don't worry, you'll figure out the answers in the next two labs. The important thing is to understand how bigger triangles lead to more threads on a screw.

Conclusion / Discussion:
1. A screw is basically an inclined plane wrapped around and around a cylinder! If it's a pointy screw, like a wood screw, it also has a small wedge at its tip. Try looking at the screw alongside a wrapped-up pencil to understand this better. Don't worry; we'll be studying this more in the next lesson.

2. Think about what you know about inclined planes. How can using an inclined plane wrapped up into the shape of a screw help people do work? How do screws help people do work? Try to think of the answers to this question in terms of force, direction, and distance along which the force is applied. [Screws decrease effort by converting a force that goes around and around to a force that goes up and down. This concept is further explored in the next lab.]

3. Look at different-sized screws. What's different about the distance between the threads and the number of threads on different screws? Can you think of a reason why there would be such differences? [The closer together the threads, the more power the screw has. But it takes more turns to screw in a screw with closer threads. Closer threads = less effort but more time, farther-apart threads = more effort but less time. Remember, there's always a trade-off with work! This concept is further explored in the next lab.]

For More Lab Fun:
1. Repeat the above experiments with pencils or cylinders of different diameters. Predict how you think a skinnier cylinder would affect the number of threads and test your answer. Do the same with a wider cylinder.

2. If you like spies and codes, have an adult help you to research the scytale (skytale) code. It uses a strip of paper wrapped around a cylinder.

Notebooking Ideas:
1. Use a definition page to define *threads*.

2. Imagine what it would be like to be an ant trying to get food to the top of a giant screw. What would walking between the threads be like? Would it be easier or harder than walking straight to the top of the screw? Draw a picture or write a story about what you imagined.

Those Screwy Planes

Hypothesis: If I wrap an inclined plane around something like a pencil, I think it will look like this:

Observations and Analysis:

1. When I wrapped the wedge-shaped triangle around a pencil, it looked like this:

Those Screwy Planes - page 2

2. This shape reminds me of a: _____

_____

3. When I wrapped the smallest triangle around the pencil, I counted _____ threads.

4. When I made the threads closer together, it had the following effect on the number of threads:
   a big difference | a little difference | no difference

5. When I made the threads farther apart, it had the following effect on the number of threads:
   a big difference | a little difference | no difference

How the shape of the triangle affects the number of threads:
(Remember to start with the 6-inch side of the triangle next to the pencil every time.)

6. When I wrapped the 4 inch by 6 inch triangle around the pencil, there were this many threads: _____

7. When I wrapped the 6 inch by 6 inch triangle around the pencil, there were this many threads: _____

8. When I wrapped the 8 inch by 6 inch triangle around the pencil, there were this many threads: _____

9. When I wrapped the 10 inch by 6 inch triangle around the pencil, there were this many threads: _____

Conclusion: The larger the triangle, the **greater | lesser** the number of threads.

For my notebook

What Do Stairs and Screws Have in Common?

You've discovered that an inclined plane can be transformed into a screw by wrapping the inclined plane around in a spiral. But how in the world does this device help us to do work? Why do we think of it as a "simple machine"? Remember that an inclined plane helps us by making it "easier" to move an object. By increasing the distance over which we have to push, an inclined plane decreases the force we need to use. Here's a thought experiment that helped me to understand how a screw makes our work easier in just the same way as an inclined plane.

Imagine trying to get from the ground floor to the second floor of a building. You could hang a rope from the ceiling of the second floor and climb up. That would take a lot of strength—or force—but you wouldn't have to travel very far. Or, you could build an inclined plane to get up to the second floor. Wait a minute! Someone might slip and fall climbing up a ramp. Perhaps you could cut little notches in the ramp, so no one slips. It would like this:

Well, that's a familiar shape. It's just a staircase. Did you realize that a staircase is a form of an inclined plane? We walk a bit farther in order to get from one floor to another, but we don't have to use as much force as we'd need if we climbed straight upward.

Now, imagine a staircase wrapped around a pole, just like you wrapped triangles around a pencil. What would it look like? It would be a spiral staircase. Just like a simple inclined plane, a spiral staircase makes work easier: We travel farther, going around and around the stairs, but it takes a lot less force at any given time to get to the top.

A <u>screw</u> is just like that spiral staircase. Imagine that you're a tiny creature that can walk along the threads of a screw. You're a pretty weak creature, so you can't climb straight to the top. But going along, around and around, at a gentle slope, you can make it. Hey! There you are, standing on top of the screw. You made it! Just in time for another thought experiment. Someone is about to start putting that screw into a piece of wood. They use a screwdriver to turn it around and around. As the screwdriver turns, you sit on the top of that screw near the edge, traveling around and around in circles. Despite getting dizzy, you realize that every time you go around in a circle, the screw gets a tiny bit farther into the wood. If you unraveled that spiral shape you were traveling in, it might be 10 centimeters long. Yet for all that turning around and around, the screw only pushed 1 centimeter down into the wood. So less force was needed to move the screw downward than if it had been pounded straight into the wood, but the force was applied over a longer distance—around and around in circles.

In the next experiment, we're going to get to the bottom of how these screws do their work.

Work Lab #7: The Nuts & Bolts of Screws - instructions

Materials:
- Lab sheets, pencil
- Ruler
- At least 2 bolts, each with a nut that will fit the bolt. The diameters of the bolts should be roughly the same, but the distance between the threads should be as different as possible.
- Permanent marker
- Short piece of thin string or thread (12 inches should do)

Aloud: You've probably seen screws before. Some are big. Some are small. Some have lots of threads all squeezed close together, and some have threads that seem big enough for an ant to crawl along between them. Why do you think we have all these sizes and shapes of screws? Let's see if we can find out.

We're going to use nuts and bolts because bolts aren't as pointy and sharp as screws, but both work the same way.

Procedure:
1. Pick up one of the nut & bolt sets and play around with it a little bit. Note what happens when the nut is held stationary and the bolt is turned. Note what happens when the bolt is held stationary and the nut is turned.

2. Talk about how two distances are involved: (1) the distance the nut travels around and around as it threads its way along the bolt; (2) the distance along the length of the bolt that the nut travels.

3. Fill in the HYPOTHESIS section of the lab sheet.

4. Pick up the bolt that appears to have the threads more spread apart than the other(s).

5. Use the permanent marker to make a mark on one side of the nut. You're going to be spinning the nut around the bolt, and you need some way to keep of track of when it has made one complete turn. Also, mark on the bolt itself a space of approximately 1 centimeter.

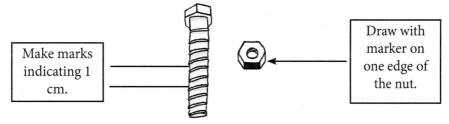

Make marks indicating 1 cm.

Draw with marker on one edge of the nut.

6. Using the ruler, count how many threads there are (approximately!) over a space of 1 centimeter. We're looking for rough numbers here, so don't ruin your eyesight counting threads. Record your findings on the lab sheet.

7. Take the string and start to wrap it around the bolt where you've marked out 1 cm. Wrap it along the threads until it's covering the distance you've marked off. Unwrap the thread, keeping track of how much you just used. Measure it and record your findings on the lab sheet.

8. Place the nut on the very end of the bolt, but high enough so that the threads are engaged and the nut will turn.

9. Using the mark you made on the nut, start turning the nut and count five turns.

10. Using the ruler, measure how far the nut has traveled.

[continued]

11. Fill in the data table on the lab sheet for this bolt.

12. Repeat these steps for as many nut/bolt sets as you'd like, but do at least two sets of nuts and bolts.

13. Complete the lab sheet.

Possible Answers:
#1: inclined plane
#2: closer together
#3: ramp (or inclined plane)
 Conclusion: really hard, not very hard.

Conclusion / Discussion:
You've just discovered one reason why screws and nuts and bolts come in many different sizes and with different types of threads. To drill into a material that's really hard, you could use a screw with close-together threads. You'd have to turn the screw driver around and around more times, but you wouldn't need to use as much force. If you needed to drill into something that wasn't so hard, you wouldn't want to do all that extra turning of the screwdriver. Because the material is soft, you don't need as much force, so you might as well have the threads a little farther apart.

More Lab Fun:
1. If you have a piece of wood and some wood screws of various sizes, you might try screwing into the wood to see how the different sizes of screws work.

2. Play around with nuts and bolts with different diameters. See if you can figure out what changes when the diameter of the bolt changes.

Notebooking Ideas:
1. Look for screws in your house. Write down all the places you find screws being used. Don't forget to look in cabinets, at your toys, in the kitchen, everywhere.

2. Get a book about Archimedes and learn about how he used a screw to get water from one place to another. Draw a picture and write about it in your notebook.

Note to Parents and Teachers: Technically, a screw is an inclined plane wrapped around in a cylinder shape with a tiny wedge (the point of the screw) at the end. Because visualizing the inclined plane/ screw relationship can be difficult, I haven't complicated the explanation by adding a wedge into the picture. Also, for the technically minded, a screw moved by a screwdriver is really a bit of a complex machine—a screw plus a lever. What's important here is just that the students understand how screws are related to inclined planes.

The Nuts & Bolts of Screws

Hypothesis: A screw with lots of close-together threads is **easier / harder** to use than a screw with just a few spread out threads.
(Hint: this is a trick question.)

Data Collected:

Number of threads in 1 cm	Length of string it takes to travel around 1 cm of the bolt	Distance traveled by the nut when turned 5 complete turns

Analysis:

1. A screw is a simple machine made by wrapping **an inclined plane / a bolt** around in a spiral.

2. It takes more string to travel along 1 centimeter of the length of the bolt when the threads are **closer together / farther apart**.

3. If I imagine unraveling the threads of 1 centimeter of the bolt, I'd have a _____ as long as the string I wrapped around the bolt.

Conclusion: A screw makes work easier because it takes less force to get the screw into an object like a piece of wood. But, we have to turn the screwdriver over and over—over a greater distance—than the screw travels into the wood. I think that screws with lots of close-together threads would be most helpful for pushing into objects that are **really hard / not very hard**. And, screws with far-apart threads would be most helpful for pushing into objects that are **really hard / not very hard**.

For my notebook

Levers: How to Move the Planet with a Really Long Stick

Do you remember the Greek scientist and mathematician **Archimedes** and his cousin King Hiero? Here's another story about them: Archimedes was the first person to describe how a simple machine called a lever works. A lever is basically a stick that can move around a point. The picture shows the kind of lever with which most of us are already familiar:

Imagine that the bucket weighs 100 pounds. It would be awfully hard to lift up. For thousands of years, people knew that they could use a long stick resting on something like a rock in order to lift things up more easily. This simple machine—a stick and something on which to rest the stick—is called a lever. Physicists have names for all the parts of a lever. The lever itself is the long stick. The weight that you're trying to move, like the bucket in our picture, is called the load. The force you apply at one end of the lever to move the other end upward is called the effort. That makes sense, because effort means the amount of work you put into trying to do something. The triangle in our picture around which the lever moves is called the fulcrum, a word that comes from the Latin word meaning "support." The fulcrum is the point around which a lever moves.

You've probably played on top of a lever before. Can you think of what you sit on in a playground that works like a lever? If you thought of a seesaw or teeter-totter you're right! You might not have realized you were experimenting with a simple machine, but by sitting on the seesaw, you've probably learned how pushing one end down lifts the other end up.

So, what does all of this have to do with Archimedes? Well, Archimedes was the first person to figure out mathematically how a lever works. He was so confident of his results that he told King Hiero if there were a place to stand and a long enough lever, he could move the entire planet! King Hiero didn't believe Archimedes, so he asked Archimedes to prove his claim by moving a huge ship all by himself. Before we find out more about whether Archimedes could move that ship, let's see if we can discover some of the same principles about levers that Archimedes did.

Work Lab #8: Large, Little, and Long Levers - instructions

Materials:
- Lab sheet, pencil
- 12-inch ruler that's stiff (not a flimsy plastic ruler) and relatively flat on one side
- Extra pencil
- About 30 pennies
- Tape

Aloud: One of the qualities that helps scientists make discoveries is curiosity about what happens in the world. Archimedes was curious about how and why levers work. Like Archimedes, we're going to take some time to observe how a lever works. You'll see that what Archimedes figured out is pretty simple; it just took someone's close observations, and thinking about what he saw to come up with a discovery that helped to change the world!

Procedure:
1. Fill in the HYPOTHESIS section of the lab sheet.

2. Lay a pencil on a table and tape both ends to the table so it won't roll around.

3. Now, place the ruler across the pencil, so that the 6-inch mark is over the pencil. You've made a lever! The pencil is going to be the fulcrum. Don't worry if it's not perfectly balanced—some rulers have extra space at one end. Just line it up at the 6-inch mark, regardless.

4. On the right side of the ruler, next to the edge, place 8 pennies in a stack. These are going to be the load you are trying to lift.

5. Find the line on the lab sheet that corresponds with placing the fulcrum at the 6-inch mark. Because this is a 12-inch ruler, the load should be about 12 to 6 inches from the fulcrum, or 6 inches from the fulcrum. Likewise, the other end of the ruler, where the effort is going to be applied, is also about 6 inches from the fulcrum. Again, don't worry about the little bits of extra space at the ends of some rulers. Fill in these values on the lab sheet.

6. Fill in the HYPOTHESIS column on the lab sheet. How many pennies do you think it will take to lift the load with the lever set up this way?

7. Now, one at a time, place pennies in a pile on the left side of the ruler, near the end. Place one penny on. Does it provide enough force at the point of effort to lift the load? Most likely, it doesn't. Keep placing pennies onto a pile on the effort side until the load lifts up, even just a little. Write down your results on the lab sheet.

8. Move the ruler so that the 5-inch mark is over the pencil. Now how many pennies do you think it will take to lift the load? Write down your guess, and then try it out. Keep filling in your chart, moving the ruler to the spots specified.

[continued]

Work Lab #8: Large, Little, and Long Levers
- instructions page 2

Possible Answers:
Conclusions: #1: does; #2: easier

Conclusion / Discussion:
1. Talk about what a big difference the position of the fulcrum makes. Can you figure out the trade-off that using a lever involves? It took less force (fewer pennies) at the point of effort when the fulcrum was closest to the load. Was there something that was made more difficult when the fulcrum was so close to the load? [We'll find the answer to this question in the next lab, so don't worry if it isn't apparent yet.]

2. Think about Archimedes's claim that he could move the whole planet with a lever. Imagine what it would be like to try to lift something really big (but smaller than the planet) with a lever. If you wanted to lift a car, how big do you think the lever would need to be? What if you wanted to lift a house?

3. Talk about the ways in which you've seen levers used.

More Lab Fun:
Get a yardstick or meterstick and perform more experiments with levers. Can you figure out a way to predict how many pennies will be needed to balance a particular load? Experiment to find the biggest load you can lift with one penny by putting the fulcrum in the best spot for lifting.

Notebooking Ideas:
Tell the story of Archimedes's claim that he could lift the world with a long enough lever. Draw a picture of what you think it might have looked like if Archimedes could try to prove his claim.

NAME _____ DATE _____

Large, Little, and Long Levers

Hypothesis: I think that where you put the lever on the fulcrum **will / won't** make a big difference in how much effort is needed to lift a load.

Data Collected:

Position on ruler of fulcrum	Distance between the load and the fulcrum, in inches	Distance between the effort and the fulcrum, in inches	**Hypotheses:** I think it will take this many pennies to lift a load of 8 pennies	Number of pennies it took to lift a load of 8 pennies
3 inches				
4 inches				
5 inches				
6 inches				
7 inches				
8 inches				
9 inches				

Conclusions:

1. Where the lever is placed on the fulcrum **does / does not** make a big difference in how much force is needed to lift a load.

2. The closer the load is to the fulcrum, the **harder / easier** it is to move the load.

For my notebook

Lugging Loads with Lots of Levers

We learned earlier that physicists have names for all the parts of a lever. Let's review these names and learn a few more. Here's a picture of a lever like the one you made in your last experiment.

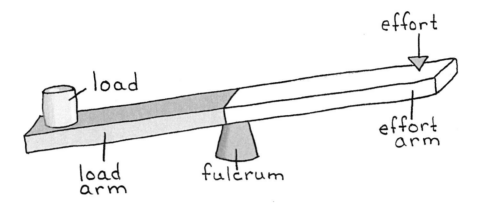

This kind of lever is called a <u>first-class lever</u>. In first-class levers, the fulcrum is in between the effort and the load. We'll learn about other classes of levers later, but for now, let's get back to our diagram of a first-class lever.

Did you notice that in the picture the lever is divided into two sections? It's really all just one lever, but the part of the lever between the fulcrum and the load is called the <u>load arm</u>. And the part of the lever between the fulcrum and the effort is called the <u>effort arm</u>.

When you made your own first-class lever out of a ruler and a pencil, you observed what Archimedes described mathematically: When the effort arm is much larger than the load arm, it takes much less force to lift a load. Another way to put this is that the closer the fulcrum is to the load, the easier it will be to lift the load. In fact, Archimedes figured out that these two lengths are related by simple division like this: If you have something that weighs 1000 pounds and you want to lift it by using only 2 pounds of force, the effort arm would have to be 500 times longer than the load arm! The 500 quantity came by dividing the size of the load by the amount of force we can use to push down on the lever, or 1000 ÷ 2 = 500.

Imagine that you want to lift a box by sitting on the effort side of a big lever. If the box weighs twice as much as you weigh, then the effort arm has to be twice as long as the load arm, like this:

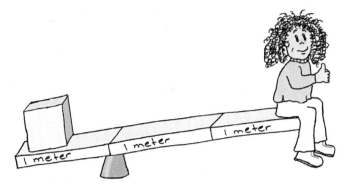

Let's say that each section of the lever is about 1 meter long, which is reasonable because the box and your body will need some space to sit on the lever. So, our lever will have to be about 3 meters long for you to lift the box, with the fulcrum placed about 1 meter away from the load end.

If the box weighs 5 times as much as you weigh, then the effort arm will have to be 5 times as long as the load arm. Now our lever needs to be 6 meters long! Can you figure out why? As you can see, the lever needs to get really big to lift a load that's many times larger than the force applied at the effort end. You might have wondered how large a lever Archimedes would have needed to move the entire planet. Thanks to what we've discovered about levers, you won't have to wonder any more. Let's figure it out!

"Give me a lever long enough and a place to stand and I will move the earth." –Archimedes

Unit 5- Work: Plane and Simple Machines

Work Lab #9- First-Class Levers—Large, Larger, and Largest
- instructions

Materials:
- Lab sheets, pencil
- Access to the Internet or owner's manual of your car (optional)
- Calculator

Aloud: Simple machines always involve a trade-off—a job may seem easier in one way, but it will also get harder in another way. For example, using a ramp to get a large box to a height of 10 feet seems easier than lifting it straight up because it requires less force to push the box up the ramp than to lift it. But the trade-off of a ramp is that you have to push the box over a longer distance. So what's the trade-off of using a first-class lever? Today, we're going to try to answer that question by figuring out what size levers we'd need to use to move some really big objects—a car, a whale, and planet Earth!

Imagine that you can get a lever of any size you need. You're going to sit on the effort end of the lever, and the load—the really, really big load—is going to be placed on the load end of the lever. How could you figure out how big the lever would need to be, and where the fulcrum should go so that your weight could lift the load? Well, first you're going to need to gather some information. Let's see if we can figure out what information you'll need.

Procedure:

Lifting a Car

1. In the box provided on the lab sheet, draw a picture of a lever that will be used to lift the car. Draw a lever with one end under the car and a picture of yourself (relative in size to the car) on the other end. Draw in the fulcrum roughly where you think it will need to be. Label the following parts of the lever: Load, Effort, Load Arm, Effort Arm, and Fulcrum. Leave a little bit of room to label the relative sizes of the load arm and effort arm later on.

2. Now, look at your diagram. Think for a moment or two about what information you might need to figure out how big the lever needs to be. Write it down in the space provided in #1.

Figuring Out the Force Applied at the Effort End:

3. Discuss how you might estimate how much force will be applied at the effort end of the lever. Think about what is going to be pushing down at the end—you'll be sitting on the lever. How much force does your body push down with? Fill out questions #2 to #4 on the lab sheet.

Figuring Out the Size of the Load:

4. Discuss what the load is going to be. You'll need to decide what type of car you're thinking of lifting up. It might be fun to use your family car. If so, you could probably figure out how much it weighs by looking in the owner's manual or looking online. If you don't want to look anything up, you can plan on lifting up my car, a Honda Accord. It weighs 2,822 pounds without anyone inside of it. Fill in #5 and #6 on the lab sheet.

Determining the Size of the Lever You'll Need:

5. Fill in #7. This is just a recap of the earlier information gathering. Now, take a moment to add these amounts to the diagram you drew.

6. Fill in #8. Add this information to your diagram as well.

7. Fill in the rest of this page (#9 & #10)

[continued]

Work Lab #9- First-Class Levers—Large, Larger, and Largest
- instructions page 2

Possible Answers:

#1: The correct answers would be: how much I weigh and how much the car weighs. Don't worry if the answers are incorrect, as the rest of the lab works through this problem.

#2: me, sitting on the lever

#3: weighing myself, knowing how much I weigh

#4: the student's weight, in pounds

#5, #6: Answers will vary depending on what type of car you choose. Make sure that the weight you use is in pounds.

#7: should be the same as #6 and #4

#8: This will depend on the weights you used. The number should be somewhere around 30 to 50ish.

#9: The answers should be the same number as you figured out in #8. (load arm x 1)

#10: the same as #8, the same as # 8 + 1 is the size of the lever needed

<u>A Whale and a Planet:</u>

8. You should now understand how to figure out the size of a lever given the weight of the load and the amount of force at the effort arm. See if you can use your knowledge to figure out how large a lever you would need to lift a whale by filling out #11-#14 on the lab sheets. (For a child weighing about 80 lbs, you should end up with a lever that's approximately 4000 feet long—almost a mile!)

Aloud: Finally, we are going to figure out how long a lever you would need to move the world. Because Earth weighs an enormous amount of pounds (13,000 with 21 zeros after it!), we are going to have to change how we do some of the math so that it will work on a regular calculator. There is a special way that mathematicians and scientists write large numbers. To show that a number like 13,000 has 21 zeros after it, they write: $13,000 \times 10^{21}$ (10 to the 21st power). So, every time you see 10^{21} it means there are 21 zeros after the number 10. When you do calculations, just use "13,000" for the weight of Earth. The information on the lab sheets will keep track of where those extra 21 zeros belong.

9. Fill in #15-#18 on the lab sheet. Complete the CONCLUSION.

Possible Answers:

#11: Answers will vary. For a child weighing 80 pounds the answer is 4,000.

#12: same as #11

#13: same as #11 (load arm x 1)

#14: same as the answer from #13 + 1 (4001 ft in the example of an 80 lb child)

#15: Answers will vary. For a child weighing 80 lbs the answer is 162.5 (plus 21 zeros as indicated on the lab sheet.) (FYI: The 5 is counted as one of the zero places.)

#16: same as #15

#17: answer from #15 plus 21 zeros as indicated on the lab sheet

#18: answer from #17 + 1

Conclusion: less, big, bigger

Conclusion / Discussion:

1. Make sure the students understand the following key ideas about levers: Levers make it possible to lift large objects with a relatively small amount of force. The bigger the difference between the load and the force at the effort arm of the lever, the bigger the lever has to be. As the lever gets larger, it has to be moved farther to get the load to move. This is the trade-off involved in using a lever.

2. Talk about whether you think Archimedes could have actually moved Earth given a really big lever. If the lever is bigger than the galaxy, how far do you think Archimedes would have had to push the lever to move Earth a few feet? How long would that take? How long does it take us just to get someplace like the moon?

First-Class Levers—Large, Larger, and Largest

LIFTING A CAR WITH A LEVER:

1. I think I'm going to need to find out the following information to figure out how big this lever needs to be: _____

_____

_____.

THE FORCE AT THE EFFORT END:

2. The force at the effort end of the lever is being provided by

_____.

3. I could figure out the amount of this force by _____

_____.

4. So the force being applied at the effort ends is _____ pounds.

THE LOAD:

5. The load is going to be a car. The type of car that we're going to imagine lifting up is a _____.

6. This type of car weighs _____ pounds.

THE LEVER:

7. The force pushing down at the load end of the lever is the weight of the car. This is _____ pounds. The force pushing down at the effort end of the lever is my weight. This is _____ pounds.

8. By dividing, I can figure out how many more times the car's weight is than mine. Here is the math:

   _____ lbs ÷ _____ lbs = _____
   (car's weight)   (my weight)   (answer)

   So the car weighs _____ times as much as I do!

9. Archimedes figured out that this is the same number of times larger that the effort arm needs to be than the load arm of the lever. So to lift the car by sitting on one end of the lever, I would need an effort arm that is _____ times as big as the load arm. If my load arm is 1 foot long, my effort arm would need to be _____ feet long.

10. The load arm of the lever I need is 1 foot long. The effort arm is _____ feet long. So, the total size of the lever I will need to lift this car by myself is _____ feet long. Wow!

LIFTING A WHALE:

A blue whale weighs about 320,000 pounds. Using this information, you should be able to figure out how big a lever you'll need to lift that whale.

11. The whale weighs _____ lbs ÷ _____ lbs (your weight) = _____ times as much as I do.

12. So, the effort arm of the lever has to be _____ times larger than the load arm.

13. If the load arm is 1 foot long (imagine that you can balance the whole whale on that short piece of wood!), then the effort arm has to be _____ feet long.

14. The whole lever, or the length of the load arm + the length of the effort arm, is _____ feet long.

You probably ended up with a lever that's close to a mile long! (A mile is 5,280 feet.) To make things simple, let's say you could lift the whale with a lever that's only 1 mile long. Looking at the diagram, can you see that you'll need to move the lever a long, long way to lift the whale just a little bit?

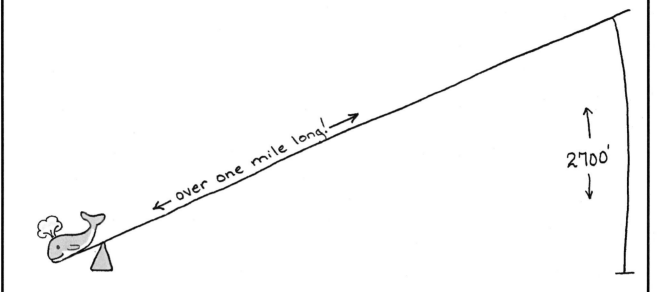

Using a type of math called <u>geometry</u>, you could figure out that to lift the whale 6 inches, you'd need to move the lever more than 2,700 feet!

LIFTING A PLANET:

For this thought experiment, we're going to need to imagine that we have a huge area in which to place Earth and our lever. In this giant space, we'll also need to assume that gravity is pretty much the same as it is on Earth. If we could actually do all of this, then Earth would weigh about 13,000,000,000,0 00,000,000,000,000 [13 septillion] pounds. Your calculator probably doesn't handle numbers that big. So, to figure out the size lever you'll need, you may need to do the math using the number 13,000. When you find an answer, add back the 21 zeroes to the end of the number. That's what $13,000 \times 10^{21}$ means in the equations on the next page.

15. Earth weighs 13,000 lbs ÷ _____ (your weight) lbs =
_____ x 10^{21} times as much as I do.

16. So, the effort arm of the lever has to be _____ x 10^{21} times larger than the load arm.

17. If the load arm is 1 foot long (imagine that you can balance the entire planet Earth on that short piece of wood!), then the effort arm has to be _____ x 10^{21} feet long.

18. The whole lever, or the length of the load arm + the length of the effort arm, is difficult to write out because the number is so large. Basically, it is the answer I got for the length of the effort arm + 1. If I weigh about 80 pounds, that lever is around this long: 162,500,000,000,000,000,000,001 (one hundred sixty-two sextillion, five hundred quintillion, one) feet. How big is that? Well, it's more than 50 times the size of our entire galaxy!

Conclusion: A first-class lever makes it easier to lift a very heavy object because it takes **less / more** force pushing on the effort end of the lever to lift the object than it would take to lift the object straight up. But, in order to move a really heavy object, you need a really **big / small** lever. This means, you need to move the lever through a much **bigger / smaller** space to lift the object just a little bit.

Work Lab #10- Second-Class Levers: Wheeling It In
- instructions

Materials:
- Lab sheets, pencil
- Stiff 12-inch ruler
- Paper cup or old yogurt container—on the smaller side
- Hole puncher
- String
- Tape
- About 50 pennies
- Shoebox, or a block about the size of a shoebox

Note to Parents and Teachers: You might want to cover up the picture of the wheelbarrow on this page until you've read the first paragraph below with your student(s).

Aloud: Now you know just about all there is to know about first-class levers. First-class levers are levers where the fulcrum is placed between the load and the effort. Examples of first-class levers include crowbars, shoehorns and seesaws. In this lab, we're going to learn about second-class levers. <u>Second-class levers</u> are levers where the load (what you are trying to lift) is placed between the fulcrum and the effort. A second-class lever looks like this:

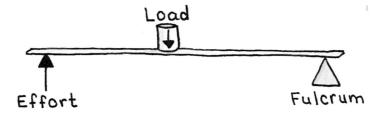

Does this diagram remind you of any simple machines you have around your house? Take a minute to think about whether there's something that has a load between where you lift and the point around which the lever moves. I admit, I had a very hard time figuring out what use second-class levers could have when I first learned about them. Here's a picture that might help:

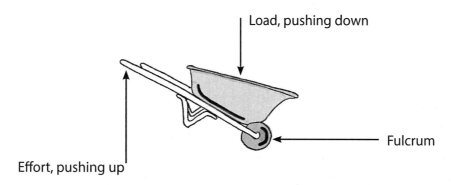

Let's see if we can build our own second-class lever to get a better idea of how they work.

[continued]

Work Lab #10- Second-Class Levers: Wheeling It In
- instructions page 2

Once again, we're going to use a ruler as a lever and try to lift up pennies. First, we're going to see how hard it is to lift 10 pennies without using the lever. This part of the experiment is called the <u>control</u>—it shows what would happen if we didn't use a lever. Then, we'll do the exact same experiment, but using the lever with the load (the pennies) in different places. By comparing our results with the control, we can see how much the second-class lever helps to make work easier.

Procedure:

CONTROL APPARATUS:

1. To set up the control part of the experiment, tie one end of the string around the center of the ruler, using a slipknot if you know how to make one.

2. Next, take the cup you're going to use. The cup is going to act as a basket into which you'll put pennies to see how many you need to lift a particular load. Punch holes in the cup at opposite sides of the top so that you can run the string through the holes and hang the basket, but don't put the string through the holes just yet.

3. Place the shoebox on its side on a table or other flat surface. Place the ruler alongside the shoebox. Drape the string over the shoebox and loop it through the holes in the cup and tie it off so that the cup hangs about halfway down the shoebox. Your setup will look something like this: (ruler is supposed to be flat on the table with the edge touching the box).

4. Stack 10 pennies on the ruler near the center where the string is tied. (If they won't stay, you could stack 5 evenly balanced on either side of the string.)

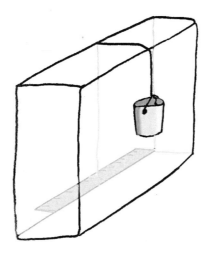

5. Sketch a picture of your apparatus in the CONTROL box on the lab sheet.

6. Fill in the HYPOTHESIS section of the lab sheet.

7. Gently add pennies, one by one, to the cup. Make sure to count the pennies as you place them into the cup. Keep adding pennies until the ruler lifts a little bit up off the surface. It should take more than 10 pennies to lift up the ruler.

8. Discuss why it didn't take exactly 10 pennies to lift up 10 pennies. (The ruler, the cup, and even the string all have weight pulling in various directions. In addition, there is friction between the box and the string resisting movement.)

9. Complete OBSERVATION and DISCUSSION for the control on the lab sheet.

[continued]

Work Lab #10- Second-Class Levers: Wheeling It In
- instructions page 3

EXPERIMENT:

10. Now we're going to rearrange the setup a little bit to make it into a second-class lever. Take all the pennies out of the cup and off of the ruler for a moment so they don't interfere with what you're doing.

11. Move the string that was around the center of the ruler down the ruler so that it is about a ½ inch from the end of the ruler. Place the ruler perpendicular to the box, so that the end with the string is next to the box and the rest of the ruler sticks out away from the box. Leave the cup hanging over the top of the box.

12. The load will, once again, be 10 pennies stacked on top of each other. Place the load somewhere near the middle of the ruler, at around the 6-inch marking.

13. Draw a picture or diagram of the apparatus so far on the Experiment Lab sheets.

14. On your picture or diagram, label the load and the effort. (Hint: the effort is where the lever, or ruler, will be lifted upward.)

15. Now, compare the diagram to what you've learned about second-class levers. Remember that the fulcrum is the part of the lever that stays still while the rest of the lever moves around the fulcrum. Where do you think the fulcrum should be in your shoebox and ruler setup? Answer question 1 on the lab sheet.

16. Let's make the fulcrum. If you thought the fulcrum should be at the end of the ruler the farthest away from the box, you were correct. In order to hold this point still, place a piece of tape along the end of the ruler as shown:

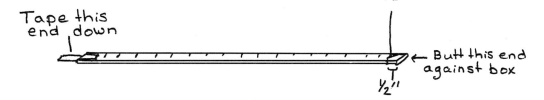

17. Add the fulcrum to your drawing. Take a moment to compare your drawing to the diagram of second-class levers and the picture of the wheelbarrow. Can you see how they have the load, effort, and fulcrum in the same places?

Aloud: We've set up a second-class lever. The fulcrum is at the end of the ruler where the tape has been placed. The effort is where the string will pull upward on the ruler; and, the load is in the middle of the ruler. You might recall that the effort arm is the distance between the effort and fulcrum. Take a moment to look at where the effort arm of your second-class lever is. And, the load arm is the distance between the fulcrum and the load. Where is the load arm of your second-class lever? Did you notice that the load arm and the effort arm overlap each other? That's okay!

18. Write down the sizes of the load and effort arms in the appropriate place on your lab sheet. Try to predict how many pennies you think you will need to place in the cup in order to lift the ruler and its load a little bit off the ground or table. Fill in your prediction on the lab sheet.

19. Now, give it a try. Add pennies one at a time to the cup. Count how many pennies you are adding. Keep adding pennies until the ruler lifts up an observable amount from the table or ground. Mark your results on the lab sheet.

[continued]

20. Move the load to the 5-inch mark. Write down the sizes of the effort arm, the load arm, and your prediction about how many pennies will be needed to lift the load. Try it out, and record your results.

21. Repeat step 12 for the remaining load positions in the data table.

22. Using your observations, fill in the remainder of the lab sheet.

Possible Answers:
Discussion: reasons include friction between the string and the box, the weight of the cup, the weight of the ruler, etc.
#2: remains the same
#3: decreases
#4: increases
#5: less
Conclusion: easier, easier

Conclusion / Discussion:
1. First, make sure that you understand how second-class levers work. The closer the load gets to the fulcrum, the easier it is to lift the load. Also, the farther the effort is from the fulcrum, the easier it will be to lift the load.

2. Talk about how first- and second-class levers are similar and how they are different. They both have the same parts—an effort point, a load, and a fulcrum. They differ in where these parts are located on the lever. In both, a larger difference between the size of the effort arm and the size of the load arm will result in a larger difference between the size of the load and how much force is needed to lift the load.

3. Talk about whether a wheelbarrow with really long handles would make the load in the wheelbarrow easier to lift. (It would.) Are there any reasons we don't see wheelbarrows with 20 foot-long handles?

4. Can you think of other simple machines that are second-class levers? Possible answers: bottle cap opener, diving board. Nail clippers and nutcrackers are made of two second-class levers put together.

Notebooking Ideas:
1. Draw pictures or diagrams of simple machines that are second-class levers. Label the different parts of the lever—the fulcrum, the load, and the effort. How do these simple machines make work easier?

2. Use a Venn Diagram page to compare first- and second-class levers. Some ideas you might want to show include: make work easier by decreasing force needed, make work harder by increasing distance, have a fulcrum, have a fulcrum in the middle, have a fulcrum at one end, etc.

Note to Parents and Teachers: You might need to watch carefully to make sure that the ruler doesn't get wedged underneath the shoebox.

Second-Class Levers: Wheeling It In

My Control Apparatus

Hypothesis: I think it will take _____ pennies placed into the cup to lift the ruler and its load of 10 pennies a little bit up off the table.

Observation: It took _____ pennies placed into the cup to lift the ruler and its load of 10 pennies a little bit up off the table.

Discussion: Some of the reasons it took more than 10 pennies to lift up 10 pennies are:

_____

_____

_____

_____

_____

_____

My Second-Class Lever Apparatus

1. To make the above apparatus into a second-class lever, I think the fulcrum should be placed _____.

Data Collected:

Position on ruler of load	Load Arm: Distance between the load and the fulcrum, in inches	Effort Arm: Distance between the effort and the fulcrum, in inches	**Hypotheses:** I think it will take this many pennies to lift a load of 10 pennies	Number of pennies it actually took to lift a load of 10 pennies
3 inches				
4 inches				
5 inches				
6 inches				
7 inches				
8 inches				
9 inches				

Analysis

2. In a second-class lever, the effort arm (the distance between the fulcrum and the effort) **remains the same / changes** when the location of the load changes.

3. When I move the load closer to the fulcrum, the size of the load arm (the distance between the load and the fulcrum) **increases /decreases**.

4. So, when I move the load closer to the fulcrum, the difference between the sizes of the load arm and the effort arm **increases /decreases**.

5. As I move the load closer to the fulcrum, it takes **more / less** force to lift the load.

Conclusion: For both first and second-class levers, lifting a load gets easier depending on how much bigger the effort arm is than the load arm. When the effort arm is much bigger than the load arm, the load is much **easier / harder** to lift. In a first-class lever, this meant that the closer the load was to the fulcrum, the easier it was to lift. In this experiment, I discovered that the same thing happens with a second-class lever. The closer the load is to the fulcrum, the **easier / harder** it is to lift.

Work Lab #11- Third-Class Levers: It's a Clean Sweep!
- instructions

Materials:
- Lab sheets, pencil
- Broom (not a push broom—just a regular household whisk broom)
- Small heavy object like a box of laundry detergent, or a gallon of water in a plastic container
- Similar-sized object that is much lighter, like an empty box of detergent or an empty container
- Tape (masking tape will work best)
- Tape measure or ruler

Aloud: So far, we've learned about two types of levers. In first-class levers, the fulcrum is in the middle—between the load and the effort. In second-class levers, the load is in the middle, between the fulcrum and the effort. What do you think is in the middle for <u>third-class levers</u>? Well, the only thing we haven't placed in the middle yet is the effort. Take a moment to imagine a lever with the effort in the middle, the fulcrum at one end, and the load at the other. What might such a lever do? Does this diagram help at all?

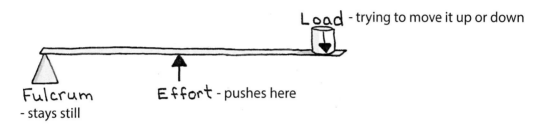

Look at the picture again and imagine a broom or a shovel. Both can be used as third-class levers! When you hold a broom or shovel, usually you put one hand at the very top of the tool. This hand holds relatively still and acts as the fulcrum to let the rest of the lever move around. Your other hand goes somewhere along the middle of the shovel or broom and exerts a force. This is the effort. At the bottom is the load you are trying to shovel or sweep along.

As we've seen, first and second-class levers make work easier because we can apply less force at the point of effort in order to move a load. The trade-off is that we have to move that force a larger distance by pushing the effort part of the lever farther than the distance the load is moved. Third-class levers make work easier in a totally different way. Rather than allowing a smaller force to move a larger load, third-class levers allow a larger force to move a smaller load over a greater distance. How does this work? Let's find out.

Procedure: (Refer to the image on the lab sheet for assistance with tape placement.)

1. Place a tape mark on the ground on a flat, smooth surface (a wood, tile, or linoleum floor will work best for this).

2. Place 3 tape marks on the broom handle. Put one about 12 inches from the top of the broom and one about 12 inches from the broom itself. Pick up the broom as you normally would. Place the third piece of tape where you usually place the hand that's not on the top of the broom handle. This tape mark should be in between the other two.

3. Put the heavy object on the tape mark you made on the ground.

4. Fill in the FIRST HYPOTHESIS section of the lab sheet.

5. Hold the broom as you normally would to sweep the floor (one hand should be at the very top). You're going to try to move the heavy object by sweeping it along. First, move your lower hand up to the top tape mark on the broom handle. Try to sweep the object a few inches from the mark. Keep the hand at the top as still as you can because it is acting as a fulcrum.

[continued]

6. Next, move your hand to where you usually place it, to the middle tape mark. Try to sweep the object again.

7. Finally, move your hand to the bottom tape mark and try one more time.

8. Repeat these steps until you have a good sense of which position required you to push harder to move the object. Fill in the FIRST OBSERVATIONS section of the lab sheet.

9. Next, you're going to experiment with how a third-class lever magnifies distance rather than force.

10. Fill in the SECOND HYPOTHESIS section.

11. Place the lightweight load on the tape line on the floor.

12. Place one hand at the top of the broom (the fulcrum) and the other hand on the top tape line on the broom. Sweep one time by moving your bottom hand in the direction you're sweeping once. You're going to be repeating this several times, and it's important to try to move your arm about the same amount each time. Go slowly, so the load doesn't go sliding away.

13. Record how far the load moved in the SECOND OBSERVATIONS section.

14. Repeat steps 11-13 for all three hand positions on the broom. Complete the lab sheet.

Possible Answers:

First Observations: bottom, top
Analysis and Conclusions #1: fulcrum; #2: hard; #3: farther
Conclusion: should state that the trade-off involved in using a third-class lever is that you push with more force over a smaller distance to move an object.

Conclusion / Discussion:

Aloud: Now you've seen how a third-class lever works. When you used a third-class lever, you needed to push harder to move a load than if you just pushed the load without the lever. But, as a trade-off, the load moved farther when you used a third-class lever.

1. Discuss why this is a useful tool. Why is it useful for a broom to push a very light load a farther distance?

2. Discuss how using a shovel works. Do you do different things with your hands when you shovel something heavy as opposed to something light? Do you move your hands from where they were if you dig something up and then have to move it somewhere else? Now that you understand how third-class levers work, can you explain why?

For More Lab Fun:

1. Go outside with a shovel and experiment with what you've learned about third-class levers. Shovels are interesting in that they typically act as first-class or third-class levers, depending on whether you're digging dirt or moving dirt.

2. If you have several shovels or brooms around your house, look at them. How are they the same? How are they different? Would some work better for tasks that involve light loads but bigger distances?

Notebooking ideas:

1. Draw a picture of a broom or a shovel showing how they work as third-class levers.

2. Design a shovel that would be really good for shoveling heavy snow. Design a different shovel that would be really good for shoveling lots of lightweight snow. If you live somewhere without snow, imagine shoveling something like dirt.

Note to Parents and Teachers: Shovels and brooms are not always used as third-class levers. But when used with one relatively stationary hand toward the top of the handle, they function as third-class levers.

Third-Class Levers: It's a Clean Sweep!

First Hypotheses:

I think it will take the *least* amount of force to move the load with one hand at the top of the broom and the other hand at the **top** / **middle** /**bottom** tape mark.

I think it will take the *most* amount of force to move the load with one hand at the top of the broom and the other hand at the **top** / **middle** /**bottom** tape mark.

First Observations:

It took the *least* force to move the load with one hand at the top of the broom and the other hand at the **top** / **middle** / **bottom** tape mark.

It took the *most* force to move the load with one hand at the top of the broom and the other hand at the **top** / **middle** / **bottom** tape mark.

Second Hypotheses:

I think the load will move the *farthest* with one hand at the top of the broom and the other hand at the **top** / **middle** / **bottom** tape mark.

I think the load will move the *least* with one hand at the top of the broom and the other hand at the **top** / **middle** / **bottom** tape mark.

Second Observations:

Upper hand at top of broom, lower hand at top tape mark	The distance the load moved:
Upper hand at top of broom, lower hand at middle tape mark	The distance the load moved:
Upper hand at top of broom, lower hand at bottom tape mark	The distance the load moved:

Analysis and Conclusions:

1. When my hand is at the top tape mark of the broom, it is closest to the **fulcrum** / **effort** of the lever.

2. With my hand at the top tape mark, it is very **hard** / **easy** to move a heavy load.

3. But, with my hand at the top tape mark, the load moves much **farther** / **less** than my hand actually moves the lever.

Conclusion: The trade-off involved in using a third-class lever is:

_____

_____

_____

_____

_____.

Lawful Levers

You now know that levers are pretty much everywhere you look. Go to the playground and sit on a seesaw, and you're using a first-class lever. Help out in the garden by pushing the wheelbarrow, and you're using a second-class lever. Sweep the floor after dinner, and you're using a third-class lever.

Levers are everywhere because they are so useful. Like all simple machines, they help us to move an object from one place to another. And, like all simple machines, they make work easier by changing something about the amount or direction of force or movement.

All levers have the same parts. There is a stiff stick of some sort: this is the lever itself. All levers have one point that holds still, around which the lever moves: this is the fulcrum. All levers move some kind of a load, and all levers have a point at which force is applied—the point of effort. But, for each class of lever, the arrangement of these parts is different.

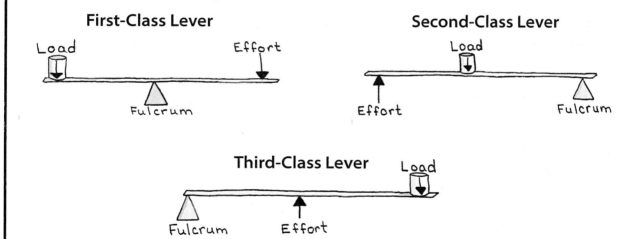

In all three classes of levers, there are some important measurements that help us to figure out how the levers can be used. The effort arm is the distance from the fulcrum to the effort. The load arm is the distance from the fulcrum to the load. In second- and third-class levers, where the fulcrum is at the end of the lever, the effort arm and load arm will overlap. That's okay. We still measure them as separate elements of the lever.

Part of the mathematics that Archimedes figured out is now known as the <u>law of the lever</u>. The law of the lever looks like this:

(size of effort arm) X (amount of force applied at effort) =
(size of load arm) X (weight of load)

All this equation means is that if you increase the size of your load, you'll need to increase either the amount of force you apply or the size of the effort arm to keep things in balance. What amazes me about this law is that it works for all three classes of levers.

You know, we still haven't found out whether Archimedes was able to move the large ship that King Hiero asked him to move. That's because, in the end, Archimedes needed some other simple machines to help him. And that's what we're going to learn about next. But first let's take a minute to see how good a Lever Detector you are!

Work Lab #12 - Lever Detector - instructions

Materials:
- Lab sheets, pencil
- Household objects that are levers (as many as you can find listed below. You don't need to have them all.) You could also make this lab into a scavenger hunt, with the students going to look at the items where they are found.
    - Bottle opener
    - Scissors
    - Claw hammer
    - Garlic press
    - Nutcracker
    - Tweezers
    - Pliers
    - Tennis/badminton/racket ball racket
    - Baseball bat
    - Fishing rod
    - Shovel
    - Rake

Aloud: You now know just about everything there is to know about levers. To finish up our exploration of levers, you're going to become a living and breathing lever detector. Your job will be to discover as many levers as you can that we use in our own lives. Then it will be up to you to figure out exactly how each of these machines gives us a mechanical advantage by altering the amount and/or direction of force we need to use to accomplish a job.

Procedure:
1. Gather devices or go look around the house for them. Examine each one as you fill in the lab sheet.

   If you choose to make this a scavenger hunt: take the lab sheet with you and look around. Every time you find a device that uses levers, examine it, think about it, and enter its information onto the sheet.

   If you have gathered items: Examine each of the items. Think about what work it helps you to perform and fill in the lab sheet.

2. See if you can add any items to the list provided.

[continued]

Work Lab #12 - Lever Detector - instructions page 2

Possible Answers: I have labeled the images with fulcrum, load, and effort (force), and offered long descriptions of the mechanical advantages. Students should not be required to provide as much detail.

Simple Machine	Class of Lever	What kind of mechanical advantage does this device give?
Scissors load / fulcrum / effort	two 1st-class levers	The fulcrum is in the middle of the lever, so the advantage of scissors comes mostly from changing the direction of force needed to cut things.
Bottle Opener effort / fulcrum / load	2nd-class lever	The fulcrum is the end of the bottle opener and the load is where the bottle cap is. The load and the fulcrum are very close together, so the force applied at the end of the bottle opener that you hold is magnified greatly, but you have to move it much farther than the bottle cap moves.
Claw hammer effort / load / fulcrum	1st-class lever	When you use the end of a hammer to remove a nail, the fulcrum is where the hammer head touches the surface of the wood—so it is between the load and the effort. The hammer helps to magnify force as well as change its direction.
Garlic press effort / fulcrum / load (inside)	2nd-class lever	The effort is applied where you squeeze the garlic press, and the load is where the press pushes down on the garlic. The fulcrum is the hinge at the very end of the press. The press magnifies the force applied.
Nutcracker fulcrum / effort / load	2nd-class lever	This is like the garlic press, with the load, or nut, between the effort and the fulcrum.
Tweezers effort / load / fulcrum	two 3rd-class levers	The fulcrum is at the end of the tweezers that is joined together. The effort is wherever you press the tweezers together with your fingers, and the load is at the end where the tweezers move. This means that for a tiny bit of motion with your fingers, you get slightly more motion at the ends of the tweezers. This helps you get more control and force over the movement of the ends of the tweezers.

[continued]

Pliers	two 1st-class levers	Pliers are similar to scissors. The fulcrum is where the pliers' two arms meet. The effort is where you squeeze the pliers. Because the distance between the effort and the fulcrum is greater than the distance from the fulcrum to the jaw end of the pliers, the force you apply is magnified and you can maneuver with more precision.
Sports racket or bat	3rd-class lever	When you swing a racket or a bat, you are applying the effort at the end where you hold the racket or bat. The load is the far end where the "machine" makes contact with a ball. Just like a broom, you have to move your hand only a little bit to create a large motion at the load end. This is quite effective for magnifying the force you apply to hitting a ball.
Fishing rod	3rd-class lever	When you pull up on a fishing rod to raise your latest catch out of the water, the rod acts as a 3rd-class lever. The effort is where your hand lifts the rod up. The load is the end where the string drops into the water. The fulcrum is where you hold the rod with your other hand, close to the end of the fishing rod. You can raise the fish a long distance above water by only moving the end of the rod you hold just a little bit. So, the rod magnifies the distance for you.
Shovel	3rd-class lever	The load for a shovel is at the bottom, where the shovel is. The fulcrum is the handle of the shovel where you put one hand. You use the other hand to lift the shovel. You can gain a mechanical advantage in at least two ways with a shovel, depending on whether you put your "effort" hand closer to the handle or farther from the handle.
Broad leaf rake or broom	3rd-class lever	As we already saw with a broom, rakes act as third-class levers. The fulcrum is the hand closest to the top of the broom or rake, and the load is where the sweeping part of the broom or rake does its work. Because you are trying to cover a large area when you sweep or rake, the mechanical advantage comes because you only need to move your hands a little bit to move the end of the broom or rake a larger distance.

[continued]

Conclusion / Discussion:

1. Make sure that you discuss how each of the devices you've found involves a trade-off. Either the load is made more difficult to move, or the distance one has to move it is increased in order to gain some other mechanical advantage.

2. Discuss what sort of thinking might have gone into inventing some of the devices you've learned about. I am always curious about how someone ever managed to come up with the idea of scissors. Do you think such inventions are obvious once you understand levers, or do you think it took some serious creativity and imagination to invent them?

More Lab Fun:

1. Some levers you may not have given much thought to are all the levers in your body. Your muscles, joints, and bones work together to create levers. Look up some joints in an anatomy book and see if you can figure out which joints are which types of levers. How do your joints give you a mechanical advantage?

2. Try to transform a lever of one class into a lever of another class. For example, how could you use a broom as a first- or second-class lever? What would it help you do? Who knows, you might create a new invention this way!

Notebooking idea:

The levers you've found around your house are fairly small in size. But levers are helpful on a large scale also. The next time you are around any large machinery, such as can be found in a factory or at a construction site or a farm, sketch some of the uses of levers you observe.

NAME _____ DATE _____

Lever Detector

Fill in the chart. I've started by filling in the first entry for you.

Challenge: Try to label the fulcrum, load, and effort on each device pictured.

Simple Machine	Class of Lever	What kind of mechanical advantage does this simple machine give?
Scissors load fulcrum effort	First-class levers (two of them)	The fulcrum is about in the middle of the lever, so the advantage of scissors comes mostly from changing the direction of force needed to cut things.
Bottle Opener		
Claw hammer		
Garlic press		
Nutcracker		

Simple Machine	Class of Lever	What kind of mechanical advantage does this simple machine give?
Tweezers		
Pliers		
Sports racket or bat		
Fishing rod		
Shovel		
Broad leaf rake or broom		

For my notebook

Dizzy Levers: Wheels & Axles

Here's a physics riddle for you: What do baby carriages, semitrucks, doorknobs and screwdrivers have in common? I don't know what answers you came up with, but the answer that I was thinking of is wheels and axles. Do you agree? Well actually, there are just a couple of little problems with my

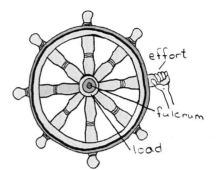

answer. First of all, I'm pretty certain that you already know what a wheel is, so I don't need to explain that. But, what is an axle? An <u>axle</u> is a stick to which a <u>wheel</u> can be attached. For our purposes, the axle is attached to the wheel in such a way that if the wheel turns, the axle turns, and if the axle turns, the wheel turns. The axle is attached to the center of the wheel.

So, now you know what an axle is. And that brings us to the second little problem with my answer to the riddle: Why would I think that screwdrivers and doorknobs have wheels and axles? To understand the answer to that question, we need to learn a bit more about why a <u>wheel and axle</u> is considered a simple machine. In other words, we need to understand how the wheel and axle makes work easier.

I don't want you to feel like we're going in circles, but the wheel and axle together make up a lever. And to make things even more complicated, depending on how the wheel and axle are used, it can be either a first-class lever or a third-class lever. Let's consider first-class levers. Remember that a first-class lever makes work easier by allowing us to apply less force over a larger distance. And, a first-class lever has the fulcrum in the middle and looks like the picture below:

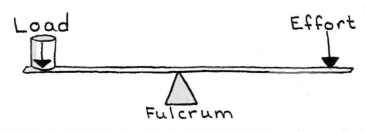

Imagine that you could spin the first-class lever around and around in a circle, with the fulcrum being the center. This makes sense because a fulcrum is the point around which a lever turns. As you turn the lever around, you are pushing on the effort point, the outside edge of the circle—like you would when turning the steering wheel on a ship.

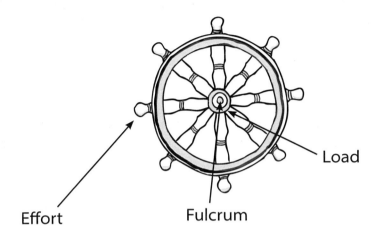

Effort

Fulcrum

Load

If you could attach an axle to the wheel, your effort would also turn the axle around. All you would need is some load tied to the axle, and you would have a spinning first-class lever with the effort, fulcrum and load all in order. Does it make work easier in the same way as a first-class lever does? Let's find out!

Work Lab #13: Going in Circles - instructions

Note: Keep the wheel and axles from this lab. You'll need them in the next couple of labs.

Materials:
- Lab sheets, pencil
- Foam board (not too thick) or corrugated cardboard, size should be at least 30" x 10" or 25" square
- Scissors or sharp knife (parents will need to help with cutting the foam or cardboard)
- 4 small wooden dowels of the sort you get at the craft store, all the same size (about 12-18 inches long and around the thickness of a pencil)
- Strong tape (like duct tape)
- Compass to draw circles, or three circular items to trace around to draw small (about 3 inches diameter), medium (about 6 inches), and large (about 10 inches) circles
- Magic marker
- Ruler or tape measure

Aloud: When you spin a first-class lever around in circles, you get a wheel and axle. Let's take some time to see if we can figure out what's so special about a stick attached to a wheel. Our first job will be to construct three wheel and axle assemblies with different-sized wheels so that we can observe how they work. The "work" we'll be trying to do is getting the axle to turn around one time.

Procedure: (steps 1-5 can be done ahead of time)

1. Using the compass or items to trace, draw three circles on either corrugated cardboard or foam board. The circles should have diameters of approximately 3, 6, and 10 inches. Don't worry about precision: you just want a small, medium, and larger circle. Also, cut out one extra circle the exact same size as your large circle for an upcoming lab (Work Lab #15) and put it aside for now.

2. Cut the circles out of the board.

3. Use a pencil to punch a hole through the centers of the circles. Smile when you realize that you're essentially using a wedge to push the foam board aside!

4. Adjust the holes until they fit the dowels.

5. Place a dowel through the center of each wheel. Move each wheel so that it's roughly in the middle of its dowel. The dowel is the axle. The wheel, obviously, is the wheel. You should have one extra dowel.

Aloud: In order to turn this into a wheel and axle, the wheel and axle must turn together. If you can turn the wheel without the axle moving, you haven't got a wheel and axle.

6. To fix the wheels on their axles, use the strong tape. It may look kind of messy, but try to tape the dowel to the wheel on both sides and work with it until the wheel and axle turn together (i.e., if you turn the wheel, the axle turns and vice versa).

7. On each wheel make a mark at some point on the edge of the wheel with the magic marker. Make another mark on the axle in roughly the same position. These marks will help you count how many turns the wheel and axle make. Also make a mark somewhere (anywhere, it doesn't matter) on the extra dowel.

8. Draw a picture of one of your wheel and axle assemblies on the lab sheet. Label the wheel and the axle on your drawing.

9. Take a moment to play around with your assemblies. Spin the wheel and observe what happens to the wheel and the axle. Spin the axle and observe what happens. Write down three things you noticed in the initial observations section of the lab sheet.

10. Fill in the hypothesis section of the lab sheet.

11. Let's find out over what distance we need to apply force to get the dowels, or axles, to go around in a circle one time. Place the dowel with no wheel attached on a flat surface. Place it with the mark you made facing straight upward. Lay it next to the ruler at 0 inches, so that you can measure how far you need to roll it to turn it around one time. Roll the dowel around once until the mark is facing upward again. Record how far you had to push the dowel to roll it around 1 time. This distance—which is just the distance around the outside of a
    [continued]

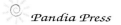

circle—is called the circumference of the circle. So, you've just measured the circumference of the dowel.

12. Now we're going to do the same thing with the wheel and axle assemblies. This time, though, we'll apply force to the wheels. Because they're fixed to the axles, they will make the axles turn as well. You might need to do this on the floor so that you'll have enough space.

13. Take the largest wheel and axle and place the wheel so that you can roll it across the floor. Adjust it so that the mark you made is at the top of the wheel. Keep track of where you start. By turning the wheel itself, without touching the axle, roll the wheel until it has gone around one time. Measure the distance over which you had to push the wheel. Record your result.

14. Repeat the experiment, this time watching both the mark you made on the axle and the mark you made on the wheel. Record how many times the axle makes a complete circle when the wheel makes a complete circle.

15. Hold both sides of the axle in your hands and spin the axle one time around. Observe the wheel and axle. Record how many times the wheel makes a circle when the axle is turned once.

16. Repeat steps 13-15 for the remaining wheel and axle assemblies. Fill in the CONCLUSION section of the lab sheet.

Possible Answers:

Initial observations: whatever the student observes is fine. Data Collected: the wheel should always spin exactly once for each turn of the axle and vice versa. Conclusion: #1 one; #2 one; #3 biggest

Conclusion / Discussion:

1. A key point is that the wheel and axle always turn together, so that one turn of the axle causes the wheel to turn once, and one turn of the wheel causes the axle to turn once.

2. Another key point is that when one pushes on the wheel to turn the assembly, one has to push over a much greater distance than when one pushes the axle. In other words, the lab makes clear, in a concrete way, that one has to apply force over a greater distance when turning the wheel.

3. Talk about what this reminds you of regarding levers: To move a load a short distance, you have to push the effort end of the lever a larger distance. The outside of the wheel is like the effort point of the lever.

4. See if you can think of some ways these properties of the wheel and axle might be helpful. Don't worry if you can't come up with anything, as we'll be experimenting more in the next labs.

More Lab Fun:

1. Play around further with the wheel and axle. If two tiny creatures were standing on the marks you made on the wheels and axles, which would travel more quickly as they turned, the one on the wheel or the one on the axle?

2. For the mathematically minded, consider the idea of the circumference of a circle to use your wheel and axle as a measuring device. Remember that the formula for circumference is C = 2 x π x radius (C = 2π r). π is approximately 3.14 and the radius is the measure from the center of the circle to one of its edges. Once you calculate the circumference of one of your wheels, you could add an extension arm to it and use it to measure distance, like the distance around a room or of a line (curved or straight). The mark on the wheel will help you keep count of each turn as you roll it across the distance. Then multiply the number of turns by the circumference of the wheel to calculate the distance the wheel traveled (e.g. 21 turns times a circumference of 31.4 inches equals a distance of 659.5 inches, or 54.95 feet).

Notebooking Idea:

1. Use a definition page to define *wheel and axle* and *circumference*.

2. If you calculated the circumference of your wheel and axle (as described in More Lab Fun #2), create an equation sheet for circumference of a circle.

NAME _____ DATE _____

Going in Circles

My Wheel & Axle

Initial Observations: When playing around with the wheel and axle assemblies that I made, I noticed that:

1. _____

_____

_____

2. _____

_____

_____

3. _____

_____

_____

Hypotheses:

1. I think that every time I spin the axle one time, the wheel will go around **less than one time / exactly one time / more than one time**.

2. I think I will have to apply force over a longer distance to get the **wheel / axle** to go around once.

Data Collected:

	Distance I had to push it to turn it around one time	Number of turns made by the axle when I turned the wheel one time	Number of turns made by the wheel when I turned the axle one time
Dowel by itself (the axle)		(does not apply)	(does not apply)
Largest wheel and axle assembly			
Medium-sized wheel and axle assembly			
Smallest wheel and axle assembly			

Conclusions:

1. Whenever the axle on a wheel and axle is pushed around in a circle one time, the wheel goes around in a circle _____ time(s).

2. Whenever the wheel on a wheel and axle is pushed around in a circle one time, the axle goes around in a circle _____ time(s).

3. To do the work of turning the axle around one time, I had to push over the greatest distance when I used the **biggest** / **medium-sized** / **smallest** wheel.

Work Lab #14: A Dizzy First-Class Lever - instructions

Note: Keep the large wheel and axle from this lab. You'll need it in the next lab.

Materials:
- Lab sheet, pencil
- Wheel and axle assemblies from the previous lab
- String, several feet long
- Something small with a bit of weight to it like a roll of duct tape or packing tape that you can tie a string around
- Someone to help out (you'll need at least two people for this lab)
- Drinking straw wide enough to fit over the dowel from the last lab (you could also make a tube out of construction paper and tape to fit over the dowel)
- Scissors

Aloud: In the last lab, we learned a little bit about how wheels and axles work. When using the wheel and axle as a first-class lever, the outside of the wheel—the part we can push on to turn the axle around—is like the effort point of the lever. The axle, the thing we were trying to move by pushing on the wheel, is the load. We push on the outside of the wheel and it does the work of moving the axle. To get the axle to turn around one time, we need to push the wheel around in a circle one time. As always, though, there's a trade-off.

Do you remember the little mark you made on the wheel to keep track of when it had travelled around in a complete circle? If you placed your finger on that mark and used it to push the wheel all the way around, it would travel a much greater distance than the corresponding mark on the axle. So just like with a first-class lever, you have to push over a longer distance at the effort point—the outside of the wheel—to get the load to move.

If the wheel and axle really function like a first-class lever, then that would mean that it would take less force to push the wheel than it does to push the axle itself. How does the wheel and axle allow us to use less force than we would need to otherwise? We're going to find out by trying to lift an object using the wheel and axle.

Procedure:
1. Cut two pieces from the straw, about 1 to 1 ½ inches.
2. Tie one end of the string around the roll of tape (or whatever you are using as a load).
3. Tie the other end of the string around the middle of the dowel with no wheel on it.
4. Tape the string to the dowel so that it doesn't turn when the dowel turns. That is, when you turn the dowel, the string should roll up on the dowel like a spool of thread.
5. Place the two pieces of straw onto either end of the dowel. This will allow the dowel to spin freely while being held by someone.
6. Have one person hold the dowel horizontally, holding one of the straw segments in one hand and the other in the other hand. The dowel should be able to spin freely. Have the second person spin the dowel so that the string starts to wind up on the dowel. Keep spinning until the roll of tape has been lifted about 1 foot off the ground. Pay attention to how hard or easy it is to lift the tape this way.
7. Switch positions so that everyone has a chance to try to lift the tape this way.
8. Fill in the HYPOTHESIS section of the lab sheet.

[continued]

Work Lab #14: A Dizzy First-Class Lever - instructions page 2

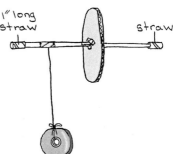

9. Remove the end of the string from the dowel. Attach it to the medium-sized wheel and axle assembly about halfway between the wheel and the end of the dowel. Tape it on as you did in step 4.

10. Again, place the straw segments onto each end of the dowel.

11. Have one person hold onto the wheel and axle using two hands to hold the two pieces of straw.

12. Have the second person raise the load about 1 foot off the ground by turning the wheel and pushing on the edge of the wheel. Compare this to the difficulty of raising the tape by turning the axle. You can easily switch between the two by turning the wheel, then turning the axle on the wheel and axle assembly. Focus on how hard you have to push the wheel or axle to move them. Give everyone a chance to try turning the wheel and axle.

13. Fill in #1 in the OBSERVATIONS section of the lab sheet.

14. Repeat steps 9-12 with the smallest-sized wheel and axle assembly.

15. Repeat steps 9-12 with the largest-sized wheel and axle assembly.

16. Finish the lab sheet.

Possible Answers:
Observations: #1: easier; #2: easier; Conclusions: #1: axle by itself; #2: one; #3: greater; #4: less; Analysis: by pushing over a greater distance, the amount of force needed is decreased.

Conclusion / Discussion:
1. Talk about how the wheel and axle works like a first-class lever. It should be clear by this point that by pushing over a greater distance, the amount of force needed is lessened.

2. Can you think of places where you've seen a construction like you made used to lift things? (Hints: water wells, truck winches.)

3. Can you figure out why it might be useful to push on the axle rather than on the wheel? What would be gained by doing this? That is, in what way would work become easier? You'll learn more about this in the next lab.

More Lab Fun:
1. Using a wheel and axle construction, you can lift lots of things. If you have a swing set or a treehouse, try to build a wheel and axle that will make lifting things up easier for you.

2. Build a wheel and axle but add a handle to the wheel by gluing or stapling stiff cardboard or foam board to the flat outside part of the wheel. Think about where you should put the handle to turn the wheel—toward the center of the wheel or toward the edge? Which will make the wheel easier to turn? Play around with some ideas to figure it out.

Notebooking Ideas:
1. Use a Venn diagram notebooking page to compare the wheel and axle and a first-class lever. Some things you might place in the diagram are: point of effort, load, increases distance, decreases force, made with a fulcrum and a stiff board, made with a circular wheel, etc.

2. Now that you know about the wheel and axle, can you think of a way Archimedes might have used the wheel and axle to move King Hiero's ship? Draw a picture of how you might have accomplished the job.

NAME _____ DATE _____

A Dizzy First-Class Lever

Hypotheses:

1. I think it will be **easier** / **harder** to lift the roll of tape by turning the wheels on the wheel and axle assemblies than it is to lift the tape by turning just the axle.

2. I think it will be **easier** / **harder** to lift the roll of tape using the largest wheel than it will be using the smallest wheel.

Observations:

1. It was **easier** / **harder** / **about the same** using the medium-sized wheel and axle assembly to lift the tape than it was using just the axle.

2. Using the largest wheel and axle to lift the tape was **easier** / **harder** / **about the same** as using the smallest wheel and axle.

Conclusions:

1. I had to push harder on the **axle by itself** / **wheel and axle assemblies** to do the same work of lifting the tape.

2. When I push on the wheel to lift the tape, every time I push it around in a circle one time, the axle goes around in a circle **one** / **two** / **three** time(s).

3. So, to lift the tape by pushing on the wheel, I have to apply force over a **greater** / **lesser** distance.

4. The trade-off is that I used **less** / **more** force pushing on the wheel.

Analysis: The wheel and axle is like a first-class lever because:

_____

_____

_____

_____

_____

Unit 5- Work: Plane and Simple Machines

Work Lab #15: Going in Circles in the Real World - instructions

Materials:
- Lab sheet, pencil
- The large wheel and axle assembly from the previous labs
- The extra-large wheel you cut out during Work Lab #13, Going In Circles
- Tape
- Ruler or tape measure

Aloud: You've seen how a wheel and axle can be used to make lifting a load easier. It takes less force to lift a load if you do your work by pushing on the wheel of a wheel and axle. That's pretty cool, but wheels and axles are even more amazing. If you push on the axle part of the wheel and axle, then your wheel and axle turns into a third-class lever. How does this make work easier? Let's find out.

Procedure:
1. We're going to rearrange your largest wheel and axle assembly a little. Detach the attached wheel and reattach it to one end of the axle. Attach the other large wheel to the other end of the axle. Secure the wheels with tape. You should have an assembly that looks like this:

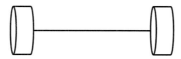

2. Mark a starting line and a finish line on a flat surface such as a hard floor or table. The starting and finish lines should be about five feet apart.

3. Fill in the HYPOTHESIS section of the lab sheet.

4. Place your assembly at the starting line.

5. Using your thumb and your index finger to spin the axle, move the wheel assembly across the floor. Don't release the wheel assembly so that it keeps going, though. Keep turning it yourself. Make a mental note of where the wheel and axle ended up.

6. Take the wheel and axle back to the starting point. Now, roll it the same distance by pushing on the wheel part of the wheel and axle. Again, don't just let the assembly roll off by itself. Move it by continuing to push on the wheel.

7. Fill in the rest of the lab sheet.

Aloud: Now you see how the wheel and axle can function either as a first-class lever or a third-class lever. When you push on the wheel, it takes less force to turn the axle, but you push over a greater distance. This is helpful for things like lifting a bucket of water out of a well. When you push on the axle, it takes more force to turn the assembly. Your fingers, though, only had to move around the circumference of the dowel a few times—a much shorter distance than moving around the wheels.

Possible Answers:
Observations: #1: a little, #2: more
Conclusion: #1: greater   #2: small, large.

[continued]

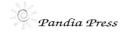

Work Lab #15: Going in Circles in the Real World
- instructions page 2

Conclusion / Discussion:

1. Discuss why using a wheel and axle as a third-class lever is helpful. Some examples of when the wheel and axle is used as a third-class lever include automobile tires, paddle wheel boats, and Ferris wheels.

2. Think about, or look at pictures of, different types of vehicles. Why do you think race cars have tires that are relatively large compared to the size of the vehicle?

More Lab Fun:

Put your knowledge of friction, the wheel and axle, and ramps together by playing around with your new rolling assembly on a ramp. What happens when you increase the friction? When you decrease it? Does the wheel and axle travel farther when the ramp is steeper? What if you make another assembly with smaller wheels? How does this affect how far the wheel and axle moves?

Notebooking Ideas:

3. Use a Venn Diagram page to compare and contrast the differences between using a wheel and axle as a first- or a third-class lever.

4. List different uses of the wheel and axle and explain why the wheel and axle makes work easier in these uses.

Going in Circles in the Real World

Hypothesis:

I think it will be easier to roll the wheel and axle assembly by turning the **axle** / **wheel**. [Hint: this is a trick question.]

Observations:

1. When I pushed on the axle to move the wheel and axle, it seemed to take **a lot** / **a little** pushing to get the wheel across a distance.

2. When I pushed on the wheel to move the wheel and axle, it seemed to take **less** / **more** pushing to get the wheel across the same distance.

Conclusion:

1. A broom is an example of a third-class lever. It makes work easier because by pushing harder over a small distance, the broom itself moves a **greater** / **lesser** distance.

2. The wheel and axle is like a third-class lever because when you push the axle, you are pushing over a **small** / **large** distance to cause the wheel to move a **small** / **large** distance.

Work Lab #16: Wheel & Axle Wrap-up - instructions

Materials:
- Lab sheets, pencil
- Household objects that are wheel & axle simple machines (as many as you can find that are pictured on the lab sheet. You don't need to have them all.)

Aloud: All of the machines you've gathered, as well as those pictured on the lab sheet, use a wheel and axle as a lever. Can you figure out how the wheel and axle is used in each case? And can you figure out if the wheel and axle functions as a first or third-class lever? If you understand how all of these work, you're a simple machine superstar!

Procedure:
1. Gather devices or go look around the house for them. Examine each one as you fill in the lab sheet. The first one is completed for you.

2. See if you can add any items to the list provided.

Possible Answers:
I have labeled what serves as the wheel and the axle on each image, and offered long descriptions of the mechanical advantages. Students should not be required to provide as much detail.

Simple Machine	Class of Lever	What kind of mechanical advantage does this device give?
Screwdriver	First	The handle is like a wheel because it is wider than the end of the screwdriver that turns the screw. It takes less force for you to turn the screw because the handle/wheel is bigger than the other end of the screwdriver. (If you increase the diameter of the handle, the wheel, the screwdriver is more effective, easier, to use.)
Hand-Turned Pencil Sharpener	First	To use a hand-turned pencil sharpener, you apply force to the outer edge of the wheel (the handle of the sharpener). You are turning the axle—the grinding part of the sharpener that's inside the machine. So, you apply force over a greater distance, but you use less force than it would take to move the grinder around the pencil tip without the handle.
Windmill	First	Wind is what applies force to the windmill. It moves the wheel part of the wheel and axle, and inside the windmill's housing, when the windmill turns, an axle turns. Less force is needed to turn the axle, but the windmill's turning covers a greater distance than the axle. Windmills can be used to generate electricity (you'll understand how when we study electromagnetism), and to grind food such as wheat.

[continued]

| Ceiling Fan | Third | In a ceiling fan, the force is applied to the axle—usually electricity is used to power the axle turning around and around. The outside of the fan moves more quickly than the axle does, and it forces air down (or up, depending on the direction of the fan), creating a breeze. |
| Doorknob | First | Just as with a pencil sharpener, you use your hand to turn the wheel part of the assembly. Inside the doorknob is the axle which turns, moving the door latch out of the way so that the door can open. If you ever have a chance to take apart a doorknob, have a look. |

Conclusion / Discussion:

As with levers, you can find wheel and axle assemblies all around you once you start looking. Here are some examples you might find in your house: rolling pin, bicycle wheel, record turntable, handheld egg beater, and a washing machine. How do wheels and axles help make work easier in cars? (There's more to think about than just the four wheels!) How about in lawn mowers? In Ferris wheels? Where else can you discover wheels and axles?

More Lab Fun:

1. What happens if you create a new simple machine by attaching the axle to another part of the wheel—farther toward one edge of the wheel? Does this device make work easier? In what ways? Can you think of ways to use this device?

2. If you have a ceiling fan with a switch that reverses its direction, experiment with it. What difference does it make if the fan changes direction? Why should ceiling fans go in one direction in the winter and another in the summer?

Notebooking ideas:

If you are enjoying thinking about simple machines, you might consider looking up Roentgen's Berlin secretary cabinet online. It is a wooden desk that was made with all sorts of hidden compartments, drawers, and panels that seem to open magically when a key is turned. In reality, a number of simple machines operate inside the desk to make all this happen. Sketch an idea for a "mechanical desk" of your own using some of the simple machines we've learned about.

Note to Parents and Teachers:

You might want to look ahead to Work Lab #17 for the next section on pulleys. The preparation involves letting some glue dry overnight.

NAME _____ DATE _____

Wheel & Axle Wrap-up

Fill in the chart. I've started by filling in the first entry for you. Challenge: Label what acts as the wheel and the axle on each device pictured.

Simple Machine	Class of Lever	What kind of mechanical advantage does this device give?
Screwdriver wheel axle	First	The handle is like a wheel because it is wider than the end of the screwdriver that turns the screw. It takes less force for you to turn the screw because the handle (the wheel) is bigger than the other end of the screwdriver.
Pencil Sharpener 		
Windmill 		

Simple Machine	Class of Lever	What kind of mechanical advantage does this device give?
Ceiling Fan		
Doorknob		

Unit 5- Work: Plane and Simple Machines

Pulleys

Simple machines seem to be getting more and more complicated! We started out with what was basically a stiff board—a ramp or inclined plane. Then we moved the inclined plane and created a wedge. By wrapping the wedge around in circles, we made a screw. We learned about levers, levers, and more levers—three classes of them to be exact. By spinning our levers around in circles, we discovered how the wheel and axle makes work easier.

The last simple machine we're going to learn about is the <u>pulley</u>. The pulley seems to do everything. It can hold still or move around. It spins in circles. It can make work easier in two different ways. It loves to work with other pulleys to make work even easier. And it was the pulley, the last of the simple machines, which Archimedes needed to move that ship for King Hiero.

A pulley is a wheel that has a groove in it where a piece of string, rope, or chain can move back and forth. It looks like this:

How does a pulley make work easier? The answer to that question is actually pretty complicated because pulleys can be used in a variety of different ways.

Let's think about one of the simplest uses of a pulley: the flagpole. You've probably seen flags flying high up on a flagpole. How do the flags get up there? How can they be taken down? One way to get the flag to the top of the pole would be to put it in your backpack, climb the pole, and attach it. That sounds kind of dangerous to me—climbing up a pole with a backpack on. Maybe, instead of carrying the flag up, you could carry some rope up and then pull the flag up with the rope. The climb might be a bit less dangerous, but it's still not a job I'd want to do.

You might remember, though, that one way simple machines make work easier is by changing the direction of force. Maybe it would be easier to pull downward from the ground to lift the flag upward. That's exactly what a pulley does, and that's exactly how real flagpoles work. At the very top of the pole is a pulley with a rope running through the groove of the pulley. One end of the rope is attached to the flag. The rope runs through the groove on the pulley, and the other end of the rope is tied up to the flagpole. When people want to raise the flag, they attach it to one end of the rope and pull on the other end of the rope. Up goes the flag. To lower the flag, people untie the rope from the pole and let the force of gravity pull the flag down. At the same time, the piece of rope that was attached to the pole goes upward. Therefore, this side of the rope has to be extra long.

A pulley that's attached to something like the top of a flagpole is called a <u>fixed pulley</u>. It makes work easier by changing the direction of the force needed to do work. By changing the direction of the force, it also changes the place a person has to stand to do the work. In the case of the flagpole, a person just has to stand on the ground rather than climbing to the top of the pole. Do pulleys also alter the amount of force needed or the distance over which the force must be applied, like other simple machines do? In the next few labs, we'll find out.

Unit 5- Work: Plane and Simple Machines

Work Lab #17: Fixed Pulleys- Which Way Did It Go?
- instructions

Notes:
- Keep the pulleys you make in this experiment. You'll need them again.
- This lab requires some preparation the day before.

Materials:
- Lab sheets, pencil
- A clothes hanger and a place to hang it from (in a closet with some space is fine. The hanger is what you'll use to hold your pulley up off the ground, so it should be the sort that is triangle-shaped and has a bar from which you can hang things. A wooden hanger is best, as the wire hangers tend to bend too easily.)
- Some easily bendable metal wire (about 12")
- Wire cutter
- A corrugated cardboard box or sheet (you need at least 1 square foot)
- Drawing/drafting compass (or 2 circular items to trace to make approximately 4- and 3-inch circles)
- Scissors or sharp craft knife (parents will need to cut the cardboard)
- 2+ short wooden dowels (about 3-4 inches) or lollipop sticks. You need at least 2 of these, more in case the kids get really interested in pulleys.
- String
- Glue (not a glue stick, as it isn't strong enough)
- Pencil or Phillips-head screwdriver (to punch a hole through the cardboard)
- 1-liter bottle of water or soda that has a top and a narrow neck around which you could tie a string or wrap a wire. It should have liquid in it so that it has a bit of weight.
- Spring scale
- Ruler or tape measure
- (If you don't want to make your own pulleys, you may be able to find some small pulleys at the hardware store. If you do purchase pulleys, you'll want at least 3 of them, and you won't need the cardboard, compass, scissors, dowels, or glue.)

Aloud: We know that pulleys can change the direction of the force needed to do work—to move something like a flag from one place to another, but it's a little harder to figure out whether a pulley can change the amount of force you need to do a certain job. Part of the difficulty is that pulleys can be used in a lot of different ways. They can be attached to something like a flagpole so that they don't move at all. These are called <u>fixed pulleys</u>. If the pulley is not attached to anything but the load, it's called a <u>moveable pulley</u>. And when you put lots of pulleys together, you have a <u>pulley block</u>. We're going to build all three of these types of pulley systems to see how they work.

Procedure:
Do ahead (at least the night before so the glue can dry):

1. You are going to construct two pulleys. You might want to make a couple of extras just in case students want to experiment with making blocks of pulleys. You'll need one of these for this experiment and the next. You'll need two for the third pulley experiment.

2. Use the drafting compass to draw the following circles on the cardboard: 4 large circles (about 4" diameter) and 2 small circles (about 3" diameter). Basically, for each pulley you want to make, you need 2 large circles and 1 smaller circle.

3. Cut the circles out. It's okay if they're not totally perfect.

4. Poke a hole through the center of each cardboard circle using the pencil or screwdriver. If you are working with your students, you might want to remind them that you are using a wedge to do this work. If you have

[continued]

Pandia Press

trouble figuring out where the center of the circle is, cut a piece of paper the same size as the circle. Fold it in half in a few different directions. Where the creases meet is the center of the circle.

5. You should now have 6 circles with holes in their centers.

6. Take one of the smaller circles and put a light layer of glue over both sides (front and back). Avoid gluing the hole you've made.

7. Sandwich the smaller circle between two larger circles, lining up the center holes as best you can. Repeat with the other circles and set aside to dry.

Lab Day:

1. Wrap some of the wire around the load (the bottle) in a way that allows you to lift the load by the wire. Shape the wire so that it makes a hook, like this:

2. Use your spring scale to determine how much force you need to lift the load without using any pulleys. Hook the scale under the wire on the load and lift slowly. When you hook things like this, you may need to bend the wire around to get it to hold on. Do whatever you need to do to lift the bottle by the wire.

    The reading on the scale is your control value—so you can see whether using a pulley is any different from not using a pulley. Record the reading on the spring scale on the Control section of the lab sheet.

3. Now, let's try lifting the load with a fixed pulley. Place a dowel or lollipop stick through the center of one of the pulleys you already made. The pulley should turn freely around the dowel.

4. Wrap wire around either end of the stick and loop it above the pulley to form a hook, like this: If the wire seems to be slipping off the stick, feel free to put some tape on to hold it. Prepare the second pulley the same way.

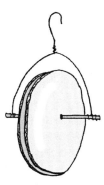

5. Hang the hanger somewhere where you have some room—a closet that's not too full, a hook on the wall, whatever will work.

[continued]

6. Hang the pulley on the hanger using the hook you made. You might wrap the hook all the way around the hanger so that it doesn't unbend when you pull on it. Place the load on the ground below.

7. Tie one end of a piece of string to the load. You can tie it to the hook you made, but it might be easier just to tie the string around the bottle for this experiment. Run the string through the groove of the pulley and down the other side. Leave a few extra feet of string. Now you have a fixed pulley attached to a load.

8. Sketch your fixed pulley setup on the lab sheet and fill in the HYPOTHESIS section of the lab sheet.

9. Make a loop in the string about 2 feet from the bottom of the pulley on the side not attached to the load. You just need a place to attach the spring scale.

10. Attach the hook on the spring scale to the loop you made.

11. Measure and record the distance from where the spring scale is attached to the string to the ground.

12. Now you're going to lift the load using the pulley. To do this, pull down on the spring scale. Remember to pull slowly because you're also measuring the force you're applying to the string. Also, pull straight down toward the ground. Pull steadily until the spring scale reaches the ground. Have someone measure about how high up the load has moved. Record your OBSERVATIONS and ANALYSIS AND CONCLUSIONS on the lab sheet.

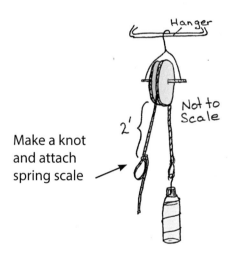

Possible Answers:

Observations: #1 & #3 should be about the same. #2 should be about the same as the value from the control. #4 up

Analysis and Conclusions: #1 about the same; #2 about the same; #3 changing the direction, does not.

Conclusion / Discussion:

1. Make sure that everyone understands that the only way in which a fixed pulley helps us to do work is by changing the direction of force applied. Can you think of any other uses for a fixed pulley? (Ideas include: raising a sail on a sail boat, getting supplies to a tree house, raising and lowering window blinds.)

[continued]

2. The force needed to lift the load with the pulley may have been slightly different than without the pulley. Can you think of reasons to account for this difference? You can discuss issues such as errors in measuring and friction between the pulley and the string. Can you think of ways you might get rid of these differences?

More Lab Fun:

1. Play around with the pulley and the load. Does it change the force needed if you pull at an angle rather than straight down on the string? Does it change the distance you need to pull?

2. Make a miniature flagpole of your own. Design a flag and attach it to the string. You'll need to solve some engineering problems such as: what do you do with the string when the flag is raised? How long should the string be so that you can still reach both ends when the flag is lowered? How can you get the flagpole to stand up straight? How can you attach a pulley to it?

Note to Parents and Teachers: This can be a little difficult to set up. Do whatever you need to get the pulley attached to the hanger so that it doesn't fall down when you lift the load.

Fixed Pulley- Which Way Did It Go?

Control: When I lift the load with just the spring scale, the spring scale reads: _____. This is how much force it takes to lift the load without using pulleys.

Experiment Setup:

Fixed Pulley

Hypothesis: I think it will take **much more** / **about the same** / **much less** force to lift the load using a fixed pulley.

Observations:

1. The distance from the point of effort (where the spring scale is attached) to the floor is: _____.

2. The force registered on the spring scale when I use the pulley to lift the load is: _____.

3. The distance that the load was lifted above the ground is: _____.

4. When I pulled down on the string, the load moved **up** / **down**.

Analysis and Conclusions:

1. Using the fixed pulley, the distance the string had to be pulled was **much more** / **about the same** / **much less** than the distance the load moved.

2. Using the fixed pulley, the force used to lift the load was **much more** / **about the same** / **much less** than the force needed to lift the load in the control portion of the experiment.

3. Therefore, a fixed pulley helps us do work by **changing the direction** / **changing the amount** of force needed to move an object. The fixed pulley **does** / **does not** change the distance over which effort needs to be applied to move a load.

Work Lab #18: Moveable Pulley- How Does It Do That?
- instructions

Materials:
- Lab sheets, pencil
- The pulley apparatus, hanger, string, and load you used in the previous experiment
- Spring scale
- Ruler or tape measure

Aloud: Pulleys are useful enough when they merely change the direction of a force applied. When you allow the pulley itself to move, though, it acts like an entirely different simple machine—one which I find almost magical. When you used a fixed pulley, the thing that was fixed—that was attached to something else so that it couldn't move—was the pulley itself. It was attached to the hanger. It could spin in circles, but it couldn't go anywhere. The string and the load could both move freely.

This time, instead of attaching the pulley to the hanger, we're going to attach the pulley to the load. Wherever the load goes, the pulley is going to go. And, wherever the pulley goes, the load will go. What do you think is going to happen when you make this moveable pulley? We're about to find out what this amazing device can do, and I think it will surprise you.

Procedure:

1. Once again, use your spring scale to determine how much force you need to lift the load without using any pulleys. This is your control value—so you can see whether using a pulley is any different from not using a pulley. It's always a good idea to repeat your control value when you start a new experiment to make sure nothing has changed. Record the reading on the spring scale on the CONTROL section of the lab sheet.

2. This time we're going to attach the pulley to the load. Hook the wire from the load around the wire from the pulley. You can wind the wires around each other so that they don't unbend. This is your moveable pulley + load. It should look like the picture to the right.

3. Tie one end of the string to the hanger. Place the load and pulley setup below the hanger on the floor. Take the other end of the string and thread it through the pulley. Fill in the HYPOTHESIS section of the lab sheet.

4. Now, let's try lifting the load with a moveable pulley. Grasp the loose string and pull it taut, without lifting the load yet. Notice how high your hand that's holding the string is. Now, lift your hand as straight up as possible a couple of feet, pulling the string. Do you see the load being lifted? Here's how it should look:

5. Have someone measure the distance your hand moved. Also measure the distance above the ground that the load moved. Record these observations. Sketch your moveable pulley setup on the lab sheet.

6. Repeat the experiment using the spring scale to measure the amount of force used. Make a loop in the string where you were holding it and attach the spring scale. Try again to lift the load with the moveable pulley, this time pulling slowly and steadily upward on the spring scale to register the force you're using. Record your result.

7. Complete the rest of the lab sheet.

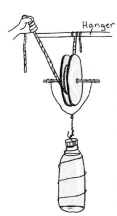

[continued]

Work Lab #18: Moveable Pulley- How Does It Do That?
- instructions page 2

Possible Answers:

Observations: #1-#4: Your arm should travel about twice as much as the load does. It should take about half as much force to move the load using the pulley. You need to pull upward to move the pulley upward.

Analysis and Conclusions: #1: about twice as much; #2: about half as much; #3: in the same direction as; #4: changing the amount; #5: does not.

Conclusion / Discussion:

1. Talk about how different the fixed pulley is from the moveable pulley. If you need help figuring out what to discuss, look at the notebooking idea below.

2. What might you use a moveable pulley for? Here's an idea if you can't think of any: How might you get a heavy load up to a tree house using a moveable pulley?

More Lab Fun:

1. Play around with the pulley and the load. Does it change the force needed if you pull at an angle rather than straight down on the string? Does it change the distance you need to pull?

2. Raise the load while observing what happens to the string. Why does your arm need to travel twice as far as the load?

3. Do you have a tree house or a swingset with a platform on it? If so, see if you can rig up a moveable pulley to deliver loads from the ground.

Notebooking Ideas:

Use a Venn Diagram page to show how fixed and moveable pulleys are different. Use one circle for fixed pulleys and the other for moveable pulleys. Put information where it belongs. You can use this list and/ or your own ideas:

- Changes the direction of the force applied
- Works in the same direction as the force
- Changes the force needed
- Doesn't change the force needed
- Uses one pulley
- Uses one string
- Helps to lift a load
- Does work

Note to Parents and Teachers: You should leave the pulley hooked to the load because you'll need it set up like this in the next experiment.

Moveable Pulley- How Does It Do That?

Control: When I lift the load with just the spring scale, the spring scale reads: _____. This is how much force it takes to lift the load without using pulleys.

Experiment Setup:

Moveable Pulley

Hypotheses:

1. I think I will have to **pull down** / **pull up** on the string to lift the load.

2. I think it will take **more** / **about the same** / **less** force to lift the load using a moveable pulley.

Observations:

1. The distance my arm moved while moving the string was:

   _____.

2. The distance the load moved was: _____.

3. The force registered on the spring scale when I used the pulley to lift the load is: _____.

4. To move the load upward, I had to pull **up** / **down**.

Analysis and Conclusions:

1. Using the moveable pulley, the distance the string had to be pulled was **about twice as much** / **about the same** / **about half as much** as the distance the load moved.

2. Using the moveable pulley, the force used to lift the load was **about twice as much** / **about the same** / **about half as much** as the force needed to lift the load in the control portion of the experiment.

3. Using the moveable pulley, the force I applied was **in the same direction as** / **in a different direction than** the direction in which the load moved.

4. Therefore, a movable pulley helps us do work by **changing the direction** / **changing the amount of force** needed to move an object.

5. The fixed pulley **does** / **does not** change the distance over which effort needs to be applied to move a load.

Work Lab #19: It's a Block! It's a Tackle! It's a Block & Tackle!
- instructions

Materials:
- Lab sheets, pencil
- The pulley apparatus, hanger, string, and load you used in the previous experiment, as well as the second pulley you made
- Spring scale
- Ruler or tape measure

Aloud: Fixed pulleys help us by changing the direction of the force applied. And moveable pulleys help us by changing the amount of force needed to move an object. Wouldn't it be wonderful if we could get both of these advantages with one pulley? Unfortunately, we can't. But don't let that get you down! We can get both of these advantages with two pulleys-one fixed and one moveable. When pulleys are combined this way, the entire pulley system is called a <u>compound pulley system</u>. It is also known as a <u>block and tackle</u>. Why is it called a block and tackle? Well, it has nothing to do with sports. It's because the group of pulleys used (you can keep adding pulleys so there are more than just two) is called a block. And the string or rope threaded through the block is called the tackle.

Can you guess who probably invented the block and tackle? It's a famous Greek scientist we've talked about before. His name starts with "A" and he once ran "naked" through the streets shouting "Eureka!" Have you figured it out yet? Let's see how his invention works.

Procedure:
1. Once again, use your spring scale to determine how much force you need to lift the load without using any pulleys and record your control value.

2. Take a moment to think about and discuss how you might arrange things so that there is one fixed pulley and one moveable pulley attached to the load. There are several ways to do it, and if the one I explain is different than yours, you should try both ideas to see how they work. Here's the setup we're going to try first.

3. Tie one end of the string to the hanger. A few inches along the bar of the hanger, attach the second pulley you made to the hanger. Place the load beneath them on the floor. Thread the free end of the string through the pulley attached to the load (the moveable pulley) and then through the pulley attached to the hanger (the fixed pulley).

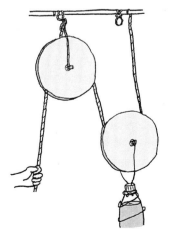

Look at this setup and sketch it on your lab sheet. Label the fixed pulley and the moveable pulley. Fill in the HYPOTHESIS section of the lab sheet.

[continued]

4. Let's try lifting the load. Grasp the loose string and pull it taut at about shoulder level, without lifting the load yet. Remember how high your hand that's holding the string is. Pull downward on the string, as straight down as possible for a couple of feet. Do you see the load being lifted?

5. Have someone measure the distance your hand moved. Also measure the distance above the ground that the load moved. Record these OBSERVATIONS.

6. Repeat the experiment using the spring scale to measure the amount of force used. Make a loop in the string where you were holding it and attach the spring scale. Try again to lift the load with the moveable pulley, this time pulling slowly and steadily down on the spring scale to register the force you're using. Record your result.

7. Complete the lab sheet.

Aloud: The fixed pulley and the moveable pulley combined give us exactly the advantage we would have expected. The fixed pulley changed the direction of the force we needed to apply. The moveable pulley changed the amount of force we needed to apply but increased the distance your arm had to pull. Is there a way to make these pulleys even better? The answer is a big "Yes!" By adding pulleys, you can keep decreasing the amount of force you need to move a load. Of course, you'll also keep increasing the distance over which you have to pull. If you're interested in how this works, take a look at the More Lab Fun section below.

Possible Answers:
Analysis and Conclusions: #1: about twice as much; #2: about half as much; #3: in a different direction than; #4: changing both the direction and the amount / does.

Conclusion / Discussion:
1. Make sure the students understand how this apparatus combines the advantages of the fixed pulley and the moveable pulley.

2. What might you use a block and tackle for? It is frequently used on large sailing vessels. Why might that be? Where else have you seen such a setup?

3. It was the block and tackle that was the final simple machine that supposedly helped Archimedes move a sailing ship over land. Use the story of Archimedes to review how all the simple machines—ramps, wedges, levers, wheels and axles, and pulleys—might have helped to accomplish this task. You can also draw a diagram of your ideas to put in your notebook.

More Lab Fun:
Make a few more pulleys: glue two of the pulleys together so that you have two grooved pulleys going around the same stick. Experiment with different setups to see if you can use even less force to lift the load. If you want some ideas, look up block and tackle setups online or at the library.

Notebooking ideas:
1. Look at #3 in the discussion section above. Draw a picture of an apparatus using lots of simple machines that Archimedes might have used to move King Hiero's ship. I imagine that you can think of ways he might have used ramps, wedges, levers, some wheels and axles, and some pulleys.

2. As you travel around, look for pulley setups and jot them down in your notebook. Construction sites, playgrounds, window blinds—all are good places to look. See if you can identify which types of pulleys are being used and write down why you think a particular type is being used for a particular job.

It's a Block! It's a Tackle! It's a Block & Tackle!

Control: When I lift the load with just the spring scale, the spring scale reads: _____. This is how much force it takes to lift the load without using pulleys.

Experiment Setup:

Compound Pulley

Hypotheses:

1. I think I will have to pull **down** / **up** on the string to lift the load.
2. I think it will take **more** / **about the same** / **less** force to lift the load using this setup.

Observations:

1. The distance my arm moved while moving the string was:

   _____.

2. The distance the load moved was: _____.
3. The force registered on the spring scale when I use the pulley to lift the load is: _____.
4. To move the load upward, I had to pull **up** / **down**.

Analysis and Conclusions:

1. Using this compound pulley, the distance the string had to be pulled was **about twice as much / about the same / about half as much** as the distance the load moved.

2. Using this compound pulley, the force used to lift the load was **about twice as much / about the same / about half as much** as the force needed to lift the load in the control portion of the experiment.

3. Using this compound pulley, the force I applied was **in the same direction as/ in a different direction than** the direction in which the load moved.

4. Therefore, this compound pulley helps us do work by **changing the direction / changing the amount / changing both the direction and the amount** of force needed to move an object. The fixed pulley **does / does not** change the distance over which effort needs to be applied to move a load.

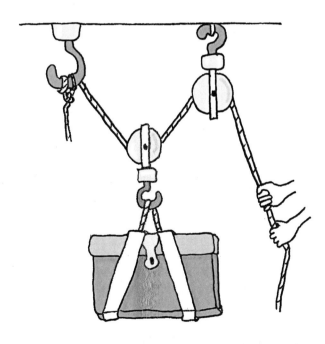

NAME _____   DATE _____

For my notebook

Simple Machines: They're Simply Fantastic!

You've learned a lot about many types of simple machines. When there's so much to remember, I find it helpful to write a summary of what I've learned. That's what I did for all the simple machines. Here's my summary. You can use mine or create your own in your notebook.

1. **Inclined Plane**

    Made of: A flat board on a slant

    Good Stuff: Changes the amount of force to get an object off the ground

    Bad Stuff: You have to push or pull over a longer distance

2. **Wedge**

    Made of: An inclined plane that moves

    Good Stuff: Changes the direction of force applied

    Bad Stuff: There is none!

3. **Screw**

    Made of: A wedge wrapped around a cylinder

    Good Stuff: Changes the direction and the amount of force applied

    Bad Stuff: You have to turn the screw over a longer distance

4. **Lever**

    Made of: A stiff board that turns around a point called a fulcrum

    Good Stuff: Changes the direction and the amount of force applied, depending on what class of lever you are using

    Bad Stuff: You have to push or pull over a longer distance

5. **Wheel and Axle**

Made of: A stick attached to a wheel through the center of the wheel

Good Stuff: Changes the direction of force applied. Can increase amount of force if the wheel is pushed; can decrease amount of force but increase speed if axle is pushed

Bad Stuff: You have to turn the wheel over a longer distance. You have to use more force to push the axle

6. **Pulley**

Made of: A wheel with a groove in it

Good Stuff: Changes the direction and/or amount of force applied, depending on the setup

Bad Stuff: If the pulley changes the amount of force applied, you need to pull over a longer distance

Unit 6

The Invisible World of Air

Unit 6- The Invisible World of Air

For my notebook

An Introduction to the Invisible

You've spent a lot of time learning about force and work and Newton's laws and simple machines. All of these are very tangible subjects: they involve things you can touch, step on, push and pull. Physics is really cool, though, because it deals not only with tangible things, but also with parts of our world that we can't even see—things that are invisible or too small to see with our eyes.

We're about to learn about one of these invisible realms. Let's see if you can guess what it is if I give you a few hints. Right now, this invisible thing is all around you. It is touching you, pushing on you from every direction and going in and out of your body! Don't get scared if this sounds mysterious, because it really isn't. Can you guess what it is?

The answer is <u>air</u>. Do you remember that one of the most important skills for a scientist is the ability to observe the world? Let's try that. Look closely at the air in the room. What? You can't see it? Well, try to smell it or taste it then. That's not working? Can you hear it? No? So answer me this: How do you know it's there?

A lot of our experiments so far have involved looking at things—watching how different forces affect objects. But we can't look directly at air, so how do we know it exists? How do we study it? Take a minute to talk about these questions.

There are a lot of different ways to study air, but most of them involve observing how air affects the world around it. We can study things like how much air weighs, how it changes when we heat it up and cool it down, and how it affects objects (like us!) that move through it.

We can study all of these behaviors of air because air is, in fact, made of something. It has mass, even though we can't see it. Air is made of tiny particles called <u>molecules</u>. As in any <u>gas</u>*, the particles in air move around all the time, bumping into each other, bumping into objects, speeding up and slowing down in response to the world around them. If we could watch air molecules in action, they'd behave a lot like marbles in a box which is being shaken, following Newton's laws by continuing in one direction until they bounce off of another marble or a solid object like the walls of the box.

All gases, including air, fill up any space into which they are placed. You can put a little air into a large space and all the molecules will spread out. Or, you can put a lot of air into a small space—like a balloon—and all the air molecules will be rushing around, literally bouncing off the walls of the balloon. It is this bouncing that causes the surface of the balloon to feel harder and harder to push inward as we blow up the balloon.

We can discover an awful lot about these air molecules even though we can't see them. Let's find out how scientists learn about a substance we can't even see.

*__Note to Parents and Teachers:__ If your students haven't yet studied the states of matter (solid, liquid, and gas), you might want to get a book from the library to introduce these ideas. You could also simply observe water in all three states—as ice, as liquid, and as steam.

Air Lab #1: It Can't Be Nothing if It Weighs Something - instructions

Materials:
- Lab sheets, pencil
- 2 balloons of the same size and shape, not yet inflated
- Short piece of string (about two feet)
- 2 rubber bands that are the same size
- Long straight stick such as a meter/yard stick

Aloud: Earlier, we learned that all matter has mass and takes up space. For matter to have mass, it has to be made of something—even if that something is tiny molecules that we can't see. If air has mass, then here on Earth gravity will pull downward on it, making something that is full of air heavier than the same object when it is not full of air. In this experiment, we're going to prove that that is just what happens.

Procedure:
1. Make a balance scale using the stick and the string. To do this, tie the string around the center of the stick. Lift the string off the ground to see if the stick balances (if it is parallel to the ground). Because of material irregularities, the exact middle of the stick may not be the place you need to place the string to get it to balance. Move the string around until the stick balances.

2. Next, we're going to prove that the two balloons which have nothing in them weigh about the same amount. Using the rubber bands, attach the uninflated balloons to the stick. Place one of the balloons one inch in from one end of the stick. Place the second balloon exactly the same amount in from the other end of the stick. Lift the string and the stick to see if it balances (it should…if it doesn't make adjustments until it does).

3. Sketch your setup in the space provided on the lab sheet and fill in the HYPOTHESIS section.

4. Remove one of the balloons from the stick, blow it up, and tie it off. Fasten it again to the stick, trying as best as you can to put it in exactly the same spot.

5. Lift the string and the stick and see what happens. Fill in the remainder of the lab sheet.

Possible Answers:
Observations: tilted toward the side with the inflated balloon
Analysis and Conclusions: #1: mass, gravity
                                   #2: mass, more
                                   #3: mass, matter

Conclusion / Discussion:
6. Review the idea that all matter has mass and takes up space. We just saw that air has mass. Did we observe anything that would suggest that air takes up space?

7. Talk about the idea of using a <u>control</u>—the balloon without air in it. How does having something to compare with the inflated balloon help make the experiment valid? Would the experiment be as valid if you used two different-shaped balloons? Two different-colored balloons? Why or why not?

[continued]

Air Lab #1: It Can't Be Nothing if It Weighs Something
- instructions page 2

More Lab Fun:
If you put regular clear tape on an inflated balloon (you just need a small piece of tape), you can poke the balloon with a pin without making the balloon pop. See if you can create a slow air leak in the balloon by placing tape on it and then slowly putting a pin through the tape. (This makes a great magic trick, too!) Remove the pin and attach the slowly leaking balloon to the balance. Watch what happens if you lift your balance as the air slowly leaves the balloon.

Notebooking ideas:
Pretend you've met someone who doesn't believe that air is really matter. Try to come up with some more ideas about how you might prove to her that air is all around us, even though we can't see it. Write down your list. You could even use some experiment pages to try out some of your ideas.

It Can't Be Nothing if It Weighs Something

Balance before inflating a balloon

Balance after inflating a balloon

Hypothesis:

I think if I repeat this balance experiment with one of the balloons inflated, the balance will **tilt toward the side with the empty balloon** / **stay balanced** / **tilt toward the side with the inflated balloon**.

Observation:

As I've shown in the drawing above, after inflating one balloon, the balance **tilted toward the side with the empty balloon** / **stayed balanced** / **tilted toward the side with the inflated balloon**.

Analysis and Conclusions:

1. All matter has **color** / **mass**. That means that all matter is made of something. Here on Earth, anything that has mass is pulled toward the center of the earth by **gravity** / **friction**.

2. When I added air to one of the balloons, it had more **mass** / **color**. This is why the balloon with the air had **more** / **less** weight.

3. I can conclude that air, even though it is invisible, has **mass** / **color**. Therefore, air is made of **nothing** / **matter**.

Air Lab #2: Is the Glass Half Empty or Half Full? - instructions

Materials:
- Lab sheets, pencil
- Glass cup—preferably a short one
- Something you can fill with water so that the cup can be entirely submersed, such as a kitchen sink, bathtub, or large plastic container
- Paper towels

Aloud: Here's a thought experiment: you're much older than you are now, and you're driving around at the store looking for a parking space. Every parking space in the lot has a car in it already. So, you decided that it would be nice just to share a parking space, and you drive your car right through a car that is already parked, so that both cars are in the same parking space. Everything is fine, right?

Well, not really. I'm guessing that there would be lots of bent and twisted metal if two cars tried to park in the same parking space at the same time. There's actually a rule in physics about this: two objects cannot occupy the same space at the same time, just like two cars cannot occupy the same parking space at the same time. This is true even of gases like air. We can compress gases—squeeze them into smaller and smaller spaces. But, air takes up space, just like all matter does. Can we prove this? Let's find out.

Procedure:

Experiment: Part I

1. Crumple up some paper towel and stuff it into the bottom of the glass. You want it just at the very bottom of the glass, and crumpled up enough that it stays there even when you turn the glass upside down.

2. Look at the glass as is and fill in the HYPOTHESIS section of the lab sheet.

3. Fill the basin or sink with water such that the water is an inch or two deeper than the height of the cup.

4. Hold the glass upside down over the water. Move the glass straight down into the water until it is resting on the bottom of the container or sink. You want to push quickly, but not so quickly that glass shatters! Hold it flush against the bottom of the container or sink.

5. Take a moment to look at the glass where it is. Can you tell if water is in it? Now, pull it back out, pulling quickly and straight up. Look at the paper towel inside. Is it dry or wet? [Parents and Teachers: it should be dry. If it isn't, you need to repeat the experiment, being very careful to push the glass straight into the water until it is flush with the bottom of the container or sink.]

6. Fill in the rest of the lab sheet.

Aloud: You've seen that water and air cannot occupy the same space at the same time. The water cannot get into the glass because there is air present, pushing the water out. But this fact gives rise to an apparent paradox—an idea that seems to contradict itself: If air and water cannot be in the same space at the same time, how in the world do we ever get water into a glass? As I'm sure you've seen hundreds of times in your life, you can fill a glass with water. Why? What happens to the air that was in the glass? Let's see if we can find out in the next part of this experiment.

[continued]

Air Lab #2: Is the Glass Half Empty or Half Full? - instructions page 2

Experiment: Part II

1. Dry off any parts of the glass that are wet. You are going to repeat the experiment; only this time, once the glass is under water, you are going to slowly lift up one side. What do you think will happen? Fill in the HYPOTHESIS section of the lab sheet.

2. Submerge the glass again, in just the same way you did in Part I of the experiment. Now, slowly lift one side of the glass and watch closely to see what happens. (You should see bubbles rising to the surface.) Keep lifting the glass until there are no more bubbles and pull it out of the water.

3. Fill in the remainder of the lab sheet.

Possible Answers:

Part I

Observations: #1: Answers will vary depending on what is observed.
#2: pretty dry / did not

Analysis and Conclusions: #1: cannot
#2: could not

Part II

Observations: #1: should observe bubbles rising and possibly water entering the cup
#2: soaking wet / did

Analysis and Conclusions: #1: could not
#2: air / air
#3: air

Conclusion / Discussion:

1. You should have all the clues you need to figure out what happens when you pour water into a glass. What happens to the air that was in the glass before the water was poured? Where does it go? (The air has room to escape the glass into the surrounding area, just like the air bubbles escaped from the glass. As you pour water, air is pushed out of the way.)

2. Can you explain why the air didn't escape in this way in the first part of the experiment?

3. We started by noting that two cars cannot occupy the same parking space simultaneously. Why is it possible for a car to pull into a parking space that's full of air?

More Lab Fun:

Try to repeat the experiment with different-sized and different-shaped glasses. See if you get different results. You could also try to submerge the cup into the water at an angle to see if that works. What if you put the cup in more slowly? More quickly? Try to explain your results given what you've just learned.

Notebooking idea:

On a blank page, draw a diagram and explain what's happening as you pour water into a cup. You might show the air molecules as little circles and show what happens to them before, during, and after the water is poured.

NAME _____ DATE _____

Is the Glass Half Empty or Half Full?

PART I

Hypotheses:

1. Other than having a crumpled-up paper towel in it, I think the glass is full of **air / water / nothing**.

2. If I were to hold this glass upside down and push it straight down into the water, I think it would be filled with **air / water / nothing**, and the paper towel would be **wet / dry**.

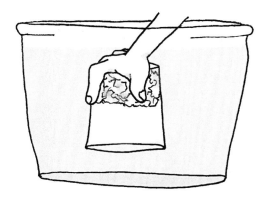

Observations:

1. When the glass was under water, I **could / could not** see whether it was filled with water. If I could see, it appeared that it **was / was not** filled with water.

2. After the glass was taken out of the water, I saw that the paper towel was **soaking wet / pretty dry**. This tells me that water **did / did not** fill up the entire glass.

Analysis and Conclusions:

1. I know that the glass had air in it before it was put into the water. I also know that two pieces of matter **can / cannot** be in the same space at the same time.

2. When the glass was pushed into the water, the air was still in the glass, so the water **could / could not** fill in that space.

PART II

Hypothesis:

When the cup is under water and lifted up just a little bit, I think the following will happen: _____

_____

_____.

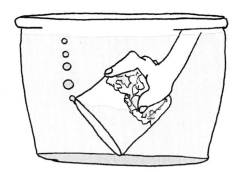

Observations:

1. When the cup was underwater and was lifted up a little bit, I saw:

_____

_____

_____.

2. After the glass was taken out of the water, I saw that the paper towel was **soaking wet** / **pretty dry**. This tells me that water **did** / **did not** fill up the entire glass.

Analysis and Conclusions:

1. As in the first part of the experiment, I know that when the glass was pushed into the water, the air was still in the glass, so the water **could** / **could not** fill the cup.

2. When I lifted the glass up a little bit, bubbles escaped. Because the only thing that was in the glass (other than the paper towel) was **water** / **air**, I can conclude that the bubbles must have been made of **water** / **air**.

3. To get into the cup, the water had to push the **air** / **water** out of the way.

NAME _____ DATE _____

For my notebook

If Hot Air Was a Superhero . . .

I like to imagine what different types of matter would be like if they were superheroes. That's strange, I know, but just go with it. Imagine water as a superhero—it could squeeze through any space, freeze, turn into steam. It would be pretty awesome. What about air? What might air be like if it was a superhero?

I suppose it would be able to squish into very small spaces by compressing all of its molecules. It would be invisible, which I imagine is very helpful to a superhero. But if air was a superhero, its true powers would only appear if we heated it up.

Do you remember what <u>molecules</u> are? A molecule is two or more atoms stuck together. Atoms and molecules make up everything in the universe including things you can't see, even gases such as air. Do you know what happens when the molecules in a gas are heated up? <u>Heat</u> is basically a form of <u>energy</u>. When you feel full of energy, what do you do? Do you sit perfectly still? No. Energy makes you want to move, to fidget, to kick, to jump and run. Energy does the same thing to molecules in a gas. When the molecules in air are heated up, they gain energy and start to move faster and faster. A fast air molecule can travel farther in the same amount of time as a slow air molecule. As the heated-up air molecules move faster and faster, they spread out as much as they can.

In an open space, as hot air molecules use their energy to speed up and move farther, there will be fewer and fewer air molecules hanging around in the area that was heated up. Fewer molecules mean less matter, and less matter means less mass. So, in an open space, hot air has less mass than the cooler air around it.

Pandia Press

Why is this important? Think about this: What happens when you put helium, a gas that is lighter than air, into a balloon? The balloon floats up. The same thing is true of hot air. Hot air rises upward because it has less mass and therefore weighs less than the air around it. In fact, this is how hot-air balloons work.

If air was a superhero, when it was heated up it would become faster and lighter. It could float up into the sky and have all sorts of adventures. In the real world, here on Earth, our weather is caused by air having such adventures—getting hotter, rising, getting cooler, falling, encountering water. From air's behavior in all these different situations, we get wind, storms, snow, clouds, and lots of other weather. Let's see if we can find some way to observe what happens when air molecules heat up and speed up in an experiment or two.

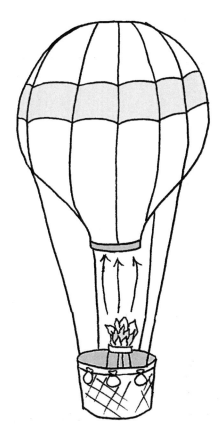

Air Lab #3: Hot Air Is Cool! - instructions

Materials:
- Lab sheets, pencil
- Empty plastic soda or water bottle (2-liter size works best), washed out and dried
- Several small balloons, roundish ones, not long ones (You only need 1 for the experiment, but I broke a few trying this myself.)
- Access to hot and cold water faucets
- Tape (optional)

Aloud: We've just learned that hot air molecules move quickly and spread out, taking up more room than cold air molecules. What do you think might happen if we were able to heat up and cool down the air inside a balloon? What would the air molecules do? How would that affect the balloon? Let's find out.

Procedure:
1. Before you blow up the balloon, try to loosen the neck (where you blow into) a little bit by stretching it a few times. You're going to need to fit this around the opening of the bottle.

2. Blow up the balloon until it's about ½ way filled.

3. Doing your best to keep the air inside the balloon, stretch the opening of the balloon over the opening of the bottle. It should be airtight (i.e., with no leaks), but if it isn't you can try taping around the area where air is escaping.

4. You should now have a bottle with a partly filled-up balloon attached to it. Fill in the HYPOTHESIS section of the lab sheet. In the "Before Experiment" box, sketch what the bottle and balloon look like before you change the temperature in the bottle.

5. Run hot water from the faucet. Be careful not to burn your hands. Hold the bottle under the water to heat up the air inside the bottle. Watch what happens to the balloon.

6. Run cold water from the faucet. Hold the bottle under the water to cool off the air inside the bottle. Observe what happens to the balloon.

7. Repeat step 5 again, just for fun. It's really amazing how much change there is when going from cold water to hot water.

8. Sketch what happened and complete the rest of the lab sheet.

Possible Answers:

Observations: #1: The balloon should get noticeably bigger. If it doesn't, continue to step 6 and then try step 5 again.
  #2: The balloon should get noticeably smaller.

Analysis and Conclusions: #1: stays the same
  #2: size
  #3: more / quickly

Conclusion / Discussion:
1. Make sure that everyone understands that the AMOUNT of air in the bottle and balloon stays the same throughout this experiment. What changes is how the air molecules are behaving. As the heat energizes them, the air molecules move more quickly, and they bounce around more and push the surface of the balloon outward.

[continued]

2. Could you use the device you've made to get an approximate measure of the temperature? What might you add to help use the bottle and balloon in this way?

More Lab Fun:

1. Put the bottle and balloon into the refrigerator for a while. Observe what happens. Then run it under hot water again. It's really quite a dramatic change.

2. Make a human model of how the air molecules were behaving. Get a few people together and draw a chalk circle outside or specify a space about the size of 3 of you lying down. Walk around slowly, bumping into each other. Then, pretend you've been energized by heat, like the air molecules. Move faster and faster. Do you naturally try to take up more space or run into the edges of the circle more frequently? This is what happened inside the balloon.

NAME _____ DATE _____

Hot Air Is Cool!

Hypotheses:

1. If I were to heat up the air in the bottle, I think the balloon would **get bigger** / **stay the same size** / **get smaller**.

2. If I were to cool off the air in the bottle, I think the balloon would **get bigger** / **stay the same size** / **get smaller**.

Observations:

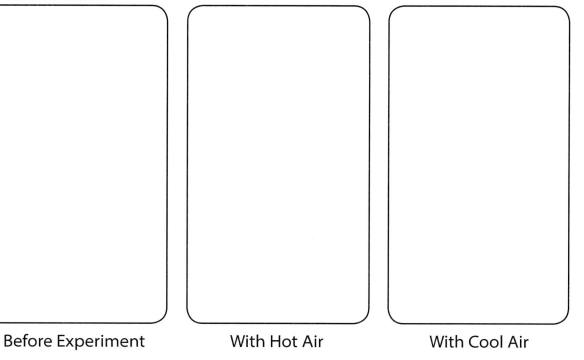

| Before Experiment | With Hot Air | With Cool Air |

1. When I heated up the air in the bottle, the balloon **got bigger** / **stayed the same size** / **got smaller** / **popped**.

2. When I cooled off the air in the bottle, the balloon **got bigger** / **stayed the same size** / **got smaller** / **popped**.

Analysis and Conclusions:

1. With the balloon sealed over the top of the bottle, the amount of air in the bottle **increases** / **stays the same** / **decreases** when I change the temperature of the air inside the bottle.

2. Therefore, the temperature of the air must change how the air affects the balloon's **size** / **color**.

3. I observed that the hot air took up **more** / **the same amount of** / **less** space than the cool air. Hot air takes up more space because its molecules are moving more **quickly** / **slowly**.

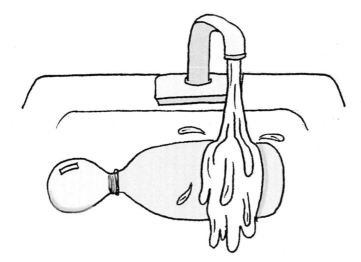

Air Lab #4: Taking Hot Air for a Spin - instructions

Materials:
- Lab sheets, pencil
- Colored pencils (optional)
- Piece of tape
- Short piece of string (about 6 inches)
- Scissors
- Access to a source of heat that doesn't involve blowing air (i.e., not a hair dryer or heating vent). If you haven't replaced your light bulbs with low-energy bulbs, a lamp will work. Otherwise, you could use a burner on the stove turned to about medium heat. Of course, an adult should be present.

Aloud: We've demonstrated that, given room, hot air <u>expands</u>: it fills a larger space than it did before it was heated. But can we also prove that because there is the same amount of air in a larger space—because the air is less dense—it rises? Of course we can.

Procedure:
1. Find the page with the spiral on it. You're going to make an <u>air current</u> detector out of it. An air current is just some air in which most of the molecules are moving in one direction, like wind. If you want a decorated air current detector, color in the spaces between the black lines with designs.

2. Cut away the parts of the page outside the spiral, so you have roughly a circle. Cut along the black line of the spiral, leaving one, continuous piece of spiraling paper.

3. Tape one end of the string to the center of the spiral. Hold the other end of the string and let the spiral drop down. Wait for it to come to rest (to stop spinning).

4. Fill in the HYPOTHESIS section of the lab sheet.

5. Go to a heat source. Hold the air current detector by the string a few inches above the heat source (you may have to hold it higher if you're using a stove-top burner). Watch what happens as the hot air interacts with the air current detector. If it doesn't spin, you might need a better source of heat.

6. Fill in the remainder of the lab sheet. (Note to Parents and Teachers: you may need to review what was learned about density before completing the analysis section of this lab. Focus on the idea that less mass in a larger space has less density than the same mass in a smaller space.)

Possible Answers:
#3: It should start to spin.
#4: does not
#5: does
#6: speed up / faster / more
#7: decreases
#8: floats
#9: rises

Conclusion / Discussion:
1. Review everything you know about how hot air behaves. The important points are:
   - Heat is a form of energy.
   - When air molecules are heated, they gain energy.
   - When air molecules gain energy, they start to move more quickly.

[continued]

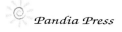

- When air molecules move more quickly, they take up more space (if there's room for them to do that).
- When air molecules take up more space, their density decreases, so they rise above the surrounding cooler air.

2. I mentioned that hot-air balloons use hot air rising. Can you think of other inventions that might make use of hot air? Use your imagination: there's even an artist that creates sculptures out of plastic garbage bags that inflate as hot air rises from the outdoor vents in New York! What ideas can you come up with?

More Lab Fun:

If you have a hot air vent (i.e., if it's winter and the heat is on), play around with your current detector. You can also see if you can make a hot air balloon using a plastic shopping bag—but this is quite a challenge.

Notebooking Ideas:

1. Use a definition page to define *air current.*

2. Draw a little cartoon air molecule. Show what happens to him (or her) as the air molecule is heated up, cooled down, and heated up again.

Taking Hot Air for a Spin

Spiral Cutout: If you wish, decorate by coloring the white spiral with designs. Then, cut around the whole spiral at the dotted line, so you have roughly a circle. Cut away the shaded parts along the black line of the spiral, leaving one, continuous piece of spiraling paper.

Unit 6- The Invisible World of Air

Hypotheses:

1. When standing still, the air current detector **spins / is relatively still**.

2. I think that if I heat up the air underneath the air current detector, the spiral will **spin / hold relatively still**.

Observation:

When I heated up the air underneath the air current detector, it **spun in circles / held relatively still**.

Analysis and Conclusions:

1. When the air in the room is all at about the same temperature, the air current detector **does / does not** move a lot.

2. When placed above a heat source, the air current detector **does / does not** move a lot.

3. This shows that, as the heat transfers energy to the air molecules, they **speed up / slow down**. As they move **faster / slower**, they need **more / less** room to move around.

4. When there are a certain number of air molecules in a particular space, and then those air molecules move faster trying to fill a bigger space, the density of the air **increases / decreases**.

5. When a less dense substance is put into a more dense substance, it **floats / sinks**.

6. Because of this, the hot air **rises / sinks** and causes the air current detector to spin.

COOL SCIENCE FACT!

In most substances, whether they are liquids, gases, or solids, heating up the substance makes the molecules inside move more quickly. You may have noticed that different substances heat up more quickly than others. The next time one of your parents can't get a glass jar with a metal lid open, suggest running the jar under hot water. The metal heats up more quickly than the glass; as its molecules move more quickly, it expands just a tiny bit, just enough to allow you to open the jar.

For my notebook

Standing Up Under Pressure

If you're near a window, take a moment to look up at the sky. It's awfully high up, the sky, isn't it? Have you ever heard the word <u>atmosphere</u>? The atmosphere is the space around the earth that is filled with air. When you look up, you're looking into the atmosphere.

Descriptions of how high up the atmosphere reaches vary because the air gets thinner and thinner (there are fewer air molecules) as you travel away from Earth's surface. For our purposes, we can say that the atmosphere extends about 70 miles above our heads. So, there are about 70 miles of air above you.

In an earlier experiment, we proved that air has mass, and therefore, on Earth, air has weight because it is pulled downward by gravity. Think about this fact: There is a column of air 70 miles high pushing down on you with all of its weight. How much weight is that? Assuming you have an average-sized head, there are more than 2000 pounds of air pushing down on you! Wow!

We call this weight—this force that air exerts by pushing on you—<u>air pressure</u>. How do people avoid being crushed by all this air pressure? You may not know it, but your body pushes outward with its own pressure, staying just about equal with the air pressure pushing inward. If air pressure weren't constantly pushing in on you, your body would push outward with so much force it would explode! This is one reason why astronauts

need entire space suits rather than just air masks—without <u>pressurized</u> space suits pushing in on them, they couldn't survive in space, where there is no atmosphere and no air pressure.

Here on Earth, air pressure causes all sorts of strange and interesting effects. Let's find out just how strong this air pressure really is.

Air Lab #5: Are You Stronger than a Piece of Paper?
- instructions

This lab and the next three make up "Under Pressure: A Quartet of Quick Experiments" that together demonstrate properties of air pressure. These four labs are short and sweet, and ideally all completed in a single lab day.

Materials:
- Lab sheet, pencil
- Sheet of paper, the bigger the better (a sheet of a newspaper would be perfect)
- Ruler—should be stiff plastic or wood
- Table surface

Aloud: Now you know that more than 2000 pounds of air pressure is pushing down on your head. An ordinary sheet of paper has more area exposed to air than the top of your head, so even more air is pushing down on it. I wonder how much difference that little bit of extra air pressure might make.

Under Pressure: A Quartet of Quick Experiments #1

Procedure:
1. Place the ruler so that it hangs off the edge of the table about 4 inches.

2. Using your hand, hit the edge of the ruler that's hanging off the edge of the table with moderate force. The ruler should go flying. That's okay, but be careful!

3. Complete CONTROL and HYPOTHESIS on the lab sheet.

4. Place the ruler in about the same position on the edge of the table as it was before. Place your sheet of paper over the ruler so that it reaches to a little less than the end of the table, like this:

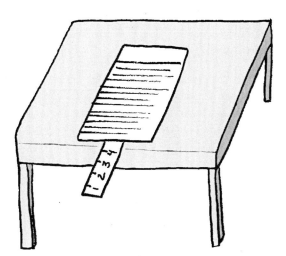

5. Repeat step #2. Did the same thing happen as when you did it the first time? Complete the lab sheet.

[continued]

Air Lab #5: Are You Stronger than a Piece of Paper?
- instructions page 2

Possible Answers:

Observation: should be, "much harder"

#1: a little

#2: larger, more

#3: air, harder

Conclusion / Discussion:

1. Talk about what would happen if, instead of hitting the ruler with a rapid downward motion, you slowly push down on the end of the ruler. Try this with and without the paper on top of the ruler. Why is it almost as easy to move the ruler in this way whether or not there is paper on top? [Hint: Think of where the air is pushing the whole time. As you lift the paper a tiny bit, air molecules rush in to fill the space underneath the paper.]

2. Why does the area on which the air is pushing matter? Imagine that the piece of paper has a column of air shaped like it is extending 70 miles above it. You can visualize how this would have more air pushing down on it than a column shaped like the top of your head.

More Lab Fun:

1. Here are some variations on the ruler experiment you might try:

    • What happens if you crumple the paper up into a tiny ball and place it on top of the ruler and then try to move the ruler? Why?
    • What happens if you move more quickly in moving the ruler? Less quickly? Why?
    • What happens if you use different-sized pieces of paper?

2. Why do you think we used a ruler? Experiment with some other objects to see if you can figure it out.

Notebooking ideas:

1. Sketch the experiment setup at the moment your hand is pushing on the ruler. Add in vectors (arrows) to show the forces acting at that moment.

2. Use a definition page to define *atmosphere* and *air pressure*.

Are You Stronger than a Piece of Paper?

Control:
When I hit a ruler that's laying partly on and partly off a table, the ruler **stays in place / falls to the ground / goes flying**.

Hypothesis:
I think that when I place a piece of paper on part of the ruler, it will be **much easier / about the same / much harder** to move the ruler.

Observation:
When I tried to hit the ruler with the piece of paper on it, it was **much easier / about the same / much harder** than without the paper to move the ruler.

Analysis and Conclusions:
1. The piece of paper weighs **a lot / a little**. Therefore, it isn't just the weight of the paper making it harder to move the ruler.

2. The surface of the paper is much **smaller / larger** than the surface of the ruler. Therefore, there is **more / less** air pressing down on the paper than was pressing down on just the ruler.

3. I think it was because of this extra weight from **friction / air** that the ruler was **harder / easier** to move when there was paper on top of it.

Unit 6- The Invisible World of Air

Air Lab #6: Differences Matter - instructions

Materials:
- Lab sheets, pencil
- Empty plastic water bottle with cap
- Access to a freezer

Aloud: In the last experiment, we discovered how strong the air pressure around us can be. Even though we can't see or feel the air pressure pushing down on us, we can observe its effects. Just adding a bit of air pressure on top of the paper (that was on top of the ruler) made a big difference in how hard it was to move the ruler.

In that experiment, we saw what happens when you add air pressure on top of an object. What do you think happens to an object, like a container, with a very different air pressure inside it than the world around it? For example, imagine a person in space with no space suit. There would be lots of pressure pushing outward against the person's skin because the human body is accustomed to a world in which there is lots of air pressure pushing in around it. But there is no air pressure in space. Scientists think a person could survive this situation! But only for a few minutes, and only if the person does not hold his breath. Take a moment to discuss why this is.

You may have figured out that the difference in air pressure between the astronaut's full lungs and the vacuum of space is huge. And since air pressure is a pretty strong force, if the astronaut tried to hold his breath, the air pushing out on his lungs would be too strong for him to survive.

Can we do an experiment to show how powerful differences in air pressure can be? Of course we can!

Under Pressure: A Quartet of Quick Experiments #2

Procedure:
1. Get the empty water bottle and seal the cap on it. Set it before the students. Discuss what forces are acting on the bottle, concentrating on the air pressure inside and outside of the bottle.

Aloud: Do you remember the term *equilibrium*? The bottle is in equilibrium because the forces acting on it all cancel each other out, so that the bottle remains where you put it. When we were studying gravity and forces, we thought about what would happen if we removed some of the forces acting on the bottle, such as the force of a table pushing up on the bottle's bottom. Another aspect of equilibrium is air pressure. The air pressure inside and outside of the bottle are close enough to each other that the bottle doesn't move. Can you think of a way to change the air pressure inside or outside of the bottle?

2. Fill in the CONTROL section of the lab sheet.

3. Place the bottle into the freezer for 30 minutes. You could complete the next 2 experiments while you're waiting. After 30 minutes, remove the bottle from the freezer and fill in the remainder of the lab sheet.

Possible Answers:
Control: #2: in equilibrium, in balance
    #3: quickly, increases
    #4: slow down / decrease
    #5: lower
Observation: squished

[continued]

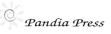

Analysis & Conclusion: #1: lower

#2: in

#3: A big difference

Conclusion / Discussion:

1. Make certain that everyone understands why a difference in air pressure exerts a net force on the bottle. It is because the forces on the bottle are no longer in equilibrium—the greater air pressure of the world outside the bottle pushes in on the lower air pressure inside the bottle.

2. Can you think of other situations in which differences in air pressure are important? Here's one of my favorites: When satellites are made, it is important that no dust or other contaminants interfere. So, satellite workers work in positive pressure environments, where the air inside the building is at a slightly higher pressure than the air outside. This prevents contaminants from floating into the building on air currents.

More Lab Fun:

1. Watch the bottle as it returns to room temperature. What happens to it?

2. Does filling the bottle about a third of the way with water change the results of the experiment? Why or why not?

3. Try the same experiment with an inflated balloon. What do you predict will happen? What does happen?

Notebooking Idea:

Invent something that uses differences in air pressure to accomplish some task. Sketch your invention in your notebook.

Differences Matter

Control:

1. Sketch the bottle and show what forces are acting on it, concentrating on the effects of the air inside and outside of the bottle.

2. This bottle is **in equilibrium** / **in motion** because the forces acting on it are out of balance / in balance.

3. We learned earlier that when air is heated up, the air molecules move more **slowly** / **quickly** and the air pressure pushing outward on an object like a balloon or bottle **increases** / **decreases**.

4. On the other hand, if the air inside an object is cooled off, we'd expect the air molecules to **speed up** / **slow down** and the air pressure to **increase** / **decrease**.

5. So, by cooling off the bottle, we can change the air pressure inside the bottle so that it is **lower** / **higher** than the air pressure around it.

Hypothesis:

I think that when I place the bottle in the freezer for a while, the bottle will **get smaller by being squished from air pressure outside it / remain the same / get larger or explode because of the air pressure pushing out on it**.

Observation:

When I removed the bottle from the freezer it was **exploded / the same as before / squished / larger**.

Analysis and Conclusions:

1. The air pressure in the bottle after it was cooled was **higher / lower** than before it was cooled.

2. Therefore, the outside air pressure pushed **in / out** on the sides of the bottle and caused it to change its shape.

3. When there's a difference in air pressure between the inside and outside of an object, there is a **big difference / almost no difference** in the forces acting on the object.

Air Lab #7: The Magic of Pressure - instructions

Materials:
- Lab sheet, pencil
- Glass, filled about ¼ with water
- Index card large enough to fit over the mouth of the glass
- Sink or basin

Aloud: We've made a lot of observations that show how air pressure behaves. We know that it pushes down on everything with considerable force, that it increases with heat, and that differences in air pressure can have a dramatic effect. But air pressure isn't just a force pushing down on us. Air pressure pushes in all directions. Take a minute to think about and discuss why that is.

Remember that air is made of tiny particles called *molecules*. The molecules don't just hold still. They're moving around constantly, bumping into walls, into people, into everything. It is this bumping that pushes out the walls of a balloon, for instance. So, if air molecules are bumping into the floor, they must then travel upward and bump into things. And, if air molecules are bumping into walls, then they must rebound off the walls and travel in a different direction. The air molecules traveling in all different directions exert pressure in all different directions as they bounce off of us and off of other objects.

Let's see if we can prove that air pressure not only exerts a downward force, but also exerts an upward force.

Under Pressure: A Quartet of Quick Experiments #3

Procedure:
1. Make sure the glass is filled part way with water. You'll want to conduct this experiment over a sink or basin.

2. Hold the glass over the sink. Talk about what will happen if you turn the glass upside down. It should be pretty obvious! Turn the glass upside down and fill in the CONTROL and HYPOTHESIS sections of the lab sheet.

Aloud: It must have seemed kind of silly to fill in a lab sheet about what happens if you tip a glass with water in it upside down. Everyone knows that water will spill out. But, in science, it is extremely important to have a <u>control</u>—a situation very much like the experiment itself with one difference that you're interested in observing. This way, you know that any differences are because of the one thing that's different. So, even when something seems obvious, scientists still conduct tests to ensure that their observations are valid.

3. Refill the glass with about the same amount of water. Place the card over the top of the glass and make sure that it is flush with the rim of the glass. Place one hand over the card to hold it in place. Turn the glass upside down, but don't remove your hand from the card just yet. Take a moment to observe any changes.

4. Now, remove your hand from the index card. What happens?

5. Complete the remainder of the lab sheet.

[continued]

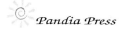

Possible Answers:

Control: pours out

Observations: #1: rested against the index card

#2: stayed where it was / stayed on the glass

Analysis and Conclusions: #1: every direction

#2: gravity

#3: air pressure / gravity

Conclusion / Discussion:

If the air pressure on the card and water is greater than the force of gravity pulling the water downward, why does water ever spill out of the cup? Why does having the index card over the top of the glass make a difference? [Stumped? Think about the experiment we did with the paper and the ruler—the index card has a bit more area for the air pressure to work against. Also, it is a solid, so the water can't just flow around it as it does the air.]

More Lab Fun:

1. Is there a point at which the force of gravity becomes stronger than the force of air pressure? That is, if you add more water to the glass and try again, can you find the point at which the force of gravity acting on the greater mass of water causes the water to spill out? Give it a try. Would a larger index card keep more water in?

2. Some kids who have tried this experiment wonder (and so do I) if it works only because the card gets a bit wet and then kind of sticks onto the rim of the glass. This is a great question. Can you design an experiment to answer this question?

3. Get a bunch of marbles and place them into a shoe box. With the top off, keep shaking the box and observe how the marbles bounce off of each other and the walls of the box. This is pretty much how air molecules behave.

Notebooking ideas:

4. Draw a picture of the upside-down glass with water and the index card and use arrows to show the forces acting on the glass, water, and card.

5. Design an invention that makes use of the fact that air pressure acts in all directions.

NAME _____ DATE _____

The Magic of Pressure

Control:

When we turn the partly filled glass upside down over the sink, the water **pours out / stays in the glass**.

Hypothesis:

I think if I repeated this experiment and changed one thing—placing the index card over the top of the cup—when the cup is turned upside down, the water will **pour out of / stay in** the glass.

Observations:

1. When I turned the glass upside down and held onto the index card, the water **rested against the index card / stayed at the bottom of the glass / spilled out**.

2. When I removed my hand from the index card, the water **stayed where it was / spilled out of the glass**, and the index card **stayed on the glass / fell off**.

Analysis and Conclusions:

1. There is air pressure pushing in on the glass from **above / every direction / below**.

2. With the glass upside down, **gravity / air pressure** is pulling the water downward.

3. Because the index card stays in place and the water doesn't spill out, the force exerted on the water and card by **gravity / air pressure** must be stronger than the force of **gravity / air pressure**.

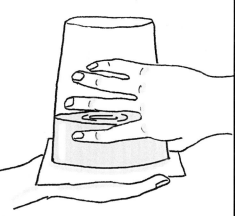

Unit 6- The Invisible World of Air

Air Lab #8: A Water Fountain That Defies Gravity! - instructions

Materials:
- Lab sheets, pencil
- An empty plastic water or soda bottle
- A straw
- Some water
- A sink or basin (There will be water spilling in this one!)
- A piece of children's clay or plasticine large enough to seal off the top of the bottle.*

* The clay needs to create a tight seal on the bottle with NO air leaking or the lab will not work. If you are unable to achieve a tight seal with the clay, try using an adhesive putty (e.g. Blu Tac), and/or cotton and super glue to seal up the bottle.

Aloud: You've discovered quite a bit about how air pressure affects the world around you. Here's a challenge: Imagine you have a bottle about ½ filled with water. You also have a straw, a piece of clay or putty, and, of course, yourself. Without tipping the bottle over, making any holes in the bottle, squeezing the bottle, or touching the water with the straw, can you figure out a way to get some water out of the bottle? Let's see if your idea is the same as mine.

Under Pressure: A Quartet of Quick Experiments #4

Procedure:
1. Fill the bottle ½ way with water. Place it on a flat surface that can get wet. Place the straw and clay near the bottle. (These are tools your students may use for their invention to get water out of the bottle.)

2. Let students ponder ways to get water out of the bottle (without actually trying them) applying what they have learned about air pressure. But remember: no tipping the bottle, squeezing it, or making holes in it. And the straw cannot touch the surface of the water.

3. Draw your best idea in the MY INVENTION portion of the lab sheet. Use vectors (arrows) to show what forces you think will be acting on the water, bottle, and straw.

4. Try your idea. Did it work? Fill in the OBSERVATIONS on the lab sheet. If your first idea and second idea didn't work, feel free to copy the lab sheet and try out more ideas.

5. When you've finished trying out your ideas, you can try one idea that I know works. Here's how: Place the clay or putty around the straw about ½ way down the straw. Place part of the straw into the bottle so that it's not touching the water and use the clay to seal the top of the bottle. Now, blow into the straw and quickly step away. What happens? Cool, huh?

6. Draw the setup of an idea that worked. Fill in the remainder of the lab sheet.

Possible Answers:
Observation: came out of the straw
Analysis and Conclusions: #1: increasing / increasing
#2: more / up

Conclusion / Discussion:
1. Talk about why increasing the amount of air in the bottle increases the air pressure within the bottle. (There are more air molecules bouncing off the sides of the bottle.) And this increase in air

[continued]

pressure forced the water molecules to move. The water molecules need to find another space to occupy, so they "climb" up the straw. Would the experiment work if you didn't use the clay or putty to seal off the top of the bottle? Why or why not?

2. You may find it difficult to get a complete seal around the straw. The experiment will not work if even the tinniest bit of air is leaking out. The trial and error that this lab requires is a good example of how science works. A lot of a scientist's job is figuring out how to set up an experiment that works and isolates the aspect of the situation the scientist is trying to learn about. In this case, creating a situation where air can only enter and leave through a single opening can be difficult. This can tell us a lot about air—the size of openings through which it can travel, for example—and about our materials. If you are unable to get a good seal using clay, try experimenting with different materials such as duck tape, or multiple materials such as clay + duck tape. If you still have no luck, try #4 in More Lab Fun.

3. Look up an invention called "Hero's Fountain" (also known as "Heron's Fountain"). This invention was made thousands of years ago by an amazing inventor in Alexandria. He also invented the world's first vending machine. His fountain seems like it continues working forever without any electricity or anyone blowing into anything, simply using air and water pressure. You can find many of his inventions online.

More Lab Fun:

1. There are instructions online for making Hero's Fountain. You'll need an adult's help, but it's not too hard and it's really quite amazing. Give it a try!

2. Does the fountain we made in the experiment work with any amount of water? Try it out with a bigger container like a gallon water or milk jug.

3. Does the fountain we made work better if you have more water in the bottle? Less? Give it a try and find out.

4. You can get a very dramatic fountain effect with a juice bag (the kind you need to poke a straw into). Squeeze out some of the excess air and then blow air into it through the provided straw. Juice will shoot out of the straw. Just be careful not to squeeze the bag while the experiment is happening so that you know the effect is more from air pressure than squeezing.

Notebooking ideas:

1. Heron made a number of inventions that used only containers, liquids, tubes (like straws), air pressure, and liquids. One of them kept a goblet full no matter how much liquid was removed! Can you design a really cool invention? Draw it out. You might even try to build it and see if you can get it to work.

2. Look up when Heron lived and add him to your timeline if you keep one. He also invented the first vending machine which dispensed "holy water" !

NAME _____ DATE _____

A Water Fountain That Defies Gravity!

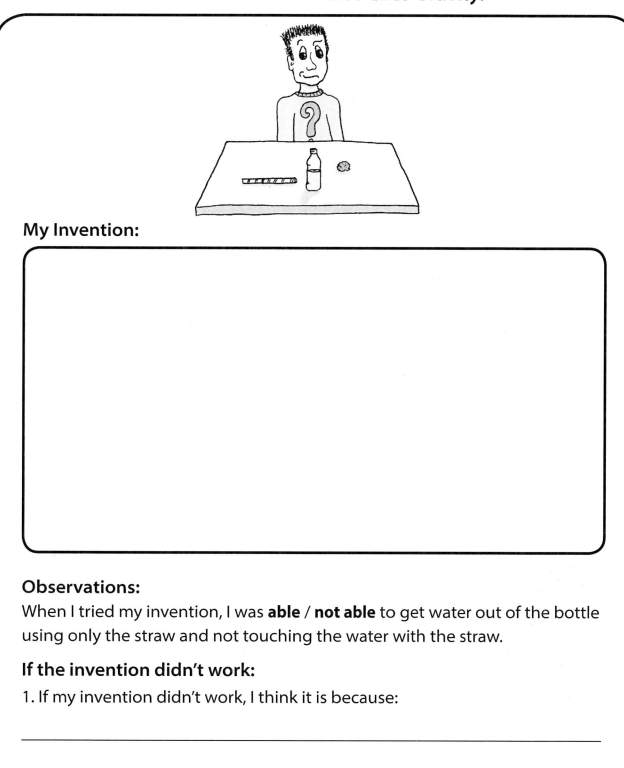

My Invention:

Observations:

When I tried my invention, I was **able / not able** to get water out of the bottle using only the straw and not touching the water with the straw.

If the invention didn't work:

1. If my invention didn't work, I think it is because:

_____

_____

_____.

2. I think I could fix this problem using the following invention:

An invention that worked:

Observation:

When I blew into the straw and moved away, the water **remained where it was** / **came out of the straw**.

Analysis and Conclusions:

1. This fountain works because when I blow into the straw, I'm **increasing** / **decreasing** the amount of air in the bottle. Since there is more air in a closed space, I must be **increasing** / **decreasing** the air pressure in the bottle.

2. With **more** / **less** air pressure pushing down on the water, the water has to go somewhere. So, it finds the only opening it can by flowing **up** / **down** the straw.

For my notebook

Air Forces without Uniforms

Just when I feel like I'm beginning to understand a lot about physics, I discover something that surprises and delights me. Have you ever heard the word "fluid"? If you have, you've probably always used it to mean a liquid, like water or juice. When it's extremely hot outside, we often hear that we should drink lots of fluids, which is good advice. However, as we've learned, physicists often define words a little differently than the rest of the world. For a physicist, a <u>fluid</u> is something which is <u>deformable</u>. That means that you can change its shape by applying pressure to it. For example, if you push on water, it moves and changes its shape. Water is a fluid. But if you push on your table, it doesn't change shape—at least, I hope it doesn't. Most <u>solids</u> are not fluids.

I thought the technical definition of fluid was quite delightful. Gases, like air, are fluids. Technically, some squishy objects, like clay, are a special type of fluid. What's so amazing about this is that objects moving through gases experience many of the same sorts of forces as objects moving through liquids.

The branch of physics that studies what happens when objects move through the air is called <u>aerodynamics</u>. "Aero" is from a word meaning *air*. "Dynamics" is from a word meaning *forces*.   Aerodynamics focuses on the four basic forces that objects, like airplanes or kites, experience when they move through the air: <u>weight</u>, <u>drag</u>, <u>thrust</u>, and <u>lift</u>. Weight and drag are the two forces that an object like an airplane has to work against to stay in the air. We already know what weight is: the force of gravity pulling down on an object. An airplane, for example, has weight, which we know is just the force of gravity trying to pull it downward. The airplane also experiences drag, the force caused by air molecules pushing against it as it moves through the air, just as friction pushes back against a moving object on the ground.

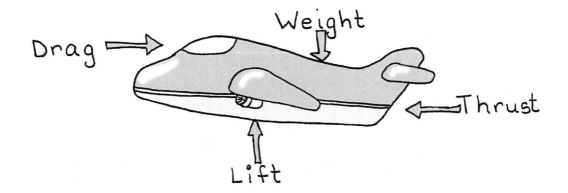

Drag and weight make it hard for an object to move through the air. Thrust and lift are the two forces that work to counteract drag and weight. Thrust is the force that pushes an object forward and can be caused by anything from a bird's wing to a jet engine. Lift is the force that tries to overcome the force of gravity and is caused by the shape of a flying object interacting with the air around it. Because of the shape of the airplane's wings, for example, the air moving over and under the wings creates differences in air pressure which raise the airplane off the ground. Our next experiments will help us understand how these four forces—weight, drag, thrust, and lift—interact.

Air Lab #9: Dropping Stuff Is a Drag - instructions

Materials:
- Lab sheets, pencils
- At least 5 pieces of copy or printer paper per student, all the same size and shape.
- A place from where you can drop paper, like the landing of a staircase or standing on a chair

Aloud: Do you remember the definition of *friction*? Take a moment to see if you can explain what friction is. Here's the official definition: Friction is a force that resists motion when two objects are in contact. In other words, if you push one object along another, like pushing a block across the floor, friction pushes back.

Drag is pretty much just friction where one of the "surfaces" is the air. Any time an object tries to move in one direction in the air, drag pushes back in the opposite direction. Because we can't see air, it's sometimes easier to think of how this works with water. When you try to move through the water, to swim or to walk, you can feel the force of the water resisting your movement. It can be hard to push all that water out of the way with your body. Because air and water are both fluids, they react to objects moving through them in similar ways. So just as your body has to push water out of the way to move through water, an object moving through air has to push air out of the way.

One of the primary ways we can change the amount of drag on an object is by changing its shape. Sometimes, like when we want to get a rocket ship to escape Earth's gravity or an airplane to fly, we try to <u>minimize</u> drag, making it as small as possible. At other times, when we want to slow down an object's movement through the air, like when we design parachutes or kites, we work to <u>maximize</u>, or increase, the drag on the object.

You probably remember Galileo's famous experiment that proved that if you drop two objects of different masses from a height, they will both hit the ground at the same time. Do you think this is true for any two objects? Well, it sort of is . . . Let's experiment and see.

Procedure:
1. Fill in the HYPOTHESIS section of the lab sheet.

2. Have two people stand up, each with a piece of paper. One person should hold the paper so that the short edge is parallel to the floor. The other should hold the paper at the same height, but flat, so that the paper's surface is parallel to the floor. Drop the papers at the same time (counting "one, two, three, go!" will help). Observe what happens. If the paper that was held with the short edge parallel to the floor flips over and drifts down, try again with a little more distance between the two people.

3. Fill in OBSERVATIONS and PRELIMINARY ANALYSIS AND CONCLUSIONS.

Aloud: We've seen that drag can significantly change how quickly an object falls. The more drag there is, the more force there is counteracting gravity to keep the object in the air. Drag can help keep an object in the air because drag is the force that resists movement through air—even if that movement is caused by gravity pulling the object downward. We're going to do some experiments to figure out what types of shapes increase and decrease drag.

[continued]

4. Using the pieces of paper, create five differently shaped objects made from paper. At least one of them should be a crumpled piece of paper. Each object should be made from exactly one piece of paper, but feel free to fold and deform the paper. Try to design shapes that you think will encounter very little drag (think of the shape of a rocket) and shapes that you think will encounter a lot of drag (think of parachutes).

5. Fill in the first two columns of the table. You should put the objects in order of what you think will be increasing drag. That is, you should put the object you think will drop most quickly at the top.

6. Time to drop things! Depending on how many people you have to drop papers and observe results, you might be able to drop all five at once to determine in what order they hit the ground. Probably, though, you'll need to compare them two at a time. Start with the object you think will fall the most quickly. Drop it at the same time as each of the others. Keep repeating the process until you have determined an ordering from the object with the least drag to the object with the most drag. Fill in the remainder of the table and the lab sheet.

Possible Answers:

Observations: #1: different speeds, #2: more slowly

Preliminary Analysis and Conclusions: #1: the same time; #2: different times; #3: downward, drag, upward; #4: greater

Predictions and Observations: #1: Answers on the table may vary. Usually, shapes that present a large surface in the direction of motion (downward) experience more drag (like a parachute, a flat piece of paper, etc.). #2 and #3: Answers may vary. Usually, shapes that present a small surface in the direction of motion (downward) experience less drag (like a rocket or airplane). Shapes that present a large surface in the direction of motion experience more drag (large flat shapes, parachutes).

Conclusion / Discussion:

1. Review Galileo's proposition that two objects subject to the same gravity fall at the same rate. What if the two pieces of paper were made of some heavy metal like lead, so that they had a lot of mass? Would the flat piece have fallen more slowly than the piece dropped edge downward? Why or why not? [It's a matter of the relative amount of upward and downward forces. There is a bit of drag on a flat piece of paper, but because paper is so light, the force of gravity on the paper is just a little bit more than the force of drag. With heavier objects, the increased mass means increased weight (gravity), to such an extent that the drag on the objects is very tiny, relative to their weight.]

2. An imprecise way of stating the results of Galileo's experiment is that any two objects dropped from a height will fall at the same rate, regardless of their mass. Now that you understand drag, how would you rephrase Galileo's results? (Hint: The shape of the objects must be taken into account.)

3. Talk about the shapes of various man-made objects that travel through the air. Do you think they are designed to maximize or minimize drag? Think about this question in terms of different car designs as well. Can you think of comparable shapes from nature, such as different birds or aquatic creatures?

[continued]

More Lab Fun:

1. Try taping some pieces of paper together and experimenting with drag. Does a larger piece of paper fall more quickly than a smaller piece? Why or why not? Does the answer depend on the shape and direction of the paper?

2. Use materials other than paper to conduct these experiments. Some fun things to try are: aluminum foil, plastic grocery bags, and plastic garbage bags. Make sure to clean up the pieces when you're finished!

3. If you have a group of students, divide up into teams. Give each team a few materials—some paper, a toilet paper role, some tape, a plastic garbage bag. Have the teams design a shape using all the materials that will minimize (or maximize) drag. Try to predict whose design will be the most effective.

Notebooking ideas:

1. Sketch man-made objects and organisms from nature that seem similar with respect to how they maximize or minimize drag.

2. Look at a picture of the International Space Station online. Sketch it in your notebook. Does it look like it would minimize drag? How about the space shuttle? Can you explain the difference?

3. Use a definition page to define *aerodynamic* and *drag*.

NAME _____ DATE _____

Dropping Stuff Is a Drag

Hypothesis:

If I drop two identical pieces of paper, one flat with respect to the ground and the other one edge down, I think the papers will **fall at the same speed, just like Galileo predicted / fall at different speeds**.

Observations:

1. When I dropped the two pieces of paper, they fell at **the same speed** / **different speeds**.

2. The paper that was held flat with respect to the floor fell **more quickly than / at the same speed as / more slowly than** the other piece of paper.

Preliminary Analysis and Conclusions:

1. Galileo predicted that when two objects are dropped from the same height, they will reach the ground at **the same time / different times**.

2. But, in this experiment, I dropped two objects at the same time and they reached the ground at **the same time / different times**.

3. This is because there is a force other than gravity acting on the papers. Gravity is pulling the papers **downward / upward** at the same rate, but **drag / inertia** is pushing the papers **downward / upward**.

4. Because gravity was equal for both pieces of paper, the force of drag on the paper that fell slowly must be **lesser / greater** than the drag on the paper that fell quickly.

Dropping Stuff Is a Drag - page 2

Predictions and Observations:

Relationship between Shape and Drag:

1. Fill in the table with objects in order of increasing drag. For example, the first row should be the object that you think will fall most quickly.

Objects in predicted order of increasing drag	Sketch or description of the shape of the paper	This object was actually the ___ quickest in falling
		1st 2nd 3rd 4th 5th
		1st 2nd 3rd 4th 5th
		1st 2nd 3rd 4th 5th
		1st 2nd 3rd 4th 5th
		1st 2nd 3rd 4th 5th

2. What sorts of shapes increase drag?

_____

_____

3. What sorts of shapes decrease drag?

_____

_____

Unit 6- The Invisible World of Air

For my notebook

How Do Planes Fly?

If you ask a pilot or someone who knows a little bit about physics that question, he might answer that airplanes fly because of <u>Bernoulli's principle</u>. In fact, when I took flying lessons, I also learned that Bernoulli's principle explained how airplane wings provide lift for an aircraft. In its shortest form, Bernoulli's principle is just an idea that a man named Bernoulli had about how the <u>velocity</u>, or speed, of a fluid is related to the fluid's pressure. If the fluid we're talking about is air, then Bernoulli's Principle means that there are fewer air molecules where the air is moving faster. And fewer air molecules in a given space means less air pressure, or force of the air pushing on object, in that space.

If you're anything like most physics students, you're probably wondering what in the world this has to do with lift and airplanes. If you look at the shape of an airplane wing, you can see that top of the wing is curved. Because of this, air has a bit farther to travel to get over the top of the wing than it does to get under the wing.

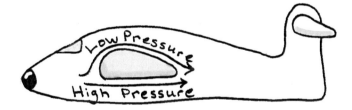

The air traveling over the top of the wing moves faster than the air underneath the wing. This means that when the plane is moving forward through the air, there is less air pressure on top of the wing than underneath the wing. If you think of air pressure as nothing more than a force providing a little push, we could restate the previous sentence as follows: When a plane is moving forward through the air, there is less force pushing down on top of the wing than pushing up from underneath the wing. Voila! There is extra force pushing up on the wing, and so the plane experiences lift. Let's see if we can demonstrate this principle in an experiment.

Air Lab #10: Hey, Bernoulli, Can You Give Me a Lift?
- instructions

Materials:
- Lab sheets, pencil
- Piece of paper
- Scissors
- Two empty soda cans

Procedure:

Section 1:

1. Cut a strip of paper about 1 inch wide from the top of the paper (so it's about 8 ½ x 1 inches).

2. Have the students hold the piece of paper close to their lower lip for a moment without blowing across it. Tell them to put the strip down for a moment.

3. Fill in the Section 1 INITIAL CONDITIONS AND HYPOTHESIS section of the lab sheet.

4. Have the students hold the paper by their lower lip again and blow hard across the top of the paper, observing what happens. They should be able adjust how hard they blow to get it to stick straight out by doing this.

5. Fill in the Section 1 OBSERVATIONS, ANALYSIS AND CONCLUSION sections of the lab sheet.

Section 2:

6. Get the two soda cans and place them on a smooth, nonsticky surface (a wood tabletop, a wood floor, etc.—not carpet or a tablecloth, though). Stand them next to each other about 1 inch apart.

7. Fill in the Section 2 HYPOTHESIS section of the lab sheet.

8. Have the students position themselves so they can blow between the two cans. Give it a try and observe what happens. The cans should move together. (Sometimes only one soda can will move depending on the angle. That's okay.)

9. Fill in the remainder of the lab sheet.

Possible Answers:

Section 1:
> Initial Conditions & Hypothesis: #1: bends downward; #2: Answers will vary.
> Observation: stuck out straight
> Analysis & Conclusion: : #1: a fluid's velocity and its pressure
> > #2: less
> > #3: faster, less
> > #4: stuck out straight

Section 2:
> Observation: moved toward each other
> Analysis & Conclusion: #1: air pressure, #2: lesser, moved toward each other

Conclusion / Discussion:

1. Make sure that students understand the following key concepts: 1) that air pressure is basically the force of air pushing on something; 2) that Bernoulli's principle describes a relationship between faster moving air and lower air pressure; and 3) that this principle can be used to explain lift on a curved airplane wing.

[continued]

2. Discuss what happens when a feather drifts to the ground. Is the feather's fall slowed by lift or drag? (Drag is the correct answer.) This example can help clarify the difference between why airplanes fly and parachutes waft gently to the ground (we hope).

3. Talk about how it is that birds can fly. From what do they derive their thrust? Their lift?

4. Are you convinced that Bernoulli's principle is a sufficient explanation for why planes fly? Why or why not?

More Lab Fun:

1. Get a hair dryer, a ping-pong ball, and a beach ball. Turn the temperature down on the hair dryer so no one gets burned. Point it upward and try to hold the balls one at a time above the stream of air. Let go. Do the balls stay suspended in the air? Can you adjust the angle of the air stream so that they do? Talk about why Bernoulli's principle explains what is happening.

2. You can also blow between and across inflated balloons to illustrate Bernoulli's principle. Try it!

Notebooking Ideas:

1. Bernoulli lived from 1700-1782 and was a mathematician. If you keep a timeline, you can put him on it!

2. Since Bernoulli lived so long ago, he wasn't really studying airplane wings, although that is the context in which most modern people think of him. He actually studied how fluids like air and water behave down here on the ground. Can you draw an invented apparatus that would demonstrate Bernoulli's principle using air pressure pushing on water? When you're finished, look up a real such invention, the Venturi meter.

NAME _____ DATE _____

Hey, Bernoulli, Can You Give Me a Lift?

SECTION 1
Initial Conditions and Hypotheses:

1. When I hold the strip of paper by my lower lip, it **sticks out straight / bends downward / bends upward**.

2. I think that when I blow across the top of the strip of paper, the paper will **stick out straight / bend downward / bend upward / disappear**.

Observation:

When I blew steadily across the top of the strip of paper, the paper **stuck out straight / disappeared / bent downward / bent upward**.

Analysis and Conclusion:

1. Bernoulli's principle describes the relationship between **airplanes and people / a fluid's velocity and its pressure / air and water**.

2. According to Bernoulli's principle, when air is moving faster, it has **more / less / the same** pressure as when air is moving slower.

3. When I blow across the top of the paper, the air above the paper strip's surface is moving **faster / slower / the same** speed as the air below the paper strip. So, according to Bernoulli's principle, there is **more / less / the same** air pressure than there is underneath the strip.

4. Because there is more force, or pressure, pushing up from the bottom of the paper than there is pushing down from the top of the paper, the strip of paper **stuck out straight / disappeared / bent downward / bent upward**.

SECTION 2
Hypotheses:

Before I knew anything about Bernoulli's principle, I would have thought that if I were to blow between two empty soda cans, the cans would **blow away from each other / move toward each other / topple over/ go flying**.

Now that I know about Bernoulli's principle, I think that if I cause air to move faster between the two soda cans, the soda cans will **blow away from each other / move toward each other / topple over/ go flying**.

Observation:

When I blew between the two soda cans, they **blew away from each other** / **moved toward each other** / **toppled over**/ **went flying**.

Analysis and Conclusions:

1. When I blew between the two soda cans, the faster-moving air between the cans caused a difference in **air pressure** / **air color** / **favorite soda flavors** between the two cans.

2. With the air moving faster between the cans, the pressure between the cans was **greater than** / **lesser than** / **the same as** the pressure on the other side of the cans. Because of this, the cans **blew away from each other** / **moved toward each other** / **toppled over**/ **went flying**.

Bernoulli's Principle, Illustrated: Use the following space to draw a picture of how Bernoulli's principle explains lift for an airplane's wing. You might draw long vectors (arrows) to illustrate faster air molecules, and draw short vectors to illustrate slower air molecules.

Air Lab #11: Take Off! - instructions

Materials:
- Lab sheets, pencil
- About 10 pieces of paper per student
- Scissors
- Tape measure
- Paper clips (optional)
- Stopwatch, watch with a second hand, or someone who can count out seconds
- A wide-open space for flying paper airplanes

Aloud: Every once in a while, you'll discover that something you once learned in science turns out not to be entirely true. This experience can be very surprising and disconcerting, but it is part of the progress of scientific knowledge, which is always becoming more and more detailed and refined. I have come to discover that many scientists no longer think that Bernoulli's principle completely explains the lift that an airplane experiences. One reason for this, which you might have thought of yourself if you've looked at lots of airplanes, is that airplanes with flat wings can fly. Without a curved wing to vary the speed of the air travelling over the top of the wing, Bernoulli's principle doesn't explain lift.

The understanding of lift that's developing combines Bernoulli's principle with Newton's laws. The science is quite complicated, but it's enough that you know that Bernoulli's principle, while still correct and helpful in explaining how planes fly, isn't the whole story. In fact, when trying to apply science to real-world situations, it can be quite difficult to grasp every single scientific principle at work. So, how do real-life inventors grapple with the wonderful complexity of physics in our world?

There's no right answer to that question. I think many inventors use a combination of an understanding of science and technology, some creativity, a lot of experimentation, and a sense of exploration and adventure. In our next experiment, that's just what you should do. Think about what you know about the forces that act on a plane—drag, lift, thrust, and weight—and design paper airplanes to fly high and far. I'll give you some starting pointers, but after that, it's up to you.

Procedure:
1. We're going to start by constructing two basic models of paper airplanes.

    a. Paper Airplane #1:

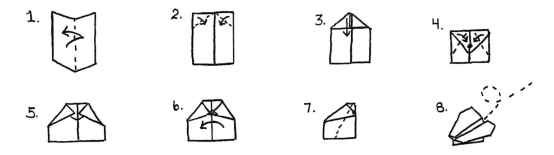

[continued]

b. Paper Airplane #2:

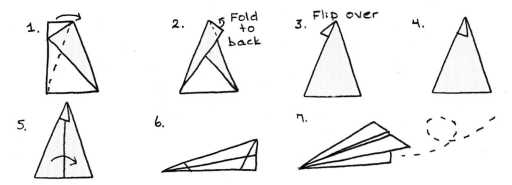

2. If you have some favorite paper airplane designs, go ahead and make one or two of them now. Try to choose designs or create your own that make sense given what you've learned about aerodynamic forces.

3. Make a simple sketch of your completed models on the lab sheet. Give each model a name so that you'll be able to refer to the models by the name later on. The second model described above is usually called a "modified dart," but you can call it anything you wish.

Examining Thrust:

Aloud: The first experiments we're going to do involve thrust. Think for a moment about what provides thrust to a paper airplane. What propels it forward? The answer, of course, is your arm. You can throw the plane with a lot of force or gently propel it on its way. Some airplane designs go farther when thrown gently, others when thrown forcefully.

4. Take each plane and stand on a spot you designate as the starting point. Have someone standing by to time how long the plane is aloft, either by counting or using a stopwatch. Throw the plane as hard as you can straight out. Measure how far it went and fill in the time aloft and distance on your lab sheet. Now, try throwing the same plane gently, again straight out. Repeat this process with the same plane, this timing aiming slightly upward, at about a 30-45 degree angle. Fill in all results on your lab sheet.

5. Repeat for each plane.

6. Examine the data you've collected so far. Can you draw any conclusions about the best airplane for distance? For time aloft? About what types of airplanes do better with more thrust or less thrust? Take a few minutes to talk about your conclusions, and then write them up in the space provided on the lab sheet. Try to refer to your data in writing up your conclusions.

The Effect of Flaps:

Aloud: You might think that airplane designers try to avoid causing drag in all situations, but drag can actually help several aspects of the aerodynamics of a plane. When an airplane lands, it often has to slow down quite quickly. You might remember that Newton's laws state that an object in motion will remain in motion unless something interferes with that motion, and that an object's tendency to stay in motion, its momentum, increases with both mass and velocity. An airplane has a lot of mass and a lot of velocity, so it is a very difficult object to slow down. Airplanes use flaps, parts of the wings that can bend down and cause increased drag, to help them slow down. Airplanes also use flaps to steer and to stabilize the airplane. Our next experiments will investigate the use of flaps on paper airplanes.

[continued]

7. On each of your airplanes, cut out two flaps—one on each wing.

8. We're going to use the results of the thrust experiments to decide how to throw each plane—gently or forcefully and at what angle. You have probably noticed that some plane designs are really good at travelling far distances while others excel at staying aloft. For each plane design, look at your data and decide how to throw the plane—you can decide whether you want to maximize the plane's ability to go far or to stay in the air for a long time. Write this information in the appropriate spot in the FLAP INVESTIGATION TABLE.

9. Now, fly some planes. You'll need to fly each plane three times, once with both flaps up, once with both flaps down, and once with the left-most flap up and the right-most flap down. As you do so, make observations and fill in the table on the lab sheet.

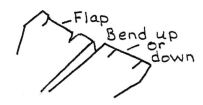

10. When you are finished filling in the table, take a few minutes to look at the data you collected and analyze it. See if you can find any patterns. When you put the left flap up on each plane, is there anything in common about how the planes behave? Are there any other patterns you notice?

11. Write your conclusions down in the space provided.

Optional Investigations:

12. If students are interested in pursuing this subject further, another factor to experiment with is the weight of the plane and where the weight is located. Use paper clips to increase the weight on the rear of the plane. Then try the nose of the plane. Try the wings as well. Are there any cases in which increased weight helps the plane to fly farther? Stay in the air longer?

Possible Answers:
Answers for these investigations will vary.

Conclusion / Discussion:

1. Usually, longer and skinnier planes like the dart fly farther, and planes with larger, wider wings stay aloft longer. Discuss why this would be true in light of how drag and lift work. Is this what happened with your planes? Why or why not, do you think?

2. Why do you think flaps affected the planes the way they did? If you are having trouble coming up with ideas, think about the fact that with a flap up or down, there will be increased drag on one side of the plane but not on the other side.

3. Talk about some man-made and natural airborne objects. Consider the shapes of jet planes, passenger planes, kites, birds that glide, predatory birds, maple leaf seeds, anything that flies through the air. Can you figure out how the shape of these objects relates to how they move through the air?

[continued]

More Lab Fun:

1. Now that you've figured out some principles of paper airplane design, work on designing some of your own. Use a similar strategy as we did in this lab to refine your design, testing throwing angle, amount of thrust, best flap position, etc.

2. Try to design a parachute for a small toy. The toy should be a little bit heavy. You can use a plastic grocery bag to make the parachute itself, and you may need to add some string to tie it to the toy. Is a circular parachute better than a rectangular parachute? Is bigger better than smaller? What can you figure out?

3. There are about a million paper airplane designs. Look some up in the library or on the Internet with an adult and try them out. You might try looking for the winners of various paper airplane contests.

Notebooking ideas:

1. In 2008, some Japanese scientists developed a paper airplane that could be dropped from the space shuttle! The goal was to make it able to glide down to Earth without burning up in the atmosphere. Their design had to strike a delicate balance between enough drag to keep the plane from plummeting to the earth and too much friction with the air that would heat up the plane. Try your hand at designing a plane that could make this trip. Draw a picture and write about what the difficulties would be.

2. As you come across different paper airplanes that work well, jot down the instructions for making them. Keep a log of which ones fly farthest, highest, or stay aloft the longest.

3. Write down the four aerodynamic forces: *drag*, *lift*, *thrust*, and *weight*. Record their definitions and applications in physics on a definition page.

Take Off!

My Paper Airplane Models: (You don't need to make 8, but you can if you want!)

_____
(name)

_____

_____   _____

_____   _____

_____   _____

Thrust Experiments:

| Plane's name | Plane thrown straight out | | | | Plane thrown at an upward angle | | | |
| | Lots of Thrust | | Gentle Thrust | | Lots of Thrust | | Gentle Thrust | |
	Time Aloft	Distance	Time Aloft	Distance	Time Aloft	Distance	Time Aloft	Distance

Conclusion: After examining different airplanes with different amounts of thrust, I have concluded:

_____

_____

_____

_____

_____

_____

_____

_____ .

Flap Investigation Experiments:

Plane's Name	Best Throw Method	Flaps Up			Flaps Down			One Flap Up, One Down		
		Time Aloft	Distance	Direction	Time Aloft	Distance	Direction	Time Aloft	Distance	Direction
	Gentle/ Forceful Angled/ Straight									
	Gentle/ Forceful Angled/ Straight									
	Gentle/ Forceful Angled/ Straight									
	Gentle/ Forceful Angled/ Straight									
	Gentle/ Forceful Angled/ Straight									
	Gentle/ Forceful Angled/ Straight									
	Gentle/ Forceful Angled/ Straight									
	Gentle/ Forceful Angled/ Straight									

Conclusion: After examining different flap positions, I have concluded:

_____

_____

_____

_____

_____.

Optional Investigations: You can fill in this table with whatever characteristics you'd like to investigate.

Plane's Name							

Conclusion:

_____

_____

_____

_____

_____ .

Unit 7

Waves and Sound

NAME _____ DATE _____

For my notebook

Let's Catch a Wave, Dude!

Have you ever watched someone surfing? I once lived by the ocean, and though I was afraid to try it for myself, I loved watching other people surfing. One thing that impressed me is how strong waves can be—they not only crash onto shore with great force, but they have enough energy to push a person standing on a surfboard amazingly fast. Even if you haven't had a chance to watch someone surfing, you've probably seen waves, either in person or in a movie or on television. Did you ever wonder what a wave is?

Physicists have thought a great deal about waves because it turns out that waves can carry everything from sound to light. Of course, when physicists think about waves, they aren't just thinking about the waves you see in a large body of water. As you've probably guessed by now, physicists have their own special and precise definition of a <u>wave</u>. Here it is, and don't worry if doesn't make much sense to you yet. It will! A wave is energy carried from one location to another in the form of a distortion through some medium. Yikes! What does that mean?

When I come across a complicated definition like that I try to break it into smaller pieces and understand each little piece. Let's try that. First, a wave is energy. What is energy? Do you remember? Physicists say that energy is the capacity of a system to do work. Work, as you know, is just the moving of an object from one place to another using a force. So energy is basically whatever goes into moving an object from one place to another. You already know this, though: It takes more energy to push a heavy object than a light object, or more energy to move an object 20 miles than it takes to move it 1 foot.

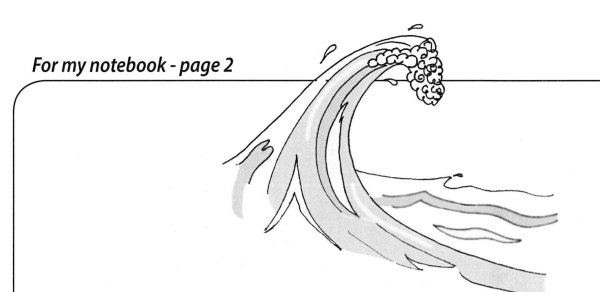

So a wave is energy carried from one location to another in the form of a <u>distortion</u>. Hmmm. What is a distortion? It's merely a fancy word for a change caused by a force. If you push in on clay and the clay's shape changes, you've caused a distortion in the clay. When a wave moves through water, it causes a distortion in the water.

We've almost understood the whole definition of a wave! A wave is energy that moves from one place to another by changing the shape of some <u>medium</u>. In this context, medium just means some substance—some form of matter—that a wave travels through. For waves in the ocean, the medium is water.

Now we've understood all the parts of the definition a wave: A wave is energy that moves through some substance by changing the substance's shape. It's not so complicated when we break it down. But, there is still plenty to learn about waves, as we'll see in our next experiments.

Sound and Waves Lab #1: Doing the Wave - instructions

Materials:
- Lab sheets, pencil
- Either a Slinky (the metal kind) or a long string of the inexpensive Mardi Gras-type beads. In a pinch, a long heavy-ish piece of rope will do. Whatever you choose will be the "medium" for your waves.
- A large, hard space so you can stretch the Slinky or string of beads out and make waves.

Aloud: When you're watching waves in the ocean, you might say things like, "Look at that really tall wave!" or "Look inside the curved top part of that wave. There's a sea otter surfing!" or "Those waves are coming into shore really close together." These kinds of descriptions are fine for most people. But, as you've discovered, physicists like to be more precise than most people when discussing scientific concepts. In order to talk intelligently and precisely about waves, physicists use different words to identify the parts of waves and how waves behave. In this experiment, we'll learn some of the names for the parts of a wave and we'll make some of our own observations about waves.

Procedure:
1. Find a nice large space. You're going to want to be able to stretch out the Slinky or the rope or string of beads. Whatever you're using is the "medium" for the waves to travel through.

2. One person should hold one end of the "medium." The other person should take the other end and walk far enough away so that there is just a little bit of slackness to the medium.

3. Start by letting one person make the waves. Sit down so your medium is resting on the floor. One person should move his or her arm back and forth slowly. Observe how the waves move along the length of the medium. Let the other person try. Play around for a while and just observe what's happening to the waves. Experiment with how fast your arm moves back and forth. Try to see if there's a difference if your arm moves back and forth over a greater distance versus over a little distance. When you've had a little time to play around with the waves, fill in the lab sheet. You may need to go back and forth between the lab sheet and making the waves to answer some of the questions.

Possible Answers:
#1: waves
#2: work
#3: energy, energy
#4: distortion
#5: medium
#6: energy, medium, distortion
#8: closer together
#9: taller
#10: moves back and forth a little as the wave passes through

Conclusion / Discussion:
1. Talk about the different characteristics of the waves you made. What types of things changed the shape of the waves? (Different arm movements, different speeds of moving the end of the rope, etc.) Can you think of ways to quantify, or measure, the different characteristics of the waves you made?

[continued]

Sound and Waves Lab #1: Doing the Wave
- instructions page 2

2. Make sure students understand that it is energy moving through the rope or Slinky. The rope itself doesn't move from one end of itself to the other—just the energy. Try to analogize this to waves in the water (we'll talk more about this in the next section as well).

More Lab Fun:

1. Interesting things happen when waves crash into each other (or objects that are in the way). Experiment with what happens if someone at each end of the rope creates a wave and those waves crash into each other. This is called wave interference.

2. You can make waves by holding the rope or Slinky in the air as well. Experiment for a while with different ways to move the ends of the rope while holding both ends off the ground. You can make the rope make three-dimensional figure eights and lots of other interesting shapes. This works especially well with strings of beads like those used on Christmas trees.

Notebooking ideas:

1. Use a definition page to define *waves*, *crest*, and *trough*.

2. Draw a picture of waves in the ocean coming into shore. Label the crest and the trough of these natural waves.

NAME _____ DATE _____

Doing the Wave

The Definition of a Wave:

1. When I moved my arm back and forth, **waves / fairies / gravity** traveled along the rope or Slinky.

2. In physics, using a force to move an object like my arm (or the end of the string) back and forth is called doing **chores / work / calculations**.

3. To get my arm to move and do work like this, I use **gravity / sound waves / energy**. When I move the end of the rope or Slinky back and forth, I'm transferring this **gravity / sound wave / energy** to the rope or Slinky.

4. The energy moves through the rope by changing the shape of the rope. This is another way of saying that the energy moves through the rope as **a distortion / air pressure**.

5. The substance that the wave is moving through is called the **small / medium / large**.

6. So, I've just demonstrated all the parts of the definition of a wave. It is **energy / work** moving through a **small / medium / large** in the form of a **distortion / color change**.

Some Other Observations:

7. Here is a rough sketch of the waves moving through the rope or Slinky:

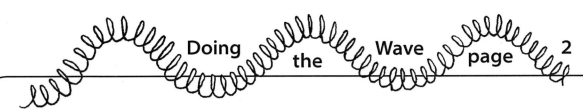

8. When I move the end of the rope back and forth really quickly, the waves look like they are **closer together / farther apart** than when I move the rope or Slinky back and forth more slowly.

A picture of the waves when I move one end of the rope or Slinky very quickly:

9. When I move my arm back and forth in very large movements, the waves seem to get **taller / shorter**.

A picture of the waves when I move one end of the rope or Slinky in large movements:

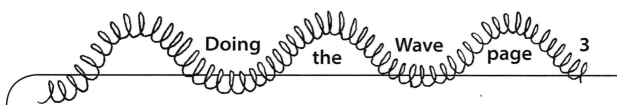

10. If I observe one spot on the rope as the waves travel along the rope, that spot **stays totally still / moves back and forth a little as the wave passes through / travels farther down the rope as the waves do**.

The Parts of a Wave:

Here is how a wave traveling through a medium is usually drawn. The wave shape shows where a spot on the rope or medium was at a given time. So, as time passes and you are making waves, if you watch one spot on the rope, it will go up and down over and over again, as this picture shows.

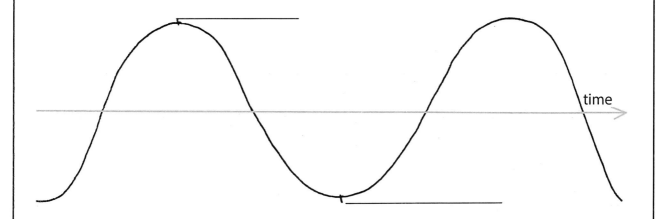

The **crest** of the wave is the very top of the wave. Label the crest of the wave on the drawing above.

The **trough** of the wave is the very bottom of the wave. Label the trough of the wave on the drawing above.

It's Sound. It's a Wave. It's a Sound Wave!

In the last lab exercise, you made waves with a physical object—a rope, a Slinky, or beads. Right now, as you're sitting and reading this, I'd like to teach you how to make another type of wave. Are you ready? This is what you need to do. Say, out loud, "Hello. I love physics." Did you say it out loud? If so, you just made <u>sound waves</u>. Try to imagine little waves of sound issuing forth from your mouth as you speak. Can you picture such waves?

I must confess that I really cannot imagine sound waves flowing out of my mouth every time I speak. Nevertheless, sound waves are real waves that you produce every time you make a noise. When you speak, energy produced by vocal chords in your throat creates a distortion, or change, in—well—what medium do sound waves travel through? When you tell your parent that you really must have chocolate ice cream, what does the sound of your voice travel through to get to your parent's ears? Take a moment to think about this question.

If your answer was "air," you are correct. The sounds you produce travel through the medium of air in the form of waves. Try speaking out loud again, but this time, place your hand under your chin over your neck first. Can you feel vibrations from inside your throat and neck? These vibrations are the energy that is going to get carried in the form of a wave to whomever might be listening to you.

"But wait," you might say. "Waves make sense in a rope and in a Slinky and in water, but not in air." We already learned that air is made of little molecules. How does a wave move through air molecules? This is a very good, scientific question. Just as the wave went through the rope or Slinky by moving each part of it back and forth a little, as the energy from sounds travels through the air, it moves each particle of air it encounters back and forth a little.

What's amazing is that the air molecules themselves don't travel along carrying sound. They pretty much stay where they are, moving back and forth a little bit in the shape of the wave. Just like when you made waves with the Slinky, it moved back and forth a little but pretty much stayed where it was on the floor as energy moved along it. If you're having trouble understanding how this can be, think of a duck floating on water. It bobs up and down as waves pass by, but doesn't get carried along with the waves. This is basically true for each water molecule affected by waves in water, and for each air molecule affected by sound waves in air.

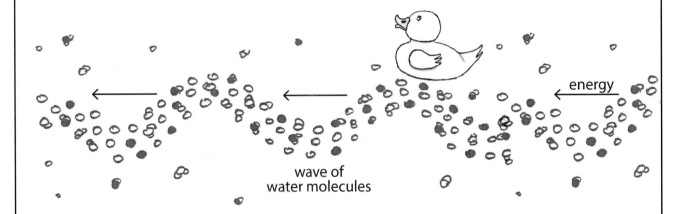

energy

wave of
water molecules

Let's try to prove this in the case of sound. Hold your hand about six inches in front of your mouth. Blow some air out. You can feel the moving air molecules on your hand, right? When you blow air, you're really causing some air molecules to move toward your hand. But, what happens if you send sound waves out toward your hand? Keep your mouth closed and make a loud humming noise with your hand in front of your mouth. There is sound energy moving outward from you, but it's definitely not moving air molecules the way blowing did. Do you think there's a way we can observe these sounds waves—or at least observe their effects?

Unit 7- Sound and Waves

Sound and Waves Lab #2: Making Big Waves - instructions

Materials:
- Lab sheets, pencil
- Whatever you used in the last lab to make waves (optional)
- Plastic, round food container—such as an old margarine or butter container
- Plastic wrap
- Rubber band large enough to fit around the top of the plastic container
- Pinch of fine sugar or salt (colored sugar works nicely, but is not necessary)

Aloud: You might recall that while learning about how air behaves, we couldn't directly observe air molecules. Instead, we had to observe how moving air molecules affected other objects that we could directly observe. We are going to use the same approach in learning about sound waves. To start out, we'll build a sound wave detector!

Procedure:
1. First, we're going to assemble the sound wave detector. Cut off a piece of plastic wrap several inches larger than the opening of the plastic container. Place the plastic wrap over the opening of the container and secure it as tightly and tautly as possible with the rubber band. (You'll need this apparatus for the next experiment, so save it.)

2. Sprinkle a pinch of salt or sugar onto the top of the plastic wrap. Try to spread it out a bit rather than having it all sitting in a clump.

Aloud: In a moment (but don't try it yet!), we're going to find out how different types of sound waves affect our sound wave detector. First, though, I'd like you just to think about what will happen to the grains of salt or sugar on your sound wave detector when sound waves hit them. It might help you to imagine that each grain will behave sort of like a very large air molecule acting as a medium for the sound waves.

3. Fill in the HYPOTHESIS section of the lab sheet.

4. With your mouth closed, hum "Happy Birthday" a few inches away from the sound detector. Watch what happens to the grains.

5. Now try singing "Happy Birthday" softly at first and then get louder and louder. Try to keep the same pitch—that is, get louder or softer, not higher or lower in tone. Observe how the behavior of the grains changes.

Note to Parents and Teachers: If you are in a small room and get too loud, the sound waves bouncing off the walls may result in the grains moving barely at all as noises get really loud. Try to avoid this. The goal is to observe increasing motion as sounds get louder.

6. Fill in the remainder of the lab sheet. You should work through the "What You Aren't Seeing" section carefully with students to ensure they understand it.

7. OPTIONAL: To further explore amplitude, you might want to pull out the slinky or rope you used to make waves on the floor. Have students try to determine what needs to change to vary the amplitude of the waves you make by moving the end of the rope.

[continued]

Possible Answers:

#1, 2: Answers will vary.

#3: vibrated and jumped around

#4: increased

#5: energy, distorting

#6: move and jump but mostly end up in the same general place

#7: sound waves

#8: more than, bigger

#9: quieter, louder

Conclusion / Discussion:

1. Review how sounds travel through the air in waves. Make sure that students understand that sound doesn't actually push individual air molecules all the way from the sound maker to the person who hears the sound. Instead, individual molecules are moved by the sound wave similar to how a beach ball is moved when it bobs up and down on water.

2. Sound needs a medium to travel through. What do you think this means about sound in a vacuum like outer space? Can sound travel through a vacuum? If the moon were to explode, would we hear it? (The answer is, "no!")

3. A larger amplitude means a louder sound. What do you think it takes to make a louder sound— more or less energy? If you haven't done so already, you might try using your rope or Slinky to make waves with larger amplitudes. Which takes more "work"—more moving of the end of the rope from one place to another? More work means more energy, so louder sounds require more energy to produce them.

More Lab Fun:

Experiment with your sound detector in different situations. Does it work differently in a small room with lots of echoes like a tiled bathroom? Does it work differently outside? If you play a musical instrument, see if the sound detector can detect sounds from the instrument. What happens when you vary the loudness?

Notebooking ideas:

1. Use a definition page to define *amplitude*.

2. Draw a picture of a sound wave traveling through the air. What do you imagine is happening to the air molecules as the sound moves through the air? Try to represent this in a picture or diagram.

Note to Parents and Teachers: Strictly speaking, sound is a "compression" or "pressure" wave traveling through the air. Where the waveform is at its crest, or highest point, air pressure is increased because of the vibration of the particles. As these particles transfer energy to particles next to them, the waveform travels through the air, though the particles do not. This information may be helpful for students who really want to understand how a wave can travel through a medium made of particles.

NAME _____ DATE _____

Making Big Waves

Hypotheses:

1. When I make a sound, **electricity / waves / air molecules** travel through the air outward from the source of the sound.

2. When these sound waves hit the grains of salt or sugar on my sound wave detector, I think the grains will _____

_____

_____

_____.

Observations:

3. When I made noises, the grains of salt or sugar on my sound wave detector **were perfectly still / vibrated and jumped around**.

4. As the sound got louder and louder, the motion of the grains **decreased / stayed the same / increased**.

Analysis and Conclusions:

5. When I make a noise, the **energy / electricity / wind** from the sound travels through the air molecules by moving, or **eating / distorting / transforming**, them a little bit.

6. When this energy hits the grains of salt or sugar, it causes them to **flow through the air to a person listening to me / taste good / move and jump but mostly end up in the same general place**.

7. In this way, the grains are registering, or detecting, **sound waves / air molecules / wind**.

8. When the sound was louder, the grains moved **less than / more than / the same as** when the sound was quieter. This suggests that the sound waves for louder sounds are **smaller / bigger / the same size as** when the sound was quieter.

What You Aren't Seeing:

Amplitude is the term used to describe the height of a wave. In the picture of waves below, label "amplitude" on the dotted line.

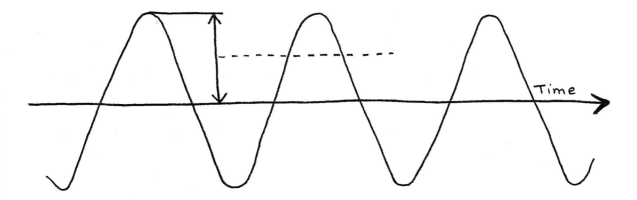

The sound waves from louder noises have a larger amplitude than the sound waves from quieter noises. Compare the sound waves drawn below. Identify which sound is "louder" and which is "quieter" based on the size of their amplitudes.

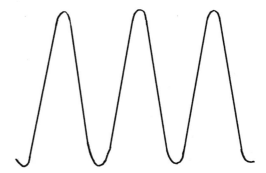

9.   This noise is **louder / quieter**.

This noise is **louder / quieter**.

For my notebook

The Speeds of Sound

We've been talking a lot about sound waves that travel through air. For most of our lives, this is how we encounter sound waves: something making a noise and the noise traveling through the air to our ears in the form of a wave. However, sound can also travel through other substances as well. Perhaps you've tried to say words when you were underwater. Although the sounds are distorted, or changed, you can still hear them. In fact, it takes less energy to transmit sound waves through many solids and liquids than it takes to transmit sound waves through the air.

Here's an example: Imagine you are in a huge room and you need to make a noise to get the attention of someone at the opposite end of the room. Fortunately, you have some choices because there happens to be a metal pipe running from your side of the room to the opposite side of the room. Does it take more energy to shout so loudly that the sound travels through the air, or to tap on the pipe so that the sound travels through the metal? Most likely, it will take less energy to send the sound waves through the solid than it would take to send them through a gas like air.

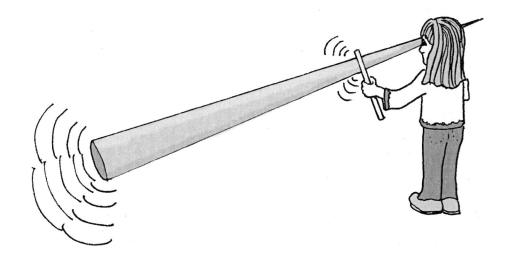

In fact, sound waves generally travel more easily through liquids and solids than through gases because the molecules in liquids and solids are closer together. So, we've discovered another characteristic of sound waves in addition to amplitude—the speed of the sound waves.

If you've ever heard someone talking about the speed of sound, though, you might be wondering how there can be different speeds of sound for different mediums. That's an excellent question! It turns out that for a particular medium, such as air, the speed of sound is constant. Whenever sound travels through air it moves 1,126 feet every second. This is true for loud sounds, quiet sounds, high sounds, and low sounds. Usually, when people are talking about the speed of sound, they are talking about the speed of sound in air.

Try this: Sing the "ABC" song up to the letter F and listen to what your voice is doing. Place your hand on your neck and do it again, feeling the differences in vibration as your voice moves from lower notes to higher notes. When you sing "A" you are singing a lower note than when you sing "F." Can you feel a difference in the vibrations on your neck when you sing higher and lower notes? We just learned that the speed of sound is constant, and we know that the amplitude of sound waves affects only the loudness of the sound, not whether the sound is a high note or a low note. So, what do you think is different about the sound waves produced for high notes as opposed to low notes?

As you might have guessed, we're going to perform a few experiments to see if we can answer this question.

Sound and Waves Lab #3: Hitting the High Notes - instructions

Materials:
- Lab sheets, pencil
- Your sound wave detector from the previous experiment

Aloud: Have you been thinking about how sound waves are shaped? Have you been pondering what we could change in a sound wave (other than the speed and the amplitude) to change whether sound is higher or lower in pitch? If you haven't, take a moment now to think about these questions. You've probably come up with one of two answers. We could change the length of each wave, which is known as the wavelength, to see how that changes sounds. Or, we could change the frequency of the waves—how close together the waves come. Wavelength and frequency are both scientific terms for characteristics of waves. <u>Wavelength</u> is defined as the distance from the crest of one wave to the crest of the next wave. <u>Frequency</u> is a measure of how quickly the crests of waves pass a particular point. You might be thinking that wavelength and frequency must be related somehow. Let's see if we can figure out how.

Procedure:
1. Fill in #1 and #2 on the lab sheet.

Aloud: Do you notice a similarity between the pictures of different wavelength waves and different frequency waves you made? Think about keeping the speed of the wave (how quickly it moves through its medium) and the amplitude of the wave constant. If you then decrease the wavelength, you have also increased the frequency. Look at the drawings you made to make sure you understand this. Also, as you can see from your drawings, the opposite is true: If you increase the wavelength, then the frequency decreases.

2. Fill in #3-#6 on the lab sheet.

Aloud: Now that you understand how frequency and wavelength work together, we can try to figure out what effect they have on how things sound. As you might have guessed, increasing and decreasing frequency has an effect on whether a noise sounds like a high note or a low note.

3. Fill in the HYPOTHESIS section.

4. Check your sound wave detector to make sure that the plastic wrap is still taut (if not, just pull it taut again) and that there are still some salt or sugar grains on it. Once it's ready, make a steady hum with your voice that is pretty low a few inches from your device—like a deep man's voice. You may have to move around a bit and adjust your amplitude (how loud your voice is) a bit. Keep trying until the grains move around a bit.

5. Now, do the same thing, making your voice go higher and higher like a soprano opera singer. Go back and forth between high and low a few times. What do you notice about how the grains are affected? Fill in the rest of the lab sheet.

[continued]

Sound and Waves Lab #3: Hitting the High Notes
- instructions page 2

Possible Answers:

#1, 2:

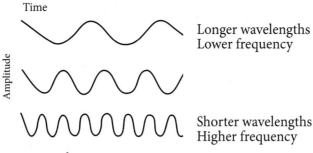

Longer wavelengths
Lower frequency

Shorter wavelengths
Higher frequency

#3: always travel at the same speed
#4: amplitude
#5: decreases
#6: decreases
Observation: more slowly than
Analysis and Conclusions: #1: waves
#2: The answer should be "more than." If not, discuss the following: every time a wave, or disturbance, hits a grain, it should move around a little bit.
#3: more, higher

Conclusion / Discussion:

1. Make certain that students understand that the speed of a wave is different from the frequency of the wave. The speed is how fast a single wave travels through a medium like the air. A very low frequency wave will travel at the same speed as a high frequency wave. So, low voices and high voices produce sound waves that travel at the same speed.

2. For mathematically minded students, you can talk about the wave equation. It looks like this: frequency x wavelength = speed. An example will help show this works: a wave with a frequency of 10 waves / second (also called 10 Hz) and a wavelength of 2 mm / wave results in this equation:

    10 waves / second x 2 mm / wave = 20 mm / second

3. You can look up the speed of sound in various materials online. It's interesting to see in which materials sound travels the quickest.

More Lab Fun:

1. Make an old-fashioned two-way communicator. Get two paper or plastic cups, a long string, and some scissors. Punch a hole in the bottom of both cups. Thread one end of the string through one of the holes and tie it off. Thread the other end of the string through the other cup hole and tie it off. Now, stretch the string out between two people. If you talk into one of the cups and your friend holds the other cup to her ear, she should be able to hear you better than if you just speak out loud. Why? (Because the sound travels better through the solid string than through air.)

2. Get a few glasses that are the same shape and size. Fill them with different amounts of water and tap lightly on the sides of the glass with a metal spoon. You can produce different musical notes depending on how much water is in the glasses. Can you figure out why this is? (Your tap on the glass generates vibrations, or waves. The more water in the glass, the more matter there is to vibrate. So, each wave produced is lower energy or lower frequency when there is more water.)

Notebooking ideas:

1. Use a definition page to define *frequency* and *wavelength*.

2. Look up the different speeds that sound travels through different mediums, such as iron, plastic, water, etc. Write these down in your notebook.

3. Could you design an experiment that would compare the speed of sound in different materials? Draw a picture of your experiment.

4. Choose a simple song like the "ABC" song. Sketch what you think the sound waves for the different notes would be, based on whether they are higher or lower notes.

Hitting the High Notes

1. The middle box below shows a sound wave. Draw in sound waves with longer and shorter wavelengths as labeled. Lines are drawn in so that you can keep the amplitude the same.

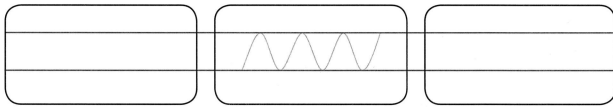

Longer wavelengths   Shorter wavelengths

2. The middle box below shows a sound wave. Draw in sound waves with lower frequencies (so that there are less waves in the box) and higher frequencies (so that there are more waves in the box).

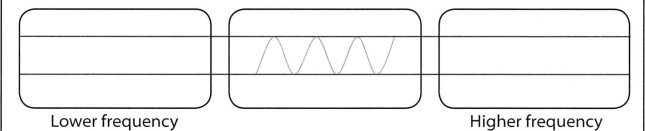

Lower frequency   Higher frequency

3. Sound waves traveling through air **travel at different speeds, depend on the sound being made / always travel at the same speed**.

4. The waves I drew above all have the same **frequency / amplitude / wavelength** because I drew them between the two lines so they all have the same height.

5. When waves have the same speed and amplitude but you increase the wavelength, the frequency **increases / stays the same / decreases**.

6. When waves have the same speed and amplitude but you increase the frequency, the wavelength **increases / stays the same / decreases**.

Hypothesis:

I think that singing a really high note will **increase / decrease / make no change to** the frequency of the sound waves produced by my voice.

Observation:

When I made a noise that was deep and low, the grains on my sound wave detector moved around **more quickly than / about the same as / more slowly than** when I made a very high noise.

Analysis and Conclusions:

1. I know that sound travels through the air in the form of **electricity / waves / gravity**.

2. If there are lots of waves closer together hitting something like my sound wave detector, I think that the waves would make the grains jump around **more than / less than / the same as** if there were only a few waves spaced farther apart.

3. Because the high notes made the grains jump around **more / less** than the low notes did, I conclude that higher notes produce sound waves with a **higher / lower** frequency than lower notes.

Cool Science Fact:

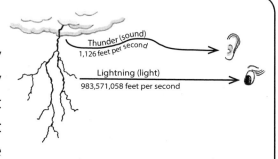

Thunder (sound)
1,126 feet per second

Lightning (light)
983,571,058 feet per second

Although sound travels incredibly quickly through the air, it travels much more slowly than light travels. You can observe this fact when there is a thunderstorm. The light from lightning travels to your eyes more quickly than the sound from the thunder, so you see lightning before you hear thunder. The closer you are to the storm, the less time that light has to outpace sound. So, by counting the seconds between the flash of lightning and the sound of thunder, you can tell whether a storm is moving toward you or away from you. If the time between the lightning and thunder is increasing, the storm is moving away from you. If it is decreasing, the storm is moving toward you.

Amplification: Can You Hear Me Now?

In 1816, about 200 years ago, a French physician named René-Théophile-Hyacinthe Laennec (pronounced Len-nek) was having a difficult time hearing the heartbeat of one his patients. He needed to find some way to amplify her heartbeat. You now know that <u>amplitude</u> is the word that physicists use to describe the height of a wave. To amplify a wave is to make the height of the wave larger—to make the sound louder.

René Laennec thought about the problem he was having hearing his patient's heartbeat. He also remembered a game that he saw some children playing one day. One child would take a hollow stick and hold it to his ear. Another child would take a small pin and scratch the other end of the stick. The hollow stick amplified the sound of the scratching pin and made it sound much louder. René Laennec wondered whether he could invent a device that would amplify heartbeats in the same way as the stick amplified the scratching pin. He rolled up some papers and placed one end against his patient's chest and the other end against his ear. Voila! René Laennec had just invented the first <u>stethoscope</u>!

Why did this simple device work to amplify the sound waves? Now that you understand how sound waves work, you can understand the answer to this question. First, think about how an amplified sound wave would look. It would have the same frequency and wavelength as the original sound, but the waves would be taller—have greater amplitudes. Do you remember making waves on a string or Slinky? When you waved your arm back and forth in larger arcs, you used more energy, putting more energy into the waves and making the amplitude of the waves greater.

When you hum a sound of a certain pitch, or frequency, you are using a certain amount of energy. If you make that sound louder, you are putting more energy into the sound wave. Usually, when you speak or make a noise, the sound waves travel outward in all directions from the producer of the sound, unless the sound waves bump into something like a wall. But, if you force all the sound waves—all the disturbances to the air molecules—into a small space, you will be using pretty much the same amount of energy to make fewer waves—giving those waves more energy and more amplitude.

By forcing most of the heartbeat sound waves into the tube he made, René Laennec made it so that larger amplitude waves traveled through his simple stethoscope. The heartbeats sounded louder when he listened at the other end of the tube.

Today's stethoscopes work pretty much the same way. At one end is the device that's placed against your chest when a doctor or nurse listens to your heart or lungs. This has a <u>diaphragm</u>, or a thin piece of material, that vibrates in response to the sound waves. The sound waves are sent through a hollow tube to the earpieces that the doctor or nurse wears. No electronics are involved!

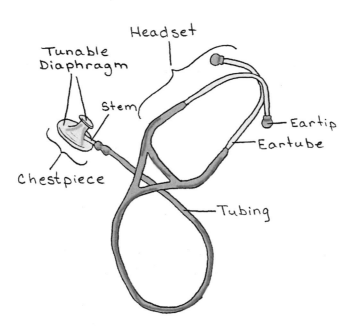

By manipulating sound waves, we can make a lot of different and useful devices. In the final few lab exercises about sound, that's just what we're going to do.

Sound and Waves Lab #4: Can You Hear Me Now?
- instructions

Materials:
- Lab sheets, pencil
- 8 sheets of construction paper per student
- Tape
- Scissors
- Crayons or marker if you like decorating things

Aloud: One type of sound that's easy to amplify is your voice. You know exactly where the sound of your voice comes out from your body, so it's relatively simple to direct those sound waves in a particular direction. Imagine you're outside and trying to get your friend's attention. Your friend is pretty far away and there are a lot of noises around. What do you do? If you're like my children, you certainly don't walk over and tap your friend on the shoulder. Instead, you shout as loudly as you can. But, what happens if it seems your friend can't quite hear you? Take a moment and imagine yourself in this situation. You're in a nice, shady spot and don't want to get up. How would you normally make your voice just a little louder?

Did you imagine holding your hands around your mouth and shouting as loudly as you could? That's what most people do to make their voices sound louder. When you cup your hands around your mouth, you may not think about it, but you are doing the same thing as René Laennec's stethoscope—directing sound waves and amplifying them. Cupping your hands around your mouth forces all the energy of the sound into the sound waves traveling forward from your mouth, amplifying them in that direction. Let's make a device that improves this ability.

Procedure:
1. Tape the first four pieces of paper together to make a larger rectangle. Do the same with the second four pieces of paper.

2. From *one* of the pieces, cut out the largest semicircle that you can. Don't worry if it's not perfect. You just need a piece that's roughly a semicircle. You can recycle the rest of that piece of paper.

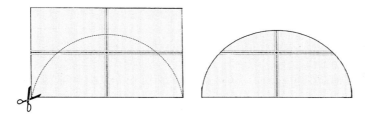

[continued]

3. If you want to decorate your devices, go ahead and color one side of the papers. We're going to be rolling them into different shapes, so abstract designs will work best.

4. Roll the rectangle into a cylinder with a diameter of about 4-5 inches and tape it into place.

5. Roll the semicircle into a cone shape. The straight edge will be the narrow end of the cone and the curved side will be the wider base of the cone. Tape this together so it will stay in place.

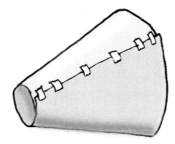

6. You are going to experiment with how well talking into these shapes helps to amplify your voice. Think about what you think is going to be most effective.

7. Fill in the HYPOTHESIS section of the lab sheet (#1-#3).

8. Have one person take the rolled-up papers and the second person stand across the room. You are going to compare how well the sound waves travel from one person to the other. The first person with the rolled-up papers should say, in a normal voice, a sentence. It can be as silly as you'd like. Next, the same person should pick up the cylinder, hold one end to his mouth, and point the other end toward the second person. He should say the same sentence in the same voice. The second person needs to decide if the voice sounds louder with or without the cylinder.

9. Continue to compare your normal voice to the cylinder and to the cone when you talk through the narrow end and the cone when you talk through the wide end. Which is loudest? Which is quietest? Keep testing until you can fill in the SHAPE OBSERVATIONS table on the lab sheet.

10. Choose the best amplifier for your voice. For most people it is the cone when talking into the narrow end. You're going to repeat the experiment, this time comparing the amplification when you point the open end of the amplifier toward the second person and the amplification (or lack of it) when pointing the open end away from that person. Look at the DIRECTION OBSERVATIONS on the lab sheet and fill it in.

11. Fill in the remainder of the lab sheet.

Possible Answers:
#1-#3: Answers will vary.
Shape observations: Answers will vary, but, most likely, talking into the small end of the cone shape produced the loudest sound.

Direction observations: Answers will vary, but, most likely, pointing the open end of the device directly toward the other person will be loudest.

Analysis and Conclusions: #1: Answers will vary.
#2: Make sure students include in their answer the idea that limiting the places the sound waves can go results in more energy in the sound waves traveling through the device, which means larger amplitude and a louder sound.

[continued]

#3: Answers will vary.

#4: Make sure students include in their answer that the most energetic or largest amplitude waves are coming from the open end of the device toward the other person.

Conclusion / Discussion:

1. Most likely, the best amplification came from speaking into the small end of the cone shape. If this wasn't your result, talk about why that might be. It might have to do with the shape of the room and where the sound waves went and/or where the other person's ears were pointed. But, point out that in most cases, the cone shape is the best amplifier.

2. Why would a cone shape be the best amplifier? What happens to the sound waves as they leave your mouth and travel outward? (Their energy is focused and then sent toward the other person. The cone shape makes it easier to make sure the sound waves travel toward the other person, as opposed to the cylinder shape, which needs to be pointed with more precision.) Ask the students if they've ever seen a megaphone. If not, find a picture of one. Now you know why a megaphone is shaped like it is.

3. Make certain that students understand that sound is louder because there is more energy in louder sounds than in quieter sounds. The increased energy takes the form of increased amplitude in the sound waves.

More Lab Fun:

1. Make your own stethoscope like René Laennec's. Roll up a piece of paper into a cylinder (with a smaller diameter than the one you made for the experiment, more like a couple of inches). If you want to get fancier, you can cut up a balloon and stretch a piece over one end to act like a diaphragm. Place that end on someone's chest and listen at the other end. Can you hear a heartbeat? Try with and without your "stethoscope."

2. It can also be useful to dampen, or make less loud, sound. Soundproofing is important, for example, in designing buildings where you don't want people in one room to hear everything that is happening next door. Experiment with soundproofing by getting a piece of cardboard or poster board. Put the board between you and someone else and make some noise. Does the cardboard block the noise? Now try taping or gluing different materials onto the cardboard to see if they dampen the sound even more. One shape that has been used traditionally for soundproofing is cardboard egg cartons, with the open ends toward the sound. Try it out!

Notebooking Ideas:

1. Use a definition page to define *amplification*.

2. Invent a device to focus sound so that you can talk to a person in the room without a third person hearing you. Draw a picture of it and describe how it works.

3. Draw a picture of what happens to the sound waves as they enter and leave a megaphone. Draw another picture to compare it with what happens when you just speak normally, without a megaphone.

Can You Hear Me Now?

Hypotheses:

1. I think the cone will work better to amplify my voice if I talk into the **wide** / **narrow** end of the cone.

2. I think the cylinder will work **better** / **worse** than the cone to amplify my voice.

3. I think a **narrower** / **medium width** / **wider** cylinder will work better to amplify my voice.

Shape Observations: (circle the appropriate volume)

Cylinder	**Most quiet** | **Louder** | **Even louder** | **Loudest**
Cone (talking through narrow end)	**Most quiet** | **Louder** | **Even louder** | **Loudest**
Cone (talking through wide end)	**Most quiet** | **Louder** | **Even louder** | **Loudest**
Normal voice	**Most quiet** | **Louder** | **Even louder** | **Loudest**

Direction Observations: (circle the appropriate volume)

Pointing the open end toward the other person	**Most quiet** | **Louder** | **Even louder** | **Loudest**
Pointing the open end a little to the left of the other person	**Most quiet** | **Louder** | **Even louder** | **Loudest**
Turning a ¼ turn and pointing the open end about 90 degrees from other person	**Most quiet** | **Louder** | **Even louder** | **Loudest**
Turning ½ way around and pointing the open end in the opposite direction of the other person	**Most quiet** | **Louder** | **Even louder** | **Loudest**

Analysis and Conclusions:

The sound seemed loudest to the second person when I spoke in **a normal voice / through the wide end of the cone / through the narrow end of the cone / through the cylinder**.

I think what happens to the sound waves when I speak through the best amplifier is: _____

_____

_____

_____

_____

_____.

In terms of direction, the sound was loudest when the device was pointed **directly toward / a little away from / at a right angle from / opposite from** the other person.

I think this is because the sound waves: _____

_____

_____

_____

_____.

Unit 8

Magnetism

For my notebook

Introducing Magnetism

Many months ago, at the beginning of learning about physics, you learned about forces. Pause for a moment to see if you remember the definition of force. What did you come up with? Did you recall that a force is a push or pull that moves matter from one place to another? If you did, great! Maybe you also remember that there are two types of forces: contact forces and action-at-a-distance forces. A contact force is when one object touches another and pushes or pulls it to move it—like when you push a toy car across the floor. An action-at-a-distance force is one that acts without actually touching an object. It pulls or pushes an object from a distance. Can you think of the action-at-a-distance force you've learned about? Here's a hint: It caused an apple to fall on Isaac Newton's head.

We're about to learn about a second action-at-a-distance force. It's one you might have seen at work on your refrigerator door: <u>magnetism</u>. As you probably know, a magnet is an object that sticks to various objects. That definition just won't work for physicists, though. If we define a magnet as an object that sticks to certain other objects, we'd have to say that tape and gum are magnets. As usual, physicists have a different and more precise definition of a magnet. A <u>magnet</u> is a substance that produces a <u>magnetic field</u>.

This may sound like a circular definition, but it isn't. A <u>field</u>, in physics, is just an area in which a force exists. All of us are within Earth's <u>gravitational field</u>, which extends in a roughly spherical shape around the earth. Around magnets, there is a field, or area, where the magnet's force extends. Just like gravity, we can't see the field, and we can't see how far it extends. But, we can do experiments to see where the magnetic field extends by testing whether it can attract objects to it at particular distances.

When objects are placed near a magnet—within the magnet's magnetic field—some objects are attracted to the magnet and some objects seem entirely unaffected. If an object is affected by a magnetic field, we say that the object is <u>magnetic</u>. Magnetism is a characteristic of an object. This is pretty simple if you think in terms of concrete objects. Metal paper clips are magnetic. Your little brother or sister is not magnetic.

Magnets must have seemed quite mysterious and magical when they were first discovered. No one knows who first found a magnetic stone, or <u>lodestone</u>, but we do know that the word *magnet* comes from a region in Greece that was called Magnesia, where lodestones were found. Let's see if we can apply some science to magnets to uncover some of their mysteries.

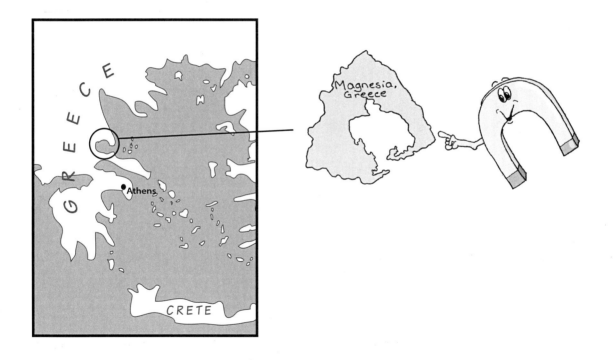

Unit 8- Magnetism

Magnetism Lab #1: Tracking Attraction - instructions

Materials:
- Lab sheets, pencil
- Several magnets, including at least: 1 bar magnet and 1 horseshoe-shaped magnet
- Students are going to gather 10 to 15 various objects around the house or classroom that may or may not be attracted to the magnets, but make sure that the following are among the objects to collect:
  - Aluminum foil
  - Metal paper clip
  - Sock

Aloud: What makes some objects magnetic while other objects are unaffected by magnets? It turns out that an object's magnetism has a lot to do with what the object is made of. What objects have you found in your life that are magnetic? Can you think of what those objects all have in common? What objects do you know of that are definitely not magnetic? Are all the magnetic objects made of the same substance? Of similar substances? Let's see if we can figure out the key to determining which objects are magnetic and which are not.

Procedure:

1. Fill in the HYPOTHESIS on the lab sheet.

2. Gather between 10 and 15 objects from around the house or classroom. Try to choose some that you think will be attracted to a magnet, some you think will not be attracted to a magnet, and some that you aren't sure about.

3. Before you test whether any of them are attracted by a magnet, fill in the first two columns on the table on the lab sheet.

4. One at a time, test whether each object is attracted to a magnet. Write your results in the table. If the results aren't what you expected, think about why. Try some of the objects with more than one magnet. If an object is magnetic, is it attracted by all the magnets you have? Finish filling in the entire table.

5. Complete the remainder of the lab sheet.

6. Fill in the Venn Diagram based on the objects you tested.

Possible Answers:
Analysis and Conclusions: #1: answers will vary.
  #2: metal
  #3: some
  #4: some
  #5: all

Venn Diagram: Some items that are metal will test magnetic. Therefore, these items (that are magnetic and metal) should be listed at the intersection of the two circles. There may be items tested that are metal but not magnetic. These items (metal but not magnetic) should be listed in the nonintersecting part of the "Things made of metal" circle. All items that are magnetic are made out of metal. Therefore, there should be no items listed in the nonintersecting part of the "Magnetic things" circle.

The following statements are true: #2 and #4

[continued]

Magnetism Lab #1: Tracking Attraction - instructions page 2

Conclusion / Discussion:

1. Make sure that the students understand that objects without any metal in them are not magnetic. Talk about which objects that were metal were magnetic. Do you know what type of metal was in those objects? Can you figure out any types of metal that are (or are not) magnetic? (Don't worry if they answer is "no." This will be discussed more in the next section.)

2. Talk about the idea of a magnetic field and how it creates an action-at-a-distance force. If you need to, play with a magnet and some paper clips to demonstrate how the magnet meets the definition of an action-at-a-distance force: Without touching the paper clip, it can exert a pull that moves the paper clip from one place to another.

More Lab Fun:

1. Walk around and discover which objects around you have magnetic parts. Try chair legs, tabletops, cabinet handles, etc. WARNING: Do not let magnets get near electronic equipment or monitors. Bad things can happen resulting in the need to purchase new electronic equipment and monitors!

2. You can also discover things around you that use magnets. Some cabinets latch using magnets. We hang things on our refrigerator doors using magnets. Can you discover any other uses for magnets around the house? If not, can you invent any?

Notebooking Idea:

Use a definition page to define *field*, *magnet*, *magnetic field*, and *magnetic*. This can get tricky, so look back at the FMN section if you need to.

NAME _____ DATE _____

Tracking Attraction

Hypothesis:

I think that all objects that are magnetic, or are attracted by

magnets, are similar because they all _____

_____ .

Predictions and Observations about Magnetism:

Object	I think this object is:	Was this object magnetic?
Sock	Magnetic / Not magnetic / I'm not sure	Yes / No
Aluminum foil	Magnetic / Not magnetic / I'm not sure	Yes / No
Paper clip	Magnetic / Not magnetic / I'm not sure	Yes / No
	Magnetic / Not magnetic / I'm not sure	Yes / No
	Magnetic / Not magnetic / I'm not sure	Yes / No
	Magnetic / Not magnetic / I'm not sure	Yes / No
	Magnetic / Not magnetic / I'm not sure	Yes / No
	Magnetic / Not magnetic / I'm not sure	Yes / No
	Magnetic / Not magnetic / I'm not sure	Yes / No
	Magnetic / Not magnetic / I'm not sure	Yes / No
	Magnetic / Not magnetic / I'm not sure	Yes / No
	Magnetic / Not magnetic / I'm not sure	Yes / No
	Magnetic / Not magnetic / I'm not sure	Yes / No
	Magnetic / Not magnetic / I'm not sure	Yes / No
	Magnetic / Not magnetic / I'm not sure	Yes / No

Tracking Attraction - page 2

Analysis and Conclusions:

1. My predictions about what was magnetic and what was not were incorrect about the following items: _____

   _____

   _____

2. I noticed that all the objects that were magnetic had **wood** / **fabric** / **metal** in them.

3. **All** / **Some** / **None** of the metal objects were magnetic.

4. Therefore, **all** / **some** / **no** types of metals must be magnetic.

5. I also discovered that when a material is magnetic, it is attracted by **all** / **some** / **no** magnets.

Venn Diagram - Show the Relationship between Metals and Magnetism

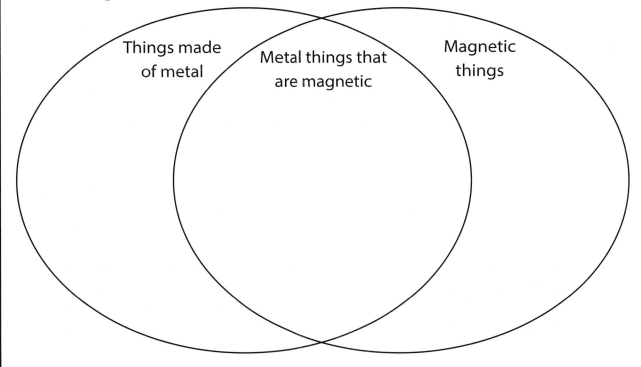

Things made of metal

Metal things that are magnetic

Magnetic things

From this diagram, which of the following statements are true?

(Circle the number for the true statements.)

1. All metal objects are magnetic.
2. Some metal objects are magnetic.
3. Some objects that are magnetic are not made of metal.
4. All objects that are magnetic are made of metal.

Magnetism Lab #2: The Measure of a Magnet - instructions

Materials:
- Lab sheets, pencil
- 5-7 magnets, including at least: 1 bar magnet and 1 horseshoe-shaped magnet
- Metal paper clips that are magnetic
- Ruler
- Flat surface such as a tabletop
- Tape

Aloud: Now you know that only some metals are magnetic or are affected by the magnetic field that a magnet produces. In fact, the metals iron, nickel, and cobalt are all magnetic. This means that there are many metals that are not magnetic, such as gold, aluminum, copper, and lead. By noting how magnets interact with various objects, you've made scientific observations that help to define how magnets work. The observations you made were <u>qualitative</u>—based on whether various objects exhibited a particular quality, or characteristic. Sometimes, qualitative observations can be quite useful in science. For example, you should now be able to explain how, scientifically, you could determine whether an object contains nickel, iron, or cobalt. Try to explain it to someone nearby right now. *

* Use a magnet to test if the object is magnetic. If it is, it might be made out of nickel, iron, or cobalt because they are magnetic.

Scientists also make use of <u>quantitative</u> observations—observations of quantities, or measurements, relating to what they are observing. Here's a pretty tough question that involves quantitative observation: How could you measure the strength of a magnet so that you could compare its strength to other magnets? Take a moment to see if you can think of a method.

Procedure:
1. Fill in #1 on the lab sheet.

2. Did you come up with a good idea for measuring the strength of a magnet? If your idea is different than the one I'm going to describe, you should try both. Here's what I thought of: Place a ruler on a flat surface like a tabletop. Place a paper clip next to the 12 inches mark on the ruler. Place the magnet you want to test next to the 0 inches mark on the ruler. (You could use the centimeter marks instead if you'd like.) Slowly move the magnet closer to the paper clip until the paper clip is attracted to the magnet. Write down how close the magnet had to be to the paper clip to attract it. Before you try this method or your method, fill out the hypothesis section of the lab sheet (#2).

3. Now, test each magnet. You should use the method I explained and, if your idea was different, you can try that as well. I've left an extra column in the observation table for you.

4. When you've finished making your observations, fill in the rest of the lab sheet.

[continued]

Possible Answers:
Your answers will vary depending on what magnets you use.

Conclusion / Discussion:

1. In this lab, students make <u>quantitative observations</u> by measuring distances. In the last lab, they made <u>qualitative observations</u> by testing the magnetic characteristics of objects. Talk about the difference between qualitative and quantitative observations. Is one "better" than the other (not really). Are there advantages of one type of observation over the other? (Some ideas: quantitative observations can be more easily compared because they are numerical; qualitative observations make clear-cut differences like magnetic vs. nonmagnetic easier to describe.)

2. Did you know before this experiment that magnets can have different strengths? Talk about your ideas as to why different magnets have different strengths and your thoughts as to how you might test these ideas. Can you think of uses of magnets that aren't too strong? What might you use a superstrong magnet for?

More Lab Fun:

1. Did you come up with a good way to test your hypothesis about why some magnets are stronger than others? If so, use some experiment pages from the Notebooking section and try it out.

2. The paper clip you used for this test didn't weigh very much. Would the results change in any way if you used a heavier object? A lighter object? See if you can find other objects to use and notice how this affects your results. Think about how you could compare your results with a paper clip to a friend's results if your friend used a different-sized paper clip or a different object. Would the numbers you came up with have any relationship to the numbers your friend came up with? Would there be a way to convert from one to the other?

Notebooking Ideas:

1. There are superpowerful magnets called neodymium magnets. I've read stories about how someone can put one in his pocket and suddenly find himself stuck to a metal table leg! Write a story or draw a comic strip about what interesting things might happen if someone discovered a superpowerful magnet and had to get it from one place to another.

2. Use a definition page to define *qualitative observations* and *quantitative observations*.

NAME _____ DATE _____

The Measure of a Magnet

1. My idea for a method to *quantitatively* measure the strength of a magnet is to: (Sketch, describe, or do both.)

_____

_____

_____

_____

_____

_____

_____

_____

_____

2. Hypotheses:

Of all the magnets I have, I think the following magnet will be strongest (sketch or describe the magnet):

Of all the magnets I have, I think the following magnet will be the weakest (sketch or describe the magnet):

3. Observations:

Magnet used: (sketch or describe)	Distance from which the magnet attracted the paper clip using the ruler method:	Measurement of magnet's strength using the method I came up with:

4. Analysis and Conclusions:

The strongest magnet was: _____

The weakest magnet was: _____

The strongest magnet was **different from** / **the same as** the magnet I thought would be strongest.

The weakest magnet was **different from** / **the same as** the magnet I thought would be weakest.

My hypothesis about why some magnets are stronger than others is:

_____

_____

An experiment that would test this hypothesis is: (sketch or describe)

NAME _____ DATE _____

For my notebook

Magnets and Poles

Anyone who has ever played with several magnets together has discovered that sometimes magnets pull each other together or <u>attract</u> each other, and sometimes they push one another away or <u>repel</u> one another. Every magnet, big or small, powerful or weak, horseshoe shaped or straight, has two different areas called <u>poles</u>. One pole of the magnet is called the <u>south pole</u> and the other end of the magnet is called the <u>north pole</u>. Poles are areas of a magnet where the magnetic field is the strongest, which means the magnet is strongest at the two poles.

Some magnets have labels on them indicating that one end is north and the other end is south. If you were to play with labeled magnets for a while, you'd quickly discover that when you place the north end of one magnet next to the north end of a second magnet, the two magnets repel each other, or push each other away. The magnets behave the same way, repelling each other, if you place the south end of one next to the south end of the other. You'd also discover that if you placed the south end of one magnet next to the north end of the other, the magnets would attract each other instead of repelling each other. In this case, the magnets would snap together quickly because of the combined force of each magnet pulling on the other. A short way to remember this is to remember that "opposites attract and likes repel."

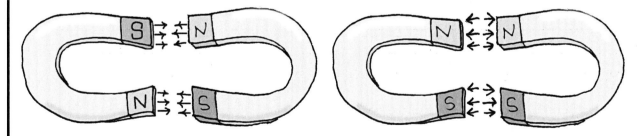

Why do magnets behave this way? The answer is pretty complex, but it has to do with what's happening inside the atoms that make up magnets. Inside atoms are tiny particles called <u>electrons</u>. Magnetism is caused by characteristics of electrons, including in what direction they are spinning and where they are moving. Just like you, atoms are more <u>stable</u>—less easy to change—when things are balanced. When you stand on one leg, it's easier to fall over than when you balance on two legs. When some atoms have electrons spinning one way and about the same number of atoms have electrons spinning the opposite way, the atoms are more balanced and stable.

It turns out that the electrons creating a south pole are out of balance in one direction. In a north pole end of a magnet, the electrons are out of balance in the opposite direction. If you put a north pole next to a south pole, there are a bunch of atoms with electrons spinning in opposite directions. All these atoms attract each other because the electrons in the north pole atoms will balance out the electrons in the south pole atoms, leading to more stability. But, when two south poles are placed next to each other, the electrons are doubly out of balance, and they repel each other to achieve a more stable state than when they are next to each other.

Balanced

Electrons Paired
Moving in opposite directions

Unbalanced

Electrons moving in same direction

You would do the same thing if you were trying to balance on one foot and someone also trying to balance on one foot pushed against you; you'd push back or repel the other person to try to maintain your stability.

In real atoms with real electrons, the situation is much more complicated. Electrons are strange and amazing particles, and you can look up more about them in the library or on the Internet. Still, even though this description of how magnetism works is greatly simplified, it gives the basic idea of what's actually at the heart of magnetism. Let's learn a little bit more about how the north and south poles of magnets behave.

Magnetism Lab #3: Searching for Poles - instructions

Materials:
- Lab sheets, pencil
- 5-10 magnets, including at least: 2 bar magnets, 1 horseshoe-shaped magnet, and a round (disc) magnet (like on the back of many refrigerator magnets)
- Two colors of tape, or a tape that you can write on and two colors of markers
- Iron filings (see supplies list for how to get these)
- Short piece of string (6-12 inches)

Aloud: Much of how a magnet behaves depends on what it's made of and how it is shaped. Did you figure out after the last experiment that a magnet's strength depends on what it is made of? If so, good for you! In any case, it's true. The type of material making up a magnet determines its strength. How a magnet is shaped also has a big effect on how a magnet behaves. Look at the collection of magnets you have. You now know that they all have two poles, one south and one north, where the magnetic field is at its strongest.

You might be able to make an intelligent guess regarding where the poles on the rectangular magnets are, but where are the poles on the round magnets? On the horseshoe magnet, are the poles the two ends sticking out, or are the two ends a single pole and bottom of the U shape the other pole? How can we use what we know about magnets and magnetic fields to identify the poles on a magnet?

Procedure:
1. On the table on the lab sheet, fill in the columns labeled: Magnet Shape, Hypothesis of Pole Locations. You should make a rough sketch of the magnet's shape (a circle, a rectangle, a horseshoe shape) in the "Magnet Shape" column. Repeat the sketch in the "Hypothesis of Pole Locations" column, but also indicate with an "X" where you think the two poles of the magnet are located. Don't worry about whether the poles are north or south just yet.

Aloud: We are going to use two approaches to finding the poles of the magnets because different approaches work better depending on which magnet is being tested. The first approach involves getting an impression of how the magnetic field around the magnet is shaped using iron filings. This approach works best with bar-shaped and horseshoe-shaped magnets. The second approach involves seeing what parts of a magnet with unknown poles are attracted to a pole on a bar magnet. Let's try each approach once, and then you can experiment with both approaches on all the magnets you have. As we go, we're also going to label the poles of the magnets using tape.

WARNING: Do not try to pick up iron filings directly with the magnets or they'll be stuck to the magnet and hard to remove. If the filings spill, there is an easy way to clean them up. Place a piece of paper over them and collect them through the paper with a magnet. With the magnet against the paper, flip the paper over so the filings are on top of the paper and then remove the magnet. Also, be sure to wash your hands after handling magnets and metal filings.

Method 1: Iron Filings:
2. Get the iron filings ready to use. If you are using loose filings, place them on a white piece of paper or card stock. If you are worried about their spilling, you can try to place this setup in a clear plastic bag, but this can interfere with the filings being able to move freely.

3. Finding the poles: Start with a bar magnet. Hold it under the paper or card stock and move it

[continued]

around. You should see the filings react to the presence of the magnet by standing up, moving with it, etc. If you have a lot of filings, the filings may pile up around the magnet. Have some fun playing with the magnet and the filings, and then focus on finding where the poles are. You'll want to move the magnet to an area of the paper with few filings to see what parts of the magnet pick up filings first. These will be the poles of the magnet. Usually, the filings will stand up straight around the poles as well. In almost all bar magnets, the poles are at either end of the magnet, slightly in from the very end of the magnet. It can take a few tries of moving the magnet back and forth to get a good sense of where the poles are.

4. Viewing the field: Slowly move the magnet around to pick up more filings through the paper. Sometimes, you can get a sense of how the magnetic field is shaped, depending on the strength and construction of the magnet. If you have a well-made magnet, the filings should look something like this:

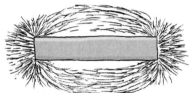

If you get a good sense of the field, sketch it in the table under the Pole Locations column.

5. Fill in the chart for the bar magnet you used, specifying the test you used and the location of the poles.

6. Label the poles using the tape. Pick one color of tape to place on one pole and use the other color of tape to place on the other pole. Just use a little tiny piece of tape so you can remember which end is which. If your magnet has labeled north and south poles, you can jot down on your lab sheet which color you used for north and which for south.

Method 2: The "String Test"

7. This method works best for disc-shaped magnets and other magnets for which you have no real idea of where the poles are. Tie a string around one of the disc magnets so that it can turn freely when hanging up.

8. Hold the string so that the magnet is hanging down and can swing around freely. Pick up a bar magnet and hold it several inches from the hanging magnet, so it's too far away to affect the hanging magnet. Slowly move one end of the bar magnet toward the hanging magnet until it starts to pull at the hanging magnet. As you move it slowly closer, the magnets should snap together. Where they are attached is most likely the pole. It might help you to know that usually disc magnets are south on one face and north on the other. When you figure out what part of the magnet is attracted to one end of the bar magnet, label it with tape. Remember that opposites attract. Let's say you labeled one end of the bar magnet with red tape and the other with blue tape. If the blue taped end attracted part of the magnet on the string, label that part of the magnet on the string with red tape.

9. Try to find the other pole using the other end of the bar magnet. Label the second pole on the magnet on the string. Fill in the rest of the table for the magnet you tested on the string.

[continued]

Testing All Magnets:

10. Continue to test magnets using one or both of the methods above, label the poles with the appropriate colored tape, and fill in the remainder of the table on the lab sheet. It can be quite hard to figure out where the poles are on some magnets—especially those that are circular or spherical. Do the best you can while playing around with both methods. Remember that the pole of a magnet is not necessarily a small point but can be the whole side of a magnet.

11. Try the horseshoe magnet using both methods. When using the filings with the horseshoe magnet, try it both with the horseshoe flat against the paper and with the ends of the horseshoe against the paper.

When You're Finished:

12. Fill in the remainder of the lab sheet.

13. Play around with your labeled magnets. Do all the poles you've identified with the same color of tape repel each other? Do the poles you've identified with different colors attract each other? They should.

Note to Parents and Teachers: In trying these experiments out myself, I discovered that it can be very challenging to pinpoint the poles on some magnets, especially the inexpensive magnets you can get at dollar stores (which also are sometimes labeled incorrectly). Emphasize for students that science is about experimenting, observing, and asking questions, not about easy answers. If they can't find the poles using any of the methods I described, maybe they can come up with different methods (seeing how two similarly shaped magnets interact is one good thing to try).

Possible Answers:

Your answers will vary depending on what magnets you use.

Conclusion / Discussion:

1. Were the poles where you expected? Did it help you to begin by identifying the poles on one magnet, and then to observe how that first magnet interacted with the other magnets? Scientific knowledge almost always progresses by looking at what's been done before and then uses that information. In what way does this experiment demonstrate how scientific knowledge builds on itself?

2. Although most people think of magnetic fields as looking like diagrams drawn on paper that show lines traveling from one end of a bar magnet to another, magnetic fields actually exist in three dimensions: They are not flat. That's why magnets attract things above and below them as well as next to them. Can you think of a way to diagram the magnetic field using a method similar to the one we used to measure the strength of the field? Talk about your ideas. (You can get a sense of the three-dimensional field by holding a paper with filings above a magnet and moving it around. The filings will stand up and point in the direction of the field at a particular point.)

[continued]

More Lab Fun:

1. There is actually a more precise way to map a magnetic field. If you have a compass, you can try it out. Place the compass in various positions around the magnet. Everywhere you put the compass, you'll see the arrow pointing in a particular direction. Sketch in the arrow where it was and pointing in the direction it was pointing. If you connect the arrows when you're done, you have a pretty rough idea of the shape of the magnetic field. This method, though, doesn't really indicate the strength of the field, only its direction.

2. Make a maze puzzle for a friend using two magnets. Get a shoebox and two magnets strong enough to attract each other through the box. Draw a maze on the bottom of the shoebox. Place one magnet on the start of the maze and the other magnet under the box sticking to it. Can your friend get through the maze touching only the magnet underneath the box?

Notebooking Idea:

Ring-shaped magnets can get very complicated. Some are essentially two horseshoe-shaped magnets stuck together at their ends. Can you think of other ways you might make a ring magnet out of smaller magnets with different shapes? Sketch them in your notebook.

NAME _____ DATE _____

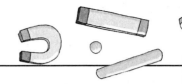

Searching for Poles

Magnet Shape	Hypothesis of Pole Locations	Tests Conducted	Pole Locations

Searching for Poles - page 2

Analysis and Conclusions:

1. It was **straightforward** / **difficult** / **impossible** to figure out where the poles were on all the magnets I tested.

2. The easiest magnet to find the poles on was shaped like (describe and/or draw): _____

   _____

3. The hardest magnet to find the poles on was shaped like (describe and/or draw): _____

   _____

4. Some ideas I have about how I could find the poles on the magnet in #3 are:

   _____

   _____

   _____

   _____

   _____

   _____

   (Maybe you should try some of these ideas!)

For my notebook

Magnets: Small, Smaller, and Smallest

You now understand quite a bit about how magnets work, how north and south poles interact with one another, and how to get a sense of where the poles on a magnet are. I'd like you to use all this information to think about an imaginary experiment. Here it is: Imagine you have a bar magnet. One end is labeled "N" and is the north pole. The other end is labeled "S" and is the south pole. Simple enough.

Now imagine a pair of supersharp scissors that can cut smoothly through anything and cut the magnet in half, like this:

You have two new pieces of material. Do you think they'll act as magnets? If so, where do you think the poles on each of the magnets are? Take a moment to answer this question before you read on.

When this experiment is actually done, two new magnets are created. What was originally the north pole is still the north pole, and what was originally the south pole is still the south pole. But, two new poles now exist—a new south pole at the end of the magnet that had the original north pole and a new north pole at the end of the magnet that had the original south pole.

In fact, you could keep cutting the magnets until they were quite tiny, and you'd keep getting new magnets with new poles! It almost seems as if the magnet is made up of lots of tiny magnets, all with tiny north and south poles lined up behind each other, like this:

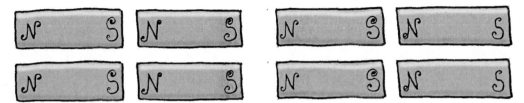

You can see why, if you cut a magnet like this in half, you'd have two new magnets, each with a north and south pole. And, you can see that you could keep cutting the magnet until it was quite small with the same results.

Magnets are not actually made up of tiny little magnets. As you may recall, the ultimate cause of magnetic fields has to do with whether the spin and movement of electrons within a substance cancel each other out, or cause magnetism, by being out of balance in a particular direction. But before scientists understood so much about electrons, they came up with the idea of <u>domains</u>, or tiny regions within a substance in which all the magnetic fields of the atoms are essentially pointing in the same direction. Domains don't tell the whole story down to the subatomic level, but they are a correct description and are still quite useful in understanding magnets and magnetism.

In a magnet, the domains would all be nicely lined up like this:

In a material like iron, which is magnetic (it can be attracted by a magnet) but is not itself a magnet, the domains might look more like this:

You can see why, with domains arranged in every direction, a material would not act as a magnet. Or, would it? Let's see what we can find out.

Magnetism Lab #4: Is It a Magnet or Isn't It? - instructions

Materials:
- Lab sheets, pencil
- The magnet you identified as strongest in Magnetism Lab #2: The Measure of a Magnet
- Metal paper clips (that are magnetic)
- Iron or steel nail (one that is attracted to magnets but is not magnetic itself)

Aloud: What is it that makes materials like iron and nickel magnetic even though they are not themselves magnets? These <u>ferromagnets</u> are different from other substances that are not magnetic because they have domains like we just learned about. In substances that are not magnetic, the electrons still create magnetic fields, but they are counteracted by other electrons in the substance. In <u>ferromagnetic materials</u>, the technical term for what we've been calling magnetic materials, there are regions, or domains, where all the magnetic fields generated by the electrons are aligned in a particular direction. In a magnet, all these domains would have their magnetic fields aligned in the same direction. But, in a ferromagnetic material, although each domain is itself like a tiny magnet with all the magnetic fields lined up, all the different domains have magnetic fields pointing every which way. Let's see if we can find out a little bit more about how the domains inside ferromagnetic materials work.

Procedure:
Part I:

1. Fill in the Hypothesis section of the lab sheet (#1-#3).

2. First, we're going to make some observations of the control for the experiment. In other words, we're going to record data about the materials before we change anything. Perform the following experiments and fill in #4-#7 on the lab sheet.

    A. See if one paper clip attracts or repels another paper clip.
    B. See if the nail and the paper clip attract or repel one another.
    C. See if the magnet attracts a single paper clip.
    D. See if the magnet attracts the nail.

3. Pick up a paper clip with the magnet. Now, try to pick up a second paper clip with the paper clip attached to the magnet. It seems as if the magnetism is flowing through one paper clip to the second. Can you pick up a third paper clip with the one attached to the magnet? How many can you pick up?

4. Go back to having one paper clip attached to the magnet and a second paper clip attracted to the first. Hold the first paper clip, and slowly move the magnet away from it. What happens? If the first paper clip still attracts the second paper clip, separate them for a moment. Try to pick up the second paper clip with the first paper clip now. What happens?

5. Finish filling in the information on the lab sheet for Part I of the experiment (up through #13).

[continued]

Part II:

Aloud: In the first part of this lab, we found that a ferromagnetic material could be temporarily magnetized. While ferromagnetic materials are within a magnetic field created by a magnet, the domains in the ferromagnetic material all line up with the magnetic field, and the ferromagnetic material becomes magnetized. In our experiment, the domains in the paper clip attached to the magnet all lined up in the same direction as those in the magnet, so that the paper clip became magnetized. However, when the paper clip was moved away from the magnet, the domains went back to being oriented in various directions, and the paper clip was no longer magnetized. Let's see if we can get those domains to stay lined up even when not in the presence of a magnetic field—that is, can we make a semi-permanent magnet out of a ferromagnetic material like a paper clip or a nail? A semipermanent magnet will be able to attract magnetic materials on its own, without being near a magnet, but might lose its ability to act as a magnet after a while.

6. Fill in the HYPOTHESIS section of the worksheet (#14 & #15).

7. Verify that the nail still doesn't attract the paper clips. If it does, drop the nail and the paper clips on the table a few times to demagnetize them (we'll redo this step later and explain why it works).

8. To magnetize the nail, rub a bar magnet along the nail repeatedly. Make sure all your strokes are in the same direction and stroke gently—don't bang the magnet against the nail every time you make a stroke. I found it worked best if I just tried to magnetize the end of the nail. Make at least 100 strokes this way.

9. See if the nail will attract a paper clip now. It may not be especially strong, but you should see some amount of magnetic attraction happening. If you don't, make another 100 strokes against the nail with the magnet.

10. Once you've magnetized the nail, even slightly, you're going to try to demagnetize it. Drop it on a table 10-15 times. Try to pick up the paper clip again. If the nail is still magnetized, drop it some more. Can you get it to completely lose its ability to act as a magnet?

11. Fill in the rest of the lab sheet.

Possible Answers:

#1, #2: ferromagnetic (If this was not the answer, go over the ideas of domains and ferromagnetic materials again with the student.)

#3: Answers will vary.

#4, #5: have no interaction with

#6, #7: attract

#8: attracts

#9, #10: Answers will vary.

#11: had no interaction with (but may vary because sometimes the paper clip becomes semi-permanently magnetized)

#12: magnetized temporarily

#13: Answer should include the idea of domains lining up in one direction.

#14, #15: Answers will vary.

#16: attracted

#17: probably less than, but may be equal to

#18: less than

#19: point in the same direction

[continued]

#20: no longer magnetic

#21: lined up

#22: in the same direction as the magnet's

#23: back to their original random directions

#24: The before picture should show domains in the nail pointing every which way. The after picture should show domains lined up in the same direction.

Conclusion / Discussion:

1. Many people have tried to magnetize a nail or paper clip or screwdriver before doing this experiment, but most don't know quite why rubbing an object with iron in it with a magnet will magnetize that object. Now that you've magnetized an object, pretend to explain to someone else how magnetizing an object works. Better yet, find someone who didn't participate in this lab and actually explain it.

2. Can you think of why it might be useful to have something temporarily, but not permanently, magnetic? We'll find out some answers to this question when we study electromagnets, but you might be able to come up with some ideas now.

3. Do you think domains would be visible in a microscope? Do you think there would be a way to make them visible in a microscope? Why or why not? It's actually pretty tough to see domains microscopically, but some pictures have been found by using microscopic metal filings and other methods such as bombarding a piece of ferromagnetic material with x-rays. You might try to look up such pictures in a recently published book or on the Internet.

More Lab Fun:

1. One experiment we didn't try is to determine whether other ways of rubbing a ferromagnetic object with a magnet will magnetize the object. What happens if you rub back and forth? Can you explain why you get the result that you do?

2. You can also try to see what happens if you leave a ferromagnetic object like a nail attached to a magnet overnight or longer. Will this force the domains to remain lined up? Why do you think you got the result you did? (This could turn out either way, depending on the object and the strength of the magnet.)

Notebooking Ideas:

1. Look in a book or online for a list of ferromagnetic materials. Write them in your notebook. Make a list of things around the house that are ferromagnetic.

2. Use a Post-it note pad to make a flipbook of domains in a nail starting out in different directions and then all lining up and attracting a paper clip. Glue your flip book into your notebook.

NAME _____ DATE _____

Is It a Magnet or Isn't It?

PART I
Hypotheses:

1. I think the paper clips are **magnetic / ferromagnetic / magnets themselves**.

2. I think the nail is **magnetic / ferromagnetic / a magnet itself**.

3. I think that because the paper clips and nail have magnetic domains, I **will / will not** be able to magnetize them. I think this because _____

   _____

   _____.

Control Observations:

4. Two paper clips **attract / have no interaction with / repel** each other.

5. The nail and the paper clip **attract / have no interaction with / repel** each other.

6. The magnet and the paper clip **attract / have no interaction with / repel** each other.

7. The magnet and the nail **attract / have no interaction with / repel** each other.

Experimental Observations:

8. When I try to pick up a second paper clip with a paper clip already attached to the magnet, the attached paper clip **attracts / has no interaction with / repels** the second paper clip.

9. I can use the attached paper clip to pick up _____ other paper clips.

10. When I attracted a paper clip to a magnet, then attracted a second paper clip to the first paper clip, I tried to remove the magnet from the first paper clip. The paper clips **still held onto each other / separated from each other**.

11.   If the two paper clips still held onto each other, when I separated them and then tried to attract one with the other, the two paper clips **attracted** / **had no interaction with** / **repelled** each other.

Analysis and Conclusions:

12.   It appears that ferromagnetic materials, like the paper clips, can become **magnetized temporarily** / **magnetized permanently** / **electrified** when exposed to a magnet's magnetic field.

13.   If I try to relate this observation to the idea of domains within ferromagnetic materials, I think that what is happening inside the paper clips is: _____

_____

_____.

PART II
Hypotheses:

14.   I think I **can** / **cannot** create a semipermanent magnet out of a ferromagnetic material like a paper clip or a nail.

15.   Using the idea of domains in a ferromagnet, describe why you think it is possible (or impossible) to create a semipermanent magnet. You can sketch a picture of the directions of the magnetic fields if you'd like as well.

_____

_____

_____

_____

_____

_____

_____

_____

_____

Observations:

16. After rubbing the nail repeatedly in the same direction with a strong magnet, I found that the nail **attracted** / **had no interaction with** / **repelled** the paper clip.

17. The strength of the attraction seemed to be **greater than** / **equal to** / **less than** the strength of the magnet I used to magnetize the nail.

18. After I dropped the nail a number of times, the nail's ability to attract the paper clip seemed to be **greater than** / **equal to** / **less than** the nail's ability to attract the paper clip before it was dropped.

Analysis and Conclusions:

19. When a ferromagnetic material like the iron in the nail is placed near a magnetic field, the domains within the material **point in different directions** / **point in the same direction** / **are destroyed**.

20. When the ferromagnetic material is removed from the field, the domains go back to pointing in different directions, so the material is **no longer magnetic** / **a permanent magnet**.

21. When I stroked the iron nail with a magnet, I think that on each stroke the domains **lined up** / **didn't line up** with the magnet's field.

22. By stroking repeatedly, I was able to create a semipermanent magnet. I think this is because the domains mostly remained oriented **in the same direction as the magnet's** / **in random directions** as I kept stroking the nail.

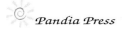

23. When I dropped the nail repeatedly, I think the domains were forced **back to their original random directions** / **to all line up**.

24. Sketch what was happening inside the nail before and after it was turned into a magnet:

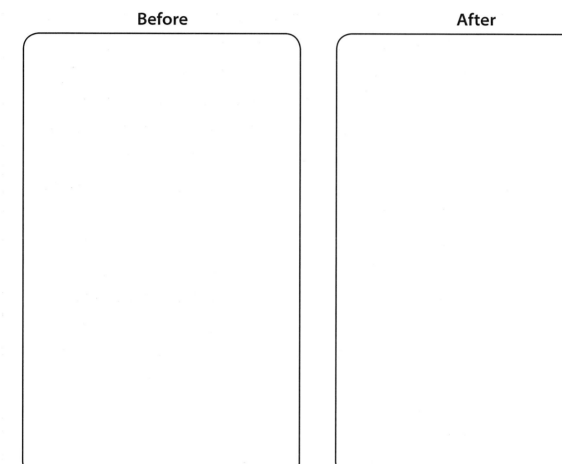

Before   **After**

For my notebook

Finding the North Pole

You've heard of the North Pole, right? If you have a globe, go find the North Pole on it. I imagine it was pretty easy to find. Much easier than if you were searching for the location of Timbuktu (which is in West Africa). Most of us have a pretty good idea of where the North Pole is located on a globe. Why do you think that particular spot on the globe is called the North Pole?

Many people will answer that the North Pole is where compasses in the northern half of the world point. Surprisingly, this answer is incorrect. Actually, the North Pole is located at one end of the <u>axis</u> of planet Earth. The axis is an imaginary pole around which Earth spins as it orbits the sun. The South Pole is located at the opposite end of this imaginary pole. Most globes spin around a stick that represents Earth's axis.

Why do many people think that compasses point to the North Pole? You may not know this, but Earth acts like it's essentially a giant magnet. Obviously, Earth is not the sort of magnet that you can see or touch. Earth, however, behaves as if there is a huge magnet running through the center of the planet, lined up almost, but not precisely, with Earth's axis. Scientists are not entirely certain about what causes Earth to behave like a magnet, but most agree that it is probably caused by molten iron spinning within the outer core as Earth rotates.

If you were reading or listening extremely carefully, you might have noticed that I wrote that the magnetism of Earth is *almost* lined up with Earth's axis. In the northern hemisphere, if you take out a compass and let the needle swing around to point north, you might be surprised to discover that it's not actually pointing directly at the North Pole. Because the axis of Earth and the magnetic field of Earth don't line up exactly, compasses point to a spot called <u>magnetic north</u>. A few years before I wrote this book, magnetic north was located more than 400 miles away from the real North Pole! You can imagine that this would make it hard to use a compass correctly to figure out where the North Pole is. In fact, precise maps show information to help line up a compass with <u>true north</u> so that it can be used correctly.

The situation is even more complicated though. Magnetic north seems to be on the move. In the last century, the magnetic north pole has travelled more than 600 miles. At the present time, it seems to be moving approximately 25 miles every year toward an area of Russia known as Siberia! Scientists think this movement is caused by variations in the spinning core of Earth. Only one thing is certain about the location of magnetic north at this point: if you try to follow it to the North Pole, you'll end up a long way from where you wanted to end up.

There is one more strange fact about magnetic north you should know. If you take out a compass and hold it next to a bar magnet, the needle of the compass, which points to magnetic north, will point to the south pole of the magnet. This means that if you think of Earth as a giant magnet, what we call the magnetic north pole is actually the south pole of the magnet. But, we call it the "north pole" because that's where the north pole of all the magnets in the northern hemisphere point. As you know, however, north poles are attracted to south poles, so calling "magnetic north" the "magnetic south" would be more accurate. Nevertheless, people are so accustomed to the names they've been using, that we still call magnetic north "magnetic north."

Magnetism Lab #5: Oh No! I Thought It Was the North Pole
- instructions

Materials:
- Lab sheets, pencil
- Cork (like a wine bottle cork)
- Bowl of water
- Needle that is magnetic
- Bar magnet with north and south poles labeled

Aloud: Even though you couldn't use a compass to get to the North Pole without also knowing where magnetic north might be at a particular time, compasses are still quite useful. Let's make a compass now by magnetizing a needle and allowing it to float freely so that it can turn to point toward magnetic north.

Procedure:
1. Find a needle or straight pin that is attracted by a magnet. Demonstrate that it can be attracted by a magnet.

2. Fill in #1-#5 on the lab sheet. If students have trouble with #5, suggest they think of ways they can use a labeled bar magnet to figure out which pole is which on the needle.

3. Construct the compass: Fill the bowl with water. Stroke the needle on one end of the bar magnet 100 times (as in the previous experiment) to magnetize it.

4. Push the needle through the cork (an adult needs to perform this step).

5. Place the cork and needle into the water. Watch how it behaves. Does it seem to turn to orient itself in a particular direction? If you slowly turn the bowl, does the needle keep pointing in the same direction?

6. Figure out which end of the needle is pointing north. Use the bar magnet by placing it a few inches from the bowl, with the SOUTH end of the bar magnet toward the bowl. Observe which end of the needle turns toward the magnet. This is the end of the needle that points north.

7. Fill in the remainder of the lab sheet.

Possible Answers:
> #1: It can be attracted by a magnet.
> #2: rubbing repeatedly in one direction with a magnet
> #3: two, north & south
> #4: North
> #5: using a bar magnet to see which end of the needle is attracted by the south pole of the bar magnet
> #6: slowly turned to point in a particular direction
> #7: north-south
> #8: north pole, south
> #9: north
> #10: Answers will vary.

[continued]

Conclusion / Discussion:

1. Many kids have done an experiment like this before. Have you? Did you learn anything new when you did the experiment this time? What was it? This is another example of how scientific knowledge accumulates based on previous experiments!

2. Make sure everyone understands the difference between the true North Pole and the magnetic north pole of Earth. Also make sure that everyone understands that the magnetic north pole is really the south pole of Earth's magnetic field. If students are having problems with this, you should do the first note-booking exercise below to clear things up.

3. There are special maps for people who go backpacking in the wild called topographic maps. If you were a mapmaker, how would you go about letting people know how to get their maps oriented correctly with a compass now that you know that magnetic north is moving around? Talk about the ideas you have about how you might accomplish this.

More Lab Fun:

1. Now that you know which part of your compass is pointing toward magnetic north, you can make a treasure hunt for some friends. Start in one spot with your compass. Give directions to where the treasure is hidden like: "Take 10 steps toward the north. Then take 20 steps toward the east." Your treasure could be a nice drawing or some cookies to share.

2. Design a compass rose for your compass. A compass rose is a pretty design that also shows the points on the compass, like the picture below, but they are often highly decorated.

3. If you have a real compass, get it out and compare it to how your compass works. What things are the same? What things are different? Why?

Notebooking Ideas:

1. Draw a picture of Earth with the imaginary axis drawn through it. Label the true North Pole and the true South Pole. Now, label the magnetic north and magnetic south poles. Next to the picture of Earth, make a picture of a compass with its needle pointing toward the magnetic north pole. Label the poles of the compass needle as well.

2. Imagine you were an early ocean adventurer. You set off for unknown parts of the world. How would you use a compass to keep track of where you traveled? If you discovered an island full of gold and treasure, how could you use the compass to return to the island after fetching a few cargo ships? Write down your answers or make them part of a story you add to your notebook.

Oh No! I Thought It Was the North Pole

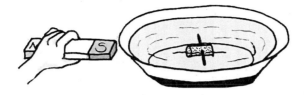

Planning your Compass:

1. I am going to make a compass needle that points to the magnetic north pole. The needle is ferromagnetic. I know this because _____
   _____
   _____.

2. Because the needle is ferromagnetic, I know that I can magnetize it by
   _____
   _____.

3. Once I magnetize the needle, it will have **one / two / three / four** poles. These poles are called the (circle the correct names): **north / south / east / west / northwest** poles.

4. The _____ pole of the needle will be attracted to magnetic north.

5. I can figure out which side of the needle is north and which side is south by _____
   _____.

Observations:

6. When I placed the cork with the magnetized needle into the bowl of water, the needle **spun wildly in circles / slowly turned to point in a particular direction / leapt out of the bowl**.

7. Because of my understanding of how Earth's magnetic field is oriented, I believe that the needle lined up to point in a **north-south / east-west** direction.

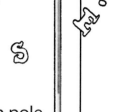

8.   To figure out which end of the needle is pointing north, I need to see which end of the needle is pointing toward the magnetic north pole. The **north pole / south pole** of the needle will point toward the magnetic north pole because the magnetic north pole of Earth is really a **north / south** pole.

9.   Whichever end of the needle is attracted to a bar magnet's south pole will be the end of the needle that points toward the magnetic **north / south** pole of Earth.

10. By using the bar magnet, I determined that the **sharp, pointy / dull** end of the needle on my compass is pointing toward the magnetic north pole.

11. Here is a picture of my compass and the bar magnet used to determine which pole is at which end of the needle (label the poles on the bar magnet and the needle):

Unit 8- Magnetism

Unit 9

Electricity

Unit 9- Electricity

For my notebook

Let's Start inside the Atom

If you've studied chemistry, you might already have learned about some of the parts that make up an <u>atom</u>. There are three basic parts to an atom: <u>protons</u>, <u>neutrons</u>, and <u>electrons</u>. In the center of an atom, is an area called the <u>nucleus</u> which contains the protons and neutrons. Protons have what is called a <u>positive charge</u>. A charge is like a tiny bit of electrical energy. Each proton has a positive charge with a value of one. So, each proton is often represented as a plus sign like this: +. Neutrons are similar to protons in size and mass, but they differ from protons because they have no charge.

Moving around the nucleus, almost at the speed of light, are electrons. Electrons are tiny when compared to protons and neutrons. And, their behavior is so fast and complex that physicists don't usually think of them as orbiting the nucleus in the usual way we think of one object orbiting another. Instead, electrons are said to form a cloud around the nucleus of the atom as they whiz around. And, as you might recall from our study of magnetism, these electrons are also spinning while they are whizzing! Each electron has a <u>negative charge</u> of one. So, each electron is often represented as a minus sign like this: — .

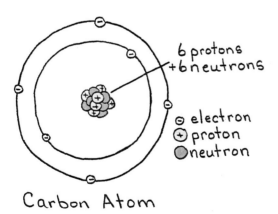

6 protons
+6 neutrons

⊖ electron
⊕ proton
⚫ neutron

Carbon Atom

Here's a simplified drawing to give you a sense of the inside of the atom. The number of protons determines what kind of atom you're looking at. In this case, there are six protons and it is a picture of a carbon atom. If there were eight protons, it would be an oxygen atom.

Do you remember the short saying we learned to help remember when magnets attract or repel each other? It was: "opposites attract and likes repel." This saying works for electrical charges as well. Two positive charges repel each other, and a negative and a positive charge attract one another. This fact gives rise to a fundamental question in physics: How does the nucleus of an atom stay together if there are a bunch of positively charged protons next to each other?

It takes a lot of strength to hold two magnetic north poles together, as you probably discovered when studying magnets. It would be even harder to keep a bunch of protons tightly packed together within the nucleus of the atom. Physicists have given a very appropriate name to the force that holds protons together: the <u>strong force</u>. I think it's really interesting to note that the strong force is about 1,000,000,000,000,000,000,000,000,000,000,000,000,000,000 (one sextillion) times as strong as gravity is.

In the next sections, we're going to be learning about <u>electricity</u>. You may have noticed that the words electricity and electron start with the same letters. That's because electricity has to do with the movement and behavior of electrons. Do you remember another force that has to do with the movement and behavior of electrons? What did you come up with? If your answer is magnetism, you are correct. Keep that thought in mind because, as we'll discover in later sections, electricity and magnetism are very closely related.

Unit 9- Electricity

Pandia Press

Electricity Lab #1: Atomic Super Models - instructions

Materials:
- Lab sheets, pencil
- Clay, two colors. Use either self-hardening clay, or polymer clay that can be baked to harden.
- Colored pencils or crayons, same colors as the clay

Aloud: As you can imagine, it can be quite difficult to study and experiment on things that are so small we can neither see nor touch them. We had this difficulty in conducting experiments with air. To solve the problem, we observed how air affects things around the air—things like balloons and glasses of water that we can see and study. How can scientists come to understand something like the atom, though, when atoms are the tiny particles that make up everything around us and not only affect everything around us but actually are part of everything around us?

This is a tough, a very tough, question. It hasn't been until the last century that scientists have begun to find ways to study what happens inside the atom, and most of the methods they use involve bombarding atoms with x-rays or other energetic waves or accelerating atoms to superfast speeds and crashing them into each other to see what happens. As you can probably guess, we're not going to be able to perform experiments like this at home or at school.

When scientists can't study something directly or even indirectly, they often make models. In fact, if you look at the history of our understanding of the atom, it proceeds from one model of the atom to the next. Let's try to duplicate some of the most famous models of the atom. We're going to proceed through history, one discovery at a time, until we get to the modern idea of the atom.

Procedure:
Democritus's Model of the Atom (ca. 400 B.C.E.)

Aloud: Democritus was an ancient Greek philosopher in an age when philosophers studied everything from morality to science. He believed that everything in the world around us was made of tiny particles. According to Democritus, these particles are so small that we cannot see them. This was an amazing thought when Democritus lived. He called these tiny particles atoms, from a Greek word meaning "uncuttable." Democritus believed that atoms could never be split or cut apart, that atoms were always in motion, and that atoms had always and would always exist. His model of an atom would consist of a solid sphere, always moving.

1. Make a model of Democritus's concept of the atom out of some clay. Make it about the size of a superball.

2. Fill in #1 on the lab sheet. Sketch the model you made in the space provided. You should be able to think of several things that Democritus was correct about in his model of the atom, as well as several things that he got wrong.

John Dalton's Model of the Atom (1804)

Aloud: Almost nothing new was discussed or discovered about atoms for many centuries after Democritus. Then, John Dalton came along at the start of the nineteenth century. John Dalton was an English scientist who looked at what was known about how different substances react with each other, and he came up with the idea that chemical reactions involved atoms of one element getting together with other atoms of other elements. Like Democritus, he didn't believe there was anything

[continued]

else going on inside the atom. But, unlike Democritus, he believed that there was one type of atom for each substance—that there were oxygen atoms, hydrogen atoms, and other atoms that combined to form more complex chemicals.

Dalton was definitely on the right track, and his work moved our understanding of atoms forward. But he had some problems. For instance, he thought that water, which is really made of two hydrogen atoms and one oxygen atom, was made of one hydrogen atom and one oxygen atom because that seemed the simplest way to combine the two atoms.

3. We're going to make a model of how Dalton believed atoms worked. Pick one color of clay to represent hydrogen atoms. Pick another color of clay to represent oxygen atoms. Dalton knew that oxygen atoms were probably larger than hydrogen atoms (they are), and that the two combined to form water. So, make a hydrogen atom out of the color you chose for hydrogen by making a tiny sphere (pea-sized or less). Then make an oxygen atom by making a larger sphere (larger than a marble-sized) out of the color you chose for oxygen. Make a model of how the atoms combined in Dalton's model to make water:

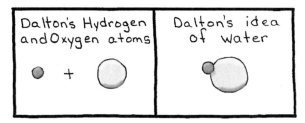

4. Fill in #2 on the lab sheet. Write in what color you are using to represent hydrogen and what color you are using to represent oxygen in the blanks. Sketch the model you made in the space provided. Record the things Dalton got right about atoms, and those he got wrong.

Avogadro's Model of the Atom (1811)

Aloud: An Italian scientist refined John Dalton's model by figuring out how to tell how many atoms of various substances are needed to combine to form a new substance. So, he was able to figure out that water actually has two hydrogen atoms for every one oxygen atom. This Italian scientist had a name that is so amazing and musical that I had to share the whole thing with you. Here it is: Lorenzo Romano Amedeo Carlo Avogadro di Quaregna e di Cerreto. Most scientists today simply refer to him as Avogadro and they still use his discoveries in chemical calculations. Like Dalton and Democritus, Avogadro didn't consider that there might be many things happening inside the atom.

5. Make a model of Avogadro's idea of the water molecule by making two small hydrogen atoms (spheres of clay) and one larger oxygen atom. Attach them to make what Avogadro might have thought a water molecule looked like, like this:

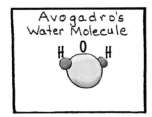

6. Fill in #3 on the lab sheet.

[continued]

THOMPSON'S MODEL OF THE ATOM (1904)

Aloud: Not too long after Dalton and Avogadro's advances, an English scientist named J.J. Thompson made a tremendous discovery. He was experimenting with cathode rays, which we know now are rays made of electrons. Back in J.J. Thompson's day, however, scientists weren't sure whether these rays were made of something mysterious like light, or made of actual particles with mass. J.J. Thompson designed experiments to prove that these rays were made of particles and, even more interesting, that these particles were negatively charged and were very small, with about 1/1000th of the mass of the smallest atom, the hydrogen atom. From these facts, he hypothesized that these particles, which he called "corpuscles," but which we call electrons, were separate parts of the atom. He knew that there must be something positively charged in the atom as well, something that had the rest of 999/1000th mass of the atom. He thought that maybe this other piece of the atom was like a sea of positive charge, with little electrically charged particles floating at random. This was called the plumpudding model of the atom, because it looked like pudding into which someone had dropped pieces of plum!

7. Make a plumpudding model of the atom. Pick a color to represent electrons, what Thompson called "corpuscles," and make several teeny-tiny spheres. Pick another color to represent the positively charged "pudding." Sprinkle the electrons onto the pudding.

8. Fill in #4 on the lab sheet.

RUTHERFORD'S MODEL OF THE ATOM (1911)

Aloud: One of J.J. Thompson's best students was a man named Ernest Rutherford. Rutherford was born in New Zealand but ended up in England studying under Thompson. Rutherford performed experiments that demonstrated that the positive charge in the atom wasn't spread around like plum pudding but was all in a small space relative to the total size of the atom. Based on this, he came up with a model for the atom that was both elegant and familiar: the planetary model. Rutherford thought that the atom was like a little solar system, with positively charged protons in the center and electrons orbiting around it like planets. You've probably seen pictures of Rutherford's model. They look like this:

Rutherford hypothesized that there were other particles in the center of the atom called "neutrons" that helped to hold the protons together, but he was unable to prove this. In fact, the existence of neutrons was eventually proven, but neutrons are not what holds protons together.

9. Make a model of Rutherford's idea of the atom. Use the color you chose in the previous model for the "pudding," and make a few spheres about the size of a marble to represent the positive protons. Use the color you used for the negatively charged particles and make several smaller spheres. Pretend they are orbiting the larger spheres. Now you have Rutherford's atom!

10. Fill in #5 on the lab sheet. On your drawing of the model, label the proton and the electrons. Use lines with arrows to show that the electrons are circling the center of the atom.

[continued]

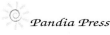

Bohr's Model of the Atom (1913)

Aloud: Rutherford's model provided another great leap forward in understanding the atom. Only a couple of years later, Niels Bohr, a Danish scientist, solved a couple of problems that had been discovered with Rutherford's model. In Bohr's model, the electrons still orbit the positively charged center of the atom, but they fill in orbitals, or particular areas that electrons can orbit in. The orbital closest to the nucleus can hold only two electrons and has electrons with the lowest amount of energy. The second orbital or shell can hold eight electrons, which have more energy than the electrons closer to the nucleus. To jump to a lower orbital, electrons have to give off some energy. To jump to a higher orbital, electrons need to absorb some energy.

Bohr's model is extremely close to how scientists think of the atom today. It is simple enough to be used by many chemists, physicists, and biologists in their work and close enough to our observations to provide accurate results in many experiments. If you take chemistry or physics in high school, much of what you learn will be based on the Bohr model.

11. Make Bohr's model of the atom. Make a large positive nucleus with eight protons squeezed together. Now, make eight tiny electrons. Rather than putting them all in equal orbits around the nucleus, place two of the electrons pretty close to the nucleus and the remainder of the electrons in an orbital that is farther out. Imagine that the electrons are all orbiting around the nucleus and that there are two more spaces that electrons could fill in the outside orbital you've made. This is Bohr's model of oxygen!

de Broglie's Model of the Atom (1926)

Aloud: Many scientists were shocked at Bohr's model of the atom. One of Bohr's requirements for how the model worked had to do with electrons moving from one shell to another. They didn't just move from one shell to another, but instantaneously jumped from one spot to another. This meant that they basically teleported around the atom in response to energy being absorbed and released. Things got even stranger when Louis de Broglie argued that electrons weren't quite particles after all. He said that sometimes they might behave like little spheres traveling around the nucleus, but other times they behave like waves. Instead of traveling in an orbital, electrons exist in an electron cloud, in some areas of which you are more likely to find an electron than others.

His theory, which seems to be correct, led to all sorts of strange and amazing ideas. Scientists named Heisenberg and Schrodinger explored these ideas further, including the idea that one could never quite know both where and how fast an electron was moving at the same time. This is the modern concept of the atom. It looks something like the picture to the right. The more dots in an area, the more likely it is that the electron is in that area, but it's impossible to say exactly where the electron will travel around the orbital.

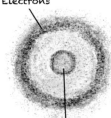

Probability Density of Electrons

Atomic Nucleus

12. It's very hard to make a clay model of the modern concept of the atom because electrons aren't believed to really exist in a particular place or shape like other objects. Still, you can try to make a model of a nucleus surrounded by an electron cloud. I'd love to see what you come up with!

13. Fill in #7. If you'd like, you can sketch the picture of the modern model of the atom given above.

[continued]

Answers could include the following:

#1: What Democritus got correct:
-Everything is made of atoms.
-Atoms are very small and cannot be seen by the human eye.

What Democritus got incorrect:
-There is nothing smaller than an atom.
-Atoms cannot be cut up and have no smaller parts within them.
-Atoms exist forever.

#2: What John Dalton got correct:
-Atoms are important to understanding chemical reactions.
-Different types of atoms exist for different substances.
-Different atoms combine in different amounts to make molecules like water.

What John Dalton got incorrect:
-Water had only 1 hydrogen atom.
-There was nothing smaller than atoms.

#3: What Avogadro got correct:
-The proportions of atoms in a molecule, for example: water has two
    hydrogen atoms and one oxygen atom.

What Avogadro got incorrect:
-There was nothing smaller than atoms.

#4: What Thompson got correct:
-There were small negatively charged particles within atoms.
-The atom was dividable into smaller components.

What Thompson got incorrect:
-The idea that the negative particles were floating in sea of positive charge.

#5: What Rutherford got correct:
-There is a nucleus of positive charge orbited by electrons which are negatively
    charged.

What Rutherford got incorrect:
-The electrons all orbit at around the same distance from the nucleus.

#6: What Bohr got correct:
-Electrons exist in orbitals around the nucleus of the atom, with only a certain
    number of electrons allowed in each orbital.
-Electrons jump instantaneously from one orbital to another. They jump to a
    higher orbital if they gain energy and to a lower orbital if they lose energy.

What Bohr got incorrect:
-Still conceives of electrons as particles orbiting a nucleus.

Probability Density
of Electrons

Atomic Nucleus

#7: What de Broglie got correct:
-Electrons act both like particles and waves simultaneously.
-Electrons exist is something like a cloud, in which there are areas that
    electrons are more likely to be found.

[continued]

Conclusion / Discussion:

1. There was A LOT of information in this section. Focus students on the idea that there have been a series of models of the atom that have changed and developed because scientists kept experimenting in order to try to prove (or disprove) existing models. Make sure that students have some sense of the starting point (atoms are tiny indivisible spheres) and the ending point (atoms are made of protons and neutrons in a nucleus with electrons in a cloud around that nucleus).

2. Why do you think scientists became so upset when it appeared that electrons could instantaneously teleport from one orbital to another? I think it's because it defied our common sense—the things we're used to seeing and experiencing never disappear from one spot and instantaneously appear in another. Many ideas in science defy common sense. Why do you think we eventually come to accept and believe these strange ideas?

More Lab Fun:

1. Make a permanent Timeline of Atomic Discovery on a strip of card stock using your clay atom models. Label each model with the date of discovery and the scientist.

2. It can be very fun to make models of various molecules. You can look up online what atoms make up things like sugar, sand, and whatever other substance you are interested in. Then, make a model of that molecule with clay.

3. If you have a group of people, try to make these models with people instead of (or in addition to) clay. Let a few people be protons, stuck in the middle (or creating a sea in the plumpudding model). Other people can be electrons, behaving as they do in the different models. If you're an electron, don't forget to try to spin while you're orbiting in the modern model!

Notebooking Idea:

If you keep a timeline, place the scientists and their discoveries on your timeline.

Atomic Super Models

1. Democritus: (ca. 460 BCE–370 BCE)

Democritus thought the atom looks like this:	What Democritus got right:	What Democritus got wrong:

2. John Dalton: (1766-1844)

Dalton thought there were different atoms for different substances. Here is a picture of a hydrogen atom (_____) and an oxygen atom (_____) combining to make what he thought was water.

Dalton thought a water molecule looks like this:	What Dalton got right:	What Dalton got wrong:

Atomic Super Models - page 2

3. Avogadro: (1776-1856)

Avogadro figured out how to tell how many atoms of what element were needed to make a substance. He came up with the correct chemical formula for water, which is two hydrogen molecules and one oxygen molecule. Here is a picture of two hydrogen atoms (_____) and an oxygen atom (_____) combined into a water molecule.

Avogadro thought a water molecule looks like this:	What Avogadro got right:	What Avogadro got wrong:

4. J.J. Thompson (1856-1940)

J.J. Thompson figured out that there were very small particles inside the atom carrying a negative charge. He posited a "plum-pudding" model of the atom. In the drawing below, the small negatively charged particles are colored _____ and the positively charged "pudding" they float in is colored _____.

Thompson thought the atom looks like this:	What Thompson got right:	What Thompson got wrong:

5. Ernest Rutherford (1871-1937)

Ernest Rutherford figured out that the positive charge of the atom was concentrated in one place, which he correctly placed in the center of the atom. He also figured out that the smaller negatively charged electrons circle the atom. In the drawing below, the negatively charged electrons are colored _____ and the positively charged protons are colored _____.

Rutherford thought the atom looks like this:	What Rutherford got right:	What Rutherford got wrong:

6. Niels Bohr (1885-1962)

Niels Bohr came up with the idea of electron orbitals, shells in which a certain amount of electrons with a certain amount of energy could orbit the nucleus. According to Bohr, the first orbital has two spaces for electrons and the second orbital has eight spaces. Here is a picture of an oxygen atom according to Bohr's model. The electrons are _____ and the protons are _____. I've made two uncolored circles to represent spots in the second orbital for two more electrons.

Bohr thought the atom looks like this:	What Bohr got right:	What Bohr got wrong:

7. Louis de Broglie (1892-1987)

De Broglie built on Bohr's idea of orbitals by describing electrons as simultaneously acting like waves and particles. Because electrons are no longer viewed to be entirely like tiny little particles, we envision there being a "cloud" in which it is more likely one will find a given electron.

de Broglie thought the atom looked like this:	What de Broglie got right:	What de Broglie got wrong:
		We don't know, yet!

Static: It's Electrifying

Congratulations! You now know more about the structure of the atom than many (perhaps most) college students. You might wonder, "Why are we learning so much about the atom when we're supposed to be studying electricity?" Understanding electricity depends on understanding electrons and how they behave which, in turn, depends on understanding the atoms they are part of.

There are two types of electricity: static electricity and current electricity. The word <u>static</u> means "not moving." The word <u>current</u> is used in the sense of a current of water, which is water that is moving in a particular direction. So, <u>static electricity</u> is electricity which is not moving, and <u>current electricity</u> is electricity that is flowing, almost like water, in a particular direction.

We're going to start out by learning about static electricity. First, I need to tell you one more thing about electrons. Electrons are like "fair-weather friends." Have you ever heard that phrase? It's usually used to describe a person who acts like a friend until some new thing comes along that's more interesting and pleasant to do, and that person leaves and becomes a fair-weather friend to someone else. Electrons are like fair-weather friends because they are always ready to change what atom or molecule they are part of.

For example, salt is made from one sodium atom and one chloride atom. The first two electron shells in sodium are totally filled, but sodium has one more electron, so this takes up a space in the third <u>electron shell</u>.

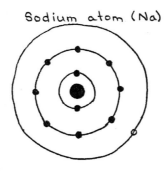

Sodium atom (Na)

Chloride is the opposite. Its first three shells are almost entirely filled up, but chloride is one electron short of filling up its third shell. When these two atoms get close to one another, the lone electron in sodium's third shell jumps to the only empty spot in chloride's third shell.

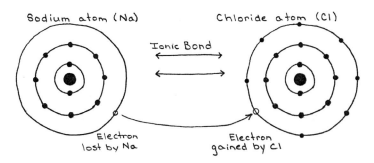

Sodium atom (Na)   Ionic Bond   Chloride atom (Cl)

Electron lost by Na   Electron gained by Cl

All of matter behaves similarly. Have you noticed that if you rub a balloon on your wool sweater the balloon will seem to stick to things like your arm or the wall? You may have been told that this is because of "static." Wool and balloons start out being mostly <u>electrically</u> <u>neutral</u>—with the same number of protons and electrons to balance each other out. However, wool has lots of electrons just waiting for a chance to jump to some other substance. And, balloons are made of latex which conveniently has some welcoming spots for stray electrons. When you rub a balloon on something made of wool, you're giving those electrons a chance to jump from the wool to the balloon. When you're finished rubbing the two together, the balloon has picked up a bunch of extra electrons and is no longer electrically neutral. Because electrons are negatively charged and the balloon now has extra electrons, the balloon has picked up a negative electric charge.

All those extra electrons aren't really doing anything. They are just sitting there on the balloon. Because the electrons aren't moving, this pool of extra electrons on the balloon is a <u>static electrical charge</u>. As you know, opposite charges attract. When this negatively charged balloon comes near a wall or your arm, it is attracted to it. Even though the wall basically has a neutral charge, the balloon is now more negative than the wall, so it is attracted to the wall. Static electricity can do some amazing things, as you're about to find out.

Electricity Lab #2: Static Detector - instructions

Materials:
- Lab sheets, pencil
- Aluminum foil
- Scissors
- Glass jar (it must be glass)
- Index card or card stock large enough to span the top of the jar
- Tape
- Balloon
- Wool sweater or piece of wool cloth
- Hole puncher (optional)

Aloud: One of the problems faced by scientists studying cool and interesting phenomena like static electricity is figuring out how to detect and measure what they are studying. Fortunately, when it comes to detecting static electricity, there is an easy-to-make device, called an <u>electroscope</u>, that detects the presence of static electricity. Here's how it works:

Two strips of aluminum foil are hung next to each other so that they can move freely. How would those two strips of foil behave if we were able to send a negative electrical charge into them? Think through this for a moment: two strips that can move freely with the same charge. What will happen? If you answered that they would repel one another, you're correct!

Electric charge can flow freely through aluminum. So, when you bring something like a negatively charged balloon with lots of extra electrons close to the aluminum foil, the electrons in the aluminum are repelled (remember, likes repel) by the balloon and travel to the ends of the aluminum foil. At this point there are two pieces of aluminum foil, the ends of which are full of negatively charged electrons. So, the two ends of the foil repel one another and move apart from each other. Let's see if we can make it work.

Procedure:
1. Most electroscopes have a large area of metal on top called a <u>collector</u>, so that whatever is being tested for static electricity can be exposed to the area of metal. For our electroscope, crumple up a ball of aluminum foil until it is about the size of a golf ball.

2. Attached to the collector (or ball) is a piece of metal through which electrical charge can travel. We can make this out of aluminum foil as well. Crumple aluminum foil into a stick shape about ½ the diameter of a pencil and several inches less than the height of the glass jar.

3. Trace the opening of the jar onto the card stock. Cut out around the shape you've traced, so that the cut-out shape is a bit larger than the opening of the jar.

4. Punch a hole in the middle of the card stock shape you've cut out with the scissors or a hole puncher. The aluminum foil stick you made should fit through the hole.

5. Put the aluminum foil stick through the hole and attach the collector to one end of the aluminum foil stick by scrunching the foil or with tape.

6. Bend the other end of the aluminum foil stick at about ½ inch at a right angle to make an L shape.

7. Cut a strip of aluminum foil about ½ inch (or 1 cm.) wide and about 5 inches (or 12 cm.) long. Fold this strip in half so that it is half as long. Unfold it.

[continued]

8. Fold about ¼ inch of the strip toward the center on each end.

9. Put everything together so that it looks like the picture below. Let the folded aluminum foil strip hang freely on the hook by the fold. Tape the lid on if you need to in order to keep it stable.

10. Fill in #1 and the first two columns of the observation chart (#2). You are going to test the balloon for static before you rub it with anything and then after you've rubbed it with wool various numbers of times. You can also find some other things around the house to test for static. Some ideas of other things to test:
    - Your hand, before and after wearing socks and rubbing them back and forth on the carpet
    - A computer screen when turned off and when turned on
    - A television when turned off and when turned on
    - Anything you've noticed in your house that seems to have a lot of static (some blankets or clothing have this quality)

11. Test the balloon by holding it close to the collector (the aluminum foil sphere). Watch what happens. Rub the wool across the balloon back and forth one time. Test the balloon again. Keep performing the tests specified in the chart and then test the objects you chose to test as well. If the strips seem stuck in the apart position, this means that they are holding onto whatever charge they have. To discharge them, just touch the collector with your hand.

12. Fill in the remainder of the lab sheet.

13. Go back to the drawing of the electroscope you made. Use arrows and "+" and "-" signs to show what happens when you bring a charged balloon near the collector of the electroscope. Label the collector as well. Try to show or explain the flow of electrons.

Answers could include the following:

Observations: Answers will vary, but the foil strips should definitely move apart when the collector is exposed to the balloon after it has been rubbed with wool quite a bit. If this doesn't happen, make sure the jar you are using is entirely dry, the strips are hanging freely, and can move easily (i.e., aren't bent firmly in a particular position).

#1: moved a little or moved a lot
#2: neutral
#3: from the wool to the balloon
#4: negative
#5: away from
#6: negative
#7: repel

[continued]

Conclusion / Discussion:

1. Many people think that when two objects that are rubbed together generate static it is because of friction between the two objects. This is not true. The rubbing just allows the two surfaces to have better contact so that electrons can jump from one surface to the other. Talk about why this is so.

2. The stronger the static charge on a surface being tested, the farther apart the ends of the aluminum foil strips should move. Why do you think this would be true? Can you think of a way you could quantitatively measure this—that is, measure with numbers rather than just a general sense of farther and closer.

3. Did any of the objects you expected to have static charges fail to move the strips? Did any objects you didn't think would hold a static charge move the strips? Talk about why this might be so.

4. Do you think static electricity is a contact force or an action-at-a-distance force? Why? (Answer: it's action-at-a-distance—think of the behavior of the foil strips inside of the electroscope.)

More Lab Fun:

1. There are dozens of fun experiments that can be done around the house with static electricity. I've listed a few, along with some hints as to why they work:

   • Get two 3-inch pieces of the tape you use for wrapping gifts. Tape each piece to a table (after you've gotten a parent's permission!) with a little hanging off the edge (so you can easily pull off the tape). Adhesives like the tape are good at collecting a static charge, so both pieces of tape are now carrying like charges. Bring them close to one another. They should repel one another dramatically.
   • Charge up the balloon again by rubbing it with wool. Turn on a water tap so a narrow, gentle stream of water is falling. Bring the balloon close to the stream of water without touching it. The static charge on the balloon should repel the water and bend the stream of water.
   • Static discharges more quickly and easily when the air is moist. As a static charge moves through the air, the water dissipates, or lessens it. You can test this on a dry day by rubbing a balloon against some wool and sticking it to a wall. Time how long it takes the balloon to fall. Try the same experiment in the bathroom after someone has taken a shower and the air is moist. What happens?

2. On a dry, winter day, put on some nice comfy socks and rub your feet against the carpet. Touch someone (who has agreed to be shocked) to see what happens. You've just made miniature lightning! Read the next FMN section to understand how this works.

Notebooking Ideas:

1. Diagram what is happening when you rub wool against a balloon as a three-panel comic strip. In the first box show both objects as neutral, with equal numbers of plus and minus charges scattered evenly. In the second panel, show the electrons moving where they move when the two are rubbed together. In the third panel, show the objects with their static charges.

2. Use a definition sheet to define *static electricity* and *current electricity*.

Unit 9- Electricity

Static Detector

Here is a picture of the electroscope I made with a balloon being held near the collector: (Leave lots of room for labeling things, which you'll do later in the lab.)

Static Detector - page 2

Observations:

What I tested	What I think will happen	What happened to the electroscope strips
The balloon, before rubbing with anything		stayed still / moved a little / moved a lot
The balloon, after rubbing with wool 1 time		stayed still / moved a little / moved a lot
The balloon, after rubbing with wool 5 times		stayed still / moved a little / moved a lot
The balloon, after rubbing with wool a lot		stayed still / moved a little / moved a lot
My hand		

Analysis and Conclusions:

1. When I tested the balloon that had been rubbed with wool many times, the foil strips **stayed still** / **moved a little** / **moved a lot**.

2. Before the balloon is rubbed with wool, it has a **positive** / **neutral** / **negative** charge.

3. Because the balloon has space for electrons and the wool has electrons that are easily transferred to other objects, when I rub the balloon with the wool, the electrons move **nowhere** / **from the wool to the balloon** / **from the balloon to the wool**.

4. After this, the balloon has a **positive** / **neutral** / **negative** static charge.

5. When I hold the balloon next to the collector on the electroscope, the negative charge on the balloon pushes the electrons in the collector **toward** / **away from** the balloon.

6. These electrons travel down the aluminum foil to the two strips, causing the strips to both have **negative** / **positive** / **different** charges.

7. Because likes **repel** / **attract**, the two strips move away from each other.

For my notebook

Electricity Rules: Playing It Safe

Electricity is amazing and cool and there are, literally, countless projects and experiments you can do with electricity. Take a moment to think about what you managed to do in the last experiment. You actually manipulated electrons—subatomic particles—into moving from one place to another. I find that utterly astonishing!

As fascinating as electricity is, however, it is also potentially dangerous. Rubbing a balloon with wool to build up a static charge may not seem particularly perilous, and it isn't. However, the same process of molecules giving and taking electrons produces powerful lightning when it occurs in the atmosphere during a thunderstorm.

This is an important and sometimes dangerous quality of static electricity. Although we think of this electricity as static and motionless, sometimes there is so much negative charge in one place compared to the positive charge in another place that the electricity manages to travel through the air! This is what happens in your house when one person happens to give another person a small "shock." As you know, the same type of electricity in the form of lightning can be dangerous if you're too close to it.

So, how can we continue to experiment with electricity—static and current electricity—in a safe manner? Here are some general rules. As we learn more about electricity, you may understand the reasons for these rules better. But, you should always follow these rules unless otherwise specified in the instructions for an experiment:

- Never play with power cords or power outlets.

- Never try to plug any of your experiments into an electrical outlet.

- Use the size battery specified in the experiment's instructions.

- Never use electrical equipment near water unless the electrical equipment is specifically designed for such use (like an underwater camera).

- Don't touch electrical things (toys, outlets, switches, etc.) while your hands are wet.

- Stay away from overhead electrical wires, and keep your kites, Frisbees and other flying toys away from them as well.

- Don't play outside when there is lightning.

If you follow these rules, you can perform all the experiments with electricity in this book safely.

Electrical Current: Going with the Flow

Earlier, we learned that there are two types of electricity: static electricity and electrical current. The difference between the two is pretty simple. Static electricity is a charge that stays still. <u>Electrical</u> <u>current</u> is a charge in motion. Many people explain that, just as water can flow through a pipe, electricity can flow through a wire.

This explanation is not entirely accurate. In a pipe, there is an outside material forming the pipe and an area on the inside, usually containing nothing but air, through which water can flow. In electrical wires, it is electrons which are flowing, and they don't flow through a hollow space in the wire: they flow through the empty spaces in atoms' <u>electron shells</u>.

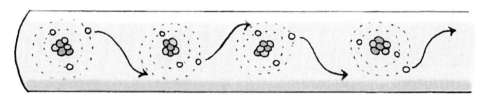

Electrons flow from atom to atom

Just as certain substances are better, or worse, at picking up static charges, there are particular substances which provide plenty of free electrons and other substances with plenty of spaces for electrons to move along. <u>Conductors</u> are those materials that allow electrical charge to move freely, that have plenty of spaces for electrons to move in and out of. Most people think of copper and aluminum as good conductors because these are the materials we most frequently use to conduct electricity. In fact, silver is one of the very best conductors of electricity, but it is far too expensive to use for wiring houses and buildings. In addition, there are nonmetallic substances that can conduct electricity such as salt water and graphite.

<u>Insulators</u> are the opposite of conductors. Insulators make it very difficult for electrons to move from atom to atom, and for the electrical

charge to move freely. Insulators are quite important in our lives. We use them to surround conductors so that we can touch the conductors without getting a shock. This is why copper wires are coated with insulating plastic or rubber. It is also why the electronics you might use every day—computers, televisions, and telephones—are covered in insulating materials, so you don't get an electric shock whenever you touch them. Can you think of other materials that make good insulators? What are telephone/electric poles usually made from? Why?

For water in a pipe to move, there has to be some force to push or pull it. If we tip the pipe so that it is slanting downward, for instance, the water inside it will flow downward because of the force of gravity pulling on it. The water flows down the pipe because it has been lifted against gravity and gained potential energy.

So, what moves electricity along an electrical conductor? Is the process similar to gravity moving water along a pipe? Well, yes and no. Usually, an electrical circuit has some sort of power source that gets the electricity moving. One type of power source that most of us have used is a <u>battery</u>. Just as you would use energy to lift one end of a pipe to create a difference in height from end to the other, a battery uses chemical energy to create a difference in the amount of positive electrical charge and negative electrical charge from one end of the battery to the other. Physicists call this a difference in <u>electrical potential</u>.

You might have noticed that one end of most batteries is labeled "+" or positive. We call this end the <u>cathode</u>. The other end of the battery is labeled "-" or minus. We call this the <u>anode</u>. Many people have a lot of trouble remembering whether the cathode is the positive or negative end of the battery. I always imagine a picture of a really happy and cool cat and think, "There goes a really positive cat." That way, I remember that the CAThode is the positive end of the battery.

When a battery is hooked up to a circuit, chemical reactions in the battery create a difference in electrical potential between the anode and the cathode. If you remember that opposite charges attract and like charges repel each other, you can understand why this difference in electrical potential pushes electricity through a circuit.

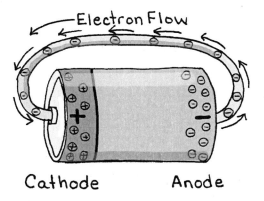

Cathode   Anode

All of the negative charges that accumulate at the anode, or negative end of the battery, repel each other. They are prevented from flowing straight through the battery to the cathode by a chemical barrier. So, they get pushed out into the wire hooked up to the anode. Where do they go? Well, there is the positive end of the battery—the cathode—attracting them on the other side of the circuit. So, they flow through whatever wires or devices are hooked up to the battery toward the cathode. By creating a difference in electrical potential, the battery pushes electrons through a circuit. When the chemicals the battery uses to create this difference are used up, the battery no longer works.

Electricity Lab #3: Going with the Flow - instructions

Materials:

- Lab sheets, pencil
- 2 pieces of insulated wire, about 6-8 inches long, with about ¼ inch of the ends stripped*
- 1 D-cell battery holder
- 1 D-cell battery
- 1 miniature light bulb** (2 to 5 volt, not an LED bulb)
- 1 miniature light bulb receptacle or socket (that fits your miniature lamp bulb)

* **Parents and Teachers:** If you have a tool chest with a wire stripper in it, feel free to use that to strip the wire ends. Otherwise, scissors work just fine. Close the scissors lightly around the end of the wire about ¼ inch from the end and roll the wire between two fingers so the scissors sort of score around the wire in a circle. Then pull the end of the insulation on the wire off.

** **What bulb should I buy?** Students are going to be making circuits to illuminate a flashlight bulb. A decade ago, this was a simple proposition, as there was really only one type of flashlight bulb available: an incandescent bulb. Now, because of environmental concerns, incandescent bulbs are no longer being produced, and LED and other bulbs such as halogen, xenon, and krypton bulbs are replacing them. Halogen, xenon, and krypton bulbs look and function similarly to the old incandescent bulbs.

The best bulb to use for this experiment is the bulb out of an old flashlight. The only bulb that absolutely won't work well is an LED bulb because the voltage requirements for LED bulbs are so low that one needs to use an extra component, a resistor, with regular batteries.

You may have to experiment with one or two bulbs, but the worst that will happen is that you will burn out a flashlight bulb or the exposed ends of the wires might become hot.

Aloud: Have you ever seen a water fountain? Not the type that you can get a drink from, but a water fountain that's large and decorative and squirts water up and around in interesting ways and patterns? Usually, the water is squirted up into a pretty fountain and then falls and flows back downward where it collects in a sort of pool. To get the water back up in the air, to move it from a place closer to the ground to a place higher up, means doing some work which, of course, means applying a force. Usually, this force arises from some sort of motor pushing the water in the direction it needs to go. If you think about it, the water travels around and around—up and out of the water spout, into the air, back to the pool, and then up and out of the water spout again. The water travels in a closed loop. In other words, no one needs to add more water or take out water for the fountain to keep functioning.

The same type of process is at work in an electrical circuit. An electrical circuit is like the water fountain, a closed loop, but instead of moving water around and around, the electrical circuit moves electricity around and around. As the electricity moves around and around, we'll learn how it accomplishes various tasks—lighting up bulbs, traveling through switches, and providing the power for so many devices that we use every day.

In a water fountain, there are many parts—a motor, pipes, a pool to collect the water. Just as with the water fountain, an electrical circuit contains many parts called components that move the electricity around and make use of the electricity. Let's start our study of circuits by learning about some electronic components.

Procedure:

1. Take a look at the battery. Different brands of batteries may look a bit different from each other, but they all have certain similarities. Fill in #1 on the lab sheet, and make sure to include the information specified on the lab sheet.

[continued]

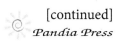
Pandia Press

Aloud: Do you remember that in the last reading you learned about the two ends of the battery--the cathode and the anode? One is the positive end of the battery and the other is the negative end of the battery. Do you remember which is which? In any case, we learned that it is the difference between the positive and negative ends of the battery--the difference in electrical potential--that causes electricity to flow through a circuit.

How does a battery create these differences in electrical potential? There's no motor inside the battery, and no little person to push charged particles around. But, there is something like a motor—something that transforms one kind of energy, in this case chemical energy, into another kind of energy, in this case electrical energy. In an alkaline battery, which is one of the most common types of batteries, the two ends of the battery are separated by special chemicals. When a battery is connected to a circuit, the chemicals start to react, and the reaction sends electrons traveling from the minus end to the plus end of the battery. This is also why batteries "run out" after a while. Once all the chemicals have reacted, all the usable chemical energy has been released, and the battery no longer works.

Label the following on your picture of a battery and fill in #2 to #5 on the lab sheet:
• Anode (low potential)
• Cathode (high potential)

2. Examine the battery holder. Notice how you can place the battery inside it so that both the anode and the cathode ends of the battery are touching metal. Once the chemical reaction starts in the battery, electricity will be able to flow into the metal parts of the battery holder. If there are wires attached to the battery holder, the electricity will be able to flow through them as well.

3. Now take a look at the wire. It should have two parts—the inside made of a conductive metal (probably copper) and the outside made of an insulating material. We strip the insulating material off the ends so that it will be easy to connect the conducting part of the wire to a battery or other component.

4. Also, take a look at the light bulb and compare it to the drawing of a light bulb provided on the worksheet.

Aloud: In the old days, all light bulbs were what are called incandescent bulbs. *Incandescent* means something which gives off light when heated. Incandescent bulbs usually have two exposed wires between which hangs a "filament" or a thin wire that resists the flow of electricity and heats up and glows as electricity flows through it. Over time, the filament becomes weak from the heat and the friction and breaks. We say that the bulb has "burnt out."

Incandescent bulbs lit up our world for more than a century, but they use a lot of energy. Because of this, most countries are phasing out the use of incandescent bulbs. One group of new light bulbs works by taking advantage of how certain gases interact with the element called tungsten. These bulbs also have a tungsten filament that glows, but because of special chemical reactions between tungsten and these gases, as the filament wears out, new tungsten is deposited on the filament and keeps it from burning out for much longer. Thus, these "halogen bulbs" are less wasteful.

Another type of light bulb that is becoming common is an LED bulb. LED bulbs light up because they are made of a special material called a semiconductor, which glows as electrons pass through it. LED bulbs use extremely low amounts of energy, don't give off as much heat, and generally last longer than incandescent bulbs. In this experiment, you should be using either an incandescent or halogen bulb.

[continued]

Electricity Lab #3: Going with the Flow - instructions page 3

Did you notice that at the base of the light bulb is a small metallic area? This is one of the contacts on the light bulb, one of the metallic areas that can connect to an electronic circuit. Do you have any idea where the other contact on the light bulb is? It can be hard to figure out because the other contact serves two purposes—it is both a contact and the area of the light bulb that screws into or sits in a socket.

So, what happens when electricity flows into one of the light bulb's contacts? Because the metallic parts of the bulb are conductors, the electricity flows up through the contact and into the filament. The metal making up the filament is called tungsten and has a special quality: it resists the flow of electricity. It doesn't stop the flow, like an insulator would, and it doesn't just conduct the electricity, as a conductor would. Instead, the moving electrons bump into the atoms of the filament as they move along, causing the atoms to vibrate. As the atoms vibrate, the filament heats up and gives off light. The electrons eventually make their way out of the filament and flow out of the other contact of the light bulb.

5. Label the following on the light bulb diagram and trace the flow of electricity. Fill in #6-#10 on the lab sheet.

   - Filament
   - Contact (the screw part)
   - Contact (the base part)
   - Inert gas (inside the bulb)

Aloud: Look at your light bulb socket. It has two contacts (sometimes screws or flaps of metals). One of these is attached to the contact on the base of the light bulb and the other connects to the screw part of the light bulb. Because these contacts are made of conductors, you can connect wires to them and the electricity will flow into and out of the contacts of the light bulb.

And, that is the last piece of knowledge you need to be able to construct your first electronic circuit. Can you figure out how to connect the battery, the battery holder, two wires, and the light bulb so that it lights up? Remember that a circuit has to be a loop—every component will have something that conducts electricity leading into it and something that conducts electricity leading out of it, just like every part of the water fountain has something that carries water into it and out of it. Try out some circuits to see which of them lights up the bulb. Using the symbols you learned, draw at least two diagrams—one of which works to light up the bulb and one that doesn't. Complete the rest of the lab sheet.

(If you have trouble drawing a circuit, look at the answer section on the next page.)

Answers could include the following:

#2: cathode

#3: anode

#4: chemical

#6:

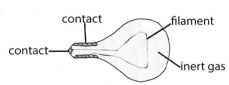

#7: tungsten, heated

#8: The electrons flowing through the filament cause friction or resistance and make the filament glow.

[continued]

#11: Answers will vary, here's an example:

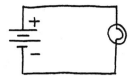

#12: Answers will vary, here's an example:

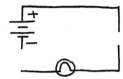

Conclusion / Discussion:

1. Make certain that students understand the idea that a circuit involves electricity flowing around in a circle and that it is the battery that "pushes" the electricity through the circuit.

2. There are many types of light bulbs today, primarily because our society is trying to find ways to use less energy to power lights. Usually, there is some trade-off involved in trying to find more efficient ways to provide power to our homes. For example, CFL bulbs, which last a long time and use less energy than incandescent bulbs, contain an element called mercury, which is very bad for the environment. Talk about ways you and your families can reduce the energy your home uses. What are the trade-offs involved in your ideas?

3. Discuss the filament inside the light bulb. Make sure that everyone understands the difference between a conductor, an insulator, and a filament, which resists the flow of electricity.

4. If batteries work because of chemical reactions, why do batteries ultimately "go dead?" (Answer: the chemicals are all used up in the reactions.)

More Lab Fun:

1. Take apart a flashlight. See if you can figure out how the circuit inside the flashlight works. Diagram the circuit, both using symbols and sketching the various components.

2. Make your own flashlight using the components we used in this experiment. You could use rolled-up construction paper to hold the components in place. Could you design a light switch for the flashlight? (We'll do that in the next experiment if you don't figure it out.) Without using an extra battery or different bulb, how can you make your flashlight brighter? (Hint: use aluminum foil as a reflector.)

Notebooking Ideas:

1. Use a definition page to define any or all of the following terms:

    electrical circuit
    electrical component
    anode
    cathode
    filament
    incandescent

2. Make a symbol key to show what each of the electronic symbols means. As you learn more symbols, add them to this page.

Going with the Flow

Batteries

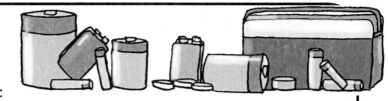

1. Sketch a picture of your battery:

Look closely at the battery and add to your drawing the following information: The type of battery (A, B, C, D, etc.), how many volts it provides (this will be somewhere on the battery), which end has a "+" sign and which end has a "-" sign, and, whether it has the word "alkaline" on it.

2. The plus end of the battery is called the **cathode / anode / balustrade**.

3. The minus end of the battery is called the **cathode / anode / balustrade**.

4. Most household batteries move electrons along with energy from
   tiny motors inside them / chemical reactions / nuclear energy.

5. It isn't practical to sketch a battery every time you want to show what you did with electricity. So, we use a symbol to represent a battery that looks like this. Try to copy this symbol to help you remember it:

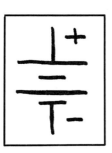

Bulbs

6. Label the filament, the two contacts, and the inert gas on the miniature light bulb pictured below. Trace over the flow of electricity from the bottom contact across the filament to the base contact.

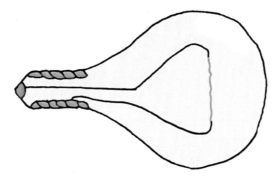

7. The filament, which is usually made of **iron / silver / tungsten**, gives off light when **cooled / heated / rubbed**.

8. Describe what happens to the electrons that flow into one end of a light bulb that causes the light bulb to light up:

_____

_____

_____

9. Light bulbs also have a special symbol. It looks like this. Try to draw one for yourself next to it.

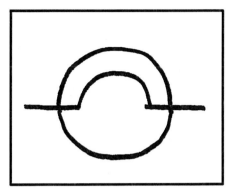 

10. There is one other symbol for you to learn. It is the symbol for a wire, and it's the easiest of all to draw because it is just a line, like this, that connects other components. Draw the symbol for a wire.

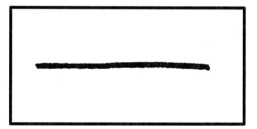 

11. Here is a circuit that lights the light bulb:

12.   Here is a circuit that does not light the bulb:

Electricity Lab #4: Switch It On - instructions

Materials:
- Lab sheets, pencil
- 4 pieces of insulated wire, about 6-8 inches long, with about ¼ inch of the ends stripped
- 2 metal paper clips
- Tape
- A piece of card stock, about 5 inches x 1 inch

From the previous lab:
- 1 D-cell battery holder
- 1 D-cell battery
- 1 miniature lamp bulb (2 to 5 volt, not an LED bulb)
- 1 miniature light bulb receptacle or socket (that fits your miniature lamp bulb)

Aloud: There's one important component of electric circuits that we haven't yet discussed. What do you think it is? Maybe this made-up story will help you figure it out. Once upon a time, there was a scientist working hard in her lab late at night. She had a small house, so her lab was in the living room. Across from her, on the couch, was a sleeping child. The scientist worked all day to create a circuit to light a very bright light bulb. She set everything up, hooked up the wires, and said, "Eureka!" The light bulb lit the room as if it were daytime. This, of course, caused the baby to wake up and start crying. And this, in turn, caused everyone else in the house to wake up. They ran into the brightly lit room and shouted, "Can you turn that thing off?"

Now do you know what component we're missing? It's a switch. Of course, we could just turn off our circuit by disconnecting all the wires, but in many cases that just isn't practical. Let's start out by making a switch so that we can turn the power off and on whenever we want in the rest of our experiments.

Procedure:
1. Make the switch. Start by attaching the end of a wire to one of the paper clips. Just loop a little of the exposed metal end of the wire around one end of the paper clip. Then, tape the paper clip onto one end of the card stock as shown:

2. Repeat with the other paper clip and another wire on the other end of the card stock. Then, fold the strip of card stock in half so that the paper clips can touch each other. Don't crease it firmly; you want it to sort of spring open on its own.

Aloud: A switch works by interrupting or conducting the flow of electrons through a circuit. One of the key reasons that a switch like the one you just made works is because air is an insulator. So, when the switch is open and the paper clips are not touching each other, no electric current could flow from one of the wires into the other because there is air—an insulator—in between the paper clips. When the switch is closed and the paper clips are touching each other, electricity can flow from one wire into the paper clip it's touching. The paper clip is a conductor, so the electricity moves through it and into the second paper clip. If the circuit is hooked to a battery, which keeps pushing electrons along, then the electrons will now move into the second wire and back into the circuit. Let's give it a try.

[continued]

3. Fill in #1-#3 on the lab sheet.

4. Build your circuit. Did it work? If not, play around with your design until you get it to work. If you are really stuck, try making the circuit that lights the bulb without the switch. Then, substitute the switch for one of the wires. When you're done, fix your circuit diagram to show what worked and fill in the rest of the lab sheet.

Possible Answers:

#3: The following circuit should work. Yours may be oriented a bit differently.

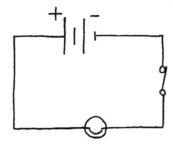

#4: cannot, an insulator

Conclusion / Discussion:

1. Take a moment to recall what batteries do and how they work. Do you remember that they push electrons because of a chemical reaction? When the battery isn't attached to any circuit, the chemicals don't react. Only when the battery is attached to a closed circuit do the chemicals react. What do you think is happening inside the battery when the switch is open? (Answer: nothing—no reaction.)

2. Now, explain out loud what happens when the switch is closed. Start with the reaction in the battery starting to push electricity through the circuit. Where do the electrons go after this and what do they do?

More Lab Fun:

1. You can use your circuit to light up lots of things. When you're done experimenting, you could install a light with a light switch into a diorama, a doll house, or a train set.

2. Did you know you can use aluminum foil as a conductor? Try to design a different switch using tape, aluminum foil, and an index card.

Notebooking Ideas:

1. If you started a page of electronics symbols, add the symbol for a switch to it.

2. Imagine you have lots of light bulbs and wires and batteries. Can you design a circuit that would work as a quiz game? You would have a piece of cardboard you could write questions on with true or false answers. The person playing would press the button she thought was correct. If she was, in fact, correct, a light bulb would light up. Draw out the circuit diagram. If you have the supplies, try to build it.

NAME _____ DATE _____

Switch It On

1. Here is a picture of the switch I made:

Opened Up

Folded Close

2. This is the symbol for a switch. Try to draw one of your own:

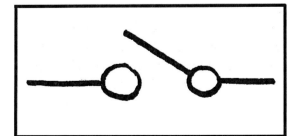

3. Using circuit symbols for a battery, a bulb, a switch, and wires, design a circuit that will light the bulb when the switch is closed and not light the bulb when the switch is opened.

4. The switch works because when the paper clips aren't touching each other, electrons **can** / **cannot** flow from one wire in the switch to the other wire. This is because the air between the paper clips is **an insulator** / **a resistor** / **a conductor**.

For my notebook

Powering Up!

When I first managed to light a bulb with a simple circuit, I thought it was amazingly cool. I sat there attaching and detaching the wire over and over to watch the light bulb turn on and off. As much as I love science, though, I couldn't stay interested in watching the bulb turn on and off forever. Eventually, I wanted to try new things. Could I make the bulb brighter? Could I hook up several light bulbs to one battery or several batteries to one light bulb?

It turns out that there are two basic ways to hook electrical components into a circuit—in <u>series</u> and in <u>parallel</u>. A series is just a sequence of things, one after the other. A circuit that is hooked up in series is just a circuit where one component is hooked to the next, which is hooked to the next. All the circuits we've made so far have been series circuits.

Two things are said to be in parallel if they are next to one another. Imagine a circuit with two batteries rather than one. We could line the batteries up one after the other and they would be in series. Or, we could somehow put them next to each other and connect both to the circuit as if the other battery weren't present. In this case, they would be hooked up in parallel. Look at the series circuit and parallel circuit illustrated below. If you removed one of the batteries in the series circuit would the bulb still light up? How about the parallel circuit? Soon you will conduct a lab to test if you're correct.

Batteries connected in series

Batteries connected in parallel

To understand how series and parallel circuits affect what's happening in a circuit, we need to understand how scientists measure the flow of electrons in a circuit. Do you remember that the D-Cell batteries we've been using are labeled as 1.5 volt batteries? Volts provide a measure of how strongly the battery pushes electrons through the circuit. In scientific language, a volt is a measure of the difference in electrical potential from one end of the battery to the other.

Think back to the idea of electric current as similar to water flowing through a pipe. If you take a pipe that you're pouring water into and tip it just a teeny bit, the difference between the high end and low end is small, so the water flows slowly. If you tip the pipe a lot, the difference between the high and low ends is greater, and gravity accelerates the water so that it falls more quickly. In a higher voltage battery, the difference in electrical potential is greater, so electricity is pushed more forcefully through the circuit.

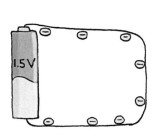 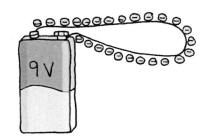

A related way to measure current is to figure out how quickly it is flowing. In electric circuits, the amount of electrical charge passing a point at a particular time is measured in amperes. Electrical power is a combination of voltage and amperes and is measured in watts. There is a mathematical formula that describes the relationship of voltage, amperes, and watts. Here it is:

POWER (OR WATTAGE) = VOLTAGE X AMPERES

If the voltage increases, so does the power. Likewise, if the amperes are increased, so does the wattage. Can you see how this is true from the equation?

Now we have some precise scientific vocabulary to talk about what happens when circuits are hooked up in series and in parallel. Let's give it a try.

Electricity Lab #5: Power Up! - instructions

Materials:
(The materials used to make the circuit and switch in the last lab can be reused here.)
- Lab sheets, pencil
- 6 pieces of insulated wire, about 6-8 inches long, with about ¼ inch of the ends stripped
- 2 D-cell battery holders
- 2 D-cell batteries
- 1 miniature lamp bulb (2 to 5 volt, not an LED bulb)
- 1 miniature light bulb receptacle or socket (that fits your miniature lamp bulb)
- The switch from the previous experiment (optional)

Aloud: Once again, we'll be making a circuit to light up a bulb. This time, though, we're going to hook up two batteries to the circuit instead of one. You now know that there are two ways we could hook these batteries up—in series and in parallel. Do you think it will make any difference to the amount of electricity reaching the light bulb?

    We're going to begin by hooking up the batteries in series. Let's see if you can design the circuit and develop a hypothesis as to what it is going to do.

Procedure:
1. Hook up the circuit with just one battery. So, you should connect the battery to the bulb to the other end of the battery. You can also include your switch if you'd like. Take a look at how bright the bulb gets. Try to keep this in mind as you proceed.

2. Think about how you would change your circuit to add a battery in series to the circuit. Draw your circuit on the lab sheet using the symbols you've learned. Your design should include:
   - 1 light bulb
   - 2 batteries
   - As many wires as you need
   - The switch you made (if you'd like)

3. Check your circuit design against the answer section. If it is incorrect, correct your drawing.

4. Fill in #1-#5 on the lab sheet.

5. Build your series circuit and try it out. Pay attention to the brightness of the light bulb. (It should be considerably brighter.)

6. Fill in #6 on the lab sheet.

7. Remove one of the batteries from the battery holder. Observe what happens to the light bulb.

8. Fill in #7-#9 on the lab sheet.

Aloud: It can be a little hard to figure out how to hook up batteries in parallel. One way to think of it is to imagine a basic circuit with one battery hooked to one light bulb. Now you're going to add a second battery on to the tail end of the first circuit, sort of like this:

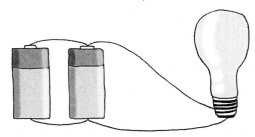

[continued]

9. Use the above drawing to create your drawing of a parallel circuit on the lab sheet, but use circuit diagram symbols. You can add your switch to the circuit if you'd like between one of the ends of the battery nearest the light bulb and the light bulb. When you're done, check that you've designed your circuit correctly against the answers.

10. Look closely at the circuit diagram and think about what is happening to the electrons in the circuit. Fill in #10-#12 on your lab sheet.

11. Build the circuit and observe the brightness of the light bulb (it should be about the same as when there is only one battery in the circuit). This can be a harder circuit to build because you have two wires connecting to each end of one of the batteries. I found it helpful to twist the ends of the wires together so they didn't fall off the connectors on the battery holder.

12. Carefully remove one of the batteries from the battery holder or circuit, leaving the wires intact. What happens? (The bulb should remain lit!)

13. Carefully replace the battery you removed and remove the other battery. What happens?

14. Fill in the remainder of the lab sheet.

Possible Answers:

Batteries in Series: (This is the basic idea. You could also add a switch at any point in the circuit.)

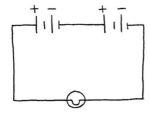

#1: 1.5
#2: pushing
#3-#5: Answers will vary.
#6: greater than
#7: did not light up
#8: more
#9: increases, increases

Batteries in Parallel:

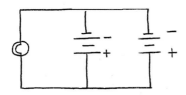

#10-#12: Answers will vary.
#13: the same as
#14: lit up
#15: lit up
#16: must not be
#17: would still light

[continued]

Electricity Lab #5: Power Up! - instructions page 3

Conclusion / Discussion:

1. Try to describe in words what happens when batteries are in series. Think about each battery as providing a certain amount of "push" to the electrons. If the electrons get one push and then another, they have twice as much "push" or voltage. When batteries are in series, you can add their voltages together to determine the total voltage in the circuit. What is it for two D-cell batteries?

2. Try to describe in words what happens when the batteries are in parallel. In this case, it's almost like there's a spare battery in the circuit. If you could measure the voltage in the parallel circuit, you'd find that it was 1.5, as if there were only one battery in the circuit. But, if you observed two circuits—one with one battery and one with two batteries in parallel, the circuit with two batteries would keep the bulb lit for twice as long. The circuit with two batteries in parallel has twice the battery capacity.

3. Can you think of some uses for having batteries in parallel? When would it be helpful to know that if one battery failed, the other could supply power? (Some thoughts: medical applications, safety lights, etc.)

4. If you try out the "for more lab fun" experiment, you'll discover that any component placed in parallel behaves like the batteries did. If you place two light bulbs in parallel and one burns out, what do you think will happen? What if the two light bulbs were in series?

More Lab Fun:

1. See what happens if you hook up two light bulbs in parallel rather than two batteries. Here's a circuit diagram of how to set it up:

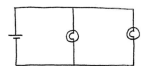

What happens if you remove one light bulb from its socket? Now, try hooking up the bulbs in series. What do you think will happen to their brightness? What does happen?

2. Can you figure out how to hook up two batteries and two light bulbs in parallel? In series? Give it a try. Does your circuit behave how you expected it to?

3. Make a second switch. What happens to switches in parallel?

Notebooking Ideas:

1. Use a definition page to define *parallel circuit* and *series circuit*.

2. A circuit can have various elements in parallel and other elements in series. Design some circuits that mix things up—batteries in series and bulbs in parallel and the reverse. Draw out the circuit diagrams. Use as many components as you'd like. If you ever get the opportunity, try out your circuits to see what happens. Remember to follow the safety rules!

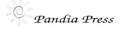

Power Up!

BATTERIES IN SERIES

Circuit Design to Test: Here is my design of a circuit to light up a bulb using two D-cell batteries in series:

Hypotheses:

1. Each of the batteries supplies electricity at 1.5 / 4 / 600 volts.

2. This means that each battery has a potential difference of 1.5 volts and is **creating** / **destroying** / **pushing** electrons with that much voltage.

3. By hooking two batteries in series, I think it will **do nothing to** / **double** / **halve** the electricity flowing into the light bulb.

4. I think the brightness of the light bulb will **decrease** / **not change** / **increase** when compared to a circuit with only one battery in it.

5. I think if I take one of the batteries out of its battery holder, the light bulb will **still light up** / **not light up** / **decrease in brightness**.

Observations:

6. When I put together this circuit, the brightness of the light bulb was **less than** / **the same as** / **greater than** it was with only one battery in the circuit.

7. When I took one of the batteries out of its battery holder, the light bulb **lit up** / **did not light up** / **decreased in brightness**.

Analysis and Conclusions:

8.   The increase in the brightness of the bulb was probably the result of its getting **more** / **less** power than it did with one battery.

9.   I know that when the voltage increases, the power **decreases** / **increases**. Therefore, I conclude that when I hook the batteries in series, the total voltage delivered to the bulb **increases** / **decreases**.

BATTERIES IN PARALLEL

Circuit Design to Test: Here is my design of a circuit to light up a bulb using two D-cell batteries in parallel:

Hypotheses:

10.   By hooking two batteries in parallel, I think it will **do nothing to / double / halve** the electricity flowing into the light bulb.

11.   I think the brightness of the light bulb will **decrease / not change / increase** when compared to a circuit with only one battery in it.

12.   I think if I remove one of the batteries in this circuit, the light bulb will **still light up / not light up / decrease in brightness**.

Observations:

13.   When I put together this circuit, the brightness of the light bulb was **less than / the same as / greater than** it was with only one battery in the circuit.

14.   When I took one of the batteries out of the battery holder, the light bulb **lit up / did not light up / decreased in brightness**.

15.   When I took the other battery out of the battery holder, the light bulb **lit up / did not light up / decreased in brightness**.

Analysis and Conclusions:

16.   Using two batteries in parallel doesn't seem to increase the brightness of the bulb, so there **must be / must not be** more power flowing into the bulb.

17.   But, there is an advantage to this circuit. If one of the batteries were missing or worn out, the light bulb **would still light / would not light**.

For my notebook

Electromagnetism

Let's pause for a moment to review a few key points about electricity and magnetism. Can you remember what, at a sub-atomic level, causes magnetism? Magnetism is caused by the movement and spin of electrons inside of magnetic materials. Having just studied electricity, you might be thinking, "Hey! That's almost exactly what causes electricity!" Electric current is caused by the movement of electrons through a conductor.

Those explanations seem remarkably similar. Can you think of any other similarities between electricity and magnetism? I can think of a major similarity. In slightly different ways, both magnets and electricity follow the rule that likes repel and unlikes attract. Magnets have two poles, and like poles repel each other while unlike poles attract each other. Electrons and protons have two opposite charges, and like charges repel each other while unlike charges attract each other.

All of these similarities are not coincidental. At the basis of both electricity and magnetism is the tiny electron and its behavior. Scientists had suspected that electricity and magnetism had something in common, but it wasn't until the 1860s that **James Clerk Maxwell**, a Scottish physicist, developed a set of mathematical equations that described the precise relationship between magnetism and electricity. These equations are now studied by physicists and engineers everywhere and are called Maxwell's equations.

Maxwell figured out that both electricity and magnetism can be described as creating a field—which you may recall is an area in which a force can affect an object. You already learned a lot about magnetic fields, but it turns out that electricity creates a field as well. This makes a lot of sense if you think about it. You saw how this worked with static electricity. When you pooled a lot of electrons in one place, like on the surface of a balloon, it created a field that could act at a slight distance if placed near an object with a like or unlike static charge. This is also true of electrical current. If you run a current through a wire, the amount of negative charge would certainly affect, and be affected by, nearby positive and negative particles.

This is where things get really cool. About 40 years before Maxwell came up with his equations, another scientist had noticed that if you generate an electrical current near a compass, the compass needle moves! He realized that electricity must somehow generate a magnetic field. Maxwell's equations showed not only that changing electrical currents create magnetic fields, but also that changing magnetic currents create electric fields or electricity!

Why is this so incredibly cool? Much of our modern machinery depends on this relationship between magnetism and electricity. Electric motors change electrical energy into physical movement (the spinning of the motor) by generating a magnetic field. Electric generators create electricity by using the physical movement of a magnet to create an electrical current. How does all this work? You're about to find out for yourself.

Electricity Lab #6: Creating a Force Field - instructions

Materials:
(You can reuse some of the supplies from the last lab here.)
- Lab sheets, pencil
- Medium-sized (about 3-4 inches) nail or screw that is attracted by a magnet
- Insulated wire (about 12 inches) with a little bit stripped at each end
- D-cell battery
- D-cell battery holder
- Paper clips
- The switch you made (optional)

Aloud: You might have gotten a bit excited at the title of this experiment. Many people have seen force fields in movies, but few think they've seen force fields in real life. A force field, though, is technically just an area in which a particular force, like magnetism, can act on an object. We're going to create an <u>electromagnet</u>, a device that acts like a magnet when the electricity is turned on but doesn't when the electricity is turned off.

An electromagnet is made by running electrical current around and around a ferromagnetic material. Look at the materials you've gathered for this experiment. Can you figure out how to make the device I just described? What in the supplies you have is ferromagnetic? Recall that ferromagnetic materials are materials that can be attracted by a magnetic field. So, the nail and the paper clips are both ferromagnetic.

We're going to use the nail to create an electromagnet. In a moment, you'll wrap the wire around and around the nail and run a current through it. This electrical current will create a slight magnetic field in addition to the electric field it will create.

Before you begin, there's one other important piece of information you need. Have you ever heard the expression short circuit? Sometimes it is used in everyday speech to mean bypassing, or going around, some procedure. If a baseball player ran from first base to home plate, she'd be said to have "short circuited" the bases. The technical use of "short circuit" is similar. A <u>short circuit</u> in an electrical circuit is when current is being sent through a circuit without anything to slow it down, such as a light bulb. Do you remember how the light bulb in the circuits we made has a filament that resists electricity, so that the electrons flowing through the filament create friction and heat it up, causing it to produce light? If we took the bulb out of the circuit, and just left wires connecting one end of a battery to the other end of the battery, the electricity would be free to flow around the circuit without anything in the way. We would have bypassed the bulb and created a short circuit.

The wires we're using are not perfect conductors. As electricity flows through them, there is a little bit of resistance, a little friction. When something like a bulb is in the circuit, the resistance of the wire can be ignored. But in a short circuit, where there is just wire connecting two ends of the battery, the resistance of the wire can cause it to heat up. So, it is very important not to leave the circuits in the next experiments hooked up unless you are actively working on them. It is also very important to take care in touching stripped wire ends, as they may heat up.

Procedure:
1. First make sure that the nail doesn't attract the paper clips. If it has been magnetized before (perhaps in a previous experiment), drop it a number of times until it becomes demagnetized or get another nail.
2. Fill in #1-#6 on the lab sheet.

[continued]

3. Leave a couple of inches of wire free, then start wrapping the wire around the nail in a coil as illustrated below. Leave a few inches of wire free at the end of the coiling as well.

4. With the battery in the battery holder, connect one free end of the wire to one end of the battery. Hold the nail over the paper clips. Observe what happens.

5. CAUTION: You are about to create a short circuit! The exposed ends of the wires may become hot. Disconnect the circuit as soon as you've made your observations!

6. Now, connect the other end of the wire to the other end of the battery and observe what happens when you hold the nail close to the paper clips. Once some paper clips are attracted to and attached to the nail, disconnect one end of the wire from the battery. What happens?

7. Pull the nail out of the coil of wire, leaving the coil intact. You've just created something called a <u>solenoid</u>. Reconnect both ends of the wire to the battery. Does your solenoid generate a strong enough magnetic field to attract the paper clips?

8. Pick up the nail, which is now not attached to anything. Has it retained the magnetic field it had? That is, does it still attract the paper clips?

9. Fill in the rest of the lab sheet.

Possible Answers:

#1: both an electric field and a slight magnetic field
#2: answers will vary
#3: a ferromagnetic, magnetic domains
#4: in random directions, is not
#5: Answers will vary.
#6 & #7: does not
#8: does
#9: does not

#10: does not attract or very slightly attracts
#11: does not
#13: changed
#14: lined up
#15: could no longer, returned to being random
#16: could not or could barely, slight

Conclusion / Discussion:

1. Talk about the difference between the solenoid and the electromagnet. The slight field created by the solenoid around the iron core (the nail) is strong enough to align the domains in the nail which, in turn, creates a powerful electromagnet.

2. How do you think electromagnets are used? They can be quite useful when extremely powerful magnets are needed because having a powerful magnet turned on all the time can be dangerous—attracting any piece of nearby iron or steel. It can help to be able to turn off and on a powerful magnet as needed. Electromagnets are also used on cranes with pulleys to lift and move metals. The magnet can be turned on to lift an object, the crane can be moved, and then the magnet can be turned off to drop the object where needed.

3. What characteristics of the electromagnet do you think affect its power? What would you do to make it stronger? Weaker? If you'd like to explore these questions more, look at the More Lab Fun section.

[continued]

Electricity Lab #6: Creating a Force Field - instructions page 3

4. How do you think solenoids are used? Some are used in conjunction with an iron core like your nail. As the core is moved in and out of the solenoid, the magnetic field created changes. This can be used to open and close a valve in machinery. In cars, solenoids are often used to get the car started. When the key is turned in the ignition, a solenoid is used to cause two contacts to connect, sending a large charge from the car's battery to start the car's engine.

More Lab Fun:

1. Explore how to increase the power of your electromagnet. Do you recall how to measure the power of a magnet (you did an experiment using a ruler to determine how far a magnet's field extended powerfully enough to attract a paper clip). Two ideas you could try to vary the magnet's power are to change the number of coils around the nail and to add a battery in series to the circuit. Use the notebook pages for experiments to develop an experiment to figure out how to change an electromagnet's power.

2. Look at #4 in the Conclusion / Discussion section above. Try to see what happens to the magnetic field you create when you move the nail part way in and out of the solenoid.

Notebooking Ideas:

1. Use a definition page to define *short circuit*, *electromagnet*, and *solenoid*.

2. Design some inventions using electromagnets and solenoids. Can you design a vending machine that uses electromagnets and/or solenoids to drop something out when a button is pushed? How about a toy that causes a model of a dancer to spin and move around using electromagnets? Draw your designs and explain how they work. You might even try to build them!

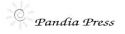

NAME _____ DATE _____

Creating a Force Field

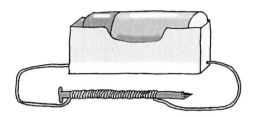

Hypotheses:

1.   I have learned that an electric current creates **an electric field** / **a slight magnetic field** / **both an electric field and a slight magnetic field**.

2.   When I wrap a wire around the nail, I think that each individual coil will generate a magnetic field pointing **in the same direction as** / **in different directions than** the other coils because all of the current will be flowing through the wire in the same direction.

3.   Inside the nail, which is **a ferromagnetic** / **plastic material**, there are lots of **batteries** / **magnetic domains**.

4.   Before anything is done to the nail, these domains are all pointing in **the same direction** / **random directions**, so that the nail **is** / **is not** a magnet.

5.   When the current passes through the coils, I think that the domains will **still point every which way** / **all line up** and that the nail will act as a magnet and **attract the paper clips** / **repel the paper clips**.

Observations:

6.   Before I do anything to the nail, it **does** / **does not** attract the paper clips.

7.   When I coil the wire around the nail and connect one end of the wire to the battery, the nail **does** / **does not** attract the paper clips.

8.   When I connect each end of the wire to the ends of the battery, the nail **does** / **does not** attract the paper clips.

9.   When I disconnect one end of the wire from the battery, the nail **does** / **does not** attract the paper clips.

10. When I hook up the solenoid to the battery, it **does attract** / **does not attract** / **very slightly attracts** the paper clips.

11. When I place the nail near the paper clips after it's disconnected from everything, it **does / does not** attract the paper clips.

12. Sketch the devices you've made. Include the battery, the nail (if needed), and the coil of wire.

This is an electromagnet.

This is a solenoid.

Analysis and Conclusions:

13. After creating the electromagnet and running current through the wire, the magnetic domains in the nail must have **changed / remained the same as they were** because the ferromagnetic nail could now act as a magnet.

14. The current running through the wire coiled around the nail must have **lined up / scrambled** the magnetic domains in the nail. Therefore, the current running through the wire must have created enough of a magnetic field to affect the magnetic domains in the nail.

15. When the current was stopped by disconnecting the electromagnet from the battery, the nail **could / could no longer** act as a magnet. Therefore, the magnetic domains must have **remained aligned / returned to being random** when not affected by the field created by the electricity in the wire.

16. The solenoid **could / could not / could barely** attract a paper clip. But, the solenoid surrounding a nail could change the domains in the nail. Therefore, the magnetic field the solenoid generates must be **nonexistent / slight / superstrong**.

Electricity Lab #7: That's Right, I Made an Electric Motor!
- instructions

Materials:
(Some of the materials used in the last lab can be reused here.)
- Lab sheets, pencils
- 2 D-cell battery holders
- 2 D-cell batteries
- 2 short lengths of insulated wire with the ends stripped (about 4-6 inches)
- 2 paper clips
- 1 long length of insulated wire with about 2-2 ½ inches of the ends stripped (about 18-20 inches total)
- Your most powerful disc-shaped magnet
- Tape
- Needle-nosed pliers or something that is strong enough to help bend the paper clips into the needed shape
- A sturdy piece of cardboard (if you want, a 12" x 12" piece would be large enough to semi-permanently mount your motor and the accompanying battery. Otherwise, a smaller piece around 4" x 4" will do).

Aloud: I think that the experiment you are about to perform is one of the most amazing experiments you can do at home with everyday materials. Think about this for a moment. You have a battery, some wire, a couple of paper clips, a magnet, and some tape. With just those objects you can make a working motor—the same kind of motor that powers everything from remote control cars to complex electronic devices like DVD players and huge powerful engines such as the engines in bullet trains.

So, what exactly is a motor? Technically, a motor is a device that creates motion. As you know, in the world of physics, you can't get something, like motion, for nothing. So a motor uses something to create motion. An <u>electric motor</u>, the kind we're going to make, changes electricity moving through a wire into rotational motion. In other words, it uses electricity to turn something very quickly. This motion could then be used to turn the wheels on a car or to spin the disc in a DVD player.

How does it work? As you know, sending current through a coiled wire creates a magnetic field. Electromagnets use this field to alter the domains inside of a nail temporarily. In an electronic motor, the magnetic field created in a wire wrapped into a coil is going to be attracted and repelled by a permanent and stationary, or non-moving, magnet. As the created field changes direction (depending on which side of the coiled wire is facing up or down), the magnet's field will push it along, attracting it one direction and repelling it in another.

This can be a difficult experiment to get working, so I've offered some suggestions for troubleshooting any problems you encounter. Keep at it because it's worth it. Once you see your own working electric motor, you'll be amazed.

Procedure:
1. Here is a diagram of how the electric motor is going to look. You might want to refer to it if you get confused by any of the step-by-step instructions.

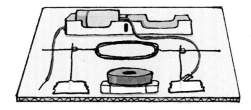

[continued]

Creating the axle supports

2. First, you will need to shape two paper clips to hold the coil of wire. Unbend a paper clip so that just the small loop remains, like this:

3. Bend the looped end of the paper clip at a right angle, so that it can act as a stand for the paper clip, like this:

4. Using pliers or some other tool to help, bend the other end of the paper clip into a small loop, like this:

5. Do the same thing with the second paper clip. You've now made two axle supports for your electric motor.

Creating the electromagnetic coil and the axles

6. In our simple motor, the electromagnetic coil and the axles are going to be made from one long piece of wire. Take your long piece of wire. Starting from a little bit past the point where the wire is stripped, wrap the wire around one or two of your fingers. It should wrap around about five times. You want the coil to end up being around 1 ½ inches long and about ½-¾ inches wide, like this:

7. You've made the electromagnetic coil. To add axles to it, wrap the ends of the wire around opposite ends of the coil once to keep the coil together, and then straighten out the stripped ends of the wire. Try to keep the loops and the stripped ends of the wires in a straight line in the middle of the coil lengthwise, like this:

8. Now you have an <u>electromagnetic coil with axles</u>.

9. To combine the coil with the axle supports, tape the right-angle part of the paper clips to the cardboard. You want the loops at the top of the paper clips to be far enough apart so that you can place the stripped ends of the coil wire through them. It should look something like the picture below. Make sure that the coil can spin freely. If it doesn't, adjust the wires and the paper clips until it does. Also, make sure that the coil isn't slipping downward in one direction or the other because the axle supports are uneven. THIS IS VERY IMPORTANT.

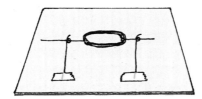

[continued]

Add the permanent, stationary magnet

10. Place the disc magnet under the axle supports. The magnet should be no more than 1-1.5 centimeters from the bottom of the coil. If the magnet is too low, roll up some tape to place underneath it. Again, make sure the coil can spin freely.

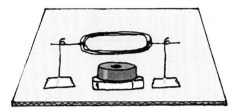

Add the power source

11. You are just about ready to power things up. Place one* battery in a battery holder near the assembly you've made. Hook up one end of each of the shorter wires to each end of the battery. Using tape, tape one end of one of the shorter wires to one of the paper clips you are using as an axle support.

Make it go

Caution: You may have noticed that this is another short circuit. The paper clips and the exposed parts of the wire will heat up. Be careful! Try to limit what you touch to the insulation around the wire.

12. You can turn on the power in one of two ways. You can add the switch you made in an earlier experiment between the unconnected wire and the second axle support, or you can simply touch the exposed end of the unconnected wire to the second axle support. Make sure you only touch the insulated parts of the wire.

13. Once there is power to the circuit, you should see the coil wobble a bit. It now has a magnetic field around it. Give the coil a little spin. If it keeps spinning on its own, wow! You've done it. You've made an electric motor. If it only spins a little then slows to a stop, disconnect a wire from the battery and read on.

*As a last resort to make your motor work, you can try to use two batteries in series to power your motor. This tends to heat the exposed wires quickly, so be extra careful.

Adjusting the motor if it's not working

14. I almost never get an electric motor to work on the first try. The problem is that it is very difficult to get the assembly together so that the coil moves very freely without slipping to the left or the right. It can also be difficult if the magnet you are using is relatively weak. Here are some things to try to get your motor working. CAUTION: Remember to make sure any exposed metal has cooled off before touching it.

   A. Adjust the axle supports so that the coil isn't leaning one way or the other. You can do this by bending the paper clips a bit, moving them a bit, whatever it takes.

   B. Adjust the coil so that the exposed wire ends you are using as axles are straight. Try to get the coil spinning as smoothly as possible by giving it a little spin with your finger and observing whether it leans or moves to one side or another. Adjust the axles and the axle supports until it is as balanced as you can make it.

[continued]

C. Move the permanent magnet closer to the coil, but not so close that the coil bumps it. I rolled up some tape to stand the magnet on to bring it closer to the coil.

D. Try changing the shape of the coil. Sometimes a more oval shape works better, sometimes a more circular shape.

E. Use less wire in your coil. The more wire, the heavier the coil, making it harder to move. You might get it working with only three to five wraparound coils.

F. As a last resort, you can try to use two batteries in series to power your motor. This tends to heat the exposed wires quickly, so be extra careful.

G. When you get your motor working, it is an amazing thing to watch!

15. Fill in the lab sheet.

Answers could include the following:

#2: motion

#3: electricity

#4: coil

#5: magnetic

#6: in the opposite direction from / opposite

#7: Answers will vary, but the basic idea is that the current through the wire on one side will create a magnetic field that is repelled by the permanent magnet, pushing it along. As the other side of the coil approaches the magnet, it will be attracted to it, getting pulled along. As the coil turns, the permanent magnet's magnetic field interacts with the coiled electromagnet's field and keeps it going. When the power is disconnected, the coil no longer has a magnetic field, so it stops turning.

Conclusion / Discussion:

1. The opposite of an electric motor is a <u>generator</u>. A generator transforms mechanical energy, or movement, into electrical energy. Usually, a magnet is moved back and forth to create a current in wires coiled around the magnet. Talk about why this works. Remember, that a moving magnet creates, or generates, electricity. If you have any hand-crank lights or radios, or emergency flashlights that you have to shake up and down to power, these operate on the same principle as a generator. When you turn the crank or shake the flashlight, you are moving a magnet inside the device to generate a current.

2. Discuss all the discoveries that went into the creation of the electric motor. First, someone had to learn about and understand magnetism. What else did it take for someone to figure out how to make a motor?

3. You probably can think of a lot of ways motors are used today. Talk about a few devices that use electric motors. What would it take to transform the rotational motion of the axle that the motor turns into whatever the device requires—spinning a disc, turning wheels on a car, etc. ?

4. I recently learned about an amazing invention called a "gravity lamp." It uses the potential energy created by a person lifting a heavy bag several feet to power a bright LED light bulb. Its inventors are hoping it can provide light in small, rural areas around the world. You might want to look it up.

More Lab Fun:

1. Make a generator using the information in discussion question #1. I won't give detailed instructions here because you know enough to figure it out yourself, but here are a few tips. To

[continued]

make a coil, wrap exposed (noninsulated) wire around an iron nail many times (at least 1000!). Alternately, if you want to move the magnet inside the coil, make a small cardboard box with an iron nail through the middle and wrap the wire around the box. This is your coil. You hook one end of the coiled wire to one of the contacts on a miniature bulb like you've been using in these experiments, and the other end of the coiled wire to the other contact on the bulb. You'll need some way to turn a magnet in circles either inside the space in the middle of the coil or next to the coil. You might use a nail with a magnet attached that you can turn in circles or ask an adult to let you use an electric drill with a magnet attached to get some speed. See if you can get the light bulb to light up.

2. Find out if you have a broken electrical device that your parents will let you take apart. Make sure that it has been unplugged for several weeks and that you have parental supervision as you work. It's also a good idea to use goggles to protect your eyes. Take apart the device and look for motors—usually small metal-encased cylinder-shaped devices with an axle sticking out on one end and power coming in through two wires. Can you see what the motor is turning and how it helps the device? Try to figure out how the rotational motion of the axle is translated into the type of motion the device requires.

Notebooking Ideas:

1. Use a definition page to design any or all of the following terms:

    electrical motor
    electrical generator

2. This is kind of a thought experiment and brain teaser. Physicists believe that it is impossible to create a <u>perpetual motion device</u>—a device that uses its own motion to power itself so that it never runs out of energy. To create such a device, we'd have to violate the fundamental rule that you can't get something—motion—for nothing. If there is some need to add energy to the device to keep it going, it is not a perpetual motion machine.

    Still, people have tried for centuries to invent such devices, and some of the devices they've come up with, while not perpetual motion devices, are still quite clever. The ideas behind generators and electrical motors suggest a direction for inventing such a machine. Can you draw out a machine that uses the motion created by a motor to power a generator that creates electricity to power the motor? Can you explain why your machine is not really a perpetual motion machine?

That's Right, I Made an Electric Motor!

1. Sketch the electric motor you made. Make sure to include and label the following parts:
   - A. Axle supports
   - B. Power supply (battery)
   - C. Electromagnetic Coil
   - D. Permanent magnet
   - E. Axles

2. A motor is a device which changes some type of energy into **gravity** / **motion** / **electricity**.

3. An electrical motor changes **electricity** / **gravity** / **friction** into motion.

Describing how a motor works:

4. When the battery is connected, electricity travels through the wires into the **permanent magnet / coil**.

5. Electricity traveling through the coil creates a **gravitational / magnetic** field.

6. On one side of the coil, the electrical current is traveling **in the same direction as / in the opposite direction from** the other side of the coil. So, the magnetic field must be **opposite / the same** on each side of the coil.

Understanding the electric motor:

7. Using this knowledge, describe why the motor's coil keeps turning as long as there is power through the wire:

    _____

    _____

    _____

    _____

    _____

8. What are some of the problems you experienced getting your motor to work and how did you solve them?

    _____

    _____

    _____

    _____

    _____

Unit 10

New Worlds to Explore

NAME _____ DATE _____

For my notebook

Everything Is Relative

So far, we've concentrated on physics as it affects our everyday lives, but we haven't studied much about the physics of the really large—the universe, or the really small—the world deep inside the atom. In both of these realms, physics becomes both strange and wondrous. Before we finish up our study of physics, I'd like to introduce you to two of the most important but also the most extraordinary areas of physics—<u>relativistic physics</u> and <u>quantum physics</u>.

Relativistic physics was almost single-handedly developed by a clerk in a government office in Switzerland, a young man who spent much of his time conducting thought experiments. This young man, **Albert Einstein**, tried to imagine what it would be like if one could travel on a flash of light. If light is what allows us to observe the visible universe, what would we observe if we could travel alongside light? Or toward light? What would we experience traveling close to the <u>speed of light</u>? As Einstein thought about these questions, he realized that no matter what perspective light is viewed from, its speed in the vacuum of space will always be the same.

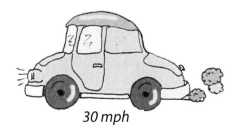

30 mph

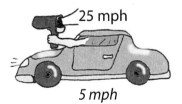

25 mph

5 mph

This was a surprising conclusion because it appears to contradict our everyday observations about motion and speed. For example, think about standing on the street and watching cars drive by at 30 miles per hour. If you had a device for measuring the speed of objects, it would indicate that the cars are traveling at 30 miles per hour. Suppose you could jump into a car of your own and chase after one of those cars. You start to drive at 5 miles per hour. Relative to you, from your frame of reference, it appears as if the car you are chasing has slowed down (really, you have sped up). If you point your speed measuring device at the car ahead of you, it will now indicate 25 miles per hour because you and your device are traveling 5 miles per hour in the same direction.

If you speed up even more, until you are traveling the same speed as another car, it will appear as if the other car is not moving relative to your car. A car traveling at the same velocity as your car is neither moving away from you nor toward you. If you point your speed measuring device at such a car, it would measure 0 miles per hour.

30 mph   0 mph   30 mph

You can easily get a sense of how observations of speed are relative—how such observations depend upon how fast and in what direction an observer is moving—by focusing on other cars while you are driving places. Watch what happens to your velocity relative to other cars as your car speeds up and slows down.

Einstein realized that, if the other cars were light, and they were therefore traveling at the speed of light, then no matter in what direction or at what speed an observer was traveling, the speed of light would appear to be the same. An observer chasing after light at high speeds doesn't see the light slow down relative to him or herself, as would an observer chasing after a car. An observer traveling away from light also doesn't observe the light speed up. Experiments have since verified that Einstein's hypothesis, derived from his thought experiments, was correct: The speed of light in a vacuum is constant regardless of the location or velocity of an observer. Take a moment to think about how this is different from the situation with everyday objects such as cars.

This was not all that Einstein realized. From this seemingly simple starting point, Einstein was able to theorize that an individual traveling close to the speed of light would experience time more slowly than an individual holding still. If you think really hard about it, you might get a glimpse of why Einstein reached this conclusion. If you flash a flashlight in space and then immediately take off after that bit of light, chasing it at a velocity very close to the speed of light, how fast would it seem like the light was traveling? According to Einstein, the light would seem to be traveling just as quickly as if you were an observer who was holding still! For that to work out, at least one of the components of velocity—distance traveled or the time it takes to travel the distance—needs to change. Einstein realized that time would have to slow down for the observer for the speed of light to remain constant. This phenomenon has been observed and verified by flying very precise clocks at high velocities. When those clocks are returned to Earth, less time has passed for them than on Earth!

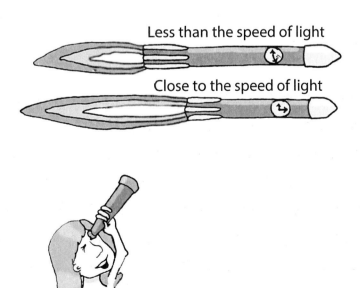

Less than the speed of light

Close to the speed of light

Perhaps even more startling, Einstein also realized that not only would time have to change, but even stranger effects must happen as objects approach the speed of light. For example, if a spacecraft travels at speeds close to the speed of light, the length of the spacecraft contracts, or gets smaller. The people on board the spacecraft don't feel smaller. However, observers watching the spacecraft would see that it appears shorter in the direction in which it is traveling.

These ideas, which Einstein derived from realizing that the speed of light must remain constant in a vacuum, are known as Einstein's <u>theory of special relativity</u>. Einstein kept thinking about special relativity. It was "special" not because it was wonderful, which it was, but because it only applied in a special case—when objects are moving at a constant velocity without any object that exerts gravity nearby (like in the vacuum of space).

Einstein had to conceive of thought experiments that would "generalize" his theory of relativity—that would explain what happens when objects accelerate or encounter gravity (like objects on Earth). The thought experiments that Einstein came up with are so simple and elegant that you can do them yourself.

New Worlds Lab #1: Dropping Rocks around the Universe - instructions

Materials:
- Lab sheets, pencil
- Your mind

Aloud: This is a thought experiment, so there is no equipment needed other than your imagination, your curiosity, and an ability to think scientifically. Here we go. This is the first thought experiment: Imagine that you are standing inside your house, inside of a soundproofed room shaped like an elevator. There are no windows in this room. The floor has the word "FLOOR" painted on it. There is an arrow pointed up toward the ceiling of the room on one of the walls. In your hand is a small rock. You let go of the rock. What happens to it?

Procedure:
1. Draw yourself (stick figure is OK) in the first room for the "First Thought Experiment" on the lab sheet. Write and draw what will happen to the rock (#1 on the lab sheet).

Aloud: If you hypothesized that the rock would fall to the ground, then your hypothesis accords with what would happen if you actually conducted this experiment. In more precise terminology, from the instant that the rock leaves your hand, Earth's gravity causes it to accelerate toward the center of the earth—from your perspective, toward the ground. The rock accelerates 10 meters per second (m/s) every second until it hits the floor. We call this "falling."

For the second thought experiment, imagine that you suddenly discover yourself in another room of the same size. Again, it has no windows and the floor has the word "FLOOR" painted on it. You don't know where the room is situated, but you are going to try to figure it out. Take a moment to think about and discuss how you might determine which planet the room is on (if any) given that you have that same rock and a way to measure its acceleration when you release it.

Now, let's continue with that thought experiment. You have that rock in your hand. You release the rock, and you are able to measure its acceleration as it falls to the floor. From the instant the rock leaves your hand, it accelerates toward the floor at the rate of 10 meters per second every second until it hits the floor. You recall that this is the same acceleration as the rock experienced when you dropped it inside of your house.

2. Draw yourself and what happened to the rock in the room for the "Second Thought Experiment" on the lab sheet. Complete the rest of the "Second Thought Experiment" (#2-#5 on the lab sheet).

Aloud: To conclude that the room must be situated on Earth, or at least on a planet with the same gravity as Earth, you had to think like a scientist. You had to consider what you knew: that Earth's gravity causes objects to accelerate toward the ground at 10 meters per second every second. You had to consider what you theoretically observed during this thought experiment: that the rock accelerated toward the floor at 10 meters per second every second.

Part of Einstein's genius is that his thinking and curiosity took this experiment a couple of steps further. Let us follow his lead with another thought experiment. In this one, you are standing in that same windowless room. Now, however, you know that you are on a spacecraft out

[continued]

in the vacuum of space. There are no planets or other objects near the spacecraft. This spacecraft is extremely advanced, so you can't even hear or feel the hum or vibration of its engines. When this thought experiment starts, the spacecraft is motionless, so you experience no gravity.

3. Complete #6 on the lab sheet, and draw yourself and what will happen to the rock in the first spacecraft in the "Third Thought Experiment" on the lab sheet.

Aloud: However, at some point, the spacecraft accelerates at a rate of 10 meters per second every second in the direction of the arrow painted on the wall of the room.

4. Complete #7 and #8 on the lab sheet, and draw what you think will happen to the rock and to you in the second spacecraft.

Aloud: As you may have recalled, when a vehicle starts accelerating, objects inside the vehicle remain at rest. Think about what happens when a car accelerates and you are sitting in it: The car moves forward, but your inertia keeps you at rest. The back of the car seat you are sitting in pushes against your back as it moves forward and you don't. Obviously, once your back hits the seat, it begins to push you forward with it.

The same thing happens if you are in a room in a spacecraft when it accelerates. Assuming you are floating upright in the room in zero gravity, as the ship accelerates forward, the floor of the room will move toward your feet, so that the floor ends up pushing against your feet. In our thought experiment, the spacecraft is moving with the same acceleration as gravity on Earth causes, so the floor pushes against your feet (and your feet push against the floor) with the same force you experience standing in your own house. With the ship accelerating, you end up standing in the room experiencing what feels like Earth's gravity.

When you release the rock, the same things happen to the rock. Initially, its inertia will keep it at rest. However, the rest of the spacecraft, including the floor of the room with you and the rock inside, is accelerating toward the rock at a rate of 10 meters per second every second. From your perspective, inside the room, the rock will appear to move—or drop—to the floor just as it would on the planet Earth. Really, it is the spacecraft and the room which are moving toward the rock.

Take a long moment to think about this thought experiment. What might have to happen for the rock to drift slowly to the floor, as if it were on the moon? (Answer: The ship would have to be accelerating less quickly.)

Finally, we've reached the thought experiment which suggests Einstein's insights into how to understand what happens beyond special relativity. His initial theories only explained what happens when objects travel at a constant velocity in the middle of space. It was his new understanding of gravity and acceleration that made it possible for him to move from special relativity to what is called general relativity. Here is the thought experiment.

Once again, you are standing in the room with your rock. You have no idea what location the room is in, but you can make some observations. Your feet are on the floor. You feel the same weight as you do on Earth. When you release the rock from your hand, it falls to the floor with an acceleration of 10 meters per second every second.

5. Fill in "Fourth Thought Experiment" (#9 and #10 on the lab sheet).

[continued]

Aloud: If you couldn't figure out how to tell where you might be, you're in good company. This was Einstein's tremendous insight: An observer experiences gravity on a planet in exactly the same way as that observer would experience acceleration in a spacecraft. By linking acceleration with gravity, Einstein was able to extend his theory to situations in which objects and observers were traveling through space and accelerating or encountering gravity. Some of the consequences of Einstein's theory of general relativity are probably familiar to you. This theory predicts the existence and behavior of black holes. General relativity also provides hypotheses pertaining to the big bang that have since been tested and verified. One of the strangest and most elegant parts of general relativity states that space is actually curved through an entirely different, fourth, dimension, and that it is this curvature that causes objects affected by gravity to accelerate.

Possible Answers:

#1: Answers will vary: both drawings should show the student in the room and the rock on the floor.

#2: accelerates toward the floor

#3: the same as

#4: on Earth

#5: Answers will vary (students will gain more insight into this concept in the Fourth Thought Experiment).

#6: something like: drop, fall, and accelerate toward the ground

#7: remain standing

#8: drop to the floor of the room

#9: a spacecraft . . .

#10: This is a trick question because there is no way to tell whether the feeling of gravity you are experiencing is caused by a large object like Earth, or is caused by acceleration.

Conclusion / Discussion:

1. Make sure that students understand Einstein's two major insights: a) that light moves at a constant speed through a vacuum; and b) that acceleration and gravity are indistinguishable from one another to an observer experiencing them. From these two insights spring many of the ideas in special and general relativity.

2. Einstein's thought experiments also had to do with people experiencing free fall. He noted that a person falling through the air would feel like he was experiencing zero gravity, as he would in space (assuming we neglect the feel of the air rushing past him). Make up a thought experiment involving the room with no windows that would illustrate this aspect of Einstein's insights.

More Lab Fun:

1. For this lab, all we've done is thought experiments. Here are a few more you can try out. As always, you can probably think of some of your own.

Galileo's thought experiment:

The ancient Greek natural philosopher Aristotle believed that objects which are heavier fall faster than objects which are lighter. As we have learned, Galileo proved him wrong by dropping objects of different masses and observing that they fall at the same rate. Or, did he? Many believe that Galileo's "experiment" was actually a thought experiment. He thought about what would happen if he dropped heavier and lighter objects tied to each other by a small length of rope. Try this thought experiment in your

[continued]

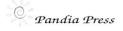

imagination: What would happen if heavier objects really did fall more quickly, as Aristotle claimed? What would happen if objects fall at the same rate regardless of mass, as Galileo claims? What could you do to verify your predictions?

Zeno's Paradox:

Zeno was another Greek philosopher. Here is his thought experiment: Achilles, a great athlete and warrior, is in a footrace with the tortoise, notoriously slow and plodding. Achilles, being a gentleman, gives the tortoise a head start of 100 meters. The race begins. Achilles rapidly crosses 100 meters. However, in the time that it takes Achilles to cross that 100 meters, the tortoise has moved a teeny bit forward. So, Achilles then tries to reach the tortoise's new position. But, in the tiny amount of time it takes Achilles to get to this new position, the tortoise has moved forward again. So, how is it possible for Achilles to catch up with the tortoise? This thought experiment has no easy answer.

Other fun thought experiments to explore are "Hilbert's Grand Hotel Paradox," which helps illuminate the idea of infinity, and Schrodinger's cat, which we will explore in the next section.

2. As we noted, Einstein's theory of special relativity predicts that people and objects traveling close to the speed of light will experience time more slowly than observers at rest. If you have a calculator that can do squares and square roots, you can actually figure out how people traveling at various speeds will experience time dilation. Here is the equation:

$$^t\text{rocket} = \frac{^t\text{earth}}{\sqrt{1-(v/c)^2}}$$

^{t}earth = how much time has passed on Earth

v = the speed of the spacecraft

c = the speed of light (about 300,000,000 meters/second)

The easiest way to play with this equation is to think of the fraction v/c as what fraction of the speed of light the rocket is traveling at. For example, its value would be .5 if the rocket were traveling at one half the speed of light. Then, pick some amount of time that people on Earth wait for the rocket—say 10 years. Plug in the numbers, and you should discover that people on the rocket will have aged only a little more than 8 ½ years. Increase the speed of the spacecraft. Try fractions like .70, .80, .90 and .99 for v/c. You will see that the time dilation increases dramatically as travelers approach the speed of light.

Notebooking ideas:

1. Many science-fiction books have played with the ideas suggested by Einstein's theories. One major theme people continue to explore is that of time dilation. Imagine that humanity has invented a way to send people across the galaxy traveling at close to the speed of light. Astronauts could go off and explore, but very little time would pass for them on their ship. Back home on Earth, their children, their spouses, their parents, and their friends will have aged years or even decades. What would this be like? How would scientists find ways to make such travel easier on everyone involved? Write down your ideas or write a story about these questions.

[continued]

New Worlds Lab #1: Dropping Rocks around the Universe
- instructions page 5

2. Think of topics for your own thought experiments. They can be everything from the everyday to the incredible. Here are some of my ideas:

- What would it be like to be a cell from a banana in a blender while a smoothie is being made? What forces would that cell experience?

- Or, what would it be like to be a particle in one of Saturn's rings? What would keep that particle in place? Would it collide with other particles? Why or why not?

- What exactly happens when one snaps two Lego pieces together? Why do they stick together? Why can they still be pulled apart?

As you can see, the possibilities are endless.

Dropping Rocks around the Universe

First thought experiment: Releasing an object while on Earth

1. When I release a rock while standing in a room inside of my house, I hypothesize that it will: _____

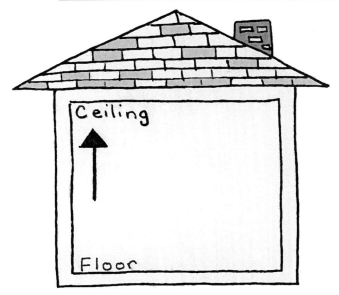

Second thought experiment: Releasing an object in an unknown location, part 1

2. When I release a rock in this location, the rock **floats in the air/ accelerates toward the floor**.

3. The behavior of the rock in this location is **the same as / different from** its behavior in the first thought experiment, when the rock was dropped inside of my house.

4. Therefore, I could conclude that the room with me and the rock inside of it are located **on the moon** / **on Jupiter** / **on Earth**.

5. Something to think about: Given the behavior of the rock, can you think of anywhere the room might be located that is not on the surface of a planet with the same gravity as Earth?

Third thought experiment: Releasing an object, first in a motionless spacecraft, and then in an accelerating spacecraft

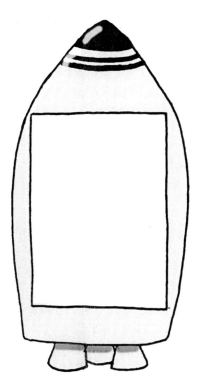

6. Before the craft starts accelerating, it is holding still, at rest in the vacuum of space. I hypothesize that if I release the rock, it will:

_____

Imagine that you grab the rock again and wait for the ship to accelerate. You are weightless in space. The ship accelerates in the same direction as the arrow on the wall of the room you are in. Think back to what you learned about inertia and momentum when one object accelerates but another object on top of it, or inside of it, does not accelerate.

7.   As the ship accelerates, my inertia—my tendency to stay at rest—keeps me in place. However, the floor of the room is moving toward my feet at 10 meters per second every second. Quickly, my feet hit the floor of the room and I'm standing. As the ship continues to accelerate at this same rate, I **start to float again / remain standing, experiencing something like Earth's gravity / am left behind, floating in space**.

8.   If I release the rock now, I hypothesize that it will **float in front of me / float to the top of the room / drop to the floor of the room**.

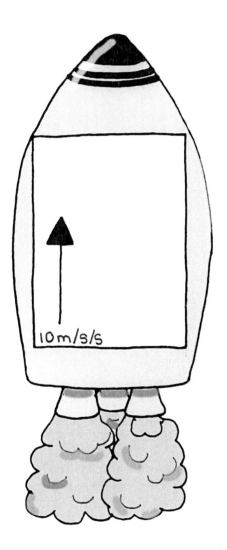

10m/s/s

Fourth thought experiment: Releasing an object in an unknown location, part 2

9.   When I imagine this situation, I drop the rock, and it falls to the ground at the same acceleration as it would on Earth. But, I also know that if my location were **Jupiter / a spacecraft accelerating at 10 meters per second every second / the moon**, the rock would behave in precisely the same way.

10.   If I wanted to figure out whether I was on Earth or in the spacecraft (assuming that the spacecraft can accelerate silently and that there are no windows in this room) I could _____

_____

_____

_____ .

(Hint: This is a bit of a trick question.)

For my notebook

Light: When Doing the Wave Just Won't Work

Einstein's insight that the speed of light is constant created an explosion in our understanding of space and time. At the other end of the spectrum, scientists were trying to understand just what the smallest piece of light might be like. Light is a curious thing. We can see the world around us because of light bouncing off of objects and into our eyes. But what is light? We can't seem to see light itself. We can't really touch it. We can block light and create a shadow. We can look at light bulbs and other sources of light. But what is the actual light stuff that these sources are giving off?

Scientists pondered this question for centuries. In science, studying things (matter and energy) that are very, very small at atomic and subatomic levels is called <u>quantum physics</u>, or quantum mechanics. An interesting thing about quantum physics is that the atomic and subatomic world can behave in surprisingly different, often illogical, ways than the world of <u>classical physics</u> that you've been mostly studying in this course.

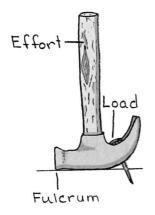

classical physics
versus
quantum physics

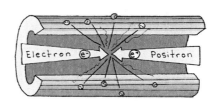

Isaac Newton was a quantum physicist who spent a lot of time studying <u>optics</u>—the behavior of light. He theorized that light consists of quickly traveling particles called "corpuscles" which could bounce perfectly off of many surfaces. This made sense to people because one could block these hypothesized light particles to create a shadow. It also made sense because the science of optics demonstrated that light travels in a straight line and bounces off of objects at a particular angle, just as tiny particles would.

Thomas Young was born about fifty years after Newton died. Young was brilliant and knew 12 languages fluently by the age of 16. Young was bothered by observations which seemed to contradict Newton's idea of light as particles. For example, if light is made of particles, how is it that light can travel around corners? You can see this for yourself on a dark night. Turn on a light in one room, and light seems to make its way around corners and into other rooms.

Thomas Young

Young set up a simple and elegant experiment. He made two tiny slits in a screen and then shined a very narrow beam of light through these slits onto a second screen. If light is made of particles, Young would have seen two lines of light on the second screen. Instead, he saw a series of bright lines separated by darker lines.

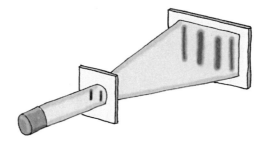

Young concluded that light must consist of waves of energy traveling through a medium just like sound does. He explained that the light waves traveling through one of the holes interfered with the light waves traveling through the other hole. In some areas, the crests of the waves combined to increase the size of the waves and the brightness of the light. In other areas, the crest and trough of the waves cancelled each other out, resulting in the darker areas on the second screen.

Over the next couple of hundred years, more and more experimental evidence accumulated to suggest that Young's idea that light is composed of waves was correct. However, a series of experiments in the early 1900s seemed to contradict this theory. These experiments involved something called the photoelectric effect. Scientists observed that when light was shined on certain sensitive metals, those metals ejected electrons.

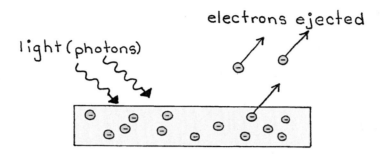

To understand what was startling about the observations of the photoelectric effect, let's consider an analogy, or model. Imagine that instead of electrons inside of atoms on a piece of metal, we have beach balls floating on the surface of water. Likewise, we'll imagine that the light shone on the metal is like the waves of water hitting the beach balls.

When scientists shined light on the metal, it was as if waves were hitting the beach balls. But, instead of all the beach balls reacting similarly, it was as if two or three of them jumped out of the water. To figure out what was going on, scientists tried to increase the intensity, or the size, of the light waves. When they did this, they were shocked. The electrons were still ejected from the material, but with no more energy than before. This would be analogous to sending first small waves and then huge waves at beach balls, but observing that they only jumped about the same height out of the water.

Then, the scientists tried to shine different-colored light at the metallic surface and were even more surprised. No matter how powerful a red light they used, no electrons moved.

Red Wave

If they used blue light, even very dim blue light, electrons were forcefully ejected from the metal. And, it wasn't a matter of shining a light on the metal for a long time: a dim blue light caused the electrons to jump just as quickly and as high as a bright blue light. In our model, this would be like sending a huge (bright red) wave and seeing no movement from the beach balls, and then sending a lot of gentle (dim blue) waves in quick succession and seeing some of the beach balls jump high out of the water, and then sending tall waves at the same frequency but seeing beach balls jump just as high as with the gentle waves.

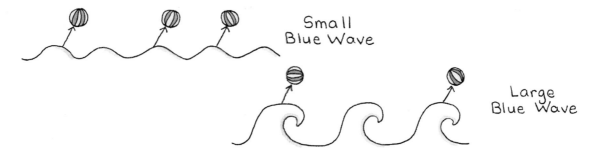

Small Blue Wave

Large Blue Wave

Whatever was happening, scientists were certain of one thing: this behavior of light made no sense given the hypothesis that light is simply a wave of energy. Young's ideas just couldn't explain the photoelectric effect. This is when that young clerk we read about previously* made his debut on the scientific scene. He posited that the photoelectric effect could be explained if light were composed of quanta, or packets, of light energy. These packets came to be called <u>photons</u>, but, as you'll see, photons don't tell the whole story about light.

*Albert Einstein

New Worlds Lab #2: Quantum Experiments - instructions

Materials:
- Lab sheets, pencil
- Your mind
- 3 sticks of pencil lead for mechanical pencils (.5 or .7 mm will work)
- Laser light (An inexpensive key chain laser or those sold as cat toys will work.)
- Dark room with clear wall space (Or, tape a piece of white paper on the wall to hide wallpaper.)

Aloud: We are going to duplicate Young's double-slit experiment. There are two primary challenges in getting this experiment to work. The first involves finding a way to make slits that are narrow enough and close enough together to work. To overcome this difficulty, we will use three sticks of pencil lead held closely together. You cannot see that there will be tiny spaces between the sticks for light to shine through, but there are. The second problem is finding a light source that is focused enough—and that is why we are using a laser rather than a flashlight.

In a moment you are going to go into a dark room and shine the flashlight or the laser pointer through the slits. The light will come out of the slits or holes and hit one of the walls of the room. Take a moment to imagine light as Newton conceived it: millions of tiny particles emerging from the flashlight and out the holes or slits. What would happen? Also, try to imagine light almost like waves of water as did Young. What would happen when the waves encounter the holes or slits and move outward from there?

Procedure:
1. Fill in "Before the Experiment" on the lab sheet.

2. You are going to hold the pencil leads all next to each other like this:
   Place them as close together as you can, holding them between your thumb and index finger. There will be a space between them, but it is too small for you to see.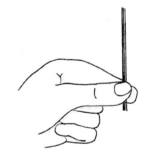

Caution: Never shine a laser light directly into eyes!

3. Go into the dark room. Shine the laser pointer or light through the leads and toward the wall. You don't need to be very far from the wall; between 1 and 4 feet should do it. You will have to play around with this a bit, holding the laser at slightly different angles, moving the leads closer to and farther from you or the wall. You should be able to see a series of alternating bright and dark areas spread out on the wall.

Troubleshooting- Try these things if the experiment is not working:
   A. Step out of the dark, rearrange the leads, and try again.
   B. Adjust your distance from the wall. I found this worked best within a couple of feet from the wall.
   C. Move the light closer to and farther from the pencil leads. Tip the leads at different angles. Tip the laser at different angles.

4. Fill in the rest of the lab sheet.

Aloud: If you were successful with this experiment, that's amazing! You've managed to reproduce one of the most important experiments in scientific history. One of the things I find fascinating about this experiment is that by varying how it is conducted and refining experimental techniques, scientists have continued to learn from it for over a century.

[continued]

New Worlds Lab #2: Quantum Experiments - instructions page 2

Possible Answers:

#1: two bright lines

#2 an interference pattern, such as alternating bright and dark lines

#5: Students may come up with a variety of answers. Make sure they considered the two factors mentioned above: that the slits be very close together and that the light be very focused. Young used a pinprick in a shade to get a beam of sunlight into the room. Rather than creating two slits, Young had the light pass around the edge of a card, creating two beams.

Conclusion / Discussion:

1. At this point, students should understand that light seems sometimes to exhibit the properties of particles and sometimes of waves. Discuss what sorts of observations are consistent with which theory (light as particles: it bounces off things, it travels in a straight line, the photoelectric effect. Light as waves: it can create interference patterns, it seems to make its way around corners).

2. Talk about why, thinking as scientists, light acting both like waves and like particles should be a problem. (Answer: because science looks for consistent theories to explain our observations.) How do you think scientists reacted to Einstein's paper positing that Young's theory that light consists of waves was wrong? They actually considered Einstein's ideas carefully, found ways to test their predictions, and verified that they were correct. In fact, this is the paper for which Einstein received the Nobel Prize!

More Lab Fun:

1. There are countless experiments you can design and conduct with light. If you have a prism or two, try shining light through it at various angles. What happens? If you have access to mirrors, see what you can determine about light and how it behaves by shining light into the mirror and seeing where it is reflected on the wall. (**Caution: do not shine the light directly into eyes, or reflect it into eyes.**) Can you detect a pattern having to do with the angle at which the light hits the mirror? What does this tell you about light?

2. The best way to understand wave interference is to find a small pond or calm lake. Try to toss in two stones simultaneously, a few feet apart from each other. Watch what happens to the waves from each stone as they hit each other.

Notebooking Ideas:

1. Sketch a picture of Young's experiment. Write down an explanation of what's happening.

2. Sketch a picture showing how weird the photoelectric effect seems by using the analogy that discussed it in terms of beach balls and waves. Explain how this provides a model of electrons and light waves.

Helpful Video Tutorials:

https://www.youtube.com/watch?v=fAVPRDnzSpE - Part 1 (wave/particle duality and the double- slit experiment)

https://www.youtube.com/watch?v=P3ABix1LJAI - Part 2 (the photoelectric effect)

https://www.youtube.com/watch?v=Bq69-MI9TA0 - A cartoon video for younger students explaining the double-slit experiment and superposition, a concept presented in the next lesson. (Some of the concepts in this video have been simplified and therefore are not entirely accurate. But this is still a nice video for younger students, or for those struggling with the concepts presented in this lab.)

http://richannel.org/the-double-slit-experiment - a more advanced explanation.

Quantum Experiments

Before the experiment:

1. If light behaves as particles, as Newton hypothesized, then when I shine light through two small slits and onto a wall, I should see: _____

   _____.

2. If light behaves as waves, as Young hypothesized, then when I shine light through the two slits, I should see: _____

   _____.

Results of the experiment:

3. Were you able to produce an interference pattern on the wall? **Yes / No**

4. If you were, sketch what it looked like:

5. How do you think Young might have performed this experiment without access to lasers which hadn't been invented, and without manufactured pencil leads? _____

   _____

   _____

   _____

   _____

For my notebook

Quantum Weirdness

We've just performed the double-slit experiment with light, and we know that the results of this experiment suggest that light is really waves. Yet, we also learned that Einstein's paper on the photoelectric effect demonstrated that light is particle-like—composed of photons or packets. However, scientists cannot be satisfied with the explanation that sometimes, for no apparent reason, light will act like waves and other times will act like particles. How could they figure out what was going on?

At the same time these questions were being asked, another set of questions, almost a mirror image, arose. Electrons, which most certainly are particles (since they consist of matter and have mass), would sometimes behave like waves. In an astonishing series of experiments, scientists duplicated Young's double-slit experiment, but this time they shot electrons at two narrow slits rather than pointing light at those slits.

First, as a control, they shot electrons through a single slit. Just as you'd predict if you shot something like teeny marbles through a slit, most bounced off the area around the slit, and some passed through the slit, hitting a wall in a pattern that was roughly the shape of the slit. Proof that electrons act like tiny particles. Well, proof until the next experiment, in which the scientists shot the electrons through two narrow slits close together. Guess what happened? The electrons hit the far wall and created an interference pattern! Just as if they were waves and not particles of matter.

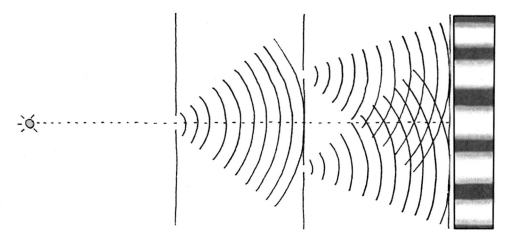

As unexpected as this was, what happened next was almost unbelievable. The physicists thought, "perhaps the electrons are bumping off the wall and hitting each other, and that's making the interference pattern." So, they conducted the double-slit experiment again, only this time they fired the electrons one at a time, so they couldn't interfere with each other. Somehow, there was an interference pattern again.

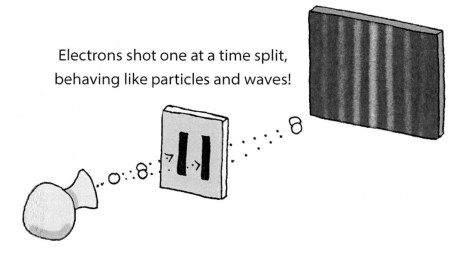

Electrons shot one at a time split, behaving like particles and waves!

A theory began to emerge. Einstein and other scientists of the time ultimately concluded that both light and electrons are characterized by duality—being two things simultaneously—waves and particles. But, for the experimental results to make sense, the physicists determined that, as each electron was shot toward the slits, it must somehow exist twice, pass through both slits, and interfere with itself. Furthermore, it must exist as a particle when it is shot, as a wave when it hits the slits, and as a particle again when it hits the wall.

If you are shaking your head and thinking, "but that can't be," you are not alone. Many scientists thought the same thing. So, another experiment was devised. This time, they would fire the electrons one at a time, but use a device to detect which slit each electron went through. Take a moment to decide what you think might have happened when they performed this experiment.

The results were incredibly strange. Now, the electrons behaved like simple particles: Each went through a particular slit and together they created a pattern of two slit-like shapes on the wall. There was no interference pattern. The only difference between when the electrons acted like waves and when the electrons acted like particles was that scientists were measuring what happened.

When being measured, electrons behaved like particles only!

These weird effects are called <u>quantum</u> effects because they occur only in the world of the smallest pieces of matter and energy—electrons and light and other similar particles. In the rest of physics, matter behaves like we expect it to. If we shoot actual marbles at a double slit, they will behave like matter. But, how can we explain what happens in the quantum world, the world of light and subatomic particles?

Physicists use mathematics to describe what happens in the world. According to their mathematics, if we shoot a particular electron toward two slits, there is a certain probability that the electron will pass through the right slit, and a certain probability that it will pass through the left slit. Most scientists think that when the electron is fired, it exists in a state called <u>superposition</u>: it exists as a set of probabilities—going through one slit, going through the other slit, bouncing off the area around the slits. Only when it is measured does the electron settle into one of its possible realities—does it actually go through one slit or the other. That is why electrons were able to create an interference pattern, even when fired one at a time: Without a device measuring them, the electrons never settled into a particular possibility, and instead existed in multiple possible states. With a measurement device, the electrons settled into particular states—a particle going through the left slit or a particle going through the right slit—thus producing two bright lines in the shape of the slits on the far wall.

As you can imagine, many scientists were utterly perplexed and couldn't accept that reality could be so bizarre at the quantum level. One

scientist, **Erwin Schrodinger** [shrow-dinger], devised a thought experiment to illustrate how absurd this quantum theory was. Unfortunately for Schrodinger, as scientists continue to experiment, they have become more and more convinced that the quantum world really is as absurd and perplexing as the electron experiments suggested. Let's try one last set of thought experiments to understand all of this weirdness.

Erwin Schrodinger

New Worlds Lab #3: Schrodinger's Cat - instructions

Materials:
- Lab sheets, pencil
- Your mind

Aloud: In order to explain how weird theories about the quantum world seemed, Schrodinger decided to invent a thought experiment that illustrated what would happen if quantum weirdness and superposition could exist not just for subatomic particles, but for us and the matter with which we interact. Because this thought experiment involves a cat who may die, you should know that it is only a thought experiment. To my knowledge, no cats or any other animals have ever actually been harmed in attempting Schrodinger's proposed experiment.

Schrodinger's experiment depends on another aspect of quantum reality: <u>radioactive decay</u>. Given a radioactive substance, there is an equal chance that a particular atom of that substance either will decay or will not decay. It's not important to know exactly what this means, only to understand that this is similar to saying that a given electron has an equal chance of passing either through the left or right slit in the double-slit experiment. So, here's the thought experiment:

Get a large metal box (not really, remember this is a thought experiment). Within that box, place the following: a cat, a very small amount of radioactive material, a device that can detect radioactive activity (whether a single atom of the radioactive material has decayed or not), a sealed flask of poisonous gas, and an apparatus that will shatter the flask and release the poisonous gas, thus killing the cat, but only if the device detects radioactivity. Close up the box, so that no observer can see what happens inside.

We start the experiment and wait patiently, as scientists do, for one hour before lifting the lid and seeing if the cat is alive or dead. An atom in the radioactive substance has an equal chance of decaying or not, but it doesn't settle into one state—decayed or not decayed—until an observer looks to see whether it has decayed. This is just like the electron, which doesn't settle into existence as either a wave or a particle until it is observed.

Schrodinger asked: if the atom is in superposition—if it is both decayed and not decayed until it is observed—does that mean that the cat is both alive and dead until someone opens the box to look? And, if that's true, what happens when the box is opened? If the atom decayed, does that mean that the cat dies the moment the experiment is observed even though the atom might have decayed five minutes earlier? Schrodinger's cat has been used to illustrate the different ways that science now views quantum events. By filling in the lab sheet, you will learn about these different schools of thought.

[continued]

Procedure:

1. Fill in #1 on the lab sheet.

Aloud: According to some scientists who came to be known as the Copenhagen School, the different possibilities of the quantum world all coexist until the result is observed, at which point they all "collapse" into one reality or another. According to these scientists, the cat truly is alive and dead until the atom is observed to have decayed or not decayed.

2. Fill in #2 on the lab sheet.

Aloud: Other scientists have proposed something known as the "Many-worlds interpretation." According to these scientists, reality splits off into different universes whenever various quantum possibilities occur. Thus, for these scientists, once the box is closed and the time comes for the atom either to decay or not, two universes split off from one another—in one, the atom decays and the cat dies. In the other, the atom does not decay and the cat lives.

3. Fill in #3 on the lab sheet.

Aloud: I've never liked the fact that, to make his point, Schrodinger thought to poison this poor cat. I've always thought a better experiment could be devised. Think of something else that could happen to the cat instead of poison. I imagine that the apparatus puts a really ridiculous cat sweater on the cat if the atom decays. What do you imagine?

4. Fill in #4 on the lab sheet.

Aloud: Science has not yet settled on exactly what happens in the quantum world. Experiments have been able to keep extremely small pieces of matter—but not quite so small as electrons—in a state of superposition for short periods of time. What do you think actually happens when an electron is fired at a double-slit apparatus? Draw a picture or describe your thoughts.

5. Fill in #5 on the lab sheet.

Possible Answers:
All answers will vary.

Conclusion / Discussion:

1. One very difficult aspect of the issues raised by quantum theories has to do with what scientists mean when they say something is "observed." Think about how you observe the world around you. All of our observations involve interactions—sound waves hitting our ear drums or photons bouncing off of objects and into our eyes. Many of the fundamental ideas in quantum theory spring from the concept that the more closely we try to measure a particular aspect of the quantum world—the position of an electron or the decay of an atom—the more the very nature of our observation—bouncing photons off of what is being observed so we can "see" it—causes changes in the system we are observing. Because of this, many people ask the following questions about Schrodinger's cat. There are no easy answers, but the question are fascinating to contemplate:

[continued]

New Worlds Lab #3: Schrodinger's Cat - instructions page 3

     A. Is it the detection device which is the actual observer and not the person who opens the box? Experimental evidence suggests that this is true. However, it doesn't solve the problem, as the next question demonstrates.

     B. If the detection device is set to operate five minutes after the atom either decays (or doesn't), is the cat both alive and dead for the five minutes between when the atom's state changes (or doesn't change) and the time the detection device operates?

     C. Can the cat be considered an observer?

     D. Are there any experimental ways to determine what is happening in the box without in any way losing information about the state of the inside of the box before we look? (So far, we think the answer is "no.")

2. Imagine what it was like to conduct the experiments described having to do with firing electrons through single and double slits. What would it have been like as each new, unanticipated result occurred? What might you have been thinking had you been present at the time?

3. The quantum world is weird and wonderful. Make sure that students understand that all this weirdness and coexistence of several realities at once only occurs at the quantum level—for objects the size of atoms and electrons and smaller. Also, talk about how science is still grappling with these issues. Science is a process of theories, experiments, thinking, sharing, and discussing. It is important for students to understand that every theory or school of thought exists only as long as it is consistent with experimental results.

4. For hundreds of years, philosophers and scientists have been asking a simple, but fascinating, question: If a tree falls in the woods and there is no one present to perceive it (or device present to record it), does the tree really make a sound? When scientists began to ponder the implications of quantum physics—how experimenters actually change the nature of the things they are observing—they recalled this philosophical question. The question gets to the heart of many ideas about how we, as human beings, interact with the world around us. On the one hand, the question is simple to answer for the scientist: If a tree falls in the woods, the energy of its impact causes sound waves to propagate through the forest and, therefore, a sound is produced. However, philosophers of science see an even deeper question here: How do we know with certainty that something has occurred if we don't perceive it directly? What is it about the scientific method, and the ideas we learn through science, that allows us to be sure that this knowledge is correct even when we haven't been the person to verify the knowledge directly? Do our certainties and beliefs ever interfere with our observations or our openness to new ideas? These are profound questions and there are no correct answers to them. Take some time to discuss how you know that a spoon will fall if you let go of it. What persuades you that this knowledge is correct? Would you know that the same thing would happen if your brother or sister or parent went to another room and tried the experiment? What would you think if someone reported that the spoon "fell" upward? What would it take to convince you that their observation was correct?

If these kinds of questions interest you, you might consider doing research into the philosophy of science. A famous book by Thomas Kuhn, called the *Structure of Scientific Revolutions*, initiated the modern debate about these questions, and scientists and philosophers have been discussing and arguing about the answers ever since.

[continued]

More Lab Fun/Notebooking Ideas:

Obviously, it would be hard to conduct your own quantum experiments. However, the ideas posited by quantum theories have inspired many writers of fantasy and science fiction. Write a story, draw a picture, or create a comic based on the idea that different realities exist in superposition. What would happen if you could travel from one reality to another? (Scientists don't believe this is possible, but it's a fun idea to think about.)

Helpful Videos:

https://www.youtube.com/watch?v=IOYyCHGWJq4 - A whiteboard video demonstration of the cat thought experiment using Einstein's version with gunpowder.

https://www.youtube.com/watch?v=uWMTOrux0LM - A funny video explaining Schrodinger's cat thought experiment, warning: possibly offensive language—parents might want to preview this video for appropriateness.

NAME _____ DATE _____

Schrodinger's Cat

1. <u>The experiment</u>: Make a sketch of Schrodinger's thought experiment. Show the effects of superposition: the atom in two states at once— decayed and not decayed; the cat in two states at once, alive and not alive. Feel free to have some fun with this drawing. I imagine one of the cats looking quite relieved!

2. <u>The Copenhagen interpretation</u>: Collapsing probabilities: Make a sketch showing how the Copenhagen School views Schrodinger's cat. Imagine that, in this case, the atom has not decayed and the cat lives on.

Schrodinger's Cat - page 2

3. <u>The Many-worlds interpretation</u>: Make a sketch showing the Many-worlds interpretation.

4. A kinder, gentler Schrodinger's cat experiment:

5. What I think happens in the quantum world:

For my notebook

Final Thoughts

The astronomer **Carl Sagan** once wrote, "Science is a way of thinking much more than it is a body of knowledge." You've spent a lot of time studying physics, and you've acquired a great deal of knowledge—everything from Newton's laws of motion to theories about space, time, and the ultimate nature of reality. Of course, any book about physics is supposed to teach you some physics. But, more than that, I hope that this book has also ignited a passion in you, a passion for closely observing the world around you and for trying to understand through thinking and experimenting how and why your world behaves the way it does. I believe that these are the most important qualities a scientist can have: curiosity, the ability to observe, and the ability to think.

Sometimes, students who know that they don't want to become a scientist wonder why they have to learn so much about subjects like physics. I have several answers for such students which I think are true for everyone. If you hold yourself open to all of the knowledge that world has to offer, you will naturally come to appreciate and enjoy life more. Looking at **Van Gogh's** painting *Starry Night* is a beautiful experience, but it is even more amazing if you know that Van Gogh somehow captured essential concepts of the physics of fluid dynamics with his swirling paint. Did you know that artists are inspired by science and scientists are inspired by artists?

Although it might seem like some of physics will never be useful to you, you never know. The photoelectric effect helped **Einstein** demonstrate the particle nature of light, but what good is that? In addition to increasing our knowledge of the building blocks of the universe and the source of all energy on Earth, understanding the photoelectric effect was a key step toward developing our ability to use solar power. Solar power can be used to create electricity so that we use less of the fuels that pollute the air and harm our health and our planet. And what about that quantum weirdness (which hardly seems real)—is it much less useful? Well, it turns out that scientists have discovered that deep within plant cells, the chlorophyll which transforms sunlight into food may actually harness superposition to direct photons in the most efficient manner. If we can understand how plants manage this, we might ultimately be able to create more efficient energy sources.

There are so many wonderful and different directions you can go from here. Carry a notebook with you and continue to make observations about the world in that notebook. Write down the date on each page, look around, and think. Write down what you see, what questions you have, ideas and connections that come to mind, and experiments you might try out some day. Read books, watch documentaries, and visit museums with science sections. If you know any scientists or engineers, talk to them about their work.

Overall, though, perhaps the most useful aspect of studying science is what **Carl Sagan** suggested—learning how to think like a scientist. If you understand how to make observations, how to think logically about what you see and learn, and how to draw conclusions from your experiences, you will have the ability to succeed at anything you want to do! Keep learning, keep observing, keep thinking, but most of all, keep being curious about everything.

Notebooking Pages

Appendix - Notebooking Pages

Physics Notebook

by _____

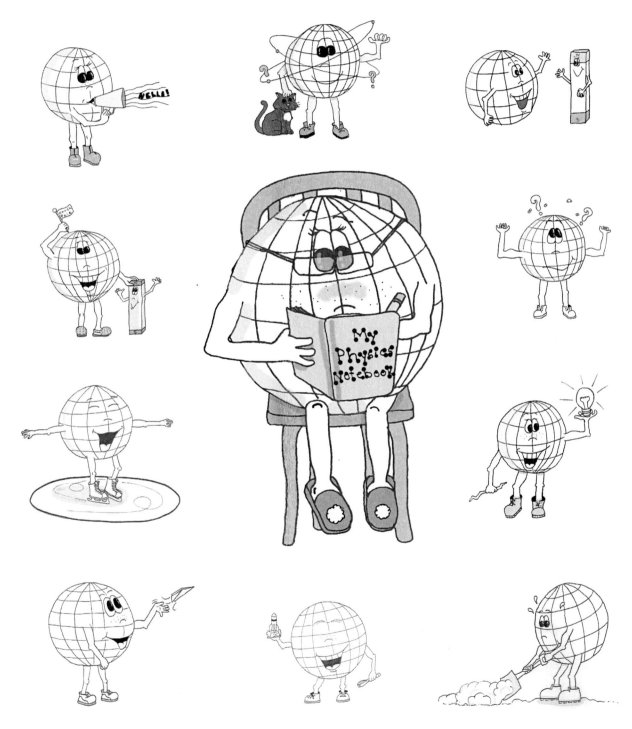

Appendix - Notebooking Pages

Appendix - Notebooking Pages

This Venn Diagram is about _____ .

Appendix - Notebooking Pages

NAME _____ DATE _____

Notebooking - Definitions

Important definitions I learned while studying _____ .

Word:

Definition: _____

_____

_____

_____

_____

Word:

Definition: _____

_____

_____

_____

_____

Word:

Definition: _____

_____

_____

_____

_____

Word:

Definition: _____

_____

_____

_____

_____

Notebooking - Definitions

Important definitions I learned while studying _____ .

Word:	Definition: _____
	_____
	_____
	_____
	_____

Word:	Definition: _____
	_____
	_____
	_____
	_____

Word:	Definition: _____
	_____
	_____
	_____
	_____

Word:	Definition: _____
	_____
	_____
	_____
	_____

NAME _____ DATE _____

Notebooking - Do Your Own Experiment!

Experiment Title: _____

(Title should explain what the experiment is about, like "Momentum & Marble Collisions.")

Materials I will need:

_____

_____

_____

The question I'm trying to answer with this experiment is:

(Make sure you include what scientific idea you are exploring—for example, momentum.)

_____

_____

_____

My Hypothesis—What I think will happen and why I think that is:

_____

_____

_____

Here is what I am going to do: (draw a picture, describe it in words, or both)

_____

_____

_____

_____

_____

_____

_____

_____

_____

_____

☐ I have reviewed what I'm going to do with an adult and the adult said it is okay.

Observations: When I did the experiment, this is what happened:

Analysis and Conclusions: What I learned from doing this experiment: (You might include: (1) whether your hypothesis was correct; (2) why you think what occurred happened; (3) what scientific idea the results show; (4) what you think could have interfered with your results; (5) what further experiments you might do to explore these ideas more.)

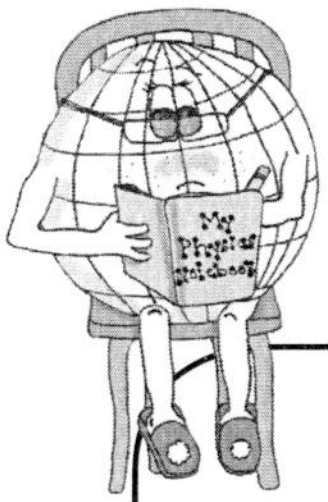

NAME ______________________________ DATE ________________

Notebooking - Equations

An Equation about ____

____

The equation:

The letters in the equation stand for:

Describe what this equation tells us about physics in your own words:

____

____

____

____

____

____

Other notes about this equation:

____

____

____

____

____

Notebooking - Equations

An Equation about _____

_____

The equation:

The letters in the equation stand for:

Describe what this equation tells us about physics in your own words:

_____

_____

_____

_____

_____

_____

Other notes about this equation:

_____

_____

_____

_____

_____

NAME _____ DATE _____

My Lab Report for _____

Statement of the Problem: (What question are you trying to answer with this lab?)

Hypothesis: (In a complete sentence, write a possible solution to the problem. Given what you know before you conduct the experiment, what do you predict the result will be?)

Materials: (A list of all the materials used in the lab.)

Procedure: (A step-by-step list. You may include sketches of the lab setup and steps. Continue on the next page and attach extra sheets if necessary.)

Observations and Data: (Describe what happened without judgement. Include any calculations, observations, sketches, graphs, and charts. Attach separate sheets if necessary.)

Conclusion: (Describe the result—the answer to the problem question. Did the result match your hypothesis? Explain why it did or did not. Discuss any errors and problems with the lab.)

Science Vocabulary

Acceleration: A change in an object's velocity.

Action: A force applied by one object to another object.

Action-at-a-distance force: A push or pull on an object that does not require physical contact with that object, such as the force of gravity or the attraction between two magnets.

Aerodynamics: The branch of physics that studies what happens when an object moves through the air.

Air: The mixture of gases surrounding the earth.

Air current: Air in which most of the molecules are moving in one direction.

Air pressure: The pressure, or force, exerted by air pushing on us from all directions.

Alkaline battery: A common type of battery that works because, when connected to a circuit, a chemical reaction is triggered which causes electrons to travel in a particular direction, creating an electrical current.

Amperes: Units with which we measure the amount of electrical charge passing a point at a particular time.

Amplify: In everyday terms, to make something louder. Technically, to increase the amplitude of a wave.

Amplitude: The height of a wave.

Anode: The part of the battery referred to as the "minus end." Electrons flow through a circuit from the anode toward the cathode.

Atmosphere: The air surrounding the planet Earth.

Atom: The smallest piece of an element that still behaves like that element. For example, you can't get anything smaller than an atom of iron and have it still be iron.

Attract: To pull something closer.

Axis (Earth's): An imaginary line or pole drawn through the earth around which the planet spins.

Axle: A stick to which a wheel can be attached.

Bernoulli's principle: The principle that there are fewer air molecules where air is moving faster. Many airplane wings are shaped to force air flowing over the top of the wing to move more quickly than air flowing past the bottom of the wing. Because of this, there is less pressure above the wing than below it, and the airplane experiences lift.

Block and tackle: A "block," or group of pulleys, along with the "tackle," or rope, that is threaded through them.

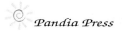

Buoyancy: The tendency of an object to float in water. Boats are, hopefully, buoyant. Most rocks are not.

Calculus: A branch of mathematics, developed in part by Isaac Newton, which provides mathematical tools for understanding the motion of objects.

Cathode: The part of the battery referred to as the "plus end." Electrons flow through a circuit from the anode toward the cathode.

Characteristics: A descriptive feature of an object or piece of matter that helps us to identify or compare objects. Some important characteristics of matter are: color, mass, density, ferromagnetism, and conductivity.

Cilia: Cilia in the inner ear are small hairlike structures which sense and respond to the motion of fluid inside the ear.

Circuit: A closed loop of conductive material (usually wires) and devices (such as bulbs or switches) through which electrical current flows.

Classical physics: A field of physics that describes most of the behavior of matter and energy that we encounter. Classical physics "breaks down" – or fails to make accurate predictions— for objects traveling at speeds close to the speed of light and for interactions that occur at the subatomic level.

Coefficient of friction: A measure of the force of friction between two specific objects or materials.

Compound pulley system: A group of pulleys used together to make work easier. Also known as a "block."

Conclusion: The decision reached by a scientist after conducting an experiment and considering the data as to whether his or her hypothesis was correct.

Conditions: In a scientific law, the description of the situation in which the law is valid. For instance, Newton's laws of motion are valid in the following conditions: when objects are not traveling close to the speed of light and when objects are not sub-atomic in size.

Conductors: Materials that allow electrical current to flow freely because of empty spaces in their electron shells.

Contact force: A push or pull on an object that requires physical contact with that object, such as pushing a shopping cart or picking up a glass of water.

Control (in an experiment): Part of an experiment done to demonstrate what happens if no conditions or variables are changed. For example, in order to determine how using a lever changes the amount of force needed to lift 10 pennies, the "control" would involve lifting the same 10 pennies in the same container or apparatus but without the lever. The experiment would change only one condition—the use of the lever.

Copenhagen interpretation: One way of viewing quantum effects which posits that a system exists in all possible states until an observer collapses the system into a particular reality.

Current: An area in a fluid or other medium that is flowing in a particular direction, such as electrical or air currents.

Current electricity: Electricity that is flowing in a particular direction.

Data: Information that is obtained through observation. Scientists make careful records of their data in lab notebooks.

Deformable: An object is deformable if you can alter its shape by pushing on it.

Density: Technically, density is an object's mass divided by its volume. Objects that have a lot of mass in a small volume have a higher density, such as heavy rocks. Objects with a small amount of matter in a large space have a lower density, such as Styrofoam.

Diaphragm: A thin sheet of material. On a stethoscope, a diaphragm is used to transmit sound waves.

Displaced: Moved out of the way.

Distortion: A change in a substance caused by some force.

Domains: In the study of magnetism, the idea that small areas of materials in which the magnetic field produced by spinning electrons points in the same direction. In a magnet, the domains are all lined up. In a magnetic metal like iron, there are many domains pointing in many directions.

Drag: One of the four main forces acting on objects as they move through the air. Drag is the force caused by air molecules pushing against an object as it moves through the air.

Effort: The amount of force needed to move the load on a lever. Effort also refers to the place on the lever where you apply force.

Effort arm: The part of a lever between the effort and the load.

Elastic potential energy: Potential energy stored in an object that has been moved despite an elastic force—such as a rubber band—pulling it in the opposite direction.

Electric motor: A device that transforms electrical energy into mechanical energy.

Electrical current: Electricity that is flowing in a particular direction.

Electrical potential: The different amount of positive electrical charge at one end of a battery or circuit as compared with the amount of negative charge at the other end. This difference drives current through a circuit because of the fact that like charges repel and unlike charges attract.

Electrical power: Measured in watts, a combination of volts and amperes—gives a sense of how much electrical energy is transferred in a circuit in a given amount of time.

Electrically neutral: Matter that is electrically neutral carries neither a positive nor a negative charge.

Electricity: A form of energy primarily having to do with the accumulation or movement of positively and negatively charged particles.

Electromagnet: A magnet created by using electrical current to orient the domains in a ferromagnetic material in one direction. The material ceases to be magnetic when the current is turned off.

Electron shell: An area around an atom's nucleus in which there is a certain likelihood of finding electrons. Electrons in higher shells have more energy than electrons in lower shells.

Electrons: Negatively charged subatomic particles that exist in a cloud around the nucleus of an atom. Electrons, although considerably smaller and less massive than protons, carry a charge of -1.

Electroscope: A device that detects the presence of static electricity.

Energy: A measure of the ability to do work. With more energy, more work can be performed.

Equal and opposite reaction: In Newton's third law of motion, an equal and opposite reaction refers to the fact that whenever a force is applied by one object to another, a reactive force arises that is in the opposite direction and of the same strength as the initial force.

Equilibrium: When all of the forces on an object result in its remaining at rest, the object is said to be in "equilibrium."

Expand: To increase the amount of space something occupies.

Ferromagnets or ferromagnetic materials: Commonly referred to as "magnetic materials." Ferromagnetic materials have domains, or regions, in which magnetic fields align and can be magnetized by using a magnet to orient most of the domains in one direction.

Field: An area in which a force exists.

Filament: The thin strand of metal in a light bulb that glows when electrical current passes through it.

First-class lever: A lever in which the fulcrum is located between the load and the effort.

First law of motion: Newton's first law of motion tells us what will happen to objects if no new force acts on them. An object at rest will remain at rest until something pushes or pulls it. An object moving at a specific velocity will remain moving at that velocity unless a force pushes or pulls it. This law is also referred to as the law of inertia.

Fixed pulley: A pulley that is attached to a stationary object such as a flagpole so that it turns but does not move.

Fluid: A substance that is deformable.

Force: Any push or pull on matter.

Four aerodynamic forces: Forces acting on an object moving through the air. The forces are weight, drag, lift, and thrust.

Frequency: A measure of how quickly waves pass by a given point.

Friction: A force that resists the motion of an object.

Fulcrum: The fixed point around which a lever moves. Derived from the Latin word meaning "support."

Gas: A state of matter in which the molecules or atoms are free to move. Gases have no fixed shape and can compress or expand to fill a space. For example, air.

Generator: A device that transforms some form of energy (usually chemical or mechanical) into electrical energy.

Gravitational field: The area around a mass to which the force of gravity extends.

Gravitational potential energy: Potential energy stored in an object that has been moved despite the force of gravity.

Gravity: A force that is a characteristic of all objects with mass. This force attracts other nearby matter.

Halogen bulb: Light bulbs that contain a special gas that reacts with a tungsten filament when electricity passes through the filament.

Heat: A type of energy transferred from an object with a higher temperature to an object with a lower temperature.

Helium: An element that, at room temperature, is a gas which is lighter than air.

Hydroplaning: The loss of friction, and therefore traction and ability to control a vehicle, which occurs when a thin layer of water builds up between a tire or a wheel and the road.

Hypothesis: A proposed explanation of why matter behaves in a certain way, usually based on a scientist's previous knowledge and observations.

Incandescent bulb: The earliest type of light bulb that made use of a filament that resists the flow of electricity. The friction from this resistance causes the filament to glow, but ultimately burns out the light bulb.

Incline: A slope.

Inclined plane: A type of simple machine made by leaning a flat surface at an angle.

Inertia: The tendency of an to object remain in the same state—at rest or in motion—until a new force acts upon it. An object with more mass has more inertia.

Inner ear: The part of the ear behind the eardrum that is responsible for detecting sound and helping us to maintain balance.

Insulators: Materials that make it very difficult for electrical current to flow.

Kinetic energy: The energy of a moving object.

Law of gravity: The scientific law that describes how objects interact because of the force of gravity between them. The law of gravity states that gravity is strong between objects when they are closer together and that gravity is stronger for objects with more mass.

Law of the lever: A mathematical formula that allows us to predict the effect of various lever configurations on the amount of force needed to move a load. In short, it states that if the size of a load is increased, either the amount of force applied at the effort or the size of the effort arm will need to be increased.

LED bulb: A newer type of light bulb that uses materials called semiconductors. These bulbs are extremely energy efficient and can glow brightly.

Lever: A stick or board that can rest on and move around a fixed object called a fulcrum.

Lift: One of the four main forces acting on an object as they move through the air. Lift is the force that tries to overcome the force of gravity and is caused by the shape of a flying object interacting with the air around it.

Liquid: A state of matter in which molecules or atoms remain in contact with one another. Liquids conform to the shape of their container. For example, water.

Load: The object that one is trying to move with a lever or pulley.

Load arm: The part of a lever between the fulcrum and the load.

Lodestone: Naturally occurring magnetic stone.

Magnet: A substance that produces a magnetic field.

Magnetic: Capable of being attracted by a magnet.

Magnetic field: An area of force surrounding a magnet or other magnetic material.

Magnetic north: The region of the earth toward which compasses point because of the earth's magnetic field. Does not correspond with true north.

Magnetism: A property of some materials that results in attracting some metals. A push or pull exerted on objects in the presence of a magnetic field.

Many-worlds interpretation: One way of viewing quantum effects, which posits that reality splits off into different universes for every possibility in a quantum interaction.

Mass: A measurement of how much matter an object is made of. Mass is often measured in grams or kilograms.

Matter: Anything that exists, has mass, and takes up some space.

Maximize: Make larger.

Maxwell's equations: Mathematical equations that describe the relationship between electricity and magnetism and demonstrate that both are aspects of a single force: electromagnetism.

Medium: Some form of matter through which waves can travel.

Minimize: Make smaller.

Molecule: A substance made of two or more atoms. For example, a water molecule is made of one oxygen atom and two hydrogen atoms.

Momentum: The degree to which an object tends to keep doing what it was doing before—either moving or remaining at rest. Momentum increases with an object's mass and velocity.

Moveable pulley: A pulley that is attached directly to the load so that it can move along with the load.

Negative charge: A tiny bit of electrical charge which scientists arbitrarily decided to call "negative." As with magnetism, negative charges repel other negative charges.

Net force: The result of all the forces acting on an object.

Neutrons: Subatomic particles in the nucleus of an atom. Neutrons carry no charge and have about as much mass as protons.

Newton's laws of motion: Three scientific laws which describe and predict how objects behave when at rest, when in motion, and when pushing on each other.

North pole: One end of a magnet that is attracted to the south pole on other magnets. The north pole of the earth's magnetic field moves around and does not actually line up exactly with the North Pole of Earth's axis as shown on globes.

Nucleus: The center of the atom.

Observation: An important step in the scientific method that involves carefully examining an experiment, object, or event with all of our senses and with measuring tools.

Optics: The field of physics that focuses on the behavior of light and its interactions with objects such as lenses and mirrors.

Parallel (circuit): When components are connected to a circuit such that the positive end of one component is hooked up to the positive end of the next component and the negative ends are also hooked up to each other, the components are said to be "in parallel." If a component in parallel breaks, the circuit will still function.

Perpetual motion device: A device that uses its own motion to power itself, so that it never runs out of energy. Such a device would violate the laws of physics as we understand those laws.

Photoelectric effect: When light is focused on certain metals, those metals eject electrons. Einstein received the Nobel Prize for his work, furthering our understanding of this effect.

Photons: Quanta, or packets, of light energy that are used to understand light's particle-like behavior.

Physicist: A scientist who studies the behavior of matter, forces, and energy.

Physics: The study of matter and the forces and energy that affect matter.

Plane: A flat surface.

Poles: Areas of a magnet where the magnetic field is the strongest.

Positive charge: A tiny bit of electrical charge which scientists arbitrarily decided to call "positive." As with magnetism, positive charges repel other positive charges.

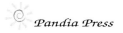

Potential energy: Energy that is stored in an object that has been moved despite another force acting on it. For example, lifting a ball into the air despite the force of gravity pulling downward on the ball stores potential energy in the ball.

Prediction: An idea about what will happen if a particular experiment is performed. Scientific hypotheses are tested by using them to make predictions and then performing experiments to find out whether the predictions are correct.

Pressurized: Maintaining a constant pressure regardless of the surrounding pressure. For example, a space suit maintains air pressure even in space, where the air pressure is absent or negligible.

Protons: Positively charged subatomic particles in the nucleus of an atom. Protons carry a charge of +1, and the number of protons in an atom determines the atom's element.

Pulley: A simple machine consisting of a wheel with a groove in it across which a string, rope, or chain can move to turn the wheel.

Pulley block: A group of pulleys used together to make work easier. Also known as a compound pulley system.

Qualitative data/observations: Describes nonnumerical data or observations of the qualities of objects such as color, texture, or whether an object is magnetic.

Quantitative data/observations: Describes numerical data or observations based on measurements such as length, mass, or distance.

Quantum effects: Phenomena that are observed among very small particles (subatomic) interacting.

Quantum physics: A field of physics that describes how matter and energy behave at the subatomic level. It is known for uncovering behaviors that seem strange or bizarre, such as that of light, which behaves both as a wave and as a particle.

Radioactive decay: The process by which certain elements emit particles from their nuclei.

Reaction: A force that results because of another force having been applied to an object.

Relativistic physics: A field of physics largely developed by Albert Einstein that more accurately describes motion, time, and space than Newton's laws of motion in certain situations such as at near light speed.

Repel: To push something away.

Rest: The state of an object when it is not moving.

Scientific law: A scientific description that has been verified in many experiments and that describes what always happens given certain starting conditions.

Scientific method: A way to ask and answer questions about the world by making observations, taking measurements, conducting experiments, and thinking about what those experiments mean.

Screw: A type of simple machine made by wrapping a wedge around a cylinder.

Second-class levers: A lever in which the load is located between the effort and the fulcrum. For example, a wheelbarrow in which the wheel is the fulcrum, the handles are the effort, and the load is in the bucket in the middle.

Second law of motion: Newton's second law of motion describes what happens when an object is acted on by a force. It states that an object will accelerate in the direction in which it is pushed and that the greater the force of the push, the greater the acceleration. In addition, it states that the greater an object's mass, the more force will be needed to move it.

Series (circuit): When the positive end of one component of a circuit is hooked up to the negative end of the next component, the components are "in series." If one component of a series breaks, the whole circuit will stop working.

Short circuit: A circuit with no devices to provide resistance or otherwise impede electrical flow. If one end of a battery is connected to the other with a wire, it creates a short circuit: the wire will become extremely hot and the battery will run out of energy quickly.

Simple machine: A device that makes work easier by altering the amount of force needed to perform the work or by altering the direction in which the force is applied.

Solid: A state of matter in which molecules or atoms are in a fixed position. Solids do not change their shape. For example, an iron bar.

Sound wave: A wave in which sound travels through a medium such as air.

South pole: One end of a magnet that is attracted to the north pole on other magnets. The south pole of the earth's magnetic field moves around and actually does not line up exactly with the south end of the axis of Earth shown on globes.

Speed of light: The speed of light in a vacuum is referred to by physicists as "c" and is a constant—the same—for all observers regardless of their position or velocity.

Stable: Not easily changed or disturbed.

Static: The state of holding still.

Static electrical charge: An accumulation of stationary electrical charge.

Static electricity: A stationary electrical charge usually caused by friction. Conceptually, it is sort of like a lake of electrons (negatively charged) or a region where many electrons are absent (positively charged).

Stethoscope: A device invented by René Laennec which amplifies sounds from the body by directing sound energy through a tube.

Strong force: The extremely strong fundamental force that holds protons and neutrons together within the nucleus of the atom.

Superposition: The idea in quantum physics that includes the concept that the same quantum particle can exist in two or more states until observed. For example, light is both a particle and a wave until an observer forces it into one state or the other.

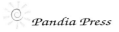

Theoretical physicist: A physicist who spends much of his or her time using mathematical models to understand how matter behaves.

Theory of general relativity: One of Einstein's three great papers that links the effects of gravity and acceleration.

Theory of special relativity: One of Einstein's three great papers which describes the effects of traveling at near-light speed, such as time dilation and length contraction.
These laws are valid in almost all circumstances on Earth. They need to be modified to work for objects traveling at very high speeds (close to the speed of light) and for objects which are extremely small (smaller than atoms).

Third-class levers: A lever in which the effort is located between the load and the fulcrum. For example, a broom is a third-class lever in which the end of the broom is the fulcrum, the place where you push with your hands is the effort, and whatever you are sweeping is the load.

Third law of motion: Newton's third law of motion states that for every action, there is an opposite and equal reaction.

Thrust: One of the four main forces acting on objects as they move through the air. Thrust is the force that pushes an object forward, such as a jet engine.

Tread: The pattern of grooves on a wheel.

Tribologist: A scientist who studies friction.

True north: The point on the globe where Earth's imaginary axis would emerge in the Arctic.

Tungsten: An element that has commonly been used to coat filaments in light bulbs because of its unique characteristics. Tungsten glows when exposed to certain chemicals and electricity but takes a long time to "burn out" as new tungsten is deposited on the filament throughout the process.

Vacuum: An area free of matter, such as in the depths of space.

Vectors: Mathematical concepts used by physicists to describe measurements that have both magnitude (size) and direction. For example, an object's speed tells us how quickly it moves from one place to another, but it does not tell us anything about the direction in which the object is moving. However, an object's velocity is a vector quantity giving us information about both the speed and direction of the object. Vectors are usually represented by arrows.

Velocity: A vector quantity that describes both an object's speed and its direction.

Volts: Units with which we measure the difference in electrical potential from one end of a battery to the other. In simpler terms, volts measure how forcefully current is pushed through a circuit.

Volume: A measurement of how much space an object takes up. Volume is often measured cubic centimeters or cubic inches for small and moderate sized objects.

Volume of water displaced: A characteristic of matter that measures how much water is pushed out of the way when an object is placed in water. It is useful for figuring out the volume of oddly shaped objects.

Watts: The units in which electrical power is measured.

Wave: Energy moved from one location to another in the form of a distortion through a medium.

Wavelength: The distance between two crests (high points) or troughs (low points) on a wave.

Wedge: A type of simple machine made by moving an inclined plane.

Weight: A measurement of the force of gravity on an object. Weight is related to mass by the mathematical formula: weight = mass x gravity. Weight is often measured in pounds.

Weight (aerodynamics): One of the four main forces acting on objects as they move through the air. Weight is the force of gravity pulling an object back toward the earth.

Wheel: A circular object.

Wheel and axle: A simple machine constructed by fixing a stick to a wheel in such a way that when the stick, or axle, moves, the wheel also moves.

Work: When a force applied to an object moves that object.

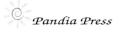

Pandia Press